Interpreting & Using
QUANTITATIVE AIDS
to BUSINESS DECISION

Chester R. Wasson
Richard R. Shreve

Austin Press
Educational division of
Lone Star Publishers, Inc.
P. O. Box 9774
Austin, Texas 78766

Library of Congress Catalog Number 75-44596
ISBN: 0-914872-08-7

Contents

i

Preface

  This book is a combined revision of three works by the senior author: UNDERSTANDING QUANTITATIVE ANALYSIS, THE ECONOMICS OF MANAGERIAL DECISION, and RESEARCH ANALYSIS FOR MARKETING DECISION. All three had developed markets as supplementary handbooks to managerial courses of several kinds, presenting the use side of quantitative tools for decision. All were written to furnish insight into the practical interpretive side of quantitative materials long familiar to those with physical science and engineering training, but missing from the background of many students in economic, social and business disciplines. When the author recaptured his copyright with the demise of the previous publisher, Appleton-Century-Crofts, it was decided to combine the fundamentals scattered through these three works and round them out to a single comprehensive handbook on the major quantitative aids proposed for use in managerial decision.

  This is thus not a central textbook for any course ordinarily given, but a supplement to many kinds of courses. It seeks to balance the usual technically oriented content of most quantitative courses with a presentation of the other side of the tools presented--the practicalities of the interpretation and use of the results of data gathering and computational analysis. Without this side of things, the technical presentations too often leave the student confused and ready to forget the technical side completely as soon as he can.

  This latter too usual result is unfortunate. Every managerial decision of any kind in our mass society must be based on some kind of quantitative input. The action which results is inescapably quantitative, since it involves matters of quantitative time and timing, the quantitative allocation of resources, (and the matching of those resources to some kind of quantitative estimate of need), and the expectation of some very specific quantitative gains or losses of some kind.

  Much faulty business and other organizational planning (and much bad legislation) results from ignoring the seeming mysteries of the quantitative elements involved and the substitution of very flawed, emotionally laden human intuition. The aura of mystery with which many cloak these quantitative tools is undeserved, a not uncommon result of incomplete familiarity rather than any inherent complexity in the approaches. Although the technicalities of the computational details are tedious and easy to forget if not used daily, the essentials needed to understand the needed inputs and the meaning of the computational results for decision are really very simple. Moreover, interpretation and use are not technical matters, nor can they wisely be either avoided or delegated. Interpretation is the very essence of the decision itself, and must take into account matters that the mere technician cannot decide--the objectives and the expectations of management itself.

If this book helps the user toward greater use and appreciation of the aids which such tools can give him, toward greater use of what the specialist can do for him and at the same time, more independence from the technician in making his decision, we will have accomplished our aim.

C.R.W.   Geneva, IL

PART I. THE FICTIONS AND REALITIES UNDERLYING NUMERICAL LANGUAGE

What kind of person are you? Do you just love to see things expressed in numbers and mathematical symbols, even when the expression means little or nothing? Or are you the sort who hastily turns the page when you see a table or graph? I hope you are neither, although you quite probably have a better feel for either the mathematical side or for the literary (qualitative) side, since the human brain does seem to process these two aspects of reality in separate areas. Certainly, if you do not take into account both sides of the information coin, you have no place in the administration of any decision position in our mass society.

Almost any decision of any sort in business or any other organized activity requires the evaluation and application of both qualitative information, with all of its nuances, and also of some form of quantitative input, either directly or indirectly, needed to place the qualitative aspects in perspective. In most cases, the administrator need not be an expert mathematician to use the quantitative information well. Indeed, the formal mathematics required in the data manipulation itself goes beyond the level of third grade arithmetic only a very minor fraction of the time. Even when the formal manipulation needed is quite complex, understanding the relationship between what goes into a calculation and the usefulness of what comes out is quite a separate matter from the complications of the computational procedure, and may not even be as well understood by the expert technician who is doing the computing by any well-informed decision maker, whatever his mathematical expertise.

What the executive needs to know, above all, are the relatively few important assumptions behind the calculation and the meaning of the results--including their limitations-- as a basis for projecting results of proposed actions.

1

The most important aspect of that understanding is a comprehension of the real limitations and value of the highly artificial language of numbers, and particularly of the weaknesses and problems involved in the process of measurement by which most of the numbers he must use are generated: the process of measurement. For this reason, the two opening chapters deal with the seldom recognized real meaning of numbers and mathematical language in general and with the standards by which all measurement information must be evaluated.

Hopefully, this material will help the reader to avoid the greatest mistake of all in the use of quantitative information: blind acceptance of the results of data gathering and calculation, the tendency to assume that figures always have solid meaning whatever the context of their use, or can ever be used without careful evaluation and reorganization in the light of the specific decision to be made on the basis of them.

IS 1+1 Always 2 ?

WALL STREET JOURNAL

"The hardware store didn't have a two-inch wrench, so I got two one-inch wrenches."

(Adapted from the Wall Street Journal of November 5, 1968, p. 5, by permission of Cartoon Features Syndicate)

1

NUMBERS AND MATHEMATICAL SYMBOLS: MEANING, IMPORTANCE AND LIMITATIONS

To a great many of us--probably even the over-whelming majority--the formal written language of quantitative expression and quantitative analysis seems to be a horribly complex, strange tongue. Conversely, fairly large numbers of people perceive quantitative expression as the most exact and beautiful essence of all truth, and in addition, a wonder-fully fascinating game. Both extreme attitudes are far too unquestioning, both equally devoid of understanding of the meaning and intellectual purpose of mathematical expression. Both overlook the information that is lost in the simplification needed to translate the disorder of the natural world into the orderly language of mathematical symbols. Both result in the unquestioning acceptance of pure nonsense when put into mathe-matical form.

This mystical acceptance of mere figures was exempli-fied some years ago when an official of a teacher's organization wished to give impact to his theme that teachers should be paid more. Without authority of any sort and without any sound definitional basis for his figures, he asserted that "90,000 teachers are leaving the profession every year." His implica-tion, of course, was that this condition was shocking. This was, indeed, the import of an article which appeared soon after in a popular national magazine, "Why Are 90,000 Teachers Leaving Every Year?" Yet even had his figure been based on some real count (which it was not) it could have actually been too low for a profession employing 1 million people. The number retiring, marrying, or dropping out to raise a family might alone have been greater than his 90,000 if he included them in his definition. The point is, neither he nor anybody else ever indicated what his figure included and

3

what it omitted. It was an arbitrary figure, quoted without content, representing no definable set of facts. Nevertheless, because it was given in <u>numerical</u> form, apparently no one challenged either his statement or his interpretation of it.

While such numerical trickery is not as rare as it should be, an even greater danger arises from lack of effort to understand quantities. The real, everyday danger is that we will lead ourselves, or let others lead us astray through faulty acceptance of half the answer. Quantity is never the whole answer to any problem, or even an adequate half answer. We get a complete answer only when we relate the quantities to those elements we define vaguely as quality, only when we arrive at an understanding of how the quantitative statement relates to the non-quantitative objectives we hope to achieve.

This book is an attempt to impart some of this understanding of quantitative methods, particularly those methods of greatest value in making decisions in the world of people and business. It is meant for all those who must apply the results of calculations to choose between courses of action, to help them find for themselves the true meaning of the calculated results and understand the limits on precision which result from purely quantitative analysis. Many if not most such choices cannot rest on the figures alone. The figures help spell out some of the limits, but they only aid, they do not replace human judgment. Indeed many of the tools which will be discussed use figures which come from judgmental sources, and are only as good as the judgment. In turn, the end results of the calculations are quite usually devices to insure that rational human judgment will be the basis of the decision rather than arbitrary feeling.

THE NEED TO UNDERSTAND QUANTITATIVE LANGUAGE

It would be difficult to say which is the surer road to error: basing decision choices solely on the simplistic calculations of formal mathematics or ignoring the efficiencies of such formal calculations and relying mainly on qualitative judgment. The latter hides the quantitative aspect under cumbersome vague generalizations and is quite likely to lose sight of the relative importance of the various factors involved. The former ignores the important differences which numbers must often disregard.

It is not hard to say, however, which is the less efficient. Every decision has some inescapable quantitative implications, and these must be dealt with in some manner. The action taken must deal in quantities, and the only usual feedback for evaluation of results is some form of quantitative measure. Relying on vague prose formulations makes consideration of alternatives much more cumbersome than the use of formal mathematics and can lead to gross misjudgment of results. Moreover, the basic language of mathematics is by far the easier side of the decision to comprehend and evaluate. Ignoring such efficiency sacrifices effort and time which need to be given to consideration of really important subjective appraisals of the qualitative side of every decision, a side not reducible to such a simplistic language. Avoiding the need for precise definition of the "how much" of the action inputs courts the dangers of too little or too much, too soon or too late.

Efficient decision making thus depends on maximum formalization of the quantitative aspects and maximum interpretative attention to the qualitative aspects. Fortunately it is not necessary to be skilled in the intricate details of mathematical calculations in order to understand their meaning for decision. Indeed, there is some reason to suspect that many of those who devote the most time to gaining such manipulative skills are the least likely to take a balanced look at the less precise qualitative side which must enter all wise decisions. Moreover, the qualitative side of a decision necessarily involves highly subjective personal values which can be assessed only by those who hold responsibility for the decision and its results. Consider the simplified example of the choice between two investments each costing $10,000: (1) one which has a 90% probability of yielding a $20,000 return in five years, (2) one which has a 9% probability of yielding a $200,000 return in the same time. The mathematics say that the two opportunities are equal--both have an <u>expected return</u> of $18,000. (0.90 x 20,000 = 18,000 and 0.09 x 200,000 = 18,000). But few of us would view them as really equal from a personal standpoint.

THE REALITIES NUMBERS DO NOT MEASURE

Some of us would see as most important the actual return, if successful, of only $20,000 in one case and $200,000 in the other, and so would choose the riskier course. Others would put greater weight on the fact that the one is almost as close to being certain as is likely in practice, the other highly improbable, and decide on the safer one. Which we would choose would therefore be dependent in part on our resources, in part on our own objectives and a very personal attitude toward risk. No mathematics yet invented can make such a decision for us. It can, however, tell us that they have the same (risk x return) product. Similar calculations would tell us that if the probability of the $200,000 return were to drop to 6%, for example, its expected return would be less than that of the more certain choice, and therefore not a rational alternative whatever our attitude toward risk.

The illustration illuminates both the values of quantitative language and the limitations which require every decision maker to be his own interpreter of meaning. Numbers help us to cut through the many details in which, for a given purpose, two phenomena or two alternatives differ, to bring into focus those attributes in which they can be compared--for that one purpose. Given the purpose, such comparisons can be objective. They are nonpersonal, since anyone with the competence to understand the situation and the language of quantity would arrive at the same ordering of value--in the example above, that the two $10,000 investments yielded comparable returns, relative to risk.

However, even the numerical description of the example indicates that the two investment alternatives do differ, both in actual return and in accompanying risk. In the quantitative statement, the two inequalities balance out, but in any personal assessment, two equally competent executives of differing temperaments would make different choices because their risk aversion values resulted in a different qualitative ranking.

In other words, quantitative language helps us to measure the nonpersonal similarities in our universe by ignoring matters in which, for a given purpose, even a nonpersonal view can detect dissimilarities. The decision process is thus freed to concentrate on the much less easily measured qualitative attributes whose relative ordering of importance depends on the personal objectives and insights of he who makes the decision. Since every decision involves both halves of reality-- both the quantitative and the qualitative--neither the choice of alternatives nor the evaluation of results can rest solely on either the quantitative side or the qualitative side. The actual computations of the quantitative side can often be delegated to skilled technicians, and often should be, since these are non-personal.

But the choices of alternatives and evaluation of results rest on criteria so personal in value that the technician's results by themselves are meaningless. The decision maker must therefore understand the language of quantity in order to know what quantities are important to his ends, and which results of highest value.

In the example above we have assumed that the figures we are using are quite solid and known, unvarying in meaning. This however, is not an inherent characteristic of numbers. Indeed, the truth is quite the opposite. Numbers have no meaning at all by themselves, and their very use requires us to ignore some of the facts. As already indicated, whatever significance they have is relative to the circumstances of their uses.

Thus, it is important that we understand just how simple and incomplete numerical information, and indeed all mathematical language is, and how dependent it is on non-mathematical information for meaning.

THE MEANING OF A NUMBER

Numbers, we all must recognize, are not natural realities. Indeed, they are not reality at all, but artificial constructs of the human mind which have been invented, paradoxically, to help us understand part of reality. A number represents a count, and we can count nothing until we are willing to shut our eyes to a basic reality of nature. That reality is that no two things in existence are exactly alike in every possible respect. Yet whenever we say there are two of anything, or two million, we are stating that each of the units in our count--people, apples, pies, dollars, or whatever--can be substituted for any other unit.

"You can't add apples and oranges" is a well-worn cliche', yet we do in fact do so often, even always, and quite legitimately. The housewife checking over her pantry may note that she has "10 cans of fruit" when in fact she has 3 cans of pears, 3 of peaches, and one can of apricots. Since any one of them can be used for her planned dessert that evening, they are fully substitutable in her mind and therefore pears can be added to apricots and both to peaches. Indeed, in recounting her summers labors, she may well add beans and peaches, saying she "put up 68 cans of fruit and vegetables". For her meal planning purposes, the beans will not substitute for the peaches, but as a measure of accomplishment, they can be equated.

We can assume such a substitutability wisely and honestly only when we define its limits, when we state the purpose, time, place, or other conditions under which we are willing to substitute one for the other.

Thus, if the bank teller offers us the choice of ten dimes or a dollar bill in exchange for our check for $1, he may be perfectly correct in saying that he is offering one dollar in each case. But if our purpose in cashing that check was to get some coins to make a telephone call, the dollar bill is not, for us, equal to the ten dimes, however equal they may be in the bank's bookkeeping. At the moment, the dollar bill is worth nothing to us because it does not fit our need for dimes.

To take a more complicated example, let us consider the population of the state of Arkennessee which the Census Bureau defines by the rather definite-looking figure of 5,397,836 people listed as of April 1, 1985. To the grocers of this fictional state, this probably represents the number of mouths they can sell to, and while each person does not consume the same amount of food, the approximation is close enough. To the state's two political parties, the Republicrats and the Demopublicans, every member of that count is important in determining the state's representation in the United States House of Representatives. At election time, however, their focus of interest shifts and both parties regard as consequential only 2,195,410 people, the number of registered voters. For the makers of hair-coloring compounds, the number is less than that--possibly the 1,090,119 teen-age girls and adult women who are not natural blondes, but dream of the romance they might have if they were.

To the makers of Pepsi-Cola, the 5 million number probably does represent the number of months in the state that are able to formulate a request for their product. Their advertising salvos, however, must be aimed at the million and a quarter teen-agers, the important one-fourth of the total which consumes well over three-fourths of their output.

8

To a harassed presidential administration seeking to pry an important bill out of Congress, Arkennessee has at the moment only ten people: its congressional delegation of 7 Demopublicans who will probably vote favorably, another who is on the fence and must be brought into line, and the 2 Republicrats who are sure to oppose the measure. In addition, the fence-straddling Demopublican happens to be heading the committee handling the legislation and counts more in the president's estimation than the other 9 members.

Obviously, any decision maker must question and analyze the measurement quality of all the figures he needs and intends to use: Where did they come from, and how measured? For what purpose were they gathered? What are they worth for his own particular purpose? After appraising the quality of his figures as obtained and analyzing their meaning in terms of the decision he must make, he asks further questions: What are the precise objectives he seeks as a result of that decision? What are his own capabilities and risk affordability? In addition, since the structure of the future is certain to differ from the structure of that past from which the figures were of necessity drawn: what is the best estimate of those differences? Finally, he must ask how must the figures be modified, how must they be tailored to fit best into the composite sketch of the future resulting from the answers to all his previous questions?

The Instability of Numerical Meaning

The meaning of a figure used for decision changes with the passage of time. The height of our year-old baby yesterday, however precise the measurement, will not be the correct measure of his height next year, and the clothes we buy for him must take into account the probable growth. Similarly, any measure we have of the popularity of dress or automobile styles today is unlikely to be an accurate guide to production schedules for those to be sold next year.

In the world of decision, we must always recognize that accuracy of meaning is highly perishable. Whatever was precisely true yesterday of customer choices, competitors' strengths, or prices, may still be approximately true tomorrow, and may be quite incorrect twelve months hence. Unfortunately, whatever figures we possess must always be out of the past, must always refer to a specific time and place which have vanished.

Our decisions can only deal with the future, a different time, usually a different place, and always with people who are no longer the same or have the same structure of desires. Such information from the past can be applied to a somewhat different present by development of generalizations which apply to the similarities of past with present and future.

Foresight about the future requires us to also recognize those aspects in which the specific situation is likely to differ from those sketched by the past and the effect on events of those differences. For this reason, all of us who seek to apply calculations must interpret for ourselves their applicability and meaning. Every decision of any consequence concerns a specific, individual situation which no generalization is likely to fit exactly. The unique aspects of decision are beyond mathematical illumination.

Indeed the tendency for measurements to change with time, place, and use is one reason for the use of the symbols which repel so many of us, rather than numbers. This repelling quality is hardly mysterious. It is our usual reaction to the strange and misunderstood--a reaction which evaporates with understanding and familiarity.

The validity of the mathematical relationships we can use depends upon their appropriateness, their accuracy depends upon the precision of the data. The meaning of the results depends on the purpose for which we use them. Thus we need to be able to learn the meaning of those results in the context of the decisions we seek to make. Fortunately no language is so simple as that of mathematics. The strangeness of its appearance, and the apparent mystery of what it says may well be due to a natural tendency to impute to the strange and unfamiliar a complexity and depth of meaning which does not exist.

Algebraic symbols probably pose the strangest and most awe-inspiring aspects of mathematics both for the non-users and those inclined to arcane expression in order to give the semblance of precision to imprecise knowledge. Such symbolism should be understood as the simplest of all shorthands, as a representation of the ultimate in imprecise meaning--the abstraction of general categories. Only three types of abbreviations are used: operating symbols which really are abbreviations for ordinary active verbs, letter abbreviations standing for generalized categories of things, and symbols denoting relationships between things. All of them are mere abbreviations which carry no more meaning than the ordinary language we all use. In many ways, they carry less solid meaning because they are abstractions intended to eliminate attention to the coloring and nuances which every living language communicates.

However little we may think in mathematical terms, all of us constantly use similar abstractions and later retranslate them into specifics. The only difference is that we do much of such thinking in terms of ordinary words, a small part in the language of mathematics. We thus deprive ourselves of the manipulative convenience of algebraic abbreviation. This is a foolish procedure, since no other language has a vocabulary as small and simple as mathematics.

THE SHORTHAND OF MATHEMATICAL EXPRESSION

Figures, Counting, and the Process of Generalization

Most of us use figures all of the time without much thought that they are abbreviations representing a very high degree of abstraction. They present counts of things, treating as equals items which we know do differ in substantial detail. If asked how many fingers we have, we may say "10 " or else "8 fingers and 2 thumbs." We do not list them separately nor indicate the unique characteristics of size, shape, position, and utility for differing tasks each of these digits has. Yet we all are fully aware of these differences, and use the actual fingers in different ways. In making our reply, therefore, we have chosen to ignore divergencies which are important in some other contexts. We have also demonstrated our complete comprehension of the foundation of all mathematical expression--the abstract generalization, the expression which deals only with the aspects of any phenomena which can, for a single purpose, be treated as the same, however much they differ in other contexts. Such a comprehension of the utility of a count is the universal building block out of which all mathematics is constructed. Every other mathematical operation is an extension and abbreviation of the counting process.

11

When we say that "we" have $18 between us, I have $8 and you have $10, we have performed a second shorthand of abstraction. Instead of starting our count all over again, we have piled a single figure representing one count--the count of your money, on top of the count of my money. Addition is thus just another shorthand for the counting process.

Similarly, subtraction is a form of counting backward. If I hand $3 of my $8 to the cashier to pay for my dinner, I can say I have "subtracted" $3 from my $8, and have only $5 left. I have actually taken dollars number 8, number 7, and number 6 out of my wallet, and know that number 5 is the highest count I have left. To most of us, I am sure, these examples seem so elementary as to appear trivial. But how many of us think of multiplication as repeated addition, and division as repeated subtraction? Yet that is precisely what they are, and they thus involve a third order of abstraction.

Consider a relatively trivial example--computing the floor area of a room to determine how many parquet blocks each 1 foot square are needed to cover it. Few of us would have any trouble with this problem. We would simply say, "multiply the length in feet by the width in feet. The product you get is the number of square feet in the room. Since each block is one foot square, that is the number of parquet blocks you need." This is right, of course.

But what we have done is to say to ourselves: This room is a rectangle. One row will contain as many blocks as there are feet in the width of the room. I will have to add as many successive rows to this first row as there are feet in the length of the room. Since each row is the same length, this means I will have to add as many rows as the room is long, in feet. I can express this process by taking the width, in 1-foot square blocks, as many times as the room is long. The quickest way to say this is "The number of foot square blocks is the same as the length times the width in feet."

All of the other operating symbols form a further layer of shorthand abstractions, derived from the initial abstraction of a count. One that bothers some people is merely another simple shorthand expression for a long series of additions-- the summation sign represented by the Greek letter sigma, Σ. Just as a figure enables us to avoid listing all of the individual items to which we have reference, so the Σ permits us to

avoid listing all of the counts we have made by indicating that
we are adding all of a whole series of values. For example,
suppose we were planning a cross-country trip with an ordinary road map having only distances between towns, and wanted
a formula for the distance between Pittsburgh and Chicago. We
could say: "Add the recorded distance from Pittsburgh to East
Liverpool to the distance from East Liverpool to Mansfield, etc. "

$$\text{A mathematician might write it:}\quad \sum_{\text{Pittsburgh}}^{\text{Chicago}} (\text{All intercity mileages})$$

Anyone familiar with mathematical notation would understand
this to be shorthand for "add all of the map readings for inter-
city distances on the road between Pittsburgh and Chicago."
This, in turn, would be understood as shorthand for an actual
listing of the intervening mileages to be found on the map,
and then summing them.

A simple extension of $\sum$ is the integral sign $\int$ --a
kind of elongated s. The meaning is the same as sigma, but
covers more complicated cases. $\int$ also is a shorthand for a
series of summations but is used where what is being summed
is an infinite series of values, such as the area under a continuous irregular curve.

Other cases of mathematical "active verbs," or operational symbols of importance are those of powers and roots.
These, of course, are simply special cases of multiplication
and division, cases in which the multiplier or divider are the
same number as the one multiplied originally.

Thus the active verbs in the language of mathematics
are not only few (plus, minus, times, divided by, and their
derivatives) but they are all derived from the same one--count.
We use the symbols of $+$, $-$, $\times$, and $\div$ simply because they are
quicker to write than the words "add" or "plus," "take the sum
of," etc.

Similarly, the items which are the subject of these
operations are usually represented by single symbols for convenience. The actualities behind these symbols are of two
types: variables and constants.

Mathematical Symbols for Quantities

Probably the most confusing aspect of mathematical
language is the fact that only actual figures and operating symbols have any real meaning. The rest are place-markers.

They are merely empty labels intended to tell us what <u>kinds</u> of figures we need if we are to carry out the operations and what to do with the figures when we have them.

Most of us can understand specific numbers, and the errors we make in arithmetic are usually just mistakes, not the result of confusion. It is easy enough for most of us to understand that if we multiply 20 feet--the length of our living room--by 16 feet, the width, that we will get the product, 320 square feet, and that this will represent its area. Even the generalized formula put into words gives most of us little trouble: "multiply the length by the width, in feet, to get the area in square feet." Some of us begin to get a little confused, however, when the mathematician starts using single letter abbreviations as convenient substitutes for our words. His choice is arbitrary, and he always clearly defines the meaning of his abbreviations, such as:

Let l be the length of the room in feet

w be the width of the room in feet

a be its area in square feet

Then, $l \times w = a$ will give the area of any rectangular room. Yet, this last says exactly the same as our earlier prose statement. We have simply made the formula easier to read and work with by substituting single letter abbreviations for the words, and a standard multiplication sign, $\times$, for the verb "multiply." The single letter symbols chosen in this case were actual initial letters of the words, but this is not always convenient and never necessary--they can be any arbitrarily chosen letters or other symbols, provided they are carefully defined in advance. They might even be the same letter with subscript numbers, as

Let x_1 be one rectilinear dimension of a room,

x_2 be the other rectilinear dimension,

x_3 be its area

Then $x_1 \cdot x_2 = x_3$

Note that this formula is identical to the other except for a different arbitrary choice of symbols (abbreviations), and the use of a different multiplication sign--the dot--instead of the cross, to save confusion with the x's. Although x_1, x_2, and x_3 are not initial letters such as l, w, and h, they serve the same purpose of abbreviations, except they may seem to be more arbitrary.

The arbitrary choice of symbols often results in quite dissimilar notation by different authors discussing the same relationships and formulas. This tendency toward diversity of expression has no doubt contributed measurably to the fog through which many of us seem to peer when confronted with calculating instructions expressed in symbols instead of the words. The tendency toward such individual choice of symbols is unfortunate, but the confusion is partly due to the habit most of us have of reading specific meaning into something that is an abstraction--in this case a mere label. However, such abstractions serve a necessary purpose in communicating knowledge, in representing the generalized knowledge we have which, while expressible in words, soon becomes too cumbersome to be readily understood.

Certain agreed-upon rules do cover the general choice of symbols, although there is considerable latitude within these rules. Distinctions are nearly always made between the kinds of symbols chosen for phenomena we call variables and those which are constants in the context of a particular calculation.

Variables

It is important to remember that both the word generalizations--such as length--and the symbols we use to represent them--such as x_1 --are simply stand-ins for numbers which are necessary to complete any calculation. Under any specific set of circumstances, the solution of any given mathematical expression depends on substituting the specific number for which the symbol is a stand-in, in the mathematical expression, in the specific instance, and then performing the actual operations (addition, multiplication, etc.) which the expression instructs us to make.

A variable is only a symbol which stands for values which change with the circumstances. It is simply an abbreviated label useful in conveying instructions to others about how to solve a problem if they have specific numbers of the sort designated by the label. We can use either the formula $1 \times w = a$, or $x_1 \cdot x_2 = x_3$ (with corresponding definitions) to communicate how anyone can make his own calculations of floor area without any advance knowledge of our own as to the specific dimensions of the various sizes of rooms. Thus 1 and x_1 both are labels for a whole series of numbers. Each

15

represents a specific value at any one time and place, but different values at different times and places, for different people.

Conventional usage has normally been to represent variables with letters from the tail end of the alphabet (x, y, or z), or to simplify notation when the variables are many, x with a numerical subscript--x_1, x_2, x_3, etc. Scientists avoid confusion between the arithmetic operating symbol, $\times$, and the variable symbol, x, by use of the dot, $\cdot$, instead of the cross $\times$, to indicate algebraic multiplication.

Constants

Some of the symbols in some of the generalized calculations we wish to communicate are fixed for whole families of circumstances, even though the value may differ for different families. For an example, let us consider the calculations for the yearly cost of operating our automobile. The number of miles we drive is obviously a variable in this calculation. The dollar cost of fuel, tires, and lubrication, for any given automobile, is probably about the same for each mile driven. In this problem, operating cost per mile is a particular kind of constant if we know the car, but varies between the VW and the Cadillac, for instance. Certain other costs are fixed over time. The license and the depreciation in sales value are yearly costs without regard to the miles driven, and the resale value depreciates inexorably with time. Thus the cost involves one value--mileage--which depends on how much we drive the car, and two values which remain relatively constant for any given car, but will differ between cars--operating costs and fixed annual costs. We can generalize the instruction which tells us how to determine automobile ownership costs for one year by a formula with four abbreviations, or symbols: one for total cost (the answer we seek), one for per-mile operating cost, one for mileage driven, and one for annual fixed costs.

Let x_1 = total annual cost of operation
x_2 = number of miles driven
a_1 = operating cost per mile--fuel, lubrication, tires, etc.
a_2 = annual fixed costs for license, depreciation, etc.

Then $x_1 = a_1 x_2 + a_2$

16

Note that we have taken our symbols for the constants, a_1 and a_2, from the first end of the alphabet. This is the standard convention. Some writers might indeed have written the formula thus, using different first-of-the-alphabet letters for each constant:

Let y = total annual cost of operation

x = number of miles driven

a = operating cost per mile

b = annual fixed cost

Then y = ax + b

In general, where the number of constants may be more than 2 or 3, it is simpler to use _a_ with subscripts, but the two formulas are the same.

In both cases, the relationship is one which any mathematician would recognize as <u>linear.</u> That is, the value of the one variable (x_1 or y) bears a constant proportional relationship to the value of the second variable (x_2 or x). The convention which dictates the first-of-the-alphabet letters be used as arbitrary symbols for constants and last of the alphabet for all variables helps us recognize the nature of this relationship immediately.

Some constants and other values have such wide importance that they are assigned special universally-used symbols never employed to represent anything else. The most widely recognized of these constants is the relationship between the diameter of a circle and its circumference, always represented by the Greek letter π. This relationship is constant--the value of π is identical whether the circle is the size of the earth or as small as the ring on your finger. In a case such as this, is simply a convenient way of indicating a single irrational number--approximately 3.1416. The symbol π is a constant which represents the end calculation of a very simple mathematical relationship, the equation, or equality, $\frac{x_1}{x_2} = \pi$ when

x_1 = circumference of any circle

x_2 = diameter of the same circle

Equalities are one of the more important mathematical relationships.

By itself, any individual symbol is an unnecessarily awkward substitute for the more meaningful word for which it stands. Its value lies in the compactness given to visualization and communication of mathematical relationships, mainly those of identities, expressed equalities, and of inequalities.

Most of us are familiar with equations--expressions which state that the items on either side of the equals sign are identical, can be substituted for each other. Any such identity or equation can be viewed as a set of instructions.

"$a = l \times w$" is really shorthand for "to find the areas of a room, multiply the length by the width."

or

$s = \dfrac{d}{t}$, where s is average speed
d is distance traveled
t is the time taken

can be read as "to find the average speed, divide the distance traveled by the time."

All such expressions permit a definite solution in any one given set of circumstances. That is, we get the desired numerical answer when we replace each variable label with the figure which applies, and carry out the actual arithmetic which the generalized instruction (equation) tells us to perform.

However, not all of the knowledge we need to use is in such clearly defined form. Quite often, it is in the form of a limitation on the value of one item, set by the values of other items in the expression. To get down to concrete cases, we may observe that we "do not really know the size of John's room, but we know it is larger than ours, and this room is 12 × 15. In a case such as this, we cannot make any statement (formulate any equation) which gives a precise statement of the size of John's room, but we can make a statement about the lower limit of size which it exceeds. We can say it is "more than 12 feet by 15 feet."

We designate such an unequal relationship by a v lying on its side: >. This inequality symbol points toward the lesser of the two values, the mouth toward the greater. Translating the original statement that John's room is larger than ours, which is 12 × 15 ft., we would write it in mathematical shorthand thus: Let x_1 = size of John's room, then

18

$x_1 > 12 \times 15$, or $12 \times 15 < x_1$.   This limits the value on the down side, but leaves it wide open in the other direction. At first blush, this may not seem a very useful kind of knowledge. A little reflection will show that we often use inequalities in our everyday decision-making. If our wife asks, when we start a trip, ·"How is the gas?" we are likely to glance at the fuel gauge and answer "We have enough to get there and to spare," without trying to estimate our exact tank level. We probably do so by some such mental arithmetic as "We usually burn a gallon in 18 miles. The map indicates that the distance is 90 miles. 90 divided by 18 is 5 gallons, and with the fuel gauge needle at the half-way mark, I know we have far more than 5 gallons."

If we were inclined to think in mathematical language, we would have thought,

Let f = our fuel supply

Then $f > \dfrac{90}{18}$

This may be enough to complete the planned trip, and thus our statement is adequate for the decision as to whether or not to purchase more fuel before we start out.

On the other hand, we may note the possibility that the return trip will be made late at night, with few stations open. We know that with the fuel gauge at the 1/2 point, we have less than 10 gallons, and therefore we decide to stop first for gas after all. In this case, also, we have made and need no precise measurement. Our inequality in this case gives us enough limiting information in both directions to arrive at a decision. In this case, our inequality would read

$$2\,\frac{(90)}{(18)} > f > \frac{90}{18}$$

which reads "f" is between 90/18 and twice 90/18. Note that it is equal to neither of these quantities, and, for our current purpose, we don't need to know its exact value.

The knowledge of merely one or two limiting values is clearly enough for decision at times. Clearly, also, the more limiting values we have, the closer we are to learning the exact value. In a nonmathematical context, we all are familiar with this principle as the basic solution of parlor charades. The answer to the standard "is it vegetable, animal, or mineral?" is enough to narrow the search a great deal. An astute questioner stands better than an even chance of pinpointing the object, without other clues, in less than 20 such limiting questions.

In business, we may know only that a price response is less than unitary elasticity or greater than unitary elasticity. This is sufficient information to enable us to decide on the proper direction for a price move predicated on that response. A best, or optimal answer can often be calculated from knowledge of a few limiting conditions. Linear programming, a useful decision tool which is discussed later, is based on this process.

Inequalities can be in terms of "more than" or "less than," or in terms of "at least," or "no more than." This last implies, of course, the possibility of an identity, and the operating symbol is $\leq$ ("less than or equal to") or $\geq$ ("equal to or greater than"). Notice that this does not mean that the quantity is actually equal to, only that it may be.

Indefinite Relationships

Sometimes we have no real knowledge of the operating nature of a relationship or of the limits. We may know only that some definite relationship does or may exist. We may have reason to believe, for example, that the flavor and other quality factors in apples depend on variety, climate, soil, and method of cultivation. However, we are not certain of the exact nature of any of these relationships. We could simply state that "apple quality is some kind of resultant of the effect of climate, apple variety, soil, and method of cultivation." Or we might make use of the mathematical abbreviation $\underline{f}$ (for "some kind of function of") and express the same vague statement in more precise-appearing terms, such as:

Let x_1 = apple qualities

x_2 = climate factors

x_3 = soil factors

x_4 = apple variety

x_5 = method of cultivation

Then $x_1 = f(a_1 x_2, \ a_2 x_3, \ a_3 x_4, \ a_4 x_5)$

We may not even be certain that we know all of the significant factors which affect apple quality. In such a case, those with a taste for mathematical expression would write it thus:

$$x_1 = f(a_1x_1, \ a_2x_2 \ \cdots \ a_kx_k)$$

The dots indicate simply that the expression represents a series, up to $\underline{k}$ in number. $\underline{k}$ is used instead of an actual number to indicate that the writer himself is ignorant of the number of factors.

The meaning of such statements of indefinite relationships is identical whether put in prose formulation or in mathematical language. In both instances that meaning is simply that "quality varies with a number of factors, but I really don't know how it varies, nor what all the factors are." Whether the mathematical expression is even as convenient as the prose in such cases is a matter of taste. A symbolic presentation undoubtedly appeals to some individuals on occasion because of the aura of precision with which it seems to cover their ignorance. They have obligingly forgotten the concomitant need to give meaning to all such expressions in the context of a specific decision.

The use of indefinite statements of relationships has none of the main value of the symbolic statement of relationships--the advantage this second order of abstraction gives us in identifying the class of relationship we are dealing with, helping us to compare relationships just as figures help us to compare the similarities in counts or measurements.

Symbolic Expression as a Means of Revealing Similarities in Relationships

The use of numbers suppresses the real dissimilarities in items to help us understand the similarities. The use of symbolic expression carries the suppression of real differences one step further by suppressing the real dissimilarities in count to reveal the real similarities in relationships. A great many of the relationships in the world fall into definite families which are easily recognized when put into symbolic form, and knowledge of the family characteristics tells us immediately a great deal about the relationship. Thus all straight lines have the family relationship $y = ax + b$. Since the mathematician realizes that either of the constants $\underline{a}$ and $\underline{b}$ can be 0, he also recognizes the form $y = b$ as a member of this family. When we have the numerical value of $\underline{a}$ available, we know something else worth knowing. The constant, $\underline{a}$, is the proportion y/x. In the graph of the equation, this is the slope of the straight

21

line, that is, its rate of increase or rate of decrease in value. Whatever the value of b, then, all lines with the same value of a are parallel. If b is not 0, we also know where the line intercepts the 2 axes of the graph. Other forms of equations identify circles of whatever size, ellipses, parabolas, sine curves, and many other families of relationships of numbers and other quantitative formulations which involve no substantial degree of personal judgment in their development.

The search for similarities of relationship is just as important when the data itself is, as is most of that needed for business decision, of a highly subjective nature. The judgmental character of much such knowledge is no reason to ignore the value of attempting to place numerical values on personal insights and experience. Just such quantification of subjective estimates is the basis of Bayesian and other newly developed tools for the mathematical comparison of decision alternatives discussed later. Judgment, however, is not the sole source of inexactness in figures. Although figures themselves arose out of the counting process, most of them represent a different process--that of measurement, and the measurement process introduces both distortions and some degree of approximation.

SUMMARY

1. The utility of the language of mathematics lies in its very limited vocabulary and the limited meanings that vocabulary attempts to convey.

2. Any form of mathematical expression ignores a large part of reality--the part which describes the unique aspects of every element of what we know. By concentrating solely on the similarities, mathematical calculations help us focus on those elements in our experience which aid in understanding new experiences and new situations. They abstract from the complexity of actuality those simpler aspects which are common to many phenomena.

3. The very abstracting process, however, limits the validity and the accuracy of any results. The user of the calculations must always weigh their meaning for the decision he is to make in terms of those qualitative values of which no mathematics can take full account. He must understand both that numbers cannot truly represent personal and subjective values and that the objective meaning itself differs with time, place,

and circumstances. He needs to realize, also, that the degree of precision expressed by numbers is quite variable--that numbers present an appearance of precision which is often false.

4. Any decision-maker must therefore have a reasonably good reading knowledge of the language of mathematics. That language is a very simple and limited one, consisting of fewer active verbs than we have fingers, ordinary figures, and the place-card markers for the latter called symbols. The latter can help us to construct abstract instructions on how to use whatever figures we may be able to furnish. The whole of the language is not really a strange one, but a series of abbreviations for words and ideas we all work with every day.

5. The basic element of mathematics is the number, a shorthand for the result of a count. Nature knows no numbers-- only individuals which are all unique in some aspect of time, place, and physical dimensions. Any number ignores some degree of uniqueness in order to help us grasp the similarities. The validity of any figure thus depends on the validity of the assumptions we are making about the identical value, for a given decision, of each of the units in the counts.

6. The operational verbs of mathematics--add, subtract, multiply, etc.--are all variants of one--to add. Addition itself is merely a shorthand extension of counting.

7. Arbitrary symbols are chosen by each writer to serve as abbreviated labels. Such label symbols enable him to convey instructions about how a given calculation can be carried out if we can get figures of the sort designated by the labels. These instructions could just as easily be expressed in ordinary words.

8. Such symbolic labels are of two general types, variables and constants. Variables, usually represented by x or some other letter from the end of the alphabet, denote figures which can vary with every different set of conditions. Constants, usually represented by a or other letters from the beginning of the alphabet, indicate that the figure used is one which may be the same for a whole family of solutions.

9. The principal reason for use of symbolic language is to render compact the statement of mathematical operations and relationships, and permit ease in manipulation, handling and comparison of relationship. The principal basic relationships are equations, inequalities, and indefinite relationships.

10.   Equations are basically instructions concerning the method by which a definite solution can be obtained once the actual numbers referred to are available.

11.   Inequalities tell us the limits to the solution we seek, but not its exact value.

12.   Indefinite relationships--generalizations of the function--simply indicate that the solution requires certain types of figures, but give no guidance as to how these shape the solution.

13.   The greatest values of symbolic statements are to enable us to identify the family to which a relationship belongs and to see how the statement of the relationship can be simplified for calculation by means of substitution and other devices.

14.   The assumptions of similarity, significance, and the relevance upon which any number or symbol rests are matters of subjective judgment and thus all quantification is to some degree subjective. Some of the most useful tools, moreover, make use of quantities which are themselves subjective in origin as well as measurement. The process of measurement introduces another source of inexactness and distortion.

2

MEASUREMENT DATA:
STANDARDS, PROBLEMS, PITFALLS

Most of the numbers we use are the results of a measurement process, not of a simple count. They answer the question "How much?", not "How many?". In measurement, unlike counting, the validity and even the value of the numbers depends on the context in which they are to be used. Their meaning is strongly colored by the fallibility of human observation. They always involve some degree of approximation and inaccuracy. The answers they give must be continually checked and interpreted in the light of each specific use.

Measurement is a much more complicated process than mere counting. Although the process of tallying requires many of the same kinds of decisions as any other measurement system, the basis of those choices are quite intuitive and obvious. When we say "3 sheep," "3 girls," "300 people," the context and the purpose of our count is usually clear, the choice of unit no strain, and the definition of that unit not one likely to give rise to ambiguity or challenge. But when we measure the production cost as $3.5436 per 1000 pieces, we go through a process on which objective agreement between equally competent observers is far from likely. Furthermore, the number itself has a far more restricted significance than the count of 3 sheep. The same 3 sheep will always tally out at 3. The same production system which produced a cost of $3.5436 may cause the cost to be $7.0872 or $1.7718 tomorrow or in some other setting. Or even at a given time, a different objective for the measurement of that cost may change the calculation to indicate that true cost figure, for that given objective, is only $.5436.

The most difficult problems in measurement usually

involve the choice of criteria to be satisfied by measurement, and the development of the instrument or method of measuring the chosen criterion. The greatest mistake is to seek greater precision than necessary.

All measurement starts with an end use or purpose and has meaning in terms only of that purpose. Accomplishment of the end purpose, however, is frequently not directly measurable, and we have to be satisfied with measuring something judged to relate to this accomplishment. In eggs, for example, we are usually interested in measuring something designated as "freshness." If pushed, we would probably define freshness as the degree an egg approaches the quality of a just-laid egg. Time passage measurement alone is not adequate for this, and many factors of handling from the moment of laying can affect it. We do know, however, that at the moment of laying, the large end has a minute air cell which increases in size as staleness increases. There are tricks of storage and shell treatment which will retard this air cell growth. But if we rule out eggs over a certain age, or with treated shells, we can use this air cell as a criterion representing all the quality factors we associate with freshness--taste, odor, stiffness of white, etc.

Whenever we desire to measure a single dimension like freshness, we can, as with eggs, usually find some criterion which works and gives us a single scale value: AA, A, B, C, for example, as in eggs. However, various users of a measurement may need other dimensions. Eggs come in a range of size, for example, as well as in varying qualities. For some people, large eggs have more relative value than small ones. For such people we need to designate size, and we do so in terms of a size label designating a given weight per dozen.

For some items, we may have to make many measurements to satisfy many users. What would an A grade automobile be? This would depend on what the purchaser sought. For some, it might be acceleration, for others, a quite incompatible item--low gas mileage. No single measure would satisfy even a majority of buyers, so those rating cars give a list of measured variables. We usually need as many criteria of measurement as we have purposes.

A mere tally is adequate measurement in the case of very few decisions in this world. A dairyman will build his barn to house exactly 100 cows and know that 100 cows will be accommodated. But a mere head count will not tell him how much milk production to plan for, even less the profit he can expect from these 100 head even with a guaranteed price. To estimate that profit potential, he needs measures of expected production from each head and of many factors involved in that production. Even in retrospect, the determination of profit achieved is a complicated measurement which differs with the objective for the measurement of that profit. Is the purpose to determine the wisdom of doubling the operation? Then every element of capital investment must be considered, every element of expected output benefit, direct and indirect, the value of every unit of labor and feed cost of any sort used estimated and included, every contingency of disease loss and price fluctuation discounted in some manner. In addition, the prospective profit from alternative uses of the same capital must be measured in the same manner. Obviously, this is a complicated process, and equally obviously will not be a really precise calculation. On the other hand, if the purpose is to report profit for tax purposes, the calculation will not and should not include the captive labor of the owner, the imputed value of fertility given to fields on which manure is spread, nor any alternative opportunity losses or profit, such as the value of home-raised feed. Still other purposes will lead to still other profit statements, each fully valid for its purpose.

The measurement process must thus start with a sharp focus on the purpose for which the resulting numbers will be used. The end result can have meaning only in terms of that one purpose and no other. Furthermore, the other steps in the process frequently result in a need for judgment as to the meaning of the resulting figure for the use intended, even when done as well as possible.

Measurement can be defined as a process which starts with some need for a quantitative comparison of alternate choices or of effects of an action relative to previous expectations. Obtaining the measurement requires:

An observer

A decision as to what kinds of factors will yield an

acceptable comparison in terms of the objective

A determination of what key aspects of these factors
are suitable for measurement

Selection and definition of a suitable unit of measurement

Development of apparatus for actual measurement using
this unit

Application of measurement tool by observer

Analysis of the measurement result in reference to the
original objective

Such a multistage process negates any possibility of
absolute accuracy even if the constant interposition of the
human element did not interfere. Nearly every stage also involves the risk--almost indeed, the certainty--of distortion
between needs and results at every stage.

PURPOSE--THE CRUCIAL ELEMENT IN MEASUREMENT

Formulation of a precise purpose to be served is easy
enough in the case of many physical tasks, but sometimes extremely difficult in business, social, and governmental affairs.
Few problems arise in developing a measurement for a clear-
cut physical operation such as determining the volume of rail-
road freight car capacity needed to bring a day's supplies of
coke, ore, and limestone from the usual sources to the steel
mill or to determine the amount of rolling mill capacity to furnish a given amount of steel of any one type to the market.
However, measuring how much of each type and size of finished
steel will constitute a profitable product mix over the larger
run is not so simple, yet a measure must be used. And the
right measure of the market share obtained by a product and
price mix can be so far from obvious that the U.S. steel industry, to take one specific example among many possible, read
its 1950's policies as successful during the very period its
price and product policies were sacrificing profitable markets
to aluminum, paper, concrete, plastics, and foreign producers.
Industry officials undoubtedly thought that they had a
measurement objective--to measure profit prospects. But they
clearly had not completed even this first step of determining
what they meant by a profit beyond the usual figure shown on the
current balance sheet. They certainly did not intend to sacri-

fice future sales volume in their most profitable categories for a temporary gain in a period of tight supply. Nevertheless, it seems clear that from the end of World War II to the late 1950's, the industry measured its success by the criterion of total tonnage sold. Little attention was paid to the inroads of aluminum on low tonnage, high profit margin products. ("Aluminum will never be a threat so long as output is in pounds. Steel can only be measured in tons," was the attitude.)

Even had the industry defined its profit ends more clearly, however, it still would have had the problem of deciding what market or industry events were relevant to attainment of a better profit structure. Was price important, and in what direction? The industry thought it was important-- important that it be higher. The result was a price per unit of benefit which brought aluminum in direct competition in casement windows, for example, and in cans. It also stimulated the use of prestressed concrete beams, and gave foreign producers a more profitable market in the U.S. Hindsight indicates that lower price should have been sought, that the industry should have set a lower-cost target to achieve profit at lower cost by improved technology (which was adopted later, when the markets were lost). Should new product development have been a measure? If so, what kind of new product development spelled potential profits? Do newer, improved production facilities mean potential profits? The industry built newer and bigger blast furnaces--much more efficient than the older ones, at $300 per ton capacity, but neglected development of new types of furnaces such as the oxygen converter, which took much less capital per ton.

In retrospect, it is always easy to see the missteps which led to trouble, either in the U.S. steel industry after World War II, or in such political quagmires as South Vietnam proved to be for the United States.

But the relationships assumed between measurement and effect desired were those which had seemed correct on many previous occasions. In other words, even when the objectives have been defined carefully and well, it is always necessary to make a fresh critical examination of the relationship between the factors thought to be criteria of accomplishment and actual attainment of that purpose.

CHOICE OF FACTORS TO MEASURE

All measurement involves simplification and compromise, but probably none requires more compromise than the choice of what to measure. Some of the compromises are forced by the limits of what is possible. The user must measure what is observable and measurable. Other compromises are the result of judgment.

Most items important to decision have innumerable aspects which might be measurable to some degree. Getting all such detail would court confusion, and much of the detail would have no relevance in the context of the given decision. The observer must choose what is simultaneously relevant, significant, and measurable. The resulting combination of judgmental choice and of choice constrained by the limits of measurability open up a number of pitfalls for the unwary. The more common problems are those of:

> Classification
>
> Indirect measures
>
> Incomplete measurement
>
> Problems of observation: the instrument, the unit, and the observer
>
> Problems of quality level
>
> Time erosion
>
> Improper interpretation of the precision necessary or that obtained.

CLASSIFICATION PROBLEMS

As already indicated, any use of quantitative expression involves a necessary assumption that somewhat unlike things are alike. Any measurement system involves classification, something not found in nature, which knows only infinite diversity. Such aggregation into classes requires judgment that the unique aspects of the various members of the class are not significant for the specific purpose sought and that the likenesses are relevant to that purpose. Put another way, the very process of classification assumes the homogeneity, relevant to the purpose pursued, of all elements making up a single quantity. When the assumption is wrong, poor decisions can result and mistaken evaluations made of results.

As already noted, from 1946 to 1957 the U.S. steel industry predicated its plans on the assumption that its market position could be measured in terms of tonnage output, assuming that each ton was of equal importance. The industry measure ignored the detail of individual product (thousands of semi-fabricated forms, shapes, sizes, and qualities), and the profitability of individual items. Because output was measured in millions of tons, the industry foresaw no significant threat in the aggressive marketing of aluminum and other structural materials. Then the recession of 1957 revealed that while aluminum had taken a relatively low percentage of the tonnage market, it had captured a large part of the steel profit by invasion of the can market, once a monopoly for tin-plated steel, and of light structurals such as casement windows, and other important areas. Paper had taken over other segments of the can market, prestressed concrete structurals a stubstantial part of construction, and plastics many items into which steel had gone. Simple tonnage proved a poor measure of competition. The classification averaged together too many items needed to be considered separately, about which different decisions needed to be made.

Governmental economic and welfare policy long made the similar mistake of measuring employment only in terms of overall average. The disorders of the 1960's showed the need for several separate classifications of workers.

Few of the classifications used in business decisions cause greater confusion than those monetary quantities labelled as costs. Far too often, these are classified in terms of actual outlays and not in terms of the alternate opportunities open to decision.

Books of account usually carry only those historical costs resulting from actual cash outlays and include all such costs without regard to those directly attributable to some one decision. But many decisions involve real costs that do not show up as any kind of cash transaction, and some of the actual cash outlays incurred are not true economic costs, relative to a specific decision.

Depreciation reserves a firm has may be used in undertaking an expansion, for example. This money, although on hand and not borrowed, has a real cost. It costs whatever return it could bring in the next best alternate use. Or we could charge its use with the interest the firm would have to pay to borrow the money--the alternative source of funds. In deciding to use the funds on hand for this expansion, the firm is sacrificing--spending, in other words--income it would otherwise receive from this money in some other profit venture, or saving the cost of the borrowing for this purpose (and probably incurring an interest cost for some other purpose).

Similarly, the new plant may occupy land bought many years before, at perhaps $100 per acre, but could now be sold for $3,000 per acre. The cost of the land for this project is no longer the original $100 per acre cost, but the $3,000 per acre the land would bring if put on the market. If the firm did not already own the property, it would have to buy it at the current market price. The real cost is $3,000 per acre even though the books may list it at $100.

Labor that would be kept on in any event to hold a skilled workforce intact obviously results in a cash payroll outlay. But this outlay is no part of the real cost of a job taken on simply to keep the force busy. Nor can any of the plant overhead outlays be charged against such a job. They would go on without reference to the decision to take or reject such an order. Only the difference in cost between doing and not doing is an economic cost.

In other words, the test of correct classification is always that of what would have happened under the alternate opportunities among which the decision maker had a choice. If a resource could have been used elsewhere, its cost value was the possible return in the highest valued alternate use. On the other hand, no decision alternative would have avoided the use of a resource, the expenditure is not, for the purpose of that decision, a cost. If any decision actually made misses making a profit which an alternative would have captured, the profit foregone will not appear on the books or on the tax report as a loss. Nevertheless, that opportunity loss is just as much a loss as though the better alternative had been chosen, as if the profit had actually been earned, then stolen by some embezzler or other thief.

All classifications must therefore always be questioned in terms of their relevance and meaning for a given purpose of measurement.

THE DISTORTIONS OF INDIRECT MEASUREMENT

Many of the things we wish to measure are not directly observable and we must measure something else which is observable and can be assumed to be a criterion as to the measure of the phenomenon whose quantity is desired. This is a problem even in the measurement of stable physical realities such as temperature.

No one has ever seen temperature--all we ever see are results of the internal, unseen phenomenon of the energy form we call heat. Centuries of observation and experiment have, however, demonstrated a very close relationship between expansion of various physical materials and heat. So we look at the height of a column of mercury, for example, and read the result as so many degrees of temperature. This reading has proved to be a very accurate measure of many physical phenomena associated with heat--for instance, the speed of a chemical reaction. Since the observed relationships have proved stable, we may even tend to think of our measurement as direct. But it is not a direct one in the sense of the measurement of length we make when we compare the length of a desk with a standard such as a foot rule or a meter stick.

The value of any indirect measurement rests on the correctness and the stability of the assumed relationship between the actual phenomenon being measured and the measurable effect which is taken as a criterion. Even in the physical world there can be problems, but they are simpler of solution than those facing decisions involving human reaction.

Sales trends, for example, are often used to measure the trend in profit because profit can only be estimated and then much later than desired, and not always with ease. Yet sales are often pushed at the expense of profit, and frequently, a greater total profit can be had by seeking sales where the volume is low, but the margin higher.

The advertiser wants to know how much effect his advertising is having on his eventual total sales, but cannot measure this separately from the other factors of product quality, competition, distribution, publicity, sales effort, etc. So he looks at the readership of his ads, or the rating of his TV shows. The two do measure, in part, the attention-getting effect of his promotion. However, experiments have indicated that the more attention some ads get, the less likely is the reader to buy the product. Even more confusing, a number of studies have shown that the relationship between purchase and advertising readership is reversed--that those who already have purchased are more likely to read the ads for a product than those who have not yet bought. The assumed cause-and-effect relationship is plausible but not true, at least universally.

For another example, the U.S. defense establishment long was led astray in evaluating its efforts in Vietnam because of reliance on the wrong indirect measures. Lacking the kind of direct measures of success available in normal warfare-- land and objectives taken--it fell back on counting of enemy personnel losses, and on proportions of votes cast for the central government. Meanwhile, the enemy was building its strength in the countryside, and revealed in the Tet offensive of 1968 that it was far from defeated.

Even when measures are direct or at least valid, the impossibility of getting a complete measure causes measurement problems.

INCOMPLETE MEASUREMENT--INDEX PROBLEMS

Measurement often has to be incomplete for one or more of a number of reasons:

--Complete measurement may be conomically impractical because it is difficult to combine several dimensions in a single number

--the multitude of measurements needed to achieve completeness is too large to justify use of all of them, economically

--the concept whose measure is sought not only includes a lot of dimensions, but all of those dimensions are not clearly defined.

Most such uses also involve indirect measurements, and in any event, the measure we get is best distinguished as an index . The decision maker needs to be especially wary in the use of indexes. He needs to keep alert to the real difference between the index values of the criteria he uses for data collection and the true values he is seeking to learn.

A good example of an incomplete measure from the physical world is the use of air temperature as an index of comfort. The physical comfort of human beings is related to temperature, but the air temperature alone does not measure probable comfort. An air temperature of well over 80 degrees F. can feel distinctly chilly if the surrounding wall surfaces are at 50 degrees F. , for example. Conversely, an air temperature of 65 degrees, even at the same relative humidity,

can feel comfortably warm if the surrounding surfaces are at
85 degrees. The relative humidity is also an extremely important factor, as anyone who has lived in coastal regions knows.
It is possible to construct some sort of comfort index, of
course, by including some kind of weighting of each of these
three factors, but human sensation is sufficiently variable that
all human observers would not agree on the exact point of comfort, or the degree by which some other point missed this target.

Constructing a comfort index is a simple task in comparison with measuring changes in the general price level.
Prices are notoriously independent of each other. At any point
of time, some are going up, some are stationary, and some
are going down, even in the wildest era of inflation. "The
general price level" is shorthand for the purchasing power of
the money we hold. This, unfortunately will differ according
to what we wish to purchase. The purchase pattern, in turn,
differs, from buyer to buyer, for one buyer from one week to
the next and one year to another, and even differs with the
shifting relative position of prices. In addition, any one average supermarket will have about 8,000 items on the shelves
(some carry 15,000 or more) and a department store may
carry 50,000 items. Moreover, the total market covers tens
of thousands of other consumer and industrial items. Clearly,
the measurement problem is formidable, and complete measurement not even definable. So we set up a few indexes of
price movement.

The best known price movement index is the Consumer
Price Index calculated monthly by the United States Bureau of
Labor Statistics. The "market basket" priced covers only 400
items of consumption--not the tens of thousands of possible
consumer items. The weights are based on average purchases
made by wage earners and clerical workers in each class of
product as determined by survey in some base year. The
weights do not change with the prices. Although meats are
included, each kind and cut has a fixed weight. If the national
supply of beef and thus actual consumption is short, the rise in
price is recorded, but the index does not reflect either the
drop in use of beef nor the corresponding rise in consumption
of pork and poultry (also in the index as fixed weights).

Furthermore, the index represents only an average for
a relatively young urban family of four (father 38, nonworking

mother, boy 13, girl 8), and thus does not correspond with the expenditures of most specific families of four even in this age and working class, nor among families of other classes with other cultural and expenditure patterns, or families with working mothers (over a third of the total), or any of the other real variations. Goods priced are very carefully and rigidly defined, but changes in design from year to year are not evaluated in terms of value/price relationships. Last year's Ford-Chevy-Plymouth average car of the selected model is considered the equivalent quality of this year's.

All of these limitations are well known to the BLS, and carefully publicized, of course. The index claims only to indicate the direction and a rough degree of the relative amount of movement in what is happening to purchasing power. It does not measure what happens to your dollar or to mine, and it is doubtful if any measure devised could. What such a measure would seek is both too big a job, and one not objectively definable. Nothing objective could measure the changes in satisfaction obtained over time. This changes with the income itself, with changes in prices and in goods, with changes in the social structure affecting the individual, and with all the changes in inner drives and taste.

All that most of our indirect measures can do for us is to give a very rough measure of the general direction of changes, and the general order of value of those changes.

The quality is never up to the level of precision the actual figures seem to imply to the uninitiated.

OBSERVATIONAL PROBLEMS--THE INSTRUMENT AND THE OBSERVER

In the final analysis, all measurement traces back to some human observer with all of his variability of judgment and of perception. All must be carried out with some kind of instrument, which can inflict mechanical defects of its own. All must be expressed in some kind of units, and these are not God-given, but defined by some very fallible humans. Finding a suitable and dependable instrument is often the most difficult part of measurement.

Humans can err and will always differ to some degree, even with themselves, in such an objective process as the reading of a thermometer or a linear measure. In fact, the

36

full name of the so-called normal curve is "normal curve of error." It is the random distribution of measurement variations obtained by a single competent observer, using the same instrument to measure the same phenomenon. Every scientist is aware of such variation and, whenever possible, averages several observations when making a measurement. In addition to such random variations, however, individual observers usually have their own biases--variations from the true value which are directional and thus do not cancel out.

One type of bias is that of point of observation--the phenomenon recognized as parallax in physical measurement. The unskilled observer, in particular, may look at an instrument from an angle, and thus line up the indicator with a different number from the one directly opposite.

A more important source of observer bias arises from differences in discrimination and perception. Experts, for example, often perceive quality differently than do laymen. Their training and experience enables them to perceive finer differences than the layman. The brewmaster can distinguish the taste differences between batches in his brewery imperceptible to most laymen. In addition, however, the expert may place more importance on some kinds of differences than do those without his interest, and thus he may measure value in a biased manner relative to the demand in the market.

Whoever does the measuring must do it in terms of some kind of instrument, and the means of measurement may itself give rise to bias and variation. For most organizational measures and decisions, money is the instrument by which inputs and outputs are usually reduced to measurable terms. Money is supposed to measure value, but it certainly does not do so in as objective and unvarying a manner as the international meter measures length. One dollar has quite a different value to two different men, to the same man under different circumstances or at two different periods of time. Moreover, what is expressed in dollars is often not money, but something whose value is simply estimated in monetary terms. As was indicated above, the cost data, always expressed in monetary terms, depends heavily on the judgment of those making the cost calculation.

Monetary value, moreover, is only a partial and biased measure of value. The price of any purchase can include varying amounts of time and convenience cost, not easily expressed in money, and of search effort.

One of the most difficult instruments to develop is one measuring "if not" characteristics. A firm with a maximum share of a convenience goods market (chewing gum or beer, for example) may feel certain that a relatively high level of advertising is necessary simply to maintain its market position. It may also know that a brief hiatus in its effort produces no measurable drop in market share. How does the president determine how much is needed, or justify a level such as $20 million for example? The Police Department may feel certain it is quite successful, and if right, all it will have to show is a low crime and arrest figure. Again, a short let-up will probably produce no noticeable effect. How can the department support the necessity of any given force level?

Two things are obvious: (a) the questions are not easy to answer, and (b) those making the budgeting decision must use some means of measuring value. Two approaches have some validity when used with eyes-open care. One that advertisers sometimes attempt is some indirect and partial effect measurements of attitude which have at least a logical relationship to functional results expected. The other method is to seek some parallel situation, one in which the forces being measured are weaker or absent, and use this as an index of the value of the force. Direct measurement of the value of the success of the Secret Service in suppressing counterfeiting, for example, is extremely difficult or impossible. But there are analog situations in industry which are not nearly as well policed--the pirating of designs in toys and garments, for instance. The incentives for such piracy are similar to those in counterfeiting money, the sanctions controlling the piracy not nearly so efficient. A little investigation of the extent of this problem would yield a rough measure of the effectiveness of the Secret Service's work.

CHOOSING THE UNIT OF MEASUREMENT

Units of measurement are always largely a matter of arbitrary choice, but the wrong choice can impede comparison or comprehension. Whenever the observer has a choice, he should choose a unit which is:
1. large enough for convenient comparison--one which does not result in astronomical numbers (such as measuring the distance from earth to moon in inches or centimeters).

2. small enough to be sensitive to real differences in terms of integral quantities--in other words, one which minimizes the need to express results in fractions.

3. greater than the usual range of uncertainty in measurement and thus expresses only those differences which are really significant.

4. homogeneous--does not include in one unit items which are, for the purpose of analysis, disparate. Thus in the analysis of markets, a county usually includes quite divergent smaller areas.

5. stable--a type of unit which does not shift in value because of extraneous forces. Generally, this means using physical measures in preference to monetary measures where there is a choice, since money values can change when no change takes place in the physical quantity represented.

6. expressed in terms of outputs and effects rather than inputs. Advertising impact is not a direct function of cost, for example, but of the change in attitude it causes. The efficiency of a labor operation is not measured by items worked on or degree of activity, but on useful or valuable outputs (which may often result in a visibly lower workload.)

Many of the figures we use for evaluation in particular raise problems of unit definition. How do we count the riders on the bus system? We can count the number of fares collected per day, for example, but this is merely a count of fares--not of riders. For some riders, one fare may mean one rider that day. For many more, two fares equals one rider. For some tourists, perhaps, one rider may have paid 8 fares in travelling about. The incidence of fares tells us nothing about how many people used the service.

Such incidence figures are easy to get, and therefore measurable. It is easy to count fares or admissions or employment service interviews. But none of these tell one important fact we often desire to measure: how many people have we been serving? For example, a sales promotion contest designed to promote sampling of the product, may have pulled in 1,000,000 entries. Did we get 1,000,000 families to try the product? Experience suggests the possibilities that the 1 million coupons may have come from only 200,000 families.

This is harder to measure, but might be possible. But even families purchasing does not really tell us what we want to know. The promotion really was of value only to the extent that those entering the contest were first-time tryers. As a unit of measure for this, the contest entries is a valueless figure.

Incidence figures, such as attendance, employment interviews, or job placements are of questionable value because of the multiple counting and the lack of quality indications. But even a complete case count may lead to double counting. An organization which reported annually on number of individuals treated proved to have an average case endurance of 13 months. Their annual report was automatically reporting double the organization's throughput.

EFFECTS ON MEASUREMENT OF TIME PERIOD, TIMING AND THE PASSAGE OF TIME

Time is the greatest source of instability of measurement. The time period covered can itself result in differences in the very important details of composition of the total. Consider an attempt to measure the market served by a ski lodge, for instance. Some of the users visit for one day only and do not return. Some stay for a single visit, but remain for a week. Some come regularly, every weekend only. Each type of visitor has different distinguishing customer characteristics, and it could be important to know how important each type is to the success of the operation. Consider the differing effects of 3 different bases for counting customers: a one-day count, a one-week tabulation, and a full-season sample taken on 20 random days.

In the full-season sample, both the every weekend guests and the one-week guests would be counted more than once, and roughly in proportion to the intensity of their patronage. Such a sample would measure the relative business value of each public from which the lodge drew its trade. The one-week sample would give less weight to the weekender, who would be counted on three days only for a single trip, than to the one-visit customer. The one-day cross section would give the same weights to the one-day, one-trip visitor, the weekender, and the one-stay, week-long visitor, distorting the relative importance of the casual customer.

Totals used in comparisons can be affected by the point

of time a measurement is taken. The differences can be quite obvious whenever a shift is made in the point of measurement, especially in accounting for costs. When is a cost incurred? Different bookkeeping systems may use any of seven points of time--the time of ordering (or of legislative authorization), the time of receipt into inventory, the date removed from inventory for use, the date of the billing, the date the check is used in payment, or the date the check is returned to the bank and debited against the account. A cash system uses one of the latter--usually the date of the check. An accrual system throws the measurement into an earlier time period. Whenever the accounting is changed from a cash to an accrual basis, expenses can jump without any change in the firms' obligations.

The passage of time can change the real length of our measuring sticks, particularly those related to money. The definition of a felony--a major crime, that is--is a monetary one. In most jurisdictions the dividing line between petty larceny and grand larceny has been $100 for many years and was $50 for generations previously. In quantity, this seems to be a relatively stable measure. But when a man stole $50 in 1910, he was taking as much as two months' wages for some skilled workers. When he steals $100 in 1976, his take is less than 3 days' pay for an unskilled worker. Such a change in significance clearly could push up the apparent level of major crime in a period when it really is decreasing.

Similarly, the significance of income tax exemptions has changed drastically in the generation since World War II. The $2,400 exemption for a family of four once eliminated any significant tax obligation for many middle class families. By the 1970's, the $3,000 exemption meant that poverty level families ("below $3,300," officially) were paying a substantial income tax.

Thus time, in its many guises, erodes the quality level of our measurements.

THE DIFFERING LEVELS OF MEASUREMENT QUALITY

By this point it should be clear that not all numerical information is of the same level of quality. The specific numerical symbol denoting a measurement, such as 3.5436, can be at any point in the complete range of precision, from no meaning at all up to the one part in 100,000 level that the figures seem to indicate, depending both on how it was arrived

at, and on the use to which it is to be put. We need to assess
both the quality of the original measurement and the meaning
of this measurement in terms of the future in which action is
contemplated before we can determine whether 3.5436 is a
meaningful quantity at all for the current purpose, whether it
means something roughly between 3 and 4, or really is 3.5436
in terms of that decision. Numbers of any kind, whether expressed in dollars, feet, or B.A. degrees granted, have to be
evaluated by the user.

Meaningless and Ambiguous Quantities

The decision maker must ask himself what meaning and
how much there is in any quantity given him as a basis for
action. However precise it looks, a figure has no meaning if it
is based on some purely arbitrary guess. It means nothing if
it expresses a ratio in which the numerator and the denominator
come from different universes, or if it is to be applied to a
different universe than that from which it is taken. The widespread circulation of figures of all kinds resulting from some
purely arbitrary and even biased guess is greater than is
commonly realized. Few business conventions go by without
quotation in some speech of at least one of the more common
meaningless statistics. Probably no harm is done in such an
atmosphere, but no serious decision should be founded on
figures whose source has not been carefully investigated.
Even more common, however, is the ambiguous statis-
tic, the figure that looks like a careful and useful calculation,
but actually has no meaning by itself and needs supplementing.
Averages, including rates, are peculiarly susceptible to
meaningless ambiguity. An excellent example familiar to
those in academic life is the grade point average by which students are ranked, and which is not uncommonly calculated to
the fifth significant figure (to the fourth decimal place).   In
this context, 3.5436 would mean an excellent course record
for a graduating senior, one in which over half the student's
grades were A. (A is valued at 4 points, B at 3, C at 2, etc.)
But as a measure of the ability and diligence of two seniors
being interviewed for a job, how good is this record? Do two
students with this same score offer equally good prospects as
employees?
One student attended a school in which the dean is interested in building up enrollments without regard for quality,

and exerts constant pressure on any teacher whose grades average low. In addition, this student has carefully detoured any electives with a reputation for difficulty and schedules instructors and courses on the basis of the instructor's reputation for grading. The other chose a school with a reputation for quality of instruction, chose courses which he felt would add most to his knowledge, including many with reputations for difficulty and volumes of work. Which would you hire, and how would you quantify the difference?

Obviously, schools must use some system of ranking students, and recruiters need some estimate of a student's achievement, but it is the height of nonsense to attach any meaning under any circumstances to digits beyond the first two (one decimal place), and even in the same school and with the same major specialization, even the first decimal place is no more than a very rough ranking for administrative convenience.

With academicians, who ought to know better, perpetuating such obvious nonsense, it is not surprising to find similar uncritical worship of the ambiguous figure in the business world. The most notorious is probably the slavish acceptance of radio and television ratings. Much too frequently, sponsorship decisions are made after the first few showings, and shows are scuttled for lack of a few decimals of total audience tune-in, at a time when neither the content of that audience nor the impact nor compatibility of the program with the advertising can be known. Again, we do need some means of ranking shows as advertising vehicles, but the figures used cannot be an unambiguous measure of what we need to know. Ratings, at best, are a very rough ranking of total set tune-ins, and there are other factors of even greater importance at times. Without knowledge of these factors, such ratings do not even rate the significance of the lowest quality of measurement value, the nominal level.

THE FOUR LEVELS OF MEASUREMENT QUALITY

Those accustomed to working with measurement recognize four general levels of measurement quality, divided into two main groups--parametric and nonparametric. The precision most of us attribute to numbers is true only of the two highest levels--the parametric levels, designated as ratio measures and as other interval measures. Most of the figures used in governmental and business decision do not meet the parametric test in the context of their use. They usually belong to the higher of the two non-parametric levels when they have any meaning at all--to the ordinal level. The lowest level is the nominal level.

The simplest way the describe the difference between the parametric and the nonparametric levels is to note that parametric numbers can be used in ordinary arithmetric computation. We can legitimately add them, subtract, divide, etc., because the interval between any two adjacent numbers in the sequence equals the interval between any other two. Nonparametric numbers look the same in print, but 2 plus 3 may not equal 5, but perhaps 21 or 2-1/2. Nonparametric numbers are essentially labels for relative position, not proportional scale lengths.

Parametric Levels of Measurement

Measurement systems in which the scale intervals are provably equal are called parametric. There are two such types: interval systems and ratio systems. The difference between the two is in the location of the zero value. The zero value is arbitrary in interval systems, such as our Fahrenheit and Celsius temperature scales. In ratio systems, such as the absolute temperature scale and the meter stick, the zero point is "real", in the sense that there are no minus values. Most physical measurements today are of one or the other of these parametric levels because of the painstaking standardization research of the past 500 years. Previously, a "foot" meant literally that-- the length of the pedal extremity of whoever was doing the measuring. Other physical measurements exhibited the same degree of imprecision and variability. Only after such approximations were discarded could physical scientists begin to make the extensive use of mathematical manipulation characteristic of today. Even so, were the materials as unstable and changing in character as is most of human economic and social behavior, it is doubtful if their neat computations would prove nearly so useful. Even the engineer finds his slide rule and computer of very limited value when he enters the area of innovation and the unique in developing really new design. By contrast, administrative decision must normally be concerned with the unique and innovative.

At first glance, most of the financial information used in business and government might seem to meet the parametric equal interval test. Clearly, any dollar in a total stack of money

44

equals any other dollar. However, the tally of expenditures and receipts in a financial statement is not really a count of dollar bills, or of money at all, but of values which have simply been estimated in dollar terms. As already indicated, all dollars listed as spent are not properly classified as true costs, and some very real financial costs have been omitted from such tallies. Moreover, money costs are not the whole of the price paid in most transactions, nor is all of the value received accurately measured or even measureable in monetary terms. The dollar tag put on the value of an asset may not reflect what it would sell for on liquidation, or even be a reasonable reflection of its income-producing potential. Furthermore, when the data given is actual, it records something out of past history. The only utility this history has is to indicate the need for some kind of management control action in the present or some plan for the future. The circumstances which gave rise to the figures will have changed by the time they are put to use, decreasing substantially whatever remaining degree of precision they may have had originally. Often, the quantities stated represent only a rough order of value, and must be treated as ordinal in value.

The Nonparametric Measures: Ordinal and Nominal

Although nonparametric measurements are most often designated with the same kind of numbers as parametric measures, the figures denoting such measurements are merely labels without any implication of proportionality. Ordinary arithmetic operations can be applied physically to such numbers of course, but the answer which results is meaningless.

Numbers or any other labels used merely for classification are designated as nominal measurement. Most nominal measures are so obvious that little temptation exists to treat them as quantities. Many such measures do not resort to numbers at all. The terms men, women, cost, profits, and loss are examples of verbal labels on nominal measurements. Like any other measurement, these terms need just as much scrutiny for the validity of the classification as any other, of course, The class labels frequently are numbers, as in catalog listings. Thus 3.5436 might be such a catalog number--a shorthand designation which enables the buyer to order exactly and the seller to recognize the item precisely, together with

45

its warehouse location and the buying official or production department head responsible for its stocking. This is probably the only level of numerical measurement that occasions no confusion.

Ordinal or ranking measurement. The greatest confusion in the use of numerical information results from the lack of recognition of the difference between numbers that do indicate some differences in value, but only the general order or rank, and numbers, like those on our common foot rule and other measuring sticks, with known intervals. Any academic grading system is a ranking, or ordinal, system, no matter how expressed (and so, unfortunately, is nearly all of the data we must use for business decision).

The nature and meaning of ordinal measurement is probably best observed in the academic grading system. Within any given classroom group, the instructor can usually do a pretty accurate job of ranking the students according to their level of understanding of the particular subject being taught and divide the students into at least the five general groups designated by the commonly used letter system: A, B, C, D and F. For administrative convenience, the university office assigns numerical values from 4 down through 0 to these grades, and makes up the Grade Point Average value already referred to. But this is a mere convenience. Only a purblind instructor will insist that an A in one of his courses has exactly the same meaning as an A in a different course of his own, e.g., that an A in his Introduction to Economics has the same meaning (whatever that is) as an A in his graduate seminar on International Problems of Economic Growth. And the difference between instructors and subjects on any campus is well known. So is the difference between schools.

But not only does one A not equal another A. Beyond the point of ranking, we have no meaningful way of comparing the relative value of two ranks. For purposes of getting that sheepskin, an A is counted at twice the value of a C--four points as compared with two. But does the A student have twice the knowledge and understanding that the C student does? Most of us would say that depends on what sort of task you ask the student to apply his knowledge to. For relatively routine tasks putting insight, imagination, and judgment to little strain, there may be little or no difference between the A students as a whole and the C students. But if they were to be assigned to a critical piece of research analysis, the C student might not be able to produce at all, and there would be wide differences between the productivity of the A students, with some of them providing an extremely useful answer, and doing it in a fourth of the time of others with a similar grade ranking. Such ordinal values, in other words, tell us only relative position, not distance between ranks, and even then, only roughly.

Nearly all of the data we must use for business decision is of this ordinal level of quality. Television ratings are of this character. They do tell something of audience size, but not necessarily much about the relative quality of the program as an advertising medium for a particular product. One of the most effective programs for one particular kind of advertising the author has ever seen was a very low-rated Saturday evening program built around films produced by the narrator, a man who pursued the hobby of time-lapse photography of plants and flowers. The rating of this show was abysmally low by any normal standards. But garden shops soon learned to stock heavily any item featured, for there was always a heavy run the following Sunday morning. Similarly, price data, sales potential estimates, and most other data on which decision output must be estimated is largely a matter of relative rank, not interval measurement.

Well-managed purchasing departments have long since learned, for example, that even for the same commodity, relative price is not equivalent to relative cost, and have developed vendor rating systems to attempt to take into account other elements of value important to the particular firm. Even for standardized commodities, price is at best an ordinal measure of value. Price information must be supplemented with information on delivery, dependability of source, uniformity of grading and other factors. Similarly, the best estimate of relative sales potentials makes assumptions about relative strength of competition, habits of consumption, and other crucial factors that are quite unlikely to be accurate. Even cost information that is meticulously accurate historically can be, at best, only an approximate projection of future costs.

Indeed, the fact that decision must anticipate a future that is somewhat different is one reason why little decision data will ever be more than a rough approximation. Tastes, technology, population and its distribution, and the identity and aggressiveness of competitors change with time, and some-

47

times overnight. Financial figures which are accurate historically become rough approximations of the future costs and
receipts relationships which need to be measured. Major
policy decisions, which inevitably deal with nonrepetitive
events, will nearly always have to make use of quantitative
information that indicates little more than a rough ordinal level
of relative value. Such data cannot be fit into neat mathematical equations.

As with every other aspect of measurement, the origin
of quantitative data does not tell us its quality. The quality as
well as the meaning is completely relative to the purpose to
which the measurement result is to be applied. The cost
accountant, for example, may have done a completely perfect
job of evaluating the cost experience of several alternative
products or programs. For the purpose of historical comparison, the data may be completely parametric. But if the same
figures are used to predict probable future costs, his figures
are approximations at best, and may even be maliciously misleading, particularly if not related to the experience curve.

The most important element in all measurement is the
user himself, and he has the task of adjudging the extent to
which data made available to him serves his purpose and the
degree of approximation the data has when used for that purpose.

EVALUATING AND USING MEASUREMENTS:
THE USE OF APPROXIMATION

Clearly all measurement involves a considerable degree of approximation. That degree of approximation, moreover, is definable only in terms of the purpose, in terms of
what the measurement is going to be used to represent. For
purposes of executive decision, the use of any quantitative data
carries an implicit assumption that the data is a sample, representing more information than it explicitly contains. Otherwise, the process would not be that of decision but the application of a known policy by a reasonably intelligent clerk. Indeed, the job of any executive could be accurately defined as
the application of judgment to interpret the meaning and degree
of approximation in the combined qualitative and quantitative
information he has available, in the light of objectives he himself has set. Others can carry out the calculations, but the

executive must determine what figures go into the computation, and what the results mean.

Since no figure is more than an approximation, a very important first step in that process of evaluating data is to determine the degree of approximation by asking himself a series of questions:

> How do we know? (Are the data real, or just some horseback guesses?)
>
> What do I intend to use the data for?
>
> For what purpose was it collected, and how did this distort the meaning, relative to my purpose for its use?
>
> Does the data contain irrelevant material?
>
> In terms of my use objectives, are the categories of classification really homogeneous? If not, how can the data be reorganized or interpreted to yield relatively homogeneous classifications which are truly relevant to my use?
>
> Do the categories used include significant quantities which are irrelevant for my purpose-- costs which are unavoidable in any case, for example?
>
> Do any of the categories used omit substantial quantities which are significant for my purpose, such as imputed opportunity costs in money or effort which are quite real, but not recorded?
>
> What is the degree of indirectness of the measurement? Are the assumed relationships between measures and the phenomena they represent valid, either originally, or in terms of my objective for their use?
>
> How incomplete is the measurement and what is the probable significance of the omissions, relative to my need?
>
> How precise is the job of measurement and how biased the observations?
>
> What effect could time factors have had in creating differences I perceive, or in changing the scale or significance of the measurements?
>
> In terms of my purpose, at what point of expression does approximation begin?

Evaluation of data in terms of level of approximation is

important both to ease of handling and to understanding of significance. Physical scientists long ago learned that no data is truly parametric beyond some discoverable level of approximation. Unfortunately, much policy decision in business and government ignores this experience.

SIGNIFICANT FIGURES: EXPRESSING FIGURES AT THEIR LEVEL OF APPROXIMATION

A well-trained scientist always indicates the degree of approximation in his data by the degree of precision in his statement. Asked to give the distance from earth to moon, he will state it as 92.8×10^6 miles, not $92,800,000$ miles. By this he means that he does not know what the figures should be in the positions in which most of us write the 0's, at least until he knows the time, place, and purpose of the measurement (such as the spot on the moon and the exact time and date on which we hope to land a rocket there).

Most nonscientists probably dislike reading approximations in terms of powers of 10, and this form complicates the typing of a table. The same end is achieved by saying the distance is 92.8 million miles, or if in the form of a table, labelling the column or row as "distance in miles (000,000 omitted)" and entering the number as **92.8**.

Such care in precision is not an academic exercise, but a method of (a) indicating the limit on the relevance and degree of certainty of the measurement and (b) focusing attention on those figures which are really significant. For this reason, the mode of expressing precision is known as "significant figures." The purpose of limiting attention to significant figures is to avoid cluttering comparisons with irrelevant detail. Thus if we desire to compare the costs of 4 programs, it is much easier to make the comparison in terms of a significant figure approximation than in a 7 figure presentation, as can be seen:

Costs	Costs (000,000 omitted)
$9,636,783	$9.6
7,187,336	7.2
3,007,996	3.0
4,998,655	5.0

The term "significant figure" relates to the number of figure symbols, <u>starting the count from the first nonzero symbol on the left.</u> After all, it is the difference in millions we need to give the most consideration, not the pennies and individual dollars at the right-hand side. Each significant figure added to our precision of statement implies accuracy to an added power of 10. Even engineers find estimates of stable inanimate nature are not better than 1 in 1,000 (three significant figures equal 10 x 10 x 10). How much less meaningful is data in the world of human whimsy?

Calculations expressed in greater precision than is justified by the measurements tend to hide meaningful differences under the spurious or redundant detail, making the data hard to analyze. Consider the following not untypical table, a disguised but precise paraphrase of one appearing in a serious and really well-planned experiment in advertising psychology (Table 2-1). In this experiment, carefully controlled small groups of subjects were exposed to visual and audio stimuli of each of three types, and each possible combination of the types (arbitrarily labeled L, M, and N in Table 2-1). From a larger group of stimuli submitted for test, each subject was asked to recall the original stimuli now presented in one of the possible combinations. (Blanks in the table indicate test-presentation situation pairs that were impossible due to physical absurdities such as recognition of an audio-only presentation from a pictorial test.) Because of the large number of test-presentation possibilities, the total of over 1,000 subjects split up into groups ranging only between 23 and 36 in number, as noted in the table.

Some significant differences were found, but note how hard it is to spot them by glancing at the table. This difficulty stems from the use of calculations going to more than the level of two significant figures, which the data permit, thus burying the only significant differences which do exist in the middle of each percentage shown. Table 2-1 reproduces the results of the experiment as originally reported, indicating the confusion caused even for an expert attempting to understand the findings when figures beyond the point of significance are included. Table 2-2 corrects the presentation of the same numerical results by reducing the numbers to the level of significance appropriate to the true accuracy of the data and clarifies the table by separating actual experimental results and the report

51

on the number of subjects involved in each experimental cell.

TABLE 2-1. THE INCORRECT ORIGINAL PRESENTATION OF DATA

Average Percentage of Recall of 25 Similar Stimuli
for 3 Different Forms of Stimulus Presentation,
and Combinations of These Forms

(n = number of subjects cooperating in each version of the test.)

Method of Initial Presentation	Method of Presentation for Test of Recall:						
	L	M	N	L&M	L&N	M&N	L,M&N
L	49.35 (n=23)	49.42 (n=24)	---	50.54 (n=23)	42.53 (n=25)	46.81 (n=23)	47.68 (n=24)
M	48.38 (n=24)	53.65 (n=24)	---	52.16 (n=24)	42.64 (n=24)	47.04 (n=23)	47.62 (n=24)
N	---	---	45.63 (n=23)	---	42.06 (n=23)	42.17 (n=25)	40.77 (n=23)
L,M&N	46.08 (n=34)	49.19 (n=36)	41.26 (n=34)	51.14 (n=35)	48.05 (n=35)	47.05 (n=34)	52.08 (n=35)
L&M	49.30 (n=31)	49.57 (n=31)	---	53.13 (n=30)	43.58 (n=30)	46.82 (n=29)	45.84 (n=36)
L&N	50.13 (n=32)	51.21 (n=28)	45.97 (n=31)	51.82 (n=24)	50.11 (n=28)	49.27 (n=31)	52.25 (n=29)
M&N	46.88 (n=28)	49.04 (n=27)	43.25 (n=26)	53.06 (n=31)	47.87 (n=28)	49.56 (n=31)	51.81 (n=31)

These calculations should not have been carried beyond the even percentage level, and even this detail strains the rules slightly for convenience of presentation. At this level, each integer represents a difference of one part in one hundred. But individual scores could only be as close as four parts in one hundred, since each subject had only twenty-five chances to be either right or wrong, i. e., 25 test pictures or other

TABLE 2-2. A CORRECT PRESENTATION OF THE DATA IN TABLE 2-1

Average Percentage of Recall of 25 Similar Stimuli, for 3 Different Forms of Stimulus Presentation, and Combinations of These Forms

(Number of subjects in individual experiments ranges from 23 to 36.)

Method of Initial Presentation	Method of Presentation for Test of Recall:						
	L	M	N	L&M	L&N	M&N	L, M&N
L	49	49	--	51	43	47	48
M	48	54	--	52	43	47	48
N	--	--	46	--	42	42	41
L&M	49	50	--	53	44	47	46
L&N	50	51	46	52	50	49	52
M&N	47	49	43	53	48	50	52
L, M&N	46	49	41	51	48	47	52

Number of Subjects in Each Individual Experiment

	L	M	N	L&M	L&N	M&N	L, M&N
L	23	24	--	23	25	23	24
M	24	24	--	24	24	23	24
N	--	--	23	--	23	25	23
L&M	31	31	--	30	30	29	36
L&N	32	28	31	24	28	31	29
M&N	28	29	26	31	28	31	31
L, M&N	34	36	34	35	35	34	35

stimuli to recognize. The original table percentages are to four significant figures, however, implying an accuracy to one part in ten thousand.

The table presented, however, is an average of scores, each possibly accurate to four parts in one hundred. If we could assume the individual's score could not vary, we might be justified in going one step further so that we would have an accuracy to about one part in six hundred (25 subjects times

25 stimuli). However, psychological measurement of this sort is almost never this precise. If we assume a normal measurement variation, the group average error has an even chance of being nearly 7 percent for groups of 25 subjects, assuming the average is correct at about 50 percent recognition.

$$\text{Standard deviation of the average} = \frac{.50 \times .50}{25} = .10$$

Chances are equal at about two-thirds this value, or .07, i.e., 7 percent. This difference is nearly as great as some of the differences in the table, as can be clearly seen from a revision of this table to even percentages. However, the consistency in the differences, when we eliminate the fictitious detail of fractional percentages, indicates that the differences are probably real.

Redundant and fictional detail has contributed to confusion in another way. For reasons with which any experienced investigator is familiar, the researchers were unable to end up with equal-sized test groups. The variation, as noted, ran from 23 to 36. Thus some differences at even the straight percentage would have shown up even if, in fact, there had been no underlying difference in the probability of recognition, due simply to the vagaries of calculation from different group totals to get the percentages. Consider, for one example, the first two recall percentages in the first row of Table 2-1 (the L-L and L-M pairs): 49.35 and 49.52. The first represents the average score for 23 subjects, the second for 24 subjects. The simple fact that these two totals differ yields a different percentage result. This can be seen if we assume that the scores for the first 23 subjects in each group are identical, giving us the average for the first group: 49.35. The 24th subject in the second group, let us assume, also, was just as likely to recall as the group average, or nearly even. But his actual score could not be closer than either 48 percent (12 recalled out of 25) or 52 percent (13 remembered out of 25). Under these assumptions the score for the larger group would have to be either 49.29 or 49.46. In actuality, it was in between these two results and closer to that of the first group than would have occurred under our assumptions. Thus the calculation beyond the even percentage confuses us by showing differences where none exist in fact.

The source of the example used here has been disguised

54

because the procedure was no worse than is the common practice in most of business figure usage. It demonstrates empirically what any mathematician or engineer would have seen from the mere numbers involved. The decimal values presented are meaningless and result in a presentation of spurious precision. For this reason alone, the calculations should not have been carried beyond even percentages.

The Rules for Evaluating the True Level of Approximation in the Original Measurements and any Resulting Computations are:

1. A measurement is meaningless past the first point of estimate available on a scale giving accurate, standardized values. If, for example, you have an accurate yardstick graduated to tenths of inches, you can measure the width of your desk with it, estimated to some simple fraction of a tenth of an inch, e.g., a third or a fifth of a tenth. If the width seems to be about a third of the way between 29.7 and 29.8 inches, you should mark it down for 29.73, "not 29.73+." You do not know whether what you estimate to be about one-third is actually more, or slightly less than .03.

2. Calculations based on counts must not be carried out to more significant figures than are contained in the total count of the base population. Statements of proportion, for example, must have the same degree of approximation as is involved in the sample size from which they are drawn (remembering that all counts are, for purposes of prognosis and prediction, samples.)

If a survey of 30 men reveals that 10 use electric razors, it is quite incorrect to say that 33.3 percent use electric razors, for by this you are stating that exactly 333 out of 1,000 would be found to shave with electricity. You do not know this to be so. If your sample, by the accidents of sampling, had turned up only 9 users of electric shavers, your calculation would have dropped to an even 30.0 percent; if 11 instead of 10, the proportion would have risen to 36.7 percent. Or if, by chance, you had simply conducted one more interview, for a total of 31 instead of 30, your discovered usage would have had to drop to 10/31 (32.3 percent) or rise to 11/31

(35.5 percent).

All you really know is that about one-third shave with electricity. You will note that this form of the statement is correct for all of the variations cited.

3. In general, any other quantity derived from a count or measure must not go beyond the precision of statement made possible by the base figure. In practice, this means that:

    a. Quantities derived by multiplication and division must be expressed in a lower level of precision than the base count, i.e., to the level that would be affected by the minimum increase or decrease in the base figures.

    b. Quantities derived by taking powers or roots may be expressed to the level of precision involved when dividing the number of significant figures in the base data by the value of the power. Pearsonian r and regression coefficients, for example, are affected because they involve calculation of squares. To justify the calculation of a coefficient to the second significant figure, therefore, the sample population studied must be in the thousands, and the other measures with which they are correlated must also be truly accurate to the fourth significant figure (to one part in 10,000). Otherwise it is quite improper, indeed untrue, to say that you have found the correlation to be .79, for example. In fact, to justify a statement that the resulting correlation is .8 requires that the base figures be accurate to one part in 100.

If such rules make an executive who is used to accounting for appropriations to the cent uncomfortable, he might reflect that he is risking his neck every day driving over a bridge designed by an engineer satisfied with the 3-significant figure precision of his slide rule. The engineer long ago learned that even in his static world of physical measurements, his data must always be treated as sample information, and that samples vary. The rest of us would do well to benefit by his experience.

HOW MUCH PRECISION DO I NEED?

This is the most useful question an observer can ask, and one which can ease many of the problems of getting a measure. Getting high precision is an expensive process, and the search is frequently a fruitless one. Quite often, we need no substantial degree of precision at all--only a rough order of value or a ranking. Almost always, a decision will be unchanged over differences of 10% or more. Indeed, many of our own human perceptions seem to recognize and respond only to differences of this general magnitude or greater. Moreover, very few decisions of any sort are irreversible, nor are many made once for all. Most involve tentative action which can be modified with the receipt of planned feedback information. We should therefore seek to obtain only that level of precision which can affect the decision we must make.

If this is done, and if it leads to the choice of a very low level--say to the nearest 10%--we may often be able to choose criteria and measuring instruments much more easily than if it were necessary to meet a demand for greater precision, and we may be able to ignore many of the lesser problems of measurement. This is especially true of formal sampling.

SUMMARY

1. A count can tell us only "how many," but we are far more often interested in the answer to "how much?" This type of number comes from a measurement process, a quite different, far more complex, much less certain, and much less objective than that of counting.

2. The validity of any measurement must be evaluated in relation to the specific purpose of its use, and the criterion of accomplishment is seldom clear and simple.

3. Measurement is a many-sided decision process with real possibilities of bias and distortion at every stage: the decision on the purpose to be served, the decision on which kinds of factors represent criteria of accomplishment of that purpose, decision on what aspects of the criteria are suitable for measurement, selection of a useful measurement unit, development of an effective measurement instrument, application of the instrument by an observer, analysis of the significance of the results in terms of the purpose. Errors in such

choices have misled many a business and governmental decision.

4. The major pitfalls in measurement are those of classification, indirect measurement, choice of instrument, selection of the unit, bias in observation, evaluation of the measurement quality achieved, ignorance of the erosive effects of time, and improper interpretation of the level of precision obtained.

5. Any number implies a classification of items on the basis of similarity. Since no two items are identical in all respects, any classification can be valid only relevant to a specific use and must be scrutinized relative to that use.

6. Much measurement must be indirect, must be measurement of some available attribute thought to be related to variations in the item whose measure is sought. The relationship always needs validation.

7. Measurement is sometimes incomplete because some factors known to be important are not measurable, or because too many factors are involved for economical investigation, or the relative importance of substantive items is not definable and stable. In such cases, we must satisfy ourselves with indexes--indicators sketching the trends and only a very rough order of value of those trends.

8. Finding an adequate instrument of measurement sometimes seems nearly impossible. Special care must be used in using monetary values as the meter, since the money value of most things can change with no change in the physical quantity involved.

9. The observer himself introduces an important source of bias into the observations.

10. Units must be chosen that are convenient, combine items which are homogeneous for the purpose of the measurement, and which are stable.

11. Time affects measurements in many ways. The choice of time period for observation can change the relative composition of a measurement. The point of time at which observation is made can affect the numbers. And the passage of time can change the significance of the classifications and the units.

12. Not all numbers have the same accuracy and precision of significance. Many quoted numbers turn out on examination to be ambiguous or meaningless, to relate to nothing definable. Only parametric measurements have the

arithmetic meaning we associate with numbers in general--
only measurements which, for the specific purpose on hand,
have truly equal intervals between the integers. Many forms
of numerical measurement do not. Ordinal values, sometimes
incorrectly treated arithmetically, simply denote a ranking
without any implication as to the distance between the various
ranks. To some degree, nearly all available data about economic and social events must be considered ordinal when used
for prediction of the future with which decision deals. The
lowest level of numerical quality is the nominal--the use of
numbers purely as identifying labels. This last use is seldom
a cause for confusion.

13. The precision of any measurement is limited, calculations should not be carried beyond this meaningful level of
precision, and significance should not be attached to figures
below this level. Moreover, few decisions require any great
level of precision, and to seek more is to multiply the expense
of measurement and to confuse the comparisons of decision
alternatives.

PART II. THE EVERYDAY TOOLS OF STA-TISTICAL ANALYSIS AND INTERPRETATION

The body of techniques we call statistics represents a higher order of abstraction than do mere numbers. All statis - tical techniques, whether so complex that they require the com- puter to be useful, or so simple that a simple exercise in mental arithmetic is enough, aim at one single purpose. That purpose is to reduce the confusion of too many numbers, which our enum- erations produce, to the simplest and most compact form pos- sible, so as to permit digestion.

The statistical tool chest contains a wide variety of imple- ments, from the computationally complex to the simplest, and new and more complex gadgets are added regularly. Most of the latter fit special needs, and are usually, unfortunately, fit only for these narrow purposes. It remains true, however, that just as the carpenter still does most of his work with a saw, hammer, and plane, all but a small fraction of the statistical tasks are well served by a handful of the computationally simplest tools of sampling, averages and measures of dispersion, and, above all, the graphic device of charting.

Simple as these tools are, computationally, the user needs a thorough understanding of both their values and limita- tions. As with tools of any sort, these simpler components of the statistical tool kit are capable of much that is not always obvious to the less skilled and understanding. They are also, like all tools, susceptible to misuse, thwarting the very deci- sion needs they are intended to meet.

3

SAMPLES:
HOW BIG IS ENOUGH?

Sampling is too commonly viewed as a specialized technical task whose results should be viewed with some measure of skepticism. Part of the reason for this may be the traditional teachings of statistics. The latter tends to imply that all samples are worthless unless chosen by a rigidly "probabilistic" procedure. Such teaching also tends to over-emphasize the error possibilities even in such cases.

Such a suspicious attitude overlooks one inescapable fact: all of the measurements of any kind we use are samples. Furthermore, when used as a basis for future expectations of economic or social events, as in any kind of planning, there is no such thing as a true probability sample. In addition, the traditional rules of sample inference are too much on the cautious side for most competitive business purposes.

The question is never whether to use a sample or not, but how to make sound use of the accidental samples and the formal sample information which is all the information we ever have. Especially when used to make plans, no observations or measurements encompass more than a small fraction of the possible aspects of any object or event. Moreover, all the information we have is about time past, which the future never duplicates. To understand what that information signifies for our plans, we need to be clear about the meaning and significance of the concepts of traditional formal sampling theory. We need also to perceive where this theory fits into the problem of drawing the kinds of samples we must use in everyday measurements. The most important of statistical concepts are those of a population or universe (also called a "sample set") and of all measurement as part of a probability distribution within such a universe or sample set.

MEASUREMENT, PROBABILITY DISTRIBUTIONS, AND POPULATIONS

Physical scientists long ago discovered that any series of readings tends to vary over some range of values when carried to the limits of the instrument's precision, even the readings of a single trained observer on a single accurate measuring instrument. When such readings are plotted as a frequency distribution, the resulting plot normally assumes a characteristic bell-shaped graph--a symmetrical plot with a heavy concentration of readings around the center. This is the Gaussian normal curve of error, or more commonly called simply the normal curve, or normal curve of probability. The central value of the curve is the arithmetic average (and also, always in such a case, the median, or center item, and the mode or most common value). This curve has a definite mathematical form. When we calculate the standard deviation, (the square root of the average of the squares of the deviations from the mean) half of all observations will be in a zone approximately two-thirds of this value of σ from the average, 95% within 2σ limits, and, 1 out of 100 observations will be outside the limits as defined as 3σ from the average.

The same kinds of distribution will normally be discovered in any situation in which all major factors effecting measurement do not change--such as the dimensions of all pieces coming from the same machine, with the same operator, using relatively uniform raw materials.

Since physical measurement is the most favorable condition for stability of observations, it should be obvious that measurements of any phenomena will vary, that all measurement, all quantitative observations of any kind, must be conceived of as probability distributions.

Not all of these distributions will exhibit the bell-shaped frequency distribution of the true normal curve. Most quantitative distributions of social and economic data seem to have a lopsided, or skew distribution. But all will have some concentration of values around some modal point, and a diminishing percentage as we proceed outward from this mode, if they are really part of the same population. This population requirement holds whether our data comes from a formal sampling procedure or is the result of accidental or nonsystematic observations over a past period.

The statistician uses population, or the technical synonyms of universe and sample set, to indicate a body of phenomena which should, for the purpose of a given measurement, yield some kind of probability distribution. A population or universe is the sum total of all possible elements that have in common the particular characteristic being studied, at one point in time, and only those individuals having the characteristic in common. The universe may be, as in the Federal Census, all the people having residence in the United States on April 1, 1980. It may be all those who bought an airline ticket to Timbuktoo during 1974. It may not be people at all, as the term population seems to imply. It may be the total of all farms on which red soft winter wheat was grown in the crop year 1975, or it may be all of the acres from which soy beans were harvested in that year.

Whether or not a collection of objects or phenomena is really a universe is not a part of nature. It depends on the nature of the later analysis to be performed on the data. For the application of statistical evaluations, the universe must contain every individual possessing the characteristic under investigation, and only those individuals. Further, the individuals must be alike in terms of this characteristic in order to be treated as statistical units. If we are sampling voters in a Department of Agriculture crop control proposal for wheat, all wheat growers would be units because they have one vote per farm. But if we wish to estimate the crop, we must count acres as the unit, even though the replies themselves must come from people. In either case, no farm which does not grow red winter wheat should be part of the universe. The statistician considers a set of phenomena a homogeneous universe when he believes one force, and only one, has any measurable influence on member events. The variations from this central value occur because an uncountable and unknowable multitude of minute factors, each of no individual consequence in the context of measurement sought, combine to cause variations in both directions.

The decision as to whether or not all measurements come from the same population is thus a judgment, although the statistician does have some negative checks. If he assumes that the central tendency of the values of a series of measurements is the result of a single influencing factor, then he assumes that, for the purpose of that one set of measurements, he is dealing with a single universe and can then make some kind of prediction concerning probable future measurement values in that universe. If he gets some anatomical measures from a sample of girls of age 12, he feels confident he can tell a garment manufacturer what sizes and what quantities of each size to make for girls of this age, in the cities and countries represented by his sample, during a period of time not very far removed from that in which the measurements were made.

Since the identification of what constitutes a population is a matter of judgment, we can define any set of quantities as a probability distribution of values if we have a good reason to believe that all of the individual values represent the effect of the same basic forces, even when the statistical purist cannot see that they are technically part of the same universe as he would define one. We all know, for example, that the various dress styles on the market are quite different in their total composition in any one year, from any other year. But we may feel that the probability distribution of taste among women, for individual dress designs available, is relatively constant, even if we cannot predict which dress style will be most popular and which least popular. We can thus take the past percentage distribution of sales by items during each season as an estimate of the kinds of distributions to expect in future seasons--as a probability distribution of what we believe that sales of any one number will be, in other words, in the population of women's styles coming out next.

This use of probability distribution of belief goes beyond the kinds of problems that traditional statistical methods deal with, but not beyond the basic significance of the terms. Many of the tools discussed in the chapters which follow make use of a series of past observations of seemingly somewhat different phenomena as a basis for estimating the probability distribution of a unique next event. If we have a sound reason for believing that such past events represent the same population, we may have a sample useful for decision even though it does not fit the rules of traditional statistics.

SAMPLES AND EVALUATION OF THEIR MEANING

A sample is some part of a population--any part, however chosen and observed. A representative sample is one

that yields closely approximate measures of those characteristics it was selected to represent. A useful sample is one
giving enough information about these characteristics so that,
when combined with what the analyst already knows, workable
inferences that are useful for decision can be drawn.

Note that while a representative sample is by definition, useful, the experienced analyst can often make use of a
nonrepresentative sample if he gets enough information about it
to fit in what he learns with existent knowledge. For example,
a really representative audit of movement of a drug brand
through retail outlets--one directly projectible to all sales--is
seldom, if ever, achieved. But the trend revealed by such
audits is usually a good reflection of the trend in movement. If
the analyst has an independent knowledge of the level of sales,
he can add this trend information to get accurate projection of
sales.

Most of us tend to apply the term sample only in relation to the formal sampling process--in relation to observations
that are labelled "sample." But there is no other kind of observation or measurement except observation of samples. The
informal and unconscious observations that we conduct all the
time, on which we base all but a minute portion of our action,
are not only samples, but often the very smallest and knowlingly
biased of samples. Nevertheless, experience usually proves
action taken on the basis of such observations can be sound.
Some of the most important decisions in our lives are made on
the basis of relatively small samples and samples that we know
to be biased.

Courtship is a sampling process. Girls and boys
associate themselves with a small number of those of the opposite sex--a select few not chosen on some sort of random probability basis, but most likely on the basis of the accidents of
propinquity. They seek each others' company during a few
hours of each week under conditions in which both are quite
aware that the behavior of the other is somewhat biased. Yet
most marriages are reasonably successful. The expectations
coming out of the courtship period are usually confirmed and
many of the divorces that do arise come out of conditions that
could not have been foreseen whatever the care taken in sampling the universe and the actions in that universe. We normally
choose our restaurants on the basis of one or two meals taken
there and make our recommendations to friends on the same

slim sample evidence. We vote for our legislators upon the most cursory analysis of their record, opinions, and character, yet usually find these legislators worth reelecting the next time.

In all these cases, we not only act on incomplete knowledge, we are consciously aware that we are so doing, although we seldom recognize the information we have as sample information. We do so because we know it is impossible to get "all of the information" even if we could afford the time and effort involved.

When we sample informally, we realize unconsciously what we should consciously recognize whenever we draw a formal sample--that all information, all samples have not one but four dimensions: numbers, the breadth of observational detail, the quality of observation of this detail, and time. All knowledge has a time bias since we can only measure what has occurred in the past. Even within that past, we usually realize that there are many things about which the numbers are so great that we cannot observe all possible happenings. But even when it might be possible to make contact with all of the numbers or happenings involved, it is not possible to take account of all possible details concerning the events themselves and surrounding events. These are infinite. We therefore limit ourselves to those we consider to have the greatest relevance to whatever kind of decision it is we have to make.

NUMBERS: WHY SMALL SAMPLES ARE OFTEN BEST

The greater the number of details we sample, the greater the job of sampling itself, since the size of the task is a product of both the numbers involved and the number of details involved in each item.

Beyond a minimum of observations, we gain more understanding of phenomena and higher accuracy of analysis by collecting more detail about each observation than by increasing the number of observations.

This has been one of the lessons of statistical quality control. With 100 percent inspection, attention is usually focused on one facet of information: which items are outside standard limits of acceptability, and how many (and even the quality of this measurement may not be good). To do this much for the entire production run is so costly that little more can be afforded in the way of useful details about the go and no-go items. If long runs are involved, 100 percent inspection is a mass production operation and must be done with an eye to mass production costs.

By contrast, statistical quality control is a small batch process. Because the total number of observations is relatively small, time and care can be spent on measuring the degree of off-standard quality and determination whence the deviation arose--from what batch of raw material, what machine, which operator, etc. Data pinpointing any need for corrective action becomes available, and the number of future off-standard pieces is reduced. Cost per item inspected will always be markedly higher than under 100 percent inspection, but total inspection cost may, just incidentally, be less. The real saving, however, lies in the control over product uniformity achieved because of broader information and the better data quality made possible by higher quality inspection personnel and the lighter stress on quantity inspection production.

Data quality results from emphasis on care and precision of measurement and close supervision of observation. There is an inverse relationship between data quality and sample size. How dramatic the gain in quality can be from the use of a formal small sample was illustrated in a mail-order tally experience. A small sample was devised to replace two 100 percent tallies of orders and customers used in making sales plans. Prior to sampling, tally results had checked so poorly with later data that they proved of little value. Sample results proved so accurate that minor errors in order handling were revealed. Yet the only difference in the information came from the quality of the personnel, their close supervision, and release from pressure for quantity production--all made possible by the small size of the sample.

When analysis begins, breadth and quality determine its accuracy, not numbers. These are matters which must be assessed on the basis of personal knowledge and judgment, and the statistician has no means of aiding this judgment. Numbers, however, can answer another kind of question for us, one worth asking: "How reliable is our data--how precise or repeatable is our measure?"* With a given sample size, i.e.,

_____

* Precision and accuracy are sometimes thought of as synonyms, but are not the same thing. <u>Accuracy</u> denotes the degree

the device used is that of "confidence limits," a measure based on the estimate of the standard deviation. With the use of this device, we can get some guidance on how large the fraction of the total universe we need to get a given level of precision. The answer deals solely with the strictly numerical or quantitative dimensions--it does not evaluate such questions as to whether the fraction came from the whole we were seeking to know, or whether the quality and breadth of the data were adequate.

CONFIDENCE LEVELS: CALCULATION AND SIGNIFICANCE

When the statistician refers to "confidence levels," he is using the term "confidence" with a more restricted and more precise meaning than we are likely to understand on the basis of common usage. When making any statement as to the confidence level of an estimate, he assumes that,
1. all possible sources of bias in the measurement have been taken account of first
2. all measurements used came from a universe that was homogenous for the purpose of the measurements
3. that measurements in that universe will vary, but that the variations are due solely to chance fluctuations caused by the sampling process, that for samples of reasonable size, the behavior of the estimate of the mean will be governed by the normal curve

_____

to which a measurement approaches the true value sought. Precision simply indicates the closeness with which repeated measurements replicate each other, regardless of bias. Thus the speedometer on my automobile dashboard may be so inaccurate that it regularly registers a speed 10 percent above my actual rate of travel. The bias may even vary as between different individual true speeds, the reading showing 70 miles/ hours when I am only travelling at 60, but indicating 27 m.p.h. when the car is moving at 26 m.p.h. The speedometer, however, is probably fairly precise: always registering 27 m.p.h. instead of 26 m.p.h. and 70 m.p.h. instead of 60 m.p.h. A measurement may be highly inaccurate but very precise. If accurate, however, it must also be precise.

4. that the measurements have been secured by a true random procedure
5. that our interest is in a long run of similar samples, not in the accuracy of a single measurement or single sample.

If the assumed conditions are met, we can make a statement about the probability that the true value of some population characteristic such as the mean will lie within a stated range around the value estimated from our sample. If we calculate the confidence level is 95% that the mean of the height of the trucks on the highway is 13 feet $\pm$ 1 foot, for instance, we are saying that 95 times out of 100, we would expect that the average of a sample of the same size, secured by the same procedure, would fall in this range. The complement of the confidence value, the error rate, can be used to express the same idea. In this case, we would say that our estimate for the average height of the trucks is 13 feet $\pm$ 1 foot with a 5% error rate.

As with all classical probability statements, our estimates are understood to refer only to the long run, in a static universe. The statement is not intended to apply to a single set of measurements. These latter are, from the traditional statistician's point of view, either wrong or right, and he cannot tell which from his confidence calculation. He does not mean that it is 95% right, nor does he consider such a condition possible. The basis for the confidence level statement is the estimate of the standard deviation, calculated from the sample data distribution. An extended discussion of these calculations can be found in any standard statistics text, so will be merely summarized to aid discussion.

Estimating the Standard Deviation and the Confidence Level

To estimate the confidence level, we need to know only the distribution of the actual sample measurements made, or a summary of this distribution, and the number in the sample taken. The size of the total population which was sampled is irrelevant so long as it is large.

The arithmetic mean $\bar{x}$ is first calculated by adding all of the observed measurements and dividing by their total number:

$\bar{x} = \Sigma \dfrac{x_i}{n}$ when $\underline{n}$ represents the number in the sample.

(meaning: divide the sum of all the individual measurements by their total number to get the average value)

The standard deviation of the sample, $\underline{s}$, is then calculated as the estimate of the standard deviation of the universe. This estimated measure of the dispersion of the values around the mean value is found from the formula:

$$s = \sqrt{\dfrac{\sum\limits_{i=1}^{n} (x_i - \bar{x})}{n - 1}}$$

Although the standard deviation is defined as the square root of the average of the square of the deviations from the mean, the denominator (n-1) is used rather than $\underline{n}$ to take account of the fact that $\underline{s}$ is based on sample data.

If we express the spread (dispersion) of data around the mean in units of standard deviation instead of in terms of the original measurement units, we can talk about how much of the data lies within some given interval such as $\bar{x} \pm 1s$ or $\bar{x} \pm 3s$. Even if we knew nothing about the distribution of the measurements in the population from which the sample was drawn and had to assume it was quite irregular and did not follow the normal curve, we would still expect 75% of all items to lie in the range $\bar{x} \pm 2s$ (See Chebyshev's theorem in any standard text.) However, if we can assume that the distribution of the population is normal, we can make more precise statements about our expectations concerning the portions of the data lying within any given number of standard deviation units from the mean. These statements of that population spread are what the statistician means by "confidence level." Figure 3-1 depicts the more commonly used values.

The estimate of the mean is also a variable whose range of value can be estimated in terms of $s_{\bar{x}}$ the standard deviation of the mean, also known as the standard error of the mean. The standard symbol so closely resembles that for standard deviation of the observations (s) and is closely related to it, that the two are often confused. The formula and the resulting value differ, however:

$$s_{\bar{x}} = \dfrac{s}{\sqrt{n}}$$

FIGURE 3-1. Normal Curve Probability Distribution Indicating Intervals of $\bar{x} \pm k\sigma$ (approximated as $\bar{x} \pm ks$)

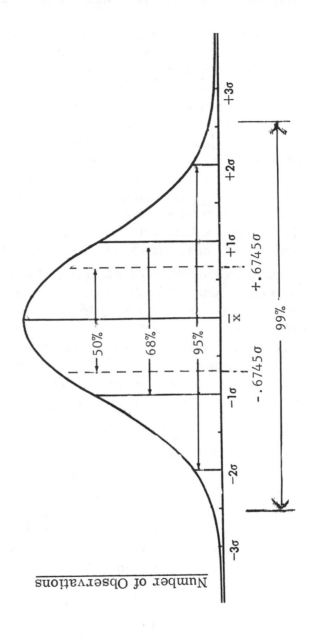

Since $\underline{n}$ is always a positive value and a moderately large one, $s_{\overline{x}}$ clearly denotes a much narrower range of value than does s.

One important property of this term is the fact that as the size of the sample n increases, the distribution of the values of $\overline{x}$ approach those of a normal distribution regardless of the shape of the distribution of x. Because of this property, except for very small sample sizes--samples of less than 10, for instance--we can refer to tables of the area under the normal curve found in most statistics texts to get estimates of the distribution of the values of the mean in terms of multiples of $s_{\overline{x}}$. These indicate that the true mean is included within an interval of $\overline{x} \pm 1.96 s_{\overline{x}}$, or roughly $2 s_{\overline{x}}$, 95% of the time if the statistician's assumption of homogeneity and lack of bias can be accepted. The 95% estimate is called the <u>confidence level</u> for the estimate of the mean, and $\overline{x} \pm k s_{\overline{x}}$, the <u>confidence interval</u>.

(In this formula, the usual convention is followed of using the symbol $\underline{k}$ to represent any arbitrarily chosen constant.) A similar calculation enables us to estimate a confidence level for a percentage or a proportion.

To see the value of this test, consider a survey of cigarette consumption by a sample of 100 smokers. The survey, let us assume, reveals an average daily usage of 24 cigarettes per smoker. The standard deviation of the sample data proves to be 20 and $s_{\overline{x}}$, the standard error of the mean, is

$$\frac{s}{\sqrt{n}} \ , \ \text{or} \ \frac{20}{\sqrt{100}} = \frac{20}{10} = 2$$

We would thus expect that .68, or about 2/3 of the time, a much larger group of samples would fall in the interval $\overline{x} \pm 1 s_{\overline{x}}$, or between 22 and 26 cigarettes per day. Moreover, we could make this estimate even though we know that the total population of smokers, like most populations of consumers, has an unbalanced distribution, with a relatively small proportion of heavy smokers and a large number of moderate smokers. Nevertheless, the rather modest sample of 100 is large enough to allow us to use normal theory to estimate the variation in the mean. This example gives us a useful basis for looking at the influence of sample size, n, upon the precision of resulting measurements.

How Important Is Sample Size?

Probably no more widespread misconceptions about measurement practice exist than the distrust of small samples. Yet we saw from the above that a relatively modest sample-- a mere 100--yielded a relatively precise estimate of a highly variable population. In fact, even if we seek a 95% level estimate, the calculations indicate that we could estimate that the true mean lies within a range between 22 and 28 ($2s_{\bar{x}} = 4$), and be wrong only 5% of the time. A larger sample, of course, would narrow the confidence interval, but not proportionately, and we might be satisfied this information were good enough for decision. Costs on data collection, never small, go up proportionately with the amount collected. Precision increases only in proportion to the <u>square root</u> of the increases in numbers. ($s_{\bar{x}}$, remember, equals $\frac{s}{\sqrt{n}}$.) To double our precision, we must quadruple our data collection cost.

This fact has an interesting corollary: whenever samples are small, additional information can be valuable in relation to cost, but as they increase in size, the additional value of the same amount of added information decreases very sharply. If the initial sample is 25, adding another 25 narrows the confidence interval by the ratio of 5/7.1 ($\sqrt{25} = 5 ; \sqrt{50} = 7.1$) but adding the same number--25--to a sample of 100 decreases the error interval merely to $\frac{11.2}{12.2}$.

One of the greatest of "common sense" errors is to assume that the larger the population, the larger must be the sample. Both experience and the cold computations of traditional statistics refute this supposition. A review of the formulas listed will show that total population does not enter into the error calculation in any manner. <u>The estimate of error does not depend on the size of the population from which the sample is drawn,</u> only on the size of the sample. It makes no difference whether the population be 5,000 or 500 million, a sample of any given size will result in the same estimate of error, so long as the population is relatively large, and the degree of homogeneity the same.

Since cost goes up in proportion to size of the sample, but its precision only increases with the square root of size, it costs us nine times as much to get 3 times the accuracy. We thus ought to weigh very carefully how much precision we really need in a sample result. This need is further reinforced by the practical fact, well known to those experienced in data collection, that as the size of the sample goes up, the quality of observation and measurement goes down, so that precision is lost through slipshod work. As taxpayers, we all have benefited from the increasing use of sampling by the United States Census over the last two decades. And as users of Census data (which nearly anyone in business is, directly or indirectly) we have profited by getting more kinds of data, and getting it quicker, and probably more accurately. Even the theoretical loss of precision occasioned by Census Bureau sampling is extremely small, for the 25% sample in use. This means that much of the information we have about the 51.24 million households in 1970 is directly true of only about 12.81 households. But calculation of our formula shows that the resulting averages are more precise than the accuracy of the quantities:

$$s_{\bar{x}} = \frac{s}{\sqrt{12,810,000}} = \frac{s}{3550}$$

Per capita income ($3932 in 1970) would be such an average. Since the s of measured income would be only some fraction of $3932, it is clear that the 2s limit of the average would not be much more than $1. This sampling deviation is much less than the inaccuracy in the reported incomes. Experience has shown that even in the total count, the Census errs by several percentage points. Furthermore, few respondents can give an accurate report on their annual income.

    The "confidence" we can have in our results as measured by the concept of confidence level is thus simply a question of how consistent we could expect results to be if the only source of error were sample variation, and if what we measure is free to vary, without restraints set by custom or other human forces.

    However, most of the data we use for business policy decision and market strategy is the result of social forces which make for uniformity and destroy independence of reaction: social custom, educational systems, sales promotion activities, legal restraints, or the mere knowledge that what we do will affect our relationships with other people, or the actions of our competitors. The proportion of voters casting a Republican ballot in the upper class section of any city is much higher than in the labor wards. The kinds of music people listen to, the kinds of recreation they seek, the department stores they patronize, will all be different in the two class extremes, and relatively uniform within a district. Thus the s in the numerators of our formulas for $s_{\bar{x}}$ will be quite small within any population stratum, and the precision with which we estimate from actual data after sampling will be relatively high. The size of the interval for a given confidence level and a fixed sample size varies with $1/s$ (that is, with $\sqrt{n}/s$). The less the standard deviation of our population, the less our sample will vary and the smaller our confidence interval and necessary sample size. If we have some knowledge that some segments of our population can be expected to produce a relatively more uniform response, we can take advantage of this uniformity by stratifying our sample: that is, by taking a specified proportion from each segment, with reference to the segment's size in the population we are sampling. If we know in advance (which we seldom do) what the s is for each chosen stratum, we can estimate the approximate interval attained for a given confidence level since s for the whole sample will now be the weighted average of the s's for the individual strata. Actually, what we have in the case of a truly stratified universe statistically is not one population, but as many as there are strata, each with a very low dispersion around its own average. Since this is a relatively common condition for a large part of human activity, this means that for activities involving people, many calculated confidence intervals are conservative statements of the degree of consistency to be expected in our counts and measurements when the sampling plan makes use of what we know about social stratification.

Since the level of confidence we ask for can seriously affect costs, and getting too much data can affect its quality, the question should be raised as to how much precision we should shoot for.

What Confidence Level Should We Shoot For and Why?

Why not shoot for as high a confidence level as we can afford? Because we meet other costs beyond the monetary-- the cost of ignoring valid information for one. This is particularly likely to happen when a confidence level is used in conjunction with an acceptance criterion. The more confidence we wish to have that our criterion will ensure that the result will be true when we accept it, the less likely we are to recognize a significant deviation from the result when such occurs. Consider the problem in the context of statistical quality control (SQC).

In its simplest form, SQC consists of checking small batches of product and comparing the variation in the averages of the batches from an overall average or specification value. These averages, which frequently are plotted on a graph for convenience, are expected to vary within some predetermined limits, usually based on the standard deviation of previous samples of the same product. The limits most commonly used are based on $2\sigma_{\overline{x}}$ or $3\sigma_{\overline{x}}$. So long as the quality of the samples does not stray outside these preset limits, quality is considered to be under adequate control and the production run is accepted. But if one single sample batch strays outside the limits, it is assumed that something is causing too much variation, and the source of the variation must be traced down to determine whether it be the machine setting, the operator, the raw material, or some environmental factor.

Why is a particular standard chosen for the control limits--why $2s_{\overline{x}}$ or why $3s_{\overline{x}}$? If you set the limits at $2s_{\overline{x}}$, you are aiming for fairly tight quality control. You know that under normal conditions, a variation of just over $2s_{\overline{x}}$ will occur once in 20 batches, but you feel that the 19 to 1 chance that this variation is abnormal justifies looking into the reason for it. There is only a 5% chance that you are sounding a false alarm. There are very real risks, on the other hand, that the process average has shifted and that your sampling has not detected it. The probability that the latter has happened depends on where the average has moved to and changes with each possible new process level. An operating characteristic curve (O. C. Curve) can be plotted to evaluate your procedures against possible alternative levels of the process average. If $3s_{\overline{x}}$ is chosen as the control limit, your false alarm rate will have dropped to 1%, but the chances of a process shift going undetected will have increased in corresponding fashion.

In other words, the confidence level has two sides. Setting a high level causes you to reject differences as unimportant which may be really significant. Setting the standard too low causes you to consider differences as important which may not be at all. You must decide where the balance should be struck. An objective evaluation involves an estimate as to the costs of too much rejection versus the cost of too easy acceptance.

This is no academic question. Not infrequently a study may indicate a percentage probability for success of an alternative is only slightly over 50%, and yet successive tests reveal the finding to be consistent, indicating a low dispersion. And in business, profits are made only by taking risks. It is a rare business situation in which the low risk course is potentially profitable. To wait until our information is copper-riveted is usually to wait until competitors have gained an advantage. Waiting for 19 to 1 odds usually means passing up a high potential opportunity.

Furthermore, the numbers dimension is only one of the important aspects of our sample. If this were not so, sampling would be a mere clerical operation, and interpretation of sample results safely left to the office boy. Unfortunately, all data has three other dimensions which cannot be evaluated by the simple logic of mathematics, but which are far more likely to affect the proper interpretation of the information than does mere sampling variation: the dimensions of time, data quality, and data breadth. Beyond this there is always the baffling question of the validity of the observations in relation to the decision to be made--whether we have, in fact, sampled the right population.

The Dimensions of Time, Quality and Breadth of the Sample

Business decisions always concern the shape of things in the future. By the time data has been gathered and analyzed, our samples tell us only the shape of things as they have been. This time element is relatively unimportant in the realm of physical measurements. The molecular weight of calcium has not changed in all the history of time. But in the affairs of men, time means change. This season's favorite color will be less popular next. The sales strategy that is working so well now will meet counter moves from competition in a few months. The advertising appeal that is so fresh and has such impact today will be stale and too freely copied by the year's end. Even the physical dimensions of today's children may be a poor guide for the clothing maker 5 years hence. The only true probability is that whatever has been is unlikely to be the same

in the future. Hence, for many business and governmental
decisions, there are no unbiased "probability" samples, and
skilled judgment is needed to estimate the nature and extent of
the time bias.

The quality dimension of our data is too often taken
for granted, and, unluckily, is in inverse ratio to the volume of
it we try to collect. Anyone with extensive experience in comparing "100% samples" with small sample results soon learns
that the precision of the small sample is almost invariably
greater than the mass measurement provided the sample truly
covers the area of interest, without respect to the problem of
data breadth discussed below. Mass measurement, like mass
production of anything else, inevitably brings pressures for
economy at the expense of care. Such pressure results in the
use of the less skilled in measurement and observation, in part
because skill is scarce as well as high paid. Nor are the differences between the mediocre quality of mass measurement
and high quality small sample measurement always small. Indeed, mass measurement can sometimes prove so inaccurate
as to be of little value, whereas a small sample can produce
quite reliable results. As already mentioned, in one case, a
one-thirtieth sample of mail order customers replaced two
different complete tallies. The result was that for the first
time in the company's history, the complex actual mailing results agreed with projections made on the basis of the tabulations. The only differences were the quality of the personnel
assigned to the job, the tightness of the supervision, and the
basis for evaluation of their work (care and precision, not
quantity primarily)--all made possible by reducing the size of
the job.

The advantage of sampling in cases like the above is
the opportunity to minimize the human error in collection.
Computers change the dimensions of the problem of 100%
sampling of course. If the measurement involves no significant degree of judgment and no human intervention on the inputs, the problem of human error disappears as, for example,
when transistors are inspected by automatic test equipment
and the data computer processed directly without clerical intervention. Similarly, if the complete tally is a computer processing of prepunched tickets for all items sold in a department
store, the results may be accurate. But where judgment is a
factor in recording the measurement, or whenever recording

of the result involves human intervention in any way, sampling is often the best answer to a data gathering problem, and the best sample is the smallest practical sample giving adequate answers for decision. Sample size is seldom as important as data breadth.

To talk of data breadth is to recognize that measurements do not occur in a sterilized vacuum. They represent a picked few of the facets of reality which occur in a certain environment under specific conditions. If we are to make the most efficient use of the information gathered, we need to know some facts about that environment and those conditions. One of the most important superiorities of statistical quality control is its necessary emphasis on data breadth. With 100% inspection, we normally measure only one aspect of quality-- "go" or "no-go," for example. As a result we learn only after the fact what part of production is not meeting standards and must be scrapped. To do more than measure this one narrow aspect for every item produced would be clearly uneconomical. But with small batch sampling for statistical quality control, we can afford both to take careful measurements and to collect collateral detail as well: the raw material batch from which the item was fabricated, the machine on which produced, the operator, and any other details concerning matters which could bias quality. Knowing this, we can pinpoint signs of unfavorable change, identify those factors that are defect causing, and eliminate the defects before more occur. Similarly, when delving into the motivations of those who might buy from us or vote for our candidate, it is always more revealing to learn a great deal more about those responding, and the bases for their responses, than to collect a mass of limited responses.

The Case for a Sample of One

The professional statistical technician would obviously be horrified by use of a sample of one for decision. He could not apply his beloved confidence measure. Nevertheless, decisions can be made on the basis of this ultimate sample limit, and frequently are. True, a sample of one is often not a valid sample, and if such a decision proves correct, it is by accident. At times, however, conclusions based on extremely limited samples are perfectly valid, even when the ultimate limit of a single observation is used. Mention has already been made of the firm which decided against a competitive counter-move on the basis of less than 20 interviews. In this case, the analyst was factoring in extensive prior research on customer attitudes with respect to the product type involved.

Even samples of one are frequently valid. To be sure, when the boss uses his wife as a single survey respondent, he is probably going to the wrong market segment. But the mail order firm president was using some well-learned experience validly when he told his dress buyers: "If I like it, don't put it in the catalog." So also was the research advisor who told a student to interview a single department store buyer to learn the probable sale price and the normal margins on some costume jewelry the latter had available for sale. And one experienced opinion researcher decided correctly on the probable outcomes of two different presidential elections on the basis of a single statement by single non-political voters in each case. In both instances, he was able to place the speaker accurately in the political spectrum, on the basis of extensive personal research on the composition and normal shifts in opinion.

Such judgments, of course, are highly subjective, and depend heavily on the insight of the analyst and his judgmental skills, as well as lengthy experience. But no conclusion is better than the judgment of the analyst making it, regardless of the technique of data collection used. Indeed, economical use of data collection resources in any sampling operation involves background knowledge and experienced judgment as much as a knowledge of the formal statistical techniques.

Validity: Does the Sample Apply?

We are pretty clear as to the nature and boundaries of the population we are sampling in most of the problems of physical measurement with which traditional statistics has been designed to cope. The production run which the quality control inspector is sampling can be well and precisely defined. But the human population with which business decision must concern itself can only rarely be defined with any precision at all, especially when that universe will exist only in the future, as a result of the actions taken by the decision maker, and will be shaped in unexpected ways by both these actions and the counteractions of competitors. The potential market for a new product, for example, is not a definite delimited entity. As a matter of experience, we can not even define what the product is, from the standpoint of the consumer, until after the latter starts to use it. That is why estimates of new product sales potentials are so imprecise in fact. One study indicated that under the best of circumstances, the average error of forecast was 122%. There can be no way of estimating the precision of our measurement if we cannot determine the degree of coincidence between the boundaries of our sample and those of the universe we intend to represent.

Fortunately, few decisions hinge on small differences, and the information from our samples, however vital, is a mere supplement needed to fill gaps in a much bigger store of accumulated experience, some of which can be taken into account by means of the subjective mathematics of Bayesian probability. Other portions are of a qualitative nature not subject to mathematical manipulation, but can lead to positive judgments. In addition, most well-planned operating procedures contain provisions for a flexible response to the feedback of results from planned action, so that the really firm decisions are subject to revision in all but the very short run.

The purpose of data collection and observation of any sort is to reach some valid conclusion as to our future course of action. Our concern is with the validity of those conclusions and our choice of action. Statistical tools can help us judge the reliability of data collection, but furnish no guidance as to the validity of the data gathered, even less of the judgments we make on the basis of that collected information. The judgments normally include a mass of background and other knowledge which we must use to make our interpretations. However well a sample meets standard statistical tests of reliability, it still may not be a valid or even useful measure of what we wish to know. Technical statistics are no help in judging validity. This is a separate analysis.

SUMMARY

1. All of the data we have is from some kind of sample and all measurements are truly represented only in terms of probability distributions.

2. Any single measurement is likely to be biased relative to the true value sought, and even the most careful measurements of a single phenomenon will vary. With physical attributes, the frequency distribution of careful measurements will generally follow the normal curve of error. Whatever is measured, when all measurements are from the same universe, there will always be a clustering around some central value and a diminution of the frequency the more the measurements deviate from this central value. In the case of most social and economic data, this distribution will tend to be lopsided, or skewed.

3. Sampling and deciding on the basis of very small samples is something we all do informally and often unconsciously all of the time. Despite this fact, many of us are suspicious of the utility of formal samples and tend to put too much stress on large quantities.

4. Primarily, most of us do not understand the purpose of sampling--to increase our knowledge and supplement it, not to limit it. In the search for the false security of numbers, we tend to overlook the importance of breadth and quality in samples, and to disregard the bias that time always introduces into their meaning.

5. Even the conservative tools of traditional statistics can help us gain a more balanced view of the requirements of sampling.

6. The most important of those tools involve confidence levels and confidence intervals. Confidence, in this context, does not mean faith, as it connotes in common usage. It simply measures the degree of repeatability of sample results under the same procedure, the precision of the measurement, but not its accuracy.

7. Confidence level calculations do tell us that although costs of data collection rise proportionately to the amount collected, the increase in precision is proportionate only to the square root of sample size.

8. As a practical matter, increase in sample size is not even as beneficial as this relationship indicates. As samples get large, the tendency is to cut down on the breadth of detail measured, and thus decrease the degree of useful knowledge. Generally, too, quality of measurement suffers in the attempt to control costs. For these reasons, small samples nearly always produce superior measurements to 100% samples.

9. The search for too much certainty--the requirement of too high a confidence level--introduces error from the
other direction: the error of assuming that some difference is
not significant when it is.

10. Sampling theory cannot help us determine the
validity of the sample, even less the validity of the interpretations we put on the results. These matters of personal judgment involve the skill of the user in supplementing informal
knowledge he already has with the added information drawn
from the sampling operation.

4

SAMPLING:
WHAT METHOD IS BEST?

Outside consultants usually find it easier to get the ear
of a prospect by promoting some specific technique of data collection or analysis. Technique is perceived as objective and
scientific, and thus, to some degree, not quite personal. The
attractive technique being promoted varies with the waves of
research fashion. One such fashion which rode the crest for a
while was that of probability sampling, to the degree that many
texts being used in statistics today recognize no other kind.

Yet mere technique, especially of data collection, is
no guarantee of usefulness of the research if that is all that is
in the offering. Any research which depends on data collection
method alone is of little value.

In point of fact, the pure random choice of chance,
"probability", design is, at best, only one aspect of any important sampling design, and not necessarily the most important
aspect, or even always necessary. In any mass population involving contact with people, pure probability designs have at
least two grave deficiencies. In the first place, it is never
possible to contact all or even nearly all of the respondents so
chosen, within the bounds of reasonable cost. A substantial
proportion will be unavailable, not only on the first call, but
even after two or three callbacks. Callback costs are expensive, and rise almost geometrically with the number involved.
Thus the cost advantage of sampling is defeated.

In addition, most mass populations or universes are
really made up of a number of quite differing segments. If the
diversity is great in terms of any characteristic being measured, there will, inevitably, be a disproportionate sampling of
the segments. As already noted, there is a 50-50 chance that
the measures from even a probability design lie outside the

limit of one standard deviation.

For many purposes, this much variation is too great. In studies of the rural relief cases made by Federal agencies during the Great Depression, for example, it was found that a probability sample of the active cases did not give a proportionate sample of the case closings. In the mail order customer sample already referred to, a true simple probability sample did not work, partly for reasons discussed further on.

If the population or universe being sampled is finite, leaving the choice to chance is almost certain to give a highly biased result of unpredictable character. Moreover, even in large populations, if the population is highly non-symmetrical, or skewed in distribution (as all economic and social data is), the very infrequently occurring high value items (such as heavy users) are unlikely to be included in truly proportionate numbers, leading to high sampling variation in the resulting averages.

For all of these reasons, therefore, experienced analysts in the economic and marketing areas have used modified probability designs whenever they had enough knowledge to segment the population under study. Probability has been used, if at all, only as the last, supplemental, step in the selection process. For small finite population, it should seldom, if ever, be the main basis of choice.

SAMPLING FINITE POPULATIONS

Populations of a very small finite number of individuals are the subject of a great deal of business research interest, especially in the area of industrial marketing research. Furthermore, the individuals making up such a finite universe are never even approximately equal in size or importance. Invariably, a handful of the biggest will account for the lion's share of whatever is being measured: for example, orders, sales, production. Inevitably, the resources and methods of operation will be so differentiated between individuals of even approximately the same size class that each firm or individual is, in a sense, a universe unto itself. An abrasives company discovered, for example, that although they had more than 100 customers in every one of its sales districts, anywhere from 60 percent to 90 percent of the business in each territory came from less than 6 customers, sometimes from a single buyer.

In such a situation, there is no sensible alternative to the hand-picked sample. Since each one of the big three or big ten will be an appreciable chunk of the universe, and each may differ measurably, the top handful must usually be studied in toto. The rest, if too large for convenient complete coverage, need to be classified into some kind of strata, and the sample should be chosen on the best knowledge of pertinent stratification characteristics. If the total number is over a couple of dozen, sampling is usually necessary. If possible, the units should be listed in some kind of pertinent sequence, and then an unbiased (random starting point) serial sample should be taken of this ordered listing. This is not a probability design. The sampling variance will be less than that of a chance determined design.

Frequently, a two-stage sampling of those smaller units is justified if the number runs into the hundreds. A fairly large sample can be covered with a brief telephoned or mailed questionnaire, for example, giving a measure of the distribution of key characteristics under study. Then a small subsample can be carefully chosen from this larger sample for intensive study (by personal interview, for instance).

SAMPLING MASS POPULATIONS

The choice of sampling system is much wider when sampling large universes or populations. The design chosen will depend on the kind of information needed, and its precision, and also on the amount of time and resources needed.

In every case, it should be remembered that the purpose of sampling is to add to available knowledge, only to the degree necessary for a decision to be made.

The amount of pertinent knowledge already available and the needs of the moment will determine the best method to use.

All mass sampling methods can be grouped under two main heads:

(a) samples making no direct use of universe knowledge, and

(b) sample designs taking into account considerable prior knowledge of universe structure and characteristics.

Only two kinds of sampling systems make no use of prior knowledge:

Accidental or convenience samples

Pure probability samples, in which chance alone determines who will be included, and no stratification is resorted to.

The simplest of all sample designs is the accidental, best illustrated by a colleague's account of one of his agency experiences: "The copy department had developed two different versions of the same ad and wanted to know which had more attention value. We simply sent some people to nearby Grant Park with copies of both. They laid out the two in front of some respondent and asked him to take one and read the headline back, alternating the left-and-right positioning of the two ads between respondents."

The accidental design may be intentional or a result of necessity. Planning executives have a last minute need for information, the decision cannot wait, and data of some sort has to be picked up when and where immediately available. There is nothing inherently wrong with such a sample, either in the planned case, as in the anecdote above, or in the emergency situation. Frequently, the reaction sought can be assumed to be relatively invariable within a given culture, as was implicit in the advertising copy case. If it is realized that this assumption is being made (and the need for a check on its validity is kept in mind), the procedure can be justified. At other times, the analyst can fit collateral detail about the respondents into knowledge he already has about universe structure, and come up with well-based recommendations for action.

Even where the value of incremental information is quite high, as it often is in emergency situations, enough general information about the universe involved may be available to permit a valid analysis. But when resources of time and money permit, this is usually not the design of choice where there is much at stake.

Probability designs lie at the opposite extreme of care in selection from accidental design, although the popular connotations of the label random often confuse this point. Such designs have been designated "probability samples" because the consistency (reliability) of results between repeated samples can be estimated in advance by means of the standard formulas of objective probability. However, the resulting estimate will prove to be a considerable overstatement of variability unless the measurement values for each individual in the sample are truly independent, which is seldom true in business or social studies.

The "true random" basis of selection at the heart of such methods does not confer any special mystical properties. They are simply devices for avoiding unintentional selection bias. Their main value lies either in those situations where the measurements sought are approximately independent, or else where the structure of their occurrence is either unknown or so poorly defined that ignorance of this structure is the safest assumption. They are thus the designs of choice for basic census operations.

In most situations facing the business analyst, however, these basic assumptions of probability theory are inapplicable and usually lead to far too conservative sample designs--designs costing more than should be allocated to a study and frequently leading to greater actual sampling variation than would some alternative design that makes maximum use of everything known about the population sampled.

Simple probability designs are sometimes used because they permit tight supervision of field workers. Thus the official of a large national research organization--himself a statistical specialist--once told the author that, as far as he was concerned, the major advantage of his probability designs was "the tight control it gives us over a widespread field force." The reason probability design does this for him, of course, is solely because such a design rules out discretion on the part of the interviewer in picking respondents. But any design that eliminates this discretion, basing choice on objective standards, does the same thing.

Whenever substantial knowledge of universe structure is available, probability may be one element in the sampling system, but an element used solely to eliminate random bias within sampling cells carefully chosen on some objective and thoroughly non-random basis.

Modified Probability Designs

Generally speaking, chance, or random selection, is a sub-element within a more complex design. Modified probability designs make use of some kind of stratification, of division of the sample into carefully defined and usually proportioned subcells.

The principal concern of statistical theory is to avoid erratic bias in the choice of sample. The procedures used to ensure lack of bias are known as random choice and the samples drawn are usually called probability samples. These are terms with very specific and limited meaning in statistics. They mean sample choices made by procedures that eliminate any foreseeable possibility for bias in selection, particularly on the part of the selector. Random, in the statistical sense, is thus quite the opposite of the terms haphazard or accidental, which are bracketed with it in vernacular usage. Random choice requires, in fact, the use of very carefully designed procedures.

The use of some kind of lottery procedure is one such device. Perhaps the simplest, for small populations, is the "pull a number out of a hat" method. One example is that of a mail-order house that wished to check a competitor's published claim that its prices were "1.9% below those in the previous catalog." The research department advised a sample stratified on a page-by-page basis.

might be listed on a page, and that special bargains received favorable position on a page, they recommended a careful randomization of choice from each page, using two boxes of numbered poker chips.

One box of chips was to contain twelve chips, numbered from 1 through 12. The other was to contain 50 chips, numbered from 1 through 50. Then, page by page, the new catalog was to be sampled as follows:

1. If the page contains but one item, find the comparable item in the previous catalog, and list the two prices. (If, in this and succeeding steps, no comparable item can be found, pass on.)

2. If the page contains more than one item, and not over twelve, number the items on the new catalog page from 1 through 12, starting at the top left and proceeding from left to right, top to bottom. Mix up the chips in the twelve-chip box

thoroughly, and pull out a chip. List the item corresponding to the chip number in the new catalog, find the comparable item in the old, and put the chip back into the box.

3. If the number of items on the page is more than 12, follow the same procedure as in step 2 above, but draw the chip from the box of 50. (In both steps, if the chip number is larger than the number of items on the page, keep drawing chips until a usable number is found.)

The estimate obtained from the above procedure was 1. 7 percent, a figure close enough to the claimed 1. 9 percent for the purpose of confirmation. The stratified form of the sample gave much more valuable information than this sample item, however. Top executives and buyers were able to see in what classes of items prices had been cut, and by how much, and where prices had been raised. Had an attempt been made to cover all or a very large portion of the items in the catalog, this kind of information would unquestionably have been buried under the mass of detail. In this case, as in most, judicious sampling resulted in more useful guidance than would a complete count.

The procedure illustrates a very important aspect of sampling and the proper place of randomization methods. In those steps in which personal bias might distort the selection, randomization was resorted to in the choosing of the item from a page. But randomization was not utilized in determining what page to take, or the number of items from a page. Here use was made of personal knowledge of catalog construction and of the relationship of page space to importance in sales volume. In general, it was known that the allocation of page space within a merchandise department is rather carefully proportioned to sales volume expected by item. Thus the page was the universe unit chosen, by using the principle of one item to a page. Even the use of randomization for choosing the item was a result of knowledge that position on the page could be a major source of bias because the items considered the more attractive buys get attention-attracting position.

The above example did result in a rather large sample since the catalog contained about thirteen hundred pages. A somewhat smaller sample might have given at least as much useful information. Had time and sample selection cost been considered too high, the widely used refinement of area sampling might have been used in a two-stage sampling scheme. The fact that items and pages are grouped into about ninety merchandise departments might have been used as the basis of stratification. Within each department, each page might have been considered as an area, and a random sample taken of the pages within a department--say one page out of four, determining which page in the series by a double toss of a coin. Then the item chosen would be selected as before.

Such multi-stage sampling is the accepted practice for sampling large populations, especially in dealing with marketing problems, where the individuals may be dispersed over a considerable area of geography and an initial listing of the units is impractical or, more usually, really impossible. Consider the problem of developing a probability sample of consumer households for a city no bigger than Wichita, Kansas. The 1960 Census enumerated over 88,000 housing units. The initial listing necessary for the construction of a single-stage random sample would be far costlier than could be justified. But by use of maps and census data, a two- or three-stage sample could be selected, at moderate cost, to meet the requirements of probability sampling. The Housing Census breaks down its listing by some ninety-four census tracts, each one homogeneous from a socioeconomic point of view. Each tract contains from 10 to 116 city blocks (with the exception of two tracts with no housing units). For each tract and each block, we have the count of housing units on the date of the census. A three-stage sample would be chosen by first getting an unbiased selection of tracts, probably first stratifying them into groups by some criterion of importance to the kind of question being studied, then picking an unbiased sample of city blocks within the chosen tracts, and finally getting the interviewer to list the homes in the chosen blocks and make an unbiased choice according to a carefully defined procedure.

In such a procedure as described, it is important to keep in mind that our sampling unit is the individual household, and that each household must have an equal chance for selection. Since blocks and tracts vary widely in the number of homes contained, the process of selection must weight the chance for selection for both blocks and tracts according to the number of contained families. This could be accomplished in two steps. First, blocks and tracts would be grouped into whatever strata were pertinent to the study then within a stratum, a cumulative total would be run, block-by-block and tract-by-tract, of the family count, in geographical sequence. This cumulative count series would then become the basis of choice, either in terms of a serial sample or on the basis of a random choice scheme. In case a serial procedure were to be followed, the grand total would be divided by the size of sample decided upon to get the interval between chosen units. Then a random starting point would be selected, probably from a table of random numbers, and the block and tract picked would be noted. Counting down in the cumulative total to the end of the interval chosen, another block would be selected at the point where this count ended, and so on to the end. To illustrate, suppose the sample called for 200 families out of a total of 88,400. Dividing 88,400 by 200 gives an interval of 442. From a table of random numbers, a three-digit number between 1 and 442 would be secured--say 137. The first block to be sampled would then be that for which the cumulative total reached is more than 136 and less than 138. Our listing may show that Block 3 in Tract 2 brings the total to 119, and that the next block, Block 4, puts the cumulative total to 143. Block 4, Tract 3 is then our starting point and will be visited by the interviewer, the homes listed in a prescribed sequence, and one home chosen according to a carefully described procedure. Adding 442 to 137 gives us 579 as the location of the next choice, which, counting down our list, turns out to be between 571, the total to which Block 26 of Tract 3 brings us, and 589, the cumulated total at the end of Block 27. The next home is then to be one of those in Block 27. We then add 442 to 579 and get 1,012 as the next point for sampling, etc.

Serial sampling is not the only method which could be used. Using the same cumulative total, we could pick a list of two hundred homes by use of a table of random numbers. In this case, we would probably first group the tracts into homogeneous strata for the purpose of sampling, and then run a cumulative total within each stratum. We would then divide our 200 into a quota for each stratum, proportioned according to the relative total count in each. Next we would turn to a table of random numbers, choose the quota of numbers needed, and locate these numbers in our cumulative totals. Say that Tracts 2, 7, 12 and 14-26 constitute a single stratum for our purposes, and that these together have a total of 11,423 homes at the time of the census. We turn to our table of random numbers and obtain 25 5-digit numbers between 1 and 11,423. We select 25 because that is the proportion which this stratum is of the total homes. We pick 5-digit numbers because the largest must contain that many digits. We then locate these numbers in the cumulative totals, in terms of tract and block as before, and proceed as we would have in the serial sample case.

Although the procedure is a little more lengthy with the table of random numbers, it is really not much more complicated. Table 4-1 is a reproduction of a segment of one such table, starting with column 21, row 4. (Column 21 begins with 1 in the number group 10053.) Let us assume we have arbitrarily chosen, before looking at the table, to start at column 22, row 4. (Column 22 begins with the first 0 in the group 10053.) This gives us the starting number, 00533 as our starting choice, indicated by the underlining. The next five digits are 12,281, which is higher than 11,423 and therefore of no use to us. But the next set of five digits is 07777 and thus within our range, for the second item. The next two sets are both too large, but 09595 that follows is the third needed number, and so on as indicated. Thus seven of the households chosen are in the blocks which contain 533, 1175, 3596, 4490, 7528, 7777, and 9594 in the list of cumulative totals. Note that although the numbers are grouped by 5's, this has no significance, but is done merely for convenience of reading and counting. Sets of five, as in this case--or 2's or 3's or 4's, as it might be in others--are simply taken in sequence from left to right and from top to bottom without regard to spacing or lines in the table, or in any other consistent sequence, vertical or horizontal.

Both serialization and random numbers are devices, in this case, to tell us which block to send the interviewer to (it could be a rural township in a study of an agricultural area). How does the interviewer identify the house he must go to? The data used to pick the block sample (or a township sample) also gives the number of housing units in each block. Specific instructions are furnished the interviewer regarding a listing of the housing units in each block to be visited: at what point to start the listing, and in what sequence. After he (or more likely, she) has listed and numbered the houses, he has a number which is furnished beforehand, selected by random within the known number to be listed, which indicates the exact house or apartment to visit.

As can be seen from the example, the key to good probability sampling procedure is availability of some form of accurate, up-to-date listing. This is also one of the major problems. Census block statistics, for example, are not avail-

Table 4-1

Segment of a Random Numbers Table

•••••	•••••	•••••	•••••	10053	31228	10777	79488	57472	10959
41378	07937	62350	82051	61684	63510	73019	18266	77263	16598
73373	43037	11991	87921	38622	23651	78815	98791	35854	94772
38863	17327	93732	24181	76505	49628	69773	10359	62152	04334
09372	51990	38141	38974	95696	51211	03442	07060	48154	83052
18120	15814	54770	66557	27710	00752	87877	00117	50449	08581
71357	11797	39062	32276	87037	96370	84776	•••••	•••••	•••••

Source: Kemeny, Schleifer, Snell, and Thompson, Finite Mathematics, (Englewood, New Jersey, Prentice-Hall, Inc., 1962), pp. 470–471. Underlining added to indicate choices for illustration.

able much before two years after the census date. Much can happen in those two years to lower the accuracy of such a listing. Wide areas of urban housing may be taken over and demolished to make way for a freeway or allow the expansion of the local university. Some buildings burn down, vacant lots get built on. A building boom may develop and populate whole suburbs that show up in the census as farms and woodlands. Even in the rural areas, large numbers of farms may be abandoned and consolidated into larger ones. Between 1950 and 1962, for example, the proportion of farmers in the labor force dropped by over three-fifths. In one case of one national sample, numbers of blocks specified by the New York headquarters for a Chicago study proved to be in the midst of rubble of what had been a dense housing area, torn down for construction of the Congress and Northwestern Expressways. Alternate blocks can be chosen to patch the sample up, but it takes little imagination to see the problems involved in fitting these into what had been, up to this point, a very precisely interdependent structure. The only real recourse is to check beforehand, and revise on the basis of the best available up-to-date information that can be had. With telephone directories issued only once per year (and out-of-date by two months when issued), even telephone surveys can run into difficulties, especially in our more transient communities.

Difficulties notwithstanding, such multistage samples have such attractive characteristics from the standpoint of maintaining tight supervision of a wide-flung interview force, and in avoidance of personal bias in respondent selection, that all reputable national research organizations have prepared a permanent probability plan for all of their sampling, or one that incorporates most of the types of specific instructions required to carry out such a sampling scheme. The temptation for cheating on selection of respondents is markedly reduced when the instructions are so specific that little room is left for misunderstanding.

However, most widespread samples are not samples of individuals, but of clusters. If you review the Wichita procedure, you can see that even in one small city, a sample of individual households could result in excessive lost time in travel, especially in studies in which call-backs are essential to catch the selected individuals at home. This travel cost problem can be minimized by selecting fewer blocks, but more homes in a block, or nearby group of blocks. If the assumption of probability statistics were completely applicable, this would cause a slight loss in efficiency of the sample, which would have to be made up by taking a larger one. However, the theoretical loss is small in relation to realized benefit, and it is also true that the assumption of sampling theory--independence of reaction--seldom is true for the subjects of most business studies. Indeed, as is argued further on, experience has shown that the cluster sample may actually be a more efficient design in some cases, if the number of clusters is kept reasonably large.

The Accidental Probability Sample

The purposely designed random choice sample requires very precise construction, but a sample that came about by accident can meet the conditions of a probability sample. The sample must simply meet the essential condition of equality of opportunity for selection of every individual in the universe under study.

In one instance, a very useful unplanned experiment evolved out of such an accidental sample in a catalog mailing to customers. The mailing list in the case in point was on a set of cardboard frame tissue stencils, the frames of which carried a buying record code for mailing selection. At one point in the feed mechanism, the addressing machine automatically selected out the predetermined stencils according to this punched code, then printed the address on a mailing label about five cycles later. An appreciable number of stencils would get broken in the machine during a run, and if this happened after selection and before printing, the rest of a tray would get selection on the basis of one stencil, and print another. Thus a considerable number of customers would get their catalogs on the basis of an irrelevant fact--the purchase record of another customer whose stencil chanced to be near to the one selected. Logically, this is a form of true random selection. The sample file of customers, on which detailed records were kept, showed that this resulted in a reversal of the intended catalog circulation policy for part of the sample. Good customers who should have received a catalog automatically were required to send in a request card, and those who were supposed to have been screened by means of a request card handling received one without having to request it. By comparison with the majority who were circulated as intended, this small, but adequate, missent sample provided a ready-made controlled test of the basic assumptions underlying the then current catalog circulation policy.

As valuable as random selection is for sample execution and evaluation, the analyst does not always have the control over selection which makes it possible, and even when he does, the gain in efficiency over a much simpler form may be miniscule if the universe being studied is highly constrained from appreciable variation by the impact of major cultural conditioning or other environmental factors.

STRATIFIED SAMPLING

The use of stratification depends on prior knowledge of some kind of stable relationship between factors used to describe the strata and the kinds of measurements sought. It also implies some means of objectively defining the strata and directly or indirectly proportioning the respondents to parallel the proportioning in the universe.

This means that there are no universal strata suitable for every kind of study, and that the choice of strata should never be routine. To use income class as the major stratification factor in studies of consumer expenditures, for example, is often wrong. Social class is so much more potent in determining how a family will apportion its spending that two families with identical incomes, but from different social levels, will have a completely different expenditure pattern relative to food, housing, and reading and educational expenditures, for example.

On some matters, age class may be quite important. In many others, age is irrelevant, or at best a poor measure. There is then no substitute for some knowledge of relationships when defining strata. Fortunately, we have a great deal of such knowledge in the case of most studies.

Where we lack such knowledge, then strata must often be identified by means of analysis of the results after collection, and sample projections modified in the light of this knowledge.

When planning any primary data collection process, therefore, the analyst needs to first define what he knows about universe structure. If he does that well, he is in a position to narrow his error range substantially, both in the collection process and through later analysis, and to define his strata and means of stratification. The latter may be direct, indirect, or by inference.

What Usable Knowledge about Universe Structure Do We Have?

Marketing deals with people in a social structure, not a group of atomistic individuals in an anarchic chaos. What people eat, drink, and wear, the kinds of cars they buy, the kinds of recreation in which they are interested, and in fact most of their major purchases are determined in very large part by the reference groups of which they are members or to whose standards they adhere. Even in our modern urban culture, variation within the group is extremely small. Variation between groups can be relatively large. If we take the time to carefully define the groups in terms of the particular kind of market and the very specific product package with which we are concerned, we can eliminate a great deal of sampling variation by using these groups as the primary basis for sampling--by stratifying the sample, in other words, on some significant basis. Variation within groups is often so small that, if the stratification is carefully done, a very large part of the total possible variation is eliminated. Consequently, if we know a great deal about the structure of our universe, we may not have much concern with sampling variation. By the same token, if we do not know much about the structure of the universe, one of the most important pieces of information that we should seek early is knowledge of that structure. Without such knowledge we are bound to incur a great deal of bias by going to the wrong groups; and we are certain to have to use methods of sampling that permit the maximum degree of variability in the sample itself.

Use of Knowledge of Structure to Reduce Error

It is a rare study which starts out with no knowledge of the universe or its structure. On those rare occasions, there is, of course, no choice but to use the procedures dictated by probability theory in order to limit the bias and sample choice. But random choice is not a substitute for knowledge.

The possibilities of both sampling error and research error in sampling can be substantially reduced by using knowledge of uniformities in the universe structure, knowledge of the interdependence of events within the universe, and knowledge of constraints upon variability of business events set by custom and the facts of economic life.

In the very finite universe of industrial market research, no valid sampling can be done except by making use of knowledge both of segmentation of the universe and of uniformities within the segments. Even in studies of mass populations, such formal and informal knowledge of uniformity-producing dependence of events can be used to take account of major factors capable of influencing them--factors which have no possible place (except in a negative sense) in the mathematics of probability.

Knowledge of universe structure is also important in reducing error of analysis. The data collection plan should therefore include special provisions for identifying the stratum from which an individual answer is obtained in order to make use of analytical error reduction.

The principal tools for making use of knowledge in reducing error are: (1) careful identification of the universe and limitation of responses to individuals in that universe, and (2) stratification. Stratification can be so effective in reducing sampling variation that whenever we have any specific reason for believing the universe is stratified in any manner, we should use whatever means we can devise to take account of such limits on response variation in designing our sample. Stratification is of three general types: direct, indirect, and inferential.

Direct Stratification

Direct stratification is the obvious method of choosing individuals or sample blocks in some specified proportion, or specified disproportion, according to carefully defined characteristics of the individual or block. These characteristics must define a group that is, for the purpose, more uniform than the universe of which it is a part. The quota design, when carefully designed and properly supervised, is one form of simple stratified sample. Excellent testimony to its value is the fact that such designs have produced a great deal of useful results even when strata were mechanically or poorly defined and sample choice was left to the whim of poorly supervised field personnel. But this success does not excuse such slovenly work. Rather, it argues for the greatest of care in making sure that the system of stratification is valid, that strata be clearly defined, and that sample selection be objective and carefully supervised.

Proper stratification is no mechanical process. Strata must be carefully designed and defined in terms of the particular measurement sought. Strata are simply areas of relative uniformity of response to a given stimulus. Thus the widely used income level stratification may be approximately valid for certain types of spending--for example, the level of rent paid--but when investigating the amount of money a family will spend for automobiles, clothing, recreation, education and even food, the strata may well include two or more quite disparate social class' spending habits.

The truck driver and the college professor may live in the same neighborhood side by side and earn somewhat similar incomes. But the college professor is much more likely to drive a Volkswagen, to spend a great deal of his money on books and magazines, and to subscribe to Harper's, than is the truck driver.

If income is used without reference to the place of the spending unit in the family life cycle, similar errors can be made. The young couple who have only been married for a year or two is an entirely different kind of spending unit with regard to appliances, sheets, tools, and furniture than the neighboring couple whose family has left home and who are themselves heading for retirement. In dealing with population classifications, it is extremely important to look behind the formal definition to the actual realities of social structure. The bedroom suburb of Boston with 5,000 people is in no sense a parallel to the small city of the same size in central Iowa. The suburb is only a politically distinguishable but not otherwise separate part of the metropolitan area of three million people while the other is a commercial center for a farming community.

Direct stratification should normally be part of the design whenever the limits of a stratum can be easily defined, when the people who are members of it can be conveniently identified, and when the stratification is known to have direct influence on the kind of marketing action sought. But every-

100

thing that we know about social structure does not fit into the requirements for direct stratification. Even when it does, if we tried to stratify by every element individually we would sometimes come up against a problem of combinations and permutations that would stump a computer. For this reason, we must often use some form of indirect stratification which takes into account a number of these factors at the same time.

Indirect Stratification

Indirect stratification makes use of relationships between some easily found and identified characteristics and those other characteristics on which stratification is sought. Such indirect stratification nearly always involves some sort of block or cluster design so chosen that the elements controlled can be expected to occur in rather uniform proportion within the cluster.

There is nothing which identifies a man as a Democrat, a Republican, or a mugwump when you look at him or when he opens the door in response to your knock. Working over their backyard barbecues, the junior executive and the young machinist are probably indistinguishable. There is no obvious caste mark on the family that does a lot of its shopping out of a mail order catalog. But for each of these and many other bases of social stratification, the resourceful analyst can very often find some type of block or cluster system, not unusually geographically defined, within each element or cell of which a relatively uniform distribution of individual types to be measured will be found. Moreover, such blocks or clusters will often group together a number of desired characteristics in sought-for combinations.

Democrats and Republicans, in any areas in which political differences are on the surface, will be found mixed in every precinct. But the proportion will vary in a highly predictable manner from one section of a city to another and from one part of the state to another. The ratio itself is a function of income, occupation, ethnic background, and other important factors. There will be little variation from one election to the next in the basic division between Democrats and Republicans in any given precinct, and within the precinct small cluster samples of voters will turn up a ratio of Democrats to Republicans in extremely close agreement with the ratio in the precinct as a whole.

Thus we can normally accomplish a simultaneous and quite feasible stratification of all these related dependent variables in desirable combinations if we select sample cells defined as groups of precincts chosen for relative uniformity of some correlate of income such as rental value, ethnic background, specific occupation composition, and past voting ratios. Cluster samples drawn from such cells will prove highly stable and highly predictive.

Similarly, a number of factors with predictable geographic occurrence have an extremely high correlation with the proportion of families who are habitual mail-order shoppers-- such factors as the size and availability of local retail stores, average income level, and population composition by age, for example. Geographically delimited cells defined on the basis of these available measurements may often yield relatively invariable sample clusters of mail-order customers in the expected ratios.

One problem can arise when the proportion of elements sought (such as the ratio of Democrats to Republicans) is related to some linear factor such as income and also to some other factor more readily definable as a spectrum phenomenon, such as occupational class, ranging from blue collar at one end to white collar at the other. In the center of the income scale, the two ends of the spectrum tend to get intermixed. The accountant and truck driver may well be next door neighbors physically, but a considerable distance apart politically and in tastes and consumption. In politics, the net division may be quite even. But a little investigation will reveal the existence of two rather sharply defined separate strata. The white collar segment may have a two-to-one Republican tendency, the blue collar the same ratio in the Democratic direction.

In such cases, it is usually well to make provision to sample the two strata separately, if some simple means can be devised. In the political polling situation, for example, an organization which picked up some of its sample at public transport waiting points in the morning rush hour made use of the fact that the two segments started their workday at different times. Equal samples were drawn at the two morning rush-hour periods. By thus separating and proportioning the two substrata, a major source of sampling variability was eliminated.

In the case of both direct stratification and indirect stratification the inference is made that there are clearly defined boundary lines between groups of variable items within a universe. However, much of the knowledge we have of social structure indicates some form of continuous variability with no clearly defined strata between the top and the bottom. This knowledge can also be put to use to reduce the possible amount of variation in the sample.

Using Knowledge of Continuous Variability

If you let stand an imperfect solution of liquids for any length of time, you will find that although all elements of the mixture are present throughout the vessel, the part at the top will have a higher proportion of the lighter elements and that at the bottom will have a denser mixture. Relative density will usually be a straight line function from top to bottom. Gasoline, for example, is such an imperfect mixture of hydrocarbons, and the difference in density from top to bottom of a large tank can be quite substantial. Knowing this, the refinery lab will sample such a tank by taking three specified samples and blending them when testing for composition--a top sample, a bottom sample, and one chosen exactly midpoint between the two. The three samples are taken in the same vertical line for convenience, and the location of the vertical is always the same: directly below an inspection port whose location is a matter of structural convenience. Any other sample chosen at equidistant points from top to bottom would serve the same purpose, one consisting of the two interquartile points and the center, for example. But a pure random sample would only be closely representative by coincidence, the coincidence that it yielded samples taken at regular intervals vertically.

In such a universe of continuously distributed measure, careful positioning of the sample in serial form will always increase accuracy. If the measurements sought are known to follow this model, then any other sampling procedure for the measurement of this particular characteristic is certainly unscientific. A great many characteristics of importance in business analysis will be known to follow such a pattern of continuous variability, although all will not be linear in form.

Consider, for example, the concept of suburbanism, a real phenomenon that has done much to affect consumer buying habits. The suburb is definable in geographic terms as a place at some distance from the center of the city complex. But where does it begin? Students tell us that the city boundary does not define it and that from an operational standpoint some areas inside this artificial political limit are true suburbs while presumably some outside partake less of the thing we call suburbanism. But distance from the central business district, at least in any one direction, will certainly give a good approximation of the suburban content of the life pattern of the inhabitants. A sample study involving business factors affected by habits or attitudes induced by suburban living would thus do well to incorporate a procedure that gave cells spaced at equidistant points along the radii from the central city.

Similarly, we might recognize a factor called ruralism as an important factor in determining the number of customers for a mail-order house and the amount and character of the business they do by mail. Ruralism in this context might be defined as the relative lack of availability of local merchants with large establishments offering both wide and deep assortments of general merchandise, such as would be found in a metropolitan area. Again, we find no boundary between rural and urban, thus defined, but a kind of continuous increase in the relative intensity in the rural element in the population or in merchandise availability as we get progressively more distant from the metropolitan center. A mail-order sample of customers would then do well to reflect this element of business potential by serializing any blocks chosen equidistant along some sequence leading out from major metropolitan areas.

Not all such types of serialization will hinge on geographic distances. In working with customer lists, for example, some element of customer size may prove to be a logical and necessary basis for serialization. In such a case, if the customers, for example, are arranged in order of size, the simplest and least variable of samples will be a systematic choice from this list taken at fixed intervals throughout, e.g., every tenth name.

Note that in handling strata, sampling units should be chosen proportionate to the population of the strata. When using knowledge of continuous variation, however, it is important that proportioning of distance be a key criteria involved in taking this factor into account. Proportioning of the total number of sample units will be an independent consideration determined by such other elements of the procedure as stratification.

Direct stratification, indirect stratification, and knowledge of continuous variability all require that we have relatively precise knowledge of the structure involved. However, we often simply have some hunches that something may be important, and if this is the case, we should also stratify on this basis.

Inferential Stratification--Using Suspicion of Possible Sources of Variation

Some possible major sources of variation are not definitely known, but are based on evidence strong enough to make it wise to take them into account. Many of these are also such that direct or even indirect stratification is not feasible because, for example, neither the strata nor their weights are clearly definable and identifiable. In such cases, care should be taken to ensure a relatively even dispersion over the sample of characteristics related to such suspected factors.

One such example would be the ensuring of adequate representation of all major groups of varying ethnic descent in a sample of consumers. We know that nationality background can affect consumer choices, purchasing habits, and attitudes in such matters as food tastes or in spending and saving habits. Stratifying a sample on the basis of nationality descent is often a hopelessly complicated task, however. But we do know that initial letters for surnames differ for different nationalities. Two-thirds of the names in the mail-order file for one small midwestern city, for example, were filed under the usually uncommon last name initial of V. The area had been settled almost exclusively by immigrants from the Netherlands. Anyone who has ever used the Minneapolis telephone directory is hardly likely to forget the page after page of Johnsons. In such a case, any effect due solely to nationality background can be minimized by making certain that the sample is distributed over such a name list, for example, in proportion to the occurrence of the surname initials in the list.

A related technique is insistence that the sample be relatively well dispersed over a geographic list or area to ensure that possible local sources of variation are not unduly weighted. An experimental agronomist, for example, was once asked what he would do if, by chance, his intended probability sample located all sample plots in one corner of the field. He replied, sensibly enough, that he would choose a new sample.

He knew that small differences in soil conditions and in micro-climate, even in the same field, could have appreciable effects on his yields.

Thus, whatever sampling design is chosen, it is usually well to incorporate either a procedure or check to ensure some kind of dispersion of the individuals or small blocks chosen.

REDUCING BIAS AND VARIATION THROUGH ANALYSIS

Sample results do not have to be accepted in the raw. If adequate provision is made for collection of collateral detail of the right kind, this detail can be used either to correct for imbalance of representation, or to signal the presence of major factors affecting universe structure which may require further investigation or analysis before inferring that the sample represents the population sampled. In a political poll, for example, some measure of party adherence and recent voting should always be obtained. When it is, it is relatively easy to re-weight the results by reference to past voting records. In marketing studies, detail on past buying and use habits should always be considered for inclusion.

At times, of course, the universe is composed of some rather sharply drawn separate substrata that were not suspected before making the study. Even in such cases, the nature of the data collected will permit internal analysis revealing possible sources of error, or even defining its extent and permitting its correction. One such case was that of a maker of a widely used feminine product. Trying to determine the reason for declining sales, the company contracted for a special, national probability, store audit. To the surprise of the company, the audit resulted in an estimate of a ten percent market share--enough to make it one of the leading brands. This was so far at variance with their own information on total sales that the company's research director knew it could not be true, but his protests were met with bland assurance that the results must be right because the agency had used a probability sample. Digging into the actual data, however, the research director discovered that, in this particular item, most outlets stocked only two or three prominent brands and that the accident of random sampling had resulted in auditing a high disproportion of the stratum of retailers who had chosen to concentrate on his particular brand. Knowing this, it was relatively simple to design the right kind of study.

Not infrequently, the only information needed from a sample is an indication of a trend, and a very biased sample, but one of known bias, may yield adequate information of this kind as readily as a truly representative design. Some years ago, the author had occasion to talk to two politicians on opposite sides of the political fence in one of the midwestern states. Both had a reputation among their acquaintances of spotting the final results of an election long before the totals seemed definitive. The answers received from each were strikingly similar. One said, "I just watch the first returns as they come in. Say one of them is in the sixth ward, up along the river. I know that is a good labor precinct. If it is going 6 to 1 for us, I know we are in. If it is only 4-1/2 to 1, we have lost." The other commented that he knew how certain precincts in the Lake District should be divided. "Take that district where I live--it is about ninety-five percent Republican and five percent Democratic, and I knew how each one stands. If the Democratic vote goes beyond that, I knew we are losing."

What each of these men was saying, of course, was that there is a basic political pattern in the electorate, and that a trend is consistent across that pattern. Since then, many observers of the political scene have come to recognize the truth of this, and have used it in projecting political trends.

More important to the business analyst, this political phenomenon is simply a special case of the general fact that human choices and actions are the result of personal perceptions. These perceptions are determined by the place of the perceivers in a social structure which determines the basic pattern of their action, plus the effect of relatively uniform external forces which are perceived by them in terms of this structure. Given a knowledge of the basic structural pattern and the place of those observed within it (place of the family in the life cycle, in the socioeconomic pyramid, etc.), even biased data can result in accurate interpretation.

USING VALIDITY CHECKS TO IMPROVE THE SAMPLE

In any kind of sample, validity checks should always be sought and used wherever possible. This is one purpose of collection of collateral detail. But the use of such checks is especially important in the case of continuing samples common to much business research, the consumer panel and the sample sales file, for example.

Some checks can be made during the sample selection process. In sampling a retailer's mailing list, for example, it is usually important to make sure that credit and cash customers are sampled in proportion, because the buying habits of these two separate strata are usually quite different. If a block sample system is necessary--which it usually is if the sample is to continue to be representative over time--these two groups can seldom be sampled separately. But the sample blocks, after selection on some objective basis, can be checked for total cash-credit proportions within strata cells, and where deviation is significant, the more deviant blocks discarded and some better balanced elements near them in the selection process substituted.

Samples can also be checked for validity at some point of time after selection, and corrected for deviant results before being put into full operation. In a sales file, for example, the sample could be checked in detail for its representative character during a trial month. If any cell proves significantly deviant at this point, the source of unacceptable deviation can be tracked down and eliminated by substitution according to some predetermined objective procedure.

TRUE FINAL ERROR A MATTER OF PERSONAL JUDGMENT

Obviously, every one of these means of error reduction carries the analyst further away from the possibility of estimating error on the basis of some mathematical formula, making the final degree of accuracy a matter of personal judgment. This is not as uncomfortable a state of events as it might seem, however. In the first place, when even average intelligence is used in their application, all of these methods limit the possibility of sample variation inherent in straight random choice. More important, they are necessary and useful to the exact degree that the assumptions of probability mathematics are inapplicable. Their purpose is to insure sample validity, something that cannot be calculated mathematically with any sampling procedure. The reliability and confidence level that can be calculated have no necessary relationship to the question of how representative the sample results are.

SAMPLE STRATIFICATION: TWO EXAMPLES

One good illustration of some of the ways in which prior knowledge may be utilized is provided by the design of the U.S. Bureau of Labor Statistics for its study of 1972-1973 consumer expenditures, used to provide a new base for the BLS Consumer Price Index (CPI). As related to the spring, 1975 American Marketing Association's Conference, the design was as follows:

"The survey consisted of two separate surveys, each with a questionnaire and a sample. In a quarterly panel survey, each consumer unit in the sample was interviewed quarterly over a 15-month period. In a diary survey, respondents completed diaries at home for two one-week periods.

"The decision to use both quarterly and diary questionnaires was based on research on collection methodology done by the BLS, the Census Bureau, and the Survey Research Laboratory of the University of Illinois.

"The research showed that quarterly surveys can indicate large purchases. Diaries are best for small, frequent, easily-forgotten purchases.

"The sample for both surveys came from the 1970 Census of Population 20 Percent Tape, which included families that had completed an extended or long-form Census Questionnaire. The sample was stratified on the basis of family size, basic family unit income, and homeownership and drawn to represent total noninstitutional U.S. population and all geographic regions.

"To reduce the risk of covering a period of unusual economic conditions, the samples were divided into subsamples, one for 1972, one for 1973.

"The first quarterly interview provided socio-economic characteristics of consumer units, inventories of their major items, and data about regularly purchased items bought since the first of the year. Interviews in the next quarters covered detailed expenses, collecting clothing and utility data every three months, small appliances every six months, and major appliances, cars, and real estate data every 12 months.

"In quarters two through five, interviewers obtained global estimates for food and beverages to be integrated with data collected by the diaries. Each family was visited five times. The last interview concerned housing expenses, work experience, changes in assets and liabilities, expenditures for goods and services requested in other quarters, and detailed estimates of family income.

"The diary questionnaire covered expenditures not covered in the quarterly interviews--food, household supplies, personal care products, and non-prescription drugs. Each family kept two consecutive one-week diaries.

"The interviewer collected socio-economic data about a consumer unit, left the diary, picked it up a week later, and left another. After the second week, while picking up the completed diary, he collected data on work experience, occupation, and income.

"The diary was divided by day of purchase and by broad classification of goods and services. Respondents were asked to make specific entries (skim, chocolate, or whole milk, fresh, dried, or canned apricots, etc.) Diaries were printed in Spanish for areas with Spanish-speaking populations.

"Cooperation was greater than the BLS had hoped, said Shiskin. Nearly 90 percent of sample units participated in the quarterly study each year. Response rates for the diary survey were 80 percent the first year and 90 percent the second." *

(Note that even with the full resources of the government, from 10% to 20% of the respondents were missed.)

Another example is that of the mail order file, already referred to previously. The problem here was especially complex. The file had to be a permanent running record, since the information needed involved purchases over a previous two-season (one year) period and the build-up of the purchase record, in terms of both frequency and amount, during the current season (6 months). The primary purposes were two in number: (a) to provide an estimate of the proportionate and absolute numbers of customers who would later be in the file at the time of mailing the next general catalog, and (b) to measure the relative profitability of each customer class during the previous season. Customer turn-over was at the rate of about 20% per year. On the basis of the kind of records available in the general file, there were 126 definable classes of customer (of

---

* "Shiskin Releases New BLS Statistics in Chicago, Tells Methodology Used," Marketing News, May 9, 1975, pp. 1, 11.

which 6 classes would be brand new entrants into the file).
This meant 126 predictions which had to be in very close accord with the right proportions, since the catalog mailing plan, and the number printed, had to be based on this prediction. For practical reasons, the total sample had to be limited to about 100,000 names. This seems large until it is realized that the average customer list would be less than 1000 each (100,000 ÷ 126).

The sample had to be a cluster sample of some sort, in order to make sure of picking up new customers--they were not identifiable at the time orders came into the house.

The first trial sample used conventional techniques: a straight probability random sample of file drawers. This sample proved worthless, a fact which would have been revealed in advance by a simple calculation of the probability of getting 126 samples simultaneously in proportion, by random methods.

At this point, another analyst decided to try a thoroughly stratified design, using knowledge of the factors which had already been shown to affect the firm's customer potential. This data had proved that the number of customers in a given community was related to:

1. Average level of consumer discretionary buying power in the county as a whole.
2. The extent of total competition as measured by:
   a. size of the local city or village
   b. size of the largest town in the county
   c. the distance to the nearest metropolitan center.
3. The service available from this firm as compared with their principal general mail order competitors measured by the parcel post zone differential. The latter was measured by the number of parcel post zones to the firm's single warehouse location, as compared with the number of parcel post zones to the nearest competitor's branch warehouse.

It was also known that the average dollar volume purchases per customer varied regionally and by state. Long experience had shown that credit-approved customers bought very substantially more than those who had not requested nor been granted credit.

The main customer file was in state-postoffice-name order. Postoffices could be identified as to county by using the Postal Guide. It was possible to get a machine count of the customers, classified as to credit-approved and otherwise, very cheaply. This count would miss the customers whose stencils were out-of-file at the time of the count (about 3 percent) because an order was being processed. It was decided to accept this error and get the count.

The sample design decided on required:

1. Creating a file card for each postoffice (about 50,000 at the time). On this card was entered,

    a. state

    b. post office name

    c. county

    d. number of customers by credit status

2. Dividing the national map into parcel post differential zones, treating each zone as a separate stratum.

3. Within the parcel post zone, locating all metropolitan area centers and using the cities as a nucleous for a subcell of surrounding counties.

4. Determining a sampling sequence for the counties in each metropolitan area by starting with the home county and arranging the county groups of cards in a spiral sequence outward to where the sequence met the spiral from another metropolitan center (in this way, knowledge of the continuity of distance variability was taken into account.)

5. Sorting the individual post-office cards into 5 population size groups, keeping the county sequence intact. Each size group was then a separate sub-stratum, taking into account the extent of local competition in all 3 dimensions.

6. Totaling the customer counts by credit status, within each sub-group of cards.

7. Choosing a random starting point, picking a serial sample of towns within each of these 5 sub-groups, within each local parcel post zone differential within the state.

8. Totaling the sample counts credit and non-credit separately and comparing them with the stratum count. Where a significant difference in number or proportion occurred, dropping out the most variant post office and substituting the nearest one which would create the correct balance of credit status.

9. Choosing equal blocks of names from each sample town, sufficient to give the total needed for the stratum, and defining the sample as all customers within that alphabetical limit of names. (Blocks were deliberately dispersed over the alphabet in different towns to eliminate a possible ethnic bias.)

10. Obtaining all of the orders, (after processing) for a period of time, checking the totals from the sample for the period, for cash and credit separately. If the proportions of total, cash and credit, did not agree with the quota, within 5%, inspect the results, cell, by cell, and draw a new sample for the most variant cell.

Obviously, the precision of such a sample could not be determined by any confidence level calculation. Too many of the rules of probability sampling had to be violated. The resulting sample, however, proved extremely accurate, and this accuracy was still good 30 years later, despite several complete turn-overs in the customer list.

The reason was simple: it was solidly based on knowledge of the relationship of stratification factors to potential purchases.

Obviously, a great deal of judgment goes into such a design, but human judgment, based on experience, is always superior to any purely mechanical operation. The sampling process is no exception, as any experimenter can testify.

SUMMARY

1. The widely touted probability sample designs are not always the best, and may even be poor designs in the case of finite populations or populations in which the measures sought exhibited a skewed distribution.

2. When sampling finite populations typical of industrial market research, hand-picked samples are nearly always necessary, one taking into account the usually large differences in size and importance of the individual members of the population.

3. Designs for sampling mass population may or may not take advantage of prior knowledge of universe structures.

4. Only accidental or convenience samples and pure probability samples are constructed without reference to such prior knowledge.

5. Convenience samples can be adequate for some needs, especially when time is of the essence.

6. Probability procedures have their greatest utility when knowledge of universe structure is not adequate for stratification. The rigid selection procedures required also facilitate supervision of field work.

7. Pure random design, however, permits too wide a sample variance for many purposes. Most research follows a modified probability design in which random selection is a minor supplemental aspect, with stratification of some kind as the major frame of the design.

8. In any scheme, "random" choice is quite different from accidental. Generally, it requires a rigid procedure based on some form of lottery (but can be produced accidentally).

9. Stratification, to be useful, cannot be a mechanical process, but must be tailored to factors related to the measures sought. It may be direct, indirect, or merely inferential in nature.

10. The purpose of stratification is to reduce sampling error by purposely dividing the population studied into segments which are more homogeneous than the population as a whole.

11. Direct stratification divides the universe into specific cells on the basis of easily identified factors known to influence the reactions we seek to measure.

12. Not all factors known to affect responses make for easy identification of stratum members. In such cases, block or cluster samples are chosen on the basis of strata measured in terms of some factor known to be related to the stratifying factor or factors sought.

13. In other cases, the stratifying factor is a continuous variable, and respondents are chosen at equal intervals along some indirect factor related to the continuous variable.

14. At times, we do not have definite knowledge that a factor is important, but have strong reasons for inferring that it does, and use some convenient indicator of this factor as a basis for stratification.

15. The sample design and sample measurements can sometimes be improved through the use of validity checks, correcting the choice when results are proved to be out of line.

5

SAMPLING RESULTS:
HOW FAR CAN YOU TRUST THEM?

No statistical technique can tell us what we want most to know: how accurate or true are the sample measurements-- how valid are they, that is?

Sampling error is of two sorts: lack of consistent measurement, and consistent bias. Reliability, i.e., the consistency of our measurements, can be determined by objective calculation. But however consistent our measurements prove to be, we must be certain of their validity, i.e., that we have measured what we intended to measure. The validity can only be estimated by means of logical analysis and is not a calculable figure. In terms of the real needs of business decision, most studies are sufficiently reliable, but a lack of validity can result in major misdirection of plans.

One good example is that of the antiacid pill which everyone liked, but which proved unsalable. The idea looked good; the pill was more convenient, and it could be taken without water. Consumers on the test panel that tried it all liked it. The company was braced for early success when they launched it in a number of test markets with heavy advertising. But it did not move off the shelves. The research conclusion that it was an attractive product had not been valid. A recheck finally uncovered the fact that users of antiacid pills felt that the water taken with such pills was an essential part of the help they gave. Research results had been consistent, but they had not been a valid measure of marketability.

SAMPLE CONSISTENCY VERSUS MEASUREMENT UTILITY

Reliability is an objectively determinable fact, a central question in traditional objective probability theory. The answer is expressed in some form of normal curve analysis--usually standard error or level of confidence, which are routine calculations. Reliability is concerned solely with sample variation resulting from two factors: (1) the actual range and degree of variation in the universe being studied and (2) the sampling plan, procedures, and sample size adopted for making observations in this universe. The resultant variation is assumed to be the algebraic sum of the effects of those extremely minute, infinitely numerous influences we subsume under the term random.

It is undeniably important that our results be consistent within some tolerable range. But the first concern of the user of research results is with their dependability as a measure of what will happen under the conditions under which decisions will be carried out--with their validity as guides for this decision. Validity is not a simple computation but a matter of carefully considered judgment. It is, in effect, a subjective probability estimate based on careful analysis of the results and the way they were obtained, as confirmed by references to as many external and internal cross-checks as the analyst can devise.

The estimate of validity is concerned with bias, not random variation--bias resulting from one or more of five different kinds of human error:

1. errors arising from the investigator's concept of the research question that needs answering and his plan for answering it
2. errors coming out of the specific procedures adopted for securing data needed to get these answers
3. errors arising out of the actual execution of the planned procedures
4. erroneous analysis and interpretation of collected information
5. errors inherent in trying to read the meaning for the future in data out of the past--extrapolation errors.

We must evaluate both reliability and validity, but never confuse the two. They are two quite different kinds of error, arising from two different sets of forces. When the statistician informs you that his sample has revealed that 40 percent ± 4 percent of the market (at the 95 percent confidence level) would buy a product, he has simply given an estimate of how much variation he would get in other repeated tests of the same kind, during the same period of time, in the same locale. He makes no statement of the stability over time of his results, and he guarantees nothing as to the extent to which he has measured what you wanted measured. He has limited himself entirely to the objective computations of expected differences between a number of samples of like kind.

For business decision, however, we want a different answer: How probable is the measurement we infer from the results of a single sample? The statistical answer gives the objective probability of repeated measures of a proposition assumed to be invariable. But the business analyst must make a subjective estimate of the variability of the item measured-- a completely different finding.

Objective probability inference makes the basic assumption that a measurement must be either wholly right, or wholly wrong. Truthfulness, is, for the objectivist technician invariable. Any measurement, survey, or experiment can have only one of four possible outcomes, in this view:

1. The proposition is in fact true, and research evidence either:
   a. leads to its full acceptance, involving no error.
   b. leads to its rejection, which we call a Type I error.
2. The proposition is in fact false, and research evidence either:
   a. indicates that it is true, leading to error labelled Type II.
   b. leads to its rejection, involving no error.

Statistical theory concerns itself solely with the relative possibility of one of these two types of error, expressed as a range of values around the parameter we seek to measure, together with a statement of the confidence level--for example, a mean of 40 percent ± 4 at the 95 percent level. Error range and confidence level are purely mechanical calculations based on the number in the sample, and must refer to some form of "true random" sample.

Such a black-and-white view of research results does not fit the needs of the decision maker. The policy maker needs to know, given a single set of observations, or at most a

very limited series of such sets: "How much certainty do I have
that a future course of action based on this measurement will
be successful?" The subjective probability with which he is
concerned starts with the assumption that the truthfulness of a
proposition can be variable, in other words.

To see the difference between these two kinds of probabilities, let us consider the hypothetical problem of interpreting the results of a consumer panel test of an interesting new
canned meat product--Mixies--a test showing that fifty-six
percent of the panel of 100 favor our product.

The statistician would reason as follows: "Assume the
true mean value for favorable reaction is L_t. Then the results
of a series of sample tests should lead to the value

$$L_t \pm k \sqrt{\frac{L_t(1 - L_t)}{n}}$$

X percent of the time," where n is the number in each sample,
k is an arbitrary constant chosen by the statistician depending
on his degree of caution, and X is his confidence limit, determined by the proportion of the so-called normal curve within
the limits

$$\pm k \sqrt{\frac{L_t(1 - L_t)}{n}}$$

Usually, he would pick 2 for the value of k, giving him a 95
percent confidence level, but he might insist on 3 (99 percent)
or less often be willing to settle for 1 (about 67 percent), or
even .6745 (50 percent). Since the true value of L_t is never
knowable in the general population under study, the statistician
is usually willing to substitute 56 percent for L_t, which he will
admit is an approximation. The traditional statistician will
thus say no more than that if you had run a very large number
of tests, you would have obtained values in the range he calculated (about 3 percent at the 95% level) X percent of the time.

But the Product Committee will not find this kind of
calculation very useful in deciding whether or not to start making and trying to sell Mixies. What this Committee will wish to
know is: If we decide to go ahead on the basis of the results
of how likely are we to get adequate product acceptance? That
is, if we decide to sell on the basis of a presumably valid test

panel result showing fifty-six percent liking, how often will decisions like this result in acceptance by about fifty-six percent or any other substantial part of the market?

There is no formula in mathematics to answer this question. It involves an inference as to results under different circumstances, at a different point in time, and assumes that the true parameter is a variable with some inherent degree of uncertainty. The analyst must find some way of estimating the answer. In other words, he must go beyond the mere measure of consistency of his measurements to assay their validity for the decision to be made. This validity will be determined by the quality of his project formulation and planning, his choice of data collection procedure, and his supervision of its operation and, most important, of his care and expert insight in analysis of the results.

Business decision led astray by simple bias alone is an extreme rarity. Unfortunately, decisions that fall far short of acceptable optimum results because of research bias are far too easy to find. In fact, few project findings really are free from large inaccuracies traceable to the aspects of data collection and interpretation which affect validity.

THE MULTIPLE SOURCES OF HUMAN RESEARCH BIAS

Research is carried out by people, and to err is human. Bias can slip in at every step from the initial investigation to the final preparation of the formal report: in problem formulation, project planning, data collection, and in the final interpretation of the collected data.

Project Conception Errors

The initial project plan itself contains the potential for three types of error:

> an error in the conception of the correct research question for investigation--the problem formulation error

> an error in choosing the sensitive variables for observation

> an error in identifying the exact nature and bound-

119

aries of the universe truly involved in the decision for which aid is sought, and in defining the sensitive members of that population for purposes of measurement.

Problem formulation is a difficult skill, and an art which comes only from experience. Almost aways, the initial statement of the problem is in action terms because the action need is the genesis of most research projects. The action itself, however, is in doubt because of some kind of information deficiency. It is this <u>underlying information question</u> which must be brought into focus if the problem is to be solved. Obviously, study of the wrong question will lead to the right answer only by accident.

The sensitive variables that must be investigated are often so far from obvious that the main research problem may be their determination. An assignment to prepare an overall branch warehouse plan turned out to be principally an investigation into what factors determined the firm's business potential. Once the analyst had satisfied himself that he knew the sensitive factors and their weights, the rest was a mere clerical exercise.

Universe boundary definition is no concern of statistical theory. It is simply assumed that they are as clearly delimited as the urn containing the balls in the lottery problem or the fifty-two cards in the poker deck. No such easy assumption can be made in business research. Consider the problem of the dress buyer seeking a style acceptance study of next season's dress line. What universe should he investigate? Obviously, just those women who wear dress sizes in the line involved. But is this a sufficient limitation? A series of tests on just this problem showed that the sample must be pinned down to actual company customers, and among them, dress customers only. A list no different than one made of his own clerical employees had a completely reversed ranking of preference from that given by customers of not too different economic level (and customer choices proved to be right)!

Since few businesses have any but the foggiest idea of the exact nature of their customer potential, the problems of the business analyst in universe delineation are apparent. Even when the universe is clearly defined, it is not safe to assume that every member is of equal value for observation. When investigating acceptance of revolutionary new products, only the tastemakers are likely to yield a correct reading on future choices. Once the universe is defined, the sensitive members must be identified.

Biases Arising Out of the Data Collection Plan

Procedural details of the data collection plan can be second only to the problem formulation as a source of bias. The total list of possibilities could be quite long, but the most important would seem to be:

1. inadequate contact of the analyst with the data collection process
2. the source of information used, and the method of respondent contact
3. in surveys, details of collection--wording, definitions, breadth of collateral detail obtained, type of response required, etc.
4. problems of memory on the part of the respondent
5. manner of presentation of the survey to the respondent--extent to which it inhibits or biases response, or adequately enlists respondent interest
6. bias in selection of respondents or of time period
7. provision of controls
8. adequacy of pretest.

We cannot stress too much the extreme importance of close personal contact of the analyst with the original data collection, including, if possible, direct participation in the process. Whether the original data derives from records or interviews, unforeseen details of record form or respondent reaction often change the interpretation that can be put on the data.

Details of the respondent's mannerisms, side remarks, tone of voice, and other sidelights of communication are as much a part of his answer as the words used. They sometimes give a reverse slant to the words themselves. In the absence of such personal contact the analyst can easily interpret the data in terms of inapplicable personal experience and analyze respondent answers in terms of a biased personal understanding of the question wording alone. He may err in estimates of the relative importance of related question responses, or otherwise be led completely astray.

The greater ability of the project director to maintain close contact with the field work is one of the major sources of superiority of the relatively small sample. There can be little question that the high accuracy of analysis achieved by two of the most widely respected private political analysts is due in no small measure to their habit of doing a large part of their own field work. For a similar reason, the disaster which befell the published straw polls in 1948 was due in no small part to the fact that they were primarily a minor sideline for their directors. * They did little or no interviewing themselves and thus missed observing the strong but subtle differences in the nature of this campaign--differences which required very careful analysis of the background of their poll results.

Direct contact with the data collection is often highly important in an analyst's data interpretation. In one instance, a study of rural family living budgets in the Lake States Cut-Over Area during the Great Depression was combined, in Washington, with similar studies from other areas, and an analysis was prepared by an analyst of the United States Department of Agriculture. The analyst interpreted the average value of a dwelling (about $1600) as reflecting extremely poor housing conditions in the area. He could hardly have been more wrong,

---

* In the 1948 Dewey-Truman race, the polls, widely featured in the press, predicted Dewey would win by a comfortable margin. Instead, Truman won by a relatively narrow electoral vote margin, and a razor-thin popular vote margin in several key states. The result was a general hue and cry against polls, many people fearing that they influenced elections through a supposed bandwagon effect. The general clamor tended to broaden into an attack on personal interview research in general, and a distinguished group of statisticians was appointed by interested learned society groups to analyze where the polls went wrong. One answer they came up with was that the polls, on the basis of past experience, had stopped interviewing six weeks ahead of the election. Previous polls had shown no substantial change after that point. However, those who looked closely at all of the election results noted that, in the key states, the presidential vote and the Truman plurality trailed the local results by a substantial margin, in areas in which the Democrats scored upsets. The presidential preference was apparently less deep-seated than the preference for local candidates--a reaction that a close observer could have noted, but would not normally be included in the questioning.

as photographs (which he did not have) of each house in the sample indicated. Although far from being housed in mansions, most of the families interviewed lived in homes that compared favorably with farm homes elsewhere. Lacking direct contact with the area in question, the analyst interpreted building costs in terms of higher construction costs in urban and rural areas he knew.

Direct contact of the analyst with a substantial part of the data collecting can be so important to gathering illuminative collateral sidelights that sample size should always be kept to a level permitting such a procedure.

Biases Due to Data Source and Method of Respondent Contact. Every method of data collection contains possibilities of gross bias under some conditions. The possibility of such error must be weighed carefully in relation to each specific research problem and plan, on the basis of experience of others as well as that of the project analyst. There are no universally true rules of what to expect, only some general guides.

Information gathered from readily available records and secondary tabulation, for example, must be scrutinized for coverage with respect to the problem under study. The information is available because it was gathered by someone else, usually for a somewhat different purpose, to fit the needs of that purpose. The readily available information locked up in the minds of key people contacted in an experience survey is not only colored by their personal experience, but censored and summarized in terms of their own particular interests.

Every means of canvass employed in surveys has its own potential bias. The most obvious bias dangers are in the mail survey, which must depend in part on some kind of mailing list, with some built-in bias possibility, and which usually secures returns from a minor fraction of the intended respondents. How great an error can result from these two types of bias became clear in the Literary Digest presidential poll fiasco of 1936. It is well established that, in terms of that particular election, the telephone-automobile list used contained an inherent bias--a bias which had not shown up in previous polls made by this publication. More important, however, was a response bias, due to the differential residential mobility of the different economic levels and the differing tendency of different socioeconomic groups to respond to a mail inquiry. Roper has related how, during the campaign, he had been approached by the Literary Digest analyst. The latter was sincerely puzzled

123

by the divergence then showing up between the Literary Digest's early returns and the results of the Roper personal poll. Roper suggested that the difference was due to response bias and suggested that the Literary Digest make a special keyed mailing of two separate lists--one to a list of buyers of new automobiles, one to buyers of used cars. When this was done, the response from new car buyers proved to be several times that received from buyers of used cars.

But the mail return may have no bias if the list itself is reasonably homogeneous from a socioeconomic standpoint. A mailed inquiry to the customers of a mail-order house, in a pretest of dress preferences of customers, gave results which checked well against later sales.

One major disadvantage of the mail survey is the complete lack of opportunity to observe the nuances of personal reaction valuable in interpreting answers and the difficulty of knowing that every respondent understands the meaning of each question in the sense intended by the analyst. It is often wise, especially when dealing with matters of opinion and emotional response, to supplement such mail studies with limited personal interviewing in which the analyst takes a major part. It certainly never hurts to encourage free comments by the respondents through provision of generous space, both in relation to key questions and in a general category at the end of the questionnaire, and to analyze carefully all such responses obtained.

In the personal interview canvass, the biggest problems are obtaining planned coverage and making certain that instructions are carried out uniformly and as intended. Finding respondents at home, or otherwise available for interview, is always a problem, especially in consumer surveys. In practice, it is seldom possible to get complete coverage of a tightly specified sampling scheme, and those missed can be a very biased sample of the total. There are methods for partial correction of such misses, such as making an intensive effort to cover a subsample of not-at-homes and checking back among those contacted for their degree of at-homeness immediately preceding the interview date and inferring from this the nature of the not-at-homes. But it should be apparent that none of these methods gives a complete correction.

Further, personal interviews make a high manpower demand, and any extensive effort requires a relatively large force of interviewers. With such a force come the supervisory problems of strict adherence to instructions, both in sample design and in the conduct of the interview. One of the best safeguards, again, is to keep the sample small enough so that the project director himself is free to undertake a substantial amount of field work and thus obtain some standard against which to check interview results.

The telephone canvass avoids the nonreponse problems of the mail survey and can minimize the expense of the callback, which makes personal interview coverage a real problem. It also removes the rather considerable incentive present in personal interview samples for the interviewer to cheat on sample selection specifications. But, in turn, the telephone inquiry enforces a relatively structured, rather brief, form of question on the survey. Attempts to gather important collateral detail may have to be skimped. Thus this method may introduce bias by means of the form of questionnaire imposed, as well as by means of the respondent's uncertainty as to the true auspices of the survey. She cannot see the questioner, and the telephone has been widely misused by selling organizations who use the word survey to get the ear of the respondent.

<u>Details of Collection as a Source of Bias.</u> Wording of questions is an important aspect of data collection, but it can never be assumed that the answers obtained are due solely to the exact wording as formulated and understood by those composing them. Besides the objective denotation found in the dictionary, many words carry a heavy emotional freight of connotation, and this can vary from locality to locality and even from person to person, both in content and depth. Also, triggered responses (strong emotional or habitual responses and associations to individual words likely to be included in a question) do exist. Some of these word associations are so general throughout the culture, we know enough to avoid using the terms involved. But the reaction to some terms may be specific to a small locality or a special group and the question framer may be innocent of any suspicion of the possibility. Anyone who grew up outside the area in which the Populist Movement took fire around the turn of the century is unlikely to understand the depth of feeling that attaches to the word interest, even yet, in such areas. Those who were not adults during the 1930's would be unable to picture the emotional depth of utter frustration and insecurity aroused in those who were by the phrase

out of a job. * To many with such strong emotional reactions
to particular individual terms, the mere inclusion of the term
sets off a train of emotionally charged associations which can
becloud the nature of the question asked and give rise to the
same general answer content regardless of word composition.
Only thorough pretesting can minimize the possibility of inclusion of such emotionally charged terms and forewarn of the
need for minute definition.

The type of response required can change the kind of
answer received. Studies have shown that pictured questions
can get a different response than those obtained from spoken
questions (James F. Engel and Hugh Wales).** The effect is
not confined to the difference between pictured and spoken questions. The highly structured yes-or-no or multiple choice
answer can force the respondent to distort his response or omit
important aspects of his attitude. The direct question may
elicit a different response from the indirect one. The good
pretest always anticipates the possibility of such bias by trying
more than one method to get at a given response.

Questions requiring recall can result in unexpected
bias if care is not taken. Accurate answers will normally result only to the extent that the respondent has had a major interest in taking conscious note of an action or observation at
the time the event took place. One way to overcome this problem is to induce the respondent to keep current records, but
this runs, in turn, into the problems of getting a representative
panel and maintaining its representativeness, as well as those
of insuring that records be actually current and not drawn up
from memory at some later time. (I once observed a salesman
making a call report for a full two week period, detailing to the
minute each call and lunch break, from memory, without notes,

---

*Just how different is illustrated by a radio news item
on July 26, 1974, during the sharp recession of that year. It
was found that substantial numbers of unemployment compen-
sation checks were being forwarded to resort areas!

**James F. Engel and Hugh Wales, "Spoken versus
Pictured Questions on Taboo Topics," Journal of Advertising
Research, Vol. 2, No. 1 (March, 1962), pp. 11-17.

as I sat beside him in a Chicago subway train.) For some purposes, a truly representative panel that will actually keep records cannot be achieved. A certain literary ability is needed, as well as a type of personality favorable to regular record keeping.

Thus, any kind of recall questions pose inherent problems of bias. So do questions that involve matters of social status, motives, and degree of conformity with community folkways and mores. The method of approaching such matters must be carefully designed to sidestep these problems, and the possibilities of bias must be carefully evaluated at each step.

Effect of Manner of Presentation of the Survey. Respondents react to the stated and suspected auspices of a survey as well as to the questions and other stimuli presented. Their feelings and attitudes toward actual or suspected survey sponsors will color the kinds of answers they give. Even where no emotional bias toward a survey sponsor is present, the degree and kind of cooperation given can be affected by the auspices of the survey. In interviews with industry officials, I have found that as a professional outsider, I sometimes got franker and more complete responses from executives under circumstances in which I told them I was not free to reveal the identity of the respondent, except that he was one of a class of possible suppliers or customers, than I would obtain when I was free to reveal the sponsor.

Bias in Selection of Respondents or Time Period. Avoidance of bias in respondent selection is far from easy, and time period bias must also be guarded against. The problem of respondent selection bias is most acute in mail surveys, but is present for every other form of respondent contact as well. The not-at-homes and the uncooperative are obviously different. In many respects, the woman who works has different opinions, attitudes, and habits from her otherwise similar neighbor, and often must be treated as a different stratum. More important, proper selection requires precise definition of the universe needing study, and the sensitive individuals within it. This is seldom completely known.

The possibility of bias in the time period should be obvious when the questions concern recent purchases of seasonal goods, involve any kinds of actions which fluctuate periodically, or come at a time when some news has in any way heightened interest in the subject of inquiry. In addition, a time bias can affect respondent selection. In fashion items, early purchasers

127

are a different breed from late adopters, for instance.

Need for Experimental Control and for Collateral
Detail. Some of the greatest errors in analysis can be traced back to lack of adequate provisions for experimental control in tests and absence of collateral detail in surveys. Experimental controls are so thoroughly discussed in all types of research literature that there is little excuse for slighting them. Unfortunately, the extent to which survey bias and error can be reduced by analysis of the right kind of collateral detail is not nearly so well understood. In a sense, careful stratification of the sample is one indirect way of furnishing collateral detail of high utility if the collected replies are identified for stratum of origin. But more direct information is even more highly useful in reducing the range of possible meaning for a measurement or observation, and in firming up the confidence the analyst can have in his projections. Such collateral information about sample composition sometimes furnishes the only means for evaluating the validity of a sample.

A good instance of the value of collateral detail in firming up an analysis was furnished by the experience of the Midwest Research Council in its 1940 presidential poll in Minnesota. On the basis of an August survey of only 700 respondents in the state, of whom nearly one-fourth were undecided, MRC was able to predict that Roosevelt would carry the state by 50,000 to 75,000 votes out of an estimated total of about 1.25 million. Roosevelt's November margin proved to be 52,000.

This estimate was based on results from a highly stratified sampling scheme, and the analysis was weighted by information given by control questions that made possible a division of respondents according to political tendency. For sampling purposes, Minnesota's precincts had been divided into a large number of groups that were relatively homogeneous from the standpoint of political history, economic factors, and type of residence. Within each cell a proportionate quota of objectively determined respondents were selected, dispersed in location over the cell according to a prescribed procedure. All respondents were classified by the interviewer as Republican, Democratic, Farmer-Labor, or split-ticket, according to their interpretations of the answers to key questions concerning primary voting habits. Final tabulations were then reweighted, within each major division of the state according to carefully calculated weights for each category. Only then was the undecided vote apportioned, separately for each category of voter, for each major subdivision of the state. Thus, collateral detail made possible by stratification and use of control questions permitted the negation of sampling variation and an accurate projection of the undecided vote, a type of projection that proved accurate, not only in this instance, but in a series of elections. Without this collateral detail, no prediction would even have been attempted.

The Effects of Operations on Research Error

Collection and processing of information can in themselves be sources of error. Five major sources of error are an ever-present danger in the collection process:
1. disregard of instructions by those collecting data
2. coverage bias due to the not-at-home problem and late reports
3. interviewer effect on response
4. communications breakdowns--misunderstanding of questions, inability to articulate a response in the form requested
5. recording errors.

No study design is better than its execution. The greater the dependence on others to do the data collection, the greater the chance that instructions may be misunderstood, interview questions reworded or presented in a manner that changes their intended meaning, inconvenient instructions side-stepped. The greater, also, the chance that some degree of interview faking or cheating may be done by interviewers, especially if instructions seem onerous, or if their only motivation is the pay. Careful training helps. Close supervision and spot-checking does too. Even better is the use, whenever possible, of interviewers with considerable interest in the research process, and also the paying of higher rates than normal to get a higher quality of personnel. And, again, execution of some of the fieldwork by the project director gives a basis for evaluation of the reports of others and a feel for the data, for which there is no substitute.

The problem of interviewer effect varies with the intensity of interest the respondent has in the subject of the interview, and also with the nature of the question or stimulus posed. Unfortunately, many business research surveys, especially in

the consumer field, deal with questions in which the consumer
has no burning interest. In such cases, the slightest suggestion of the interviewer can bias a result. The possibility of interviewer effect must be especially suspected in the case of
projective techniques of interview, where the desire of an interviewer for a fruitful result, together with the probing intended
to draw out a response can result, even unintentionally, in
leading respondents to statements that are far from spontan-
eous. Westfall has reported on a classroom experiment in
which an attempt was made to duplicate the stories reported by
a commercial agency in a TAT type of study. The picture
showed:

> two men mowing their respective lawns and stopping to
> converse over the fence between the two yards. One of
> the men was using a power mower while the other had a
> hand mower. Respondents were asked to tell a story about
> the picture.

To test the possible effects of interviewer bias,

> a class was separated into two parts in different rooms.
> In giving the instructions to one group, the instructor
> said, "One man, for example, may be saying, 'Let's quit
> and have a beer!'" More than half of the stories from
> that group mentioned beer one way or another while not
> one of the other group did. *

Two communications problems can be especially
troublesome: (1) the unsuspected variety of denotation and
connotation which different people, of differing backgrounds,
can attach to the same words and phrases, and (2) the fact that
some of the reactions for which we ask may be ones that some
respondents have never given conscious thought to, and are not
in a position to articulate. For years, the author's well educated wife insisted on translating quite (meaning "complete")
to mean not quite ("incomplete"). Many of the images we have
of jobs, people, firms, products have never been formulated
in verbal form, and if asked about them we cannot articulate
our emotional response to them.

One of the great virtues of the projective techniques
is their tendency to facilitate such answers, to enable the re-

---

* Ralph L. Westfall, "Student Involvement," Advancing
Marketing Efficiency (American Marketing Association, 1959),
p. 512.

spondent to describe his reactions. If no aid of some sort is given, the respondent's inability to articulate a response may lead him to furnish some easy, quite incorrect answer.

Some processing errors must be expected every time data has to be handled--in editing, coding, tabulating, summarizing, etc., and cross-checks are always in order. One way to minimize processing errors is to keep the number of times data is handled to the minimum. For example, when providing for mechanical processing of data by means of punch cards, one of the major advantages of the mark-sense card is the elimination of the coding and card-punching operations. The 1960 Census went even one step further by so designing their forms and machinery that a photographic record of the original schedule was translated electronically into a tape record for tabulating. Errors in coding and card-punching are frequently of the order of 3 percent.

Analytical Errors In Data Interpretation

Analytical error results from two closely related kinds of mistakes: (1) misunderstanding of the meaning of the collected information, largely through lack of adequate personal contact with the collection process and (2) lack of a correct conscious model of the relationships that hold for the universe being examined, or, worse, disregard of the necessity for such an explicit conscious model.

The need to get the feel of the data through personal contact with its collection has already been outlined. The importance and place of a theoretical model of universe relationships is reserved for the later discussion of the analytical process. Suffice it to note here that mere juggling of data without consciousness of the need for such a model is the basis for all of the superstition in the world. Moreover, a mere discovered relationship between two kinds of events gives no clue as to which is the causal factor and which is the result. To decide the latter, we need some well-based model or theory.

HOW DO WE KNOW HOW GOOD THE SAMPLE IS?

Determination of sample accuracy, as already indicated, requires two types of tests:

1. reliability--the extent of the consistency to be expected between independent measurements under the same circumstances of whatever factor is, in fact, being measured
2. validity--the extent to which we have measured the factor we thought, or hoped, we were measuring.

Validity itself is of three different levels: pragmatic validity, construct validity, and model validity. Within each type, there are two phases:

1. concurrent validity--the validity of the actual measurements
2. predictive validity--the soundness of the inferences and predictions based on the measurements.

Reliability measures the presence of random error. Validity is concerned with the presence of constant error due to the effect of major determinants of values. Of the two, only reliability is subject to estimate by objective calculation, but even this estimate tends to be conservative--that is, tends to be overstated--and then only really applies to probability designs. A better determination can be made only after the end of data collection, by comparison of replicated samples or of sample segments, and this determination can be made for any kind of design. (The conventional confidence level calculation only applies to the probability design, of course.)

Rating scales can often be tested by split-half methods. Within each stratum, reliability can be checked by observing the increase in stability of the parameters as the results for additional individuals are added in. Such measures of reliability are important, for until the measure used shows some degree of stability, analysis is crippled. But no matter how consistent the measure, we still cannot be sure of its meaning until we have substantial evidence that we have measured what we thought we had--until we have established some degree of validity for the observations and have a reasonable probability that constant errors of meaning are not present. For example, all so-called general intelligence tests have passed this and other similar technical tests. But the tests do not yield an accurate prediction of this academic performance--they are not fully valid for this purpose.

Validity cannot be measured mechanically. It is largely a matter of subjective judgment, but not necessarily pure guess. Pragmatic validity (whether a relationship works) is at least subject to test. Construct and model validity (the

132

truth of the underlying mechanism) is established through logical deduction from previous knowledge and through independent experimentation.

To establish pragmatic validity, it is necessary only to determine whether experience has demonstrated that better results come from decisions based on an inferred relationship or measure than without such an inference. Alternately, but somewhat less certainly, some degree of pragmatic validity is established if a different kind of evidence leads to a similar conclusion. Pragmatic validity itself does not require that we know why the results obtain. Thus, all surviving general mail order houses have long used the recency-frequency-amount approach to catalog circulation. Under this system, a three or four season record is kept of a customer's purchases, and catalogs mailed only to those above a certain minimum amount, recency, and frequency of purchase. More than a score of companies who failed to use this system went broke on catalog publication costs. The system provably works, but no solid theory of customer behavior gives it a firm foundation. On the contrary, there is solid evidence that some of the basic assumptions of its logic are false, and that a better system of customer classification is possible.

One weakness of pragmatic validity is that the solutions arrived at are rarely optimal in nature. A knowledge of the forces actually producing the observed results could lead to much more efficient systems of operation. Knowing that something works does not preclude the possibility that something else may not work much better. In addition, the world has seen so many spurious coincidences that it is always probable that something whose only justification is that it has worked in the past may suddenly lose its dependability because something affecting the true underlying mechanism forces a change. Conclusions drawn on the basis of pragmatic validity are never safe until the higher level of construct and model validity are established. Predictive validity can only be established through confirmation of the latter.

Construct and model validity are related. By a construct we mean a classification or designation of members of a population, of phenomena, and of characteristics that infer a certain consistency of action and relationships between the members of the population and between them and their social, material, and economic environment. Business terms like prospect, potential customer, industry, product, and market are constructs. Psychological characteristics such as drive, extroversion, aggressiveness are constructs. So are such sociological terms as conformity, social class, innovator, tastemaker. All of these terms infer a particular relationship between people. If valid, they lead us to expect a relatively consistent pattern of action between people, a degree of homogeneity of response.

By a model, we mean the assumed pattern of relationships itself, the relationship between people, and between people and their environment. We mean a certain predictability of interpersonal response under certain types of stimuli, or of similar patterns of response between events. Pure competition, oligopoly, and the two-stage process of idea adoption are models.

Thus when we classify a man as a tastemaker in a particular situation, we infer that, for certain types of innovation, he will be an early adopter, and, more, that he will be the means of introducing the innovation to other members of his social group. The model inferred by our construct of tastemaker, however, we call the two-stage process of idea adoption, and it involves a classification of a group into innovators, key influences, the majority, and the skeptics and assigns a particular role and timing for each in the process of new idea dissemination.

Like the test for pragmatic validity, part of the proof lies in determining whether predictions of expected behavior, based on the assumed relationships, are fulfilled. But in the case of construct and model validity, we do not expect as direct a correlation of behavior with prediction as we do in the case of pragmatic validity. The innovator does not necessarily lead in the choice of every type of new product, but only certain types closely related to his social values. The majority will not necessarily follow him in the adoption of every innovation he chooses, but only in those matters in which they look to this particular key influence for opinion leadership.

We thus need more than successful prediction to establish construct and model validity. We must trace out the actual pattern of relationships. For example, we must establish that the key influence actually has social contact with the following majority and that they look to him for leadership in specific areas of consumption. We must show that they adopt only after he or some other key influence puts the stamp of approval on an innovation. We must demonstrate the actual working of the interrelationships under different conditions, over considerable periods of time. In other words, we must reveal how the gears in the mechanism mesh, and in what manner. Once we have done this, as the sociologists have done in part for the innovation process*, we have a solid basis of prediction of some of the vectors in whatever process the models and constructs are applicable to, and our predictions thereby become dependable so long as this model remains valid in our changing social world.

Probably the most useful test of validity is the cross-check--the attempt to find the same answer through a completely different kind of method. If two or more completely independent approaches reach similar figures, our confidence in the measure can be much higher.

SUMMARY

1. All information is sample information and all thus subject to some degree of error from two different directions. Results from one sample to the next may not be sufficiently consistent (or, in statistical terminology, reliable). However consistent, the information itself may not be valid; we may not have been measuring what we thought we were.

2. The estimate of sampling variation simply measures how close a different sample would have been in the same circumstances. But decision must hinge on a different judgment: How much difference would a different time or different situation make in the result? We need to know the validity of the findings for the forecast purpose of a specific decision.

3. Ordinary sampling variation is seldom an influential element in the total research error which we must evaluate to measure the utility of the data for decision. Every step in the research process is a potential, and usually actual, source of error--problem formulation, research design, data collection plans and execution, analysis, and interpretation.

4. Control of project planning error is achieved by extreme care in formulating the correct research question, determining which variables are really sensitive in relation to the decision to be made, defining with care the boundaries of

---

*H. F. Lionberger, Adoption of New Ideas and Practices (Ames, Iowa, Iowa State University Press, 1959).

the universe to be investigated, and identifying the members of the population sensitive to the proposed action.

5. Maintenance of close personal contact with data collection by the analyst, and his participation in it, is the best insurance against data collection errors.

6. Every method of contact with respondents (mail, telephone, personal) has some inherent bias with respect to some kinds of information sought. Regardless of contact method, many details of collection can be a source of bias--question wording, type of response desired, need for recall, survey auspices, actual selection of respondents, or time period. Such errors can be neutralized in part by well-designed controls in the case of experiments or by maximum provision for collection of collateral information and its use in analyzing and making adjustments in returns.

7. Errors will come out of the execution of the best planned projects. Instructions are often disregarded. Some coverage bias is almost inevitable. Interviewers can affect responses even unintentionally. The communication of what is asked is seldom perfect. Recording and processing errors occur every time the data is handled.

8. Avoidance of analytical error requires the kind of insight arising out of direct contact with the actual data collection and the conscious use of an adequate model of the relationships involved.

9. Determination of final sample accuracy requires estimates of both reliability and validity.

10. Reliability may be estimated in advance by formula, but can only be computed accurately after the fact, by comparison of replicated samples or by providing for subreplication within the sample.

11. Validity of any sort is not a computation but a judgment based on some kind of supporting evidence. There are two levels: (1) pragmatic validity and (2) construct and model validity.

12. Pragmatic validity is established by the empirical test of whether or not an indicated relationship has worked in the past. However, pragmatic validity is not a completely safe basis for decision.

13. The really fundamental construct and model validity must be established by evidence that the mechanism of the relationship conceived actually exists. Once established, it forms a safe basis for decision.

6

NUMERICAL SUMMARY: AVERAGES, DISPERSION, SUMMARY TABLES

As already noted, all numbers are fictions or symbols invented to help us get some order out of the chaos of infinite variety and diversity. Their purpose is to place objects and events into classifications which, for the purposes intended, can be treated as alike. But even when we group objects in this manner, we still may have too big and too varied a universe to grasp its meaning.

For the investor and speculator, full information about the prices and quantities of each individual transaction on a stock exchange, even on a given stock on a given day, is more information than he can digest and comprehend without somehow reducing the detail. Even more bewildering would be a simple listing of every transaction in every one of the approximately 1800 issues traded on the New York Stock Exchange alone (not to mention the tens of thousands of securities of all kinds available for all corporations). If this were all we had in any attempt to assess the movements on the market, even a computer would suffer a nervous breakdown. So the investor uses two of the most common devices of traditional statistics to compress all this confusing detail into something he can comprehend and use for decision purposes: averages and measures of dispersion.

Statistics might be defined as the discipline of summarization--of compressing information into graspable limited sets of figures or other symbols such as charts. The most widely used summary devices are the single numerical ones: averages, indexes, measures of dispersion, and summary tables. Charts and graphs are largely added visualizations of these summary numbers, visualizations which furnish an added perspective and dimension. Of all such devices, the average meets the ultimate ideal for a statistical measure: within limits, it compresses the maximum amount of information into a single number. But averages of all sorts do so at a cost.

THE AVERAGES

In common usage, the term _average_ tends to connote the **typical** (most common), the midpoint, and the center of gravity of any distribution of measurements. Sometimes it is all of these, but only when the measurements are distributed symmetrically, in a bell-shaped formation. Almost none of the economic or social data important to business decision is so distributed. With the rarest of exceptions, all such data shows a lopsided distribution with a heavier concentration **nearer** one side than the other. Such business and social data exhibit a characteristically lopsided ("skewed") distribution like that in Figure 6-1. Characteristically, something like two-thirds or three-fourths of the values will be accounted for by one-third to one-fourth of the total items when we deal with matters affected by human action. For any one business firm, four-fifths of the sales volume may originate with one-fifth of the customers. Whatever the size of the individual customers, one-fifth or one-third of the orders will probably account for between four-fifths and two-thirds of the dollar volume. When dealing with production personnel, analysis will generally reveal that a large portion of the grievances or of the absenteeism are traceable to a small portion of the employees. The phenomenon is so prevalent that business writers sometimes elevate it to a principle-- the "70-30 principle" or the "80-20 principle". It is one reason for the effectiveness of management by exception.

In cases like these, the most common item (_mode_) will be, by definition at the most concentrated point. The middle item (the _median_) will be further toward the other end. The center of gravity (the _mean_) will be even further toward the other extreme.

Only one of these most common averages--the _mean_-- is a calculated one based on the actual measurements of everything in the sample set.

The _mode_ is a mere matter of observation or tabulation to find which item is the most common.

FIGURE 6-1. Typical Normal Social Curves: Percentages of Farms by Value of Product and the Percentage of Total Value of Farm Products by Value of Product per Farm, 1959

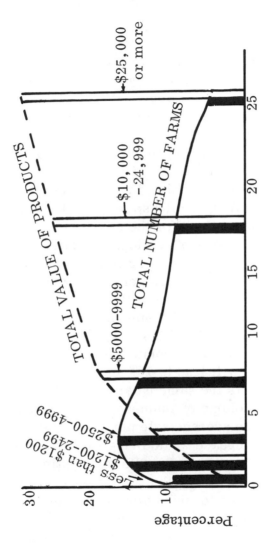

(Note that less than 30 percent of the farms produced about three-fourths of total product value)

The <u>median</u> is a mere matter of arranging items in order of value and counting to find the middle item.

The Mean as a Device for Projecting or Comparing Totals

Of course when data are so skewed, the location of the mean is far from the center of the distribution and it does not represent the more frequent or common values. If, however, we can assume that the distribution will remain relatively stable (as it quite usually does for any individual phenomenon), the mean can help us project from a group of one size to one of a different magnitude. Since the mean is related to (divided by) the total count, it is a device for comparison of the size tendency for individual items in groups of unlike total number. The mean is truly a rate: a way of comparing totals.

Consider, for instance, the estimates which the executives of Rural Mail Order House must make as it completes its catalog circulation plans for the next season. Rural's sales will depend on the number of catalogs it mails, and its profits depend on mailing only to customer lists which will average out at some profitable level of sales per catalog in the case of each particular list. Rural mailed 3 million catalogs last season and did $120 million worth of business. Meanwhile, the customer list has grown to 3.5 million customers of the type qualified to get a catalog, and the committee has concluded booming business conditions will lead to 10% more business per customer. If Rural adopts the same catalog circulation standard as last season, what volume of business should it plan for? That is easy you say: the average sale per catalog last season was $40, and the 10% increase would bring that up to $44. If we multiply $44 by 3.5 million, Rural's total estimate should be $154 million, if their economic projections are right. Of course, because of the lopsided distribution of order size (a mere 5% of the orders accounts for a fourth of the dollar sales), far less than half of the customers bought as much as $40 worth last season, but those sending in the large orders counterbalanced this, to get the average value of $40. There is no reason to doubt that the distribution will be just as skewed next season, so there is nothing wrong with this $44 projection, even though it represents a sales volume characteristic of only a minority of the customers.

The executive committee's interest in the sales average itself, but in the average as a convenient way of translating last season's total sales experience into an estimate of what next season's could be expected to be. Their real focus is on total sales, not the average, and the latter is simply a useful device in projecting a new total. At other times and for other purposes, they might be interested in the average as a device for management control. Thus if the average price paid by customers per dress in the dress department were to show a decline, they would view this variation in the average as a signal that something might be wrong with the selection of higher price merchandise in the department. Or if Rural's average rate of net profit on sales were to be substantially lower than that of its much bigger competitor, Sears Montgomery, they might begin to investigate circulation policy, or merchandising as a whole, or some other list of suspected factors. In every case, of course, they would be interested in the average as an indicator of some trouble in the total.

Sometimes, however, we forget that our true interest is in some total value and seek a rate for its empty self. We forget that a rate is only a multiplier, an "adjective," deriving whatever meaning it has from the total to which it is applied. We may forget that the reason we drove 60 miles per hour on the freeway was to make the 120-mile trip in 2 hours. At a rate of 40 miles per hour it would have required 3 hours. The 120-mile total is forgotten, however, when we speed at 60 miles per hour on a 1-mile trip through side streets where the time saving is infinitesimal and the increased risk quite substantial.

Or we may, as merchants occasionally do, look at the wrong rate and give valuable display space to a slow moving item because it gives us a high gross margin rate, perhaps a rate of 35%. We may neglect to look at the rate of inventory investment turnover, which reflects a total sales of $50 per year. Another item in the same department might have a margin of only 10% but its sales of $2,000 per year yields nearly 12 times the total margin and 6 times the return per dollar invested in inventory.

Last, it is obvious that some of us may be inclined to ignore the fact that all rates have a denominator, that they are so much per something, particularly interest rates. Although expressed in numbers, a rate is not a quantity, but an expression of a relationship of two other quantities. Rates such as averages and percentages cannot be added, subtracted, or

otherwise dealt with as quantities. If, for example, the unemployment rate is 10% in Ohio, 12% in Illinois, and 11% in Indi-
ana, we cannot assume that the average rate for the area equals
$\frac{10 + 12 + 11}{3}$, or $\frac{33}{3} = 11\%$. The total numbers of the labor
force varies in the three states, and to get the average, we
must go back to the original quantities, add the total unemployed, divide by the total of the three labor forces. Thus there
is no such thing as an interest rate of 1-1/2%, but only 1-1/2%
per month, or per year, and the two are definitely far from
the same thing. Furthermore, in these days of amortized
loans, which we pay off a little each month as the loan matures,
we need to distinguish carefully between the rate on the total
originally borrowed, and the rate on the balance still due.
How many bright-eyed young couples who would be
scandalized at an interest rate stated as 18% per annum blithely
sign up for a charge account at this same rate stated as 1-1/2%
per month? And what about your cousin who thinks he is getting money at a very low rate on the time payments on his
$3,000 car because he is being charged "only" $4.50 per $100
per year in addition to the principal of $100 per month over the
next three years? Has he forgotten that he has the use of the
full $3,000 only one month, and that in the last month of the
loan he is in effect paying 4-1/2% per year on $3,000 for the
use of a mere $100: in effect nearly 9% real interest, because
the average value he owes during the three years is just over
$1,500 (since he pays off to zero in the time the loan runs).
Even academia is not always immune to the misuse of
rates. Early in the Great Depression, one of the professional
schools boasted that "only 10% of our graduates were placed
immediately last year, but business has picked up. This year,
25% obtained jobs." The publicity neglected to mention that
the 1931 class had numbered 300 graduates, the succeeding
class only 40. Jobs landed had actually dropped from 30 to a
mere 10! The total figure to which an average refers is important.
The arithmetic mean has one particularly serious flaw.
It can be calculated from any collection of numbers, however
diverse and unrelated, and tends to emphasize the extreme
values in that collection, which may be part of a completely different universe. The mean may thus be a very untypical figure,
particularly in the kinds of skewed distributions typical of

142

social and economic data. If 297 customers from an industrial sales district buy $1000 or less each per year, averaging $500 per year, and 3 customers buy on the average $100,000 each, the average sale per customer calculates to nearly $1500. This is much less than the large customers are good for and nearly three times as much as the numerically more typical customers buy. If we want to compare typical customers we must use some other kind of average.

Averages Representing Typicality: the Median and the Mode

How would you define typicalities? If you think of the typical as being the most common, then the mode is your average, for that is exactly how the mode is measured. But the mode can be very unrepresentative of the distribution as a whole, particularly if the distribution is either skewed or U-shaped. In either case, it will be nearer one end of the extremes in value.

There also may be no real mode. If the distribution is essentially flat, the most common item may not be much more common than any other.

If we think of the average as being a central item, then the median, and only the median, is always that value, by definition. The median, however, is seldom the most common unless we have a symmetrical bell-shaped distribution. This average also gives no weight to the extremes, which may be very important in matters of design or decision (neither, of course, does the mode). In designing an automobile, for example, it is important to know more than just the dimensions of the average driver or the driver that is at the middle of the range. Some allowances must also be made for the physique of drivers that are near the extremes of the distribution of people, especially if the range is quite wide, as it is in the case of physical size of the human being.

Both the mode and the median share another defect-- they cannot be used for projecting a total, as can the mean. If we know that the median or modal purchase is $100.00 we still know nothing about the total sales. If we know the mean purchase is $100.00, multiplying $100.00 by the total number of buyers gives us the total sales. For this reason the mean is the most widely used of those best known kinds of averages. It is the basis for a wide group of averages we call indexes--

143

figures used to follow various kinds of business, economic and social trends.

INDEXES: SUMMARY AVERAGES USED TO HIGHLIGHT
TRENDS

Any of us who follows any kind of current events soon becomes familiar with at least the labels of a number of governmental and private summary measures called indexes. Among the best known are the Consumer Price Index; the Dow–Jones Industrial "Average"; the New York Stock Exchange Index; Gross National Product (GNP); the birth, death, marriage and divorce rates; the Federal Reserve Board Index of Industrial Production; the Bureau of Labor Statistics Index of Unemployment.

All of these are some kind of average (usually the mean) and generally of a weighted sample of some kind. All have proved to be extremely useful tools for summarizing and understanding the general economic or social trends involved. When we want to know what the current trend is on the stock market we ask what is happening to the Dow–Jones Industrial. We look at the GNP and the FRB Index of Industrial Production to assess what is happening to the health of the national economy. We infer what is happening to the structure of the family and the health of that institution by reference to marriage, birth, and divorce rates.

All of these indexes meet the general dictionary definition of "something that points out"--in this case the direction of movement of the activity designated. Such indexes or indicators also have the limitations implied by this label rather than by the label "measure". They are not direct measures. They are useful only as rough delineators of trends. Differences and relative value from one point of time to another are not always in fact really exact measures of the degree of actual change. In critical circumstances, they may briefly indicate even the direction of change incorrectly. Anyone basing plans and decisions on their use needs to understand these limits as well as the values of any index.

Reference has already been made in an earlier chapter to some of the limitations of indexes in general and especially in particular to the widely used Consumer Price Index (too often unofficially and incorrectly called a "cost of living" index).

The CPI represents, as do most indexes, a weighted sample of only a fraction of the items in any one family's possible purchases. These item prices are for a rigidly defined source of purchase, a given type of store in any one community, or the averages of three makes of automobiles in a single model for example. The weights assigned to each item in this very specific market basket is for a specific family composition in a very specific occupational and social class. It is in no sense typical of the habits of other kinds of families of different ages, different positions in the family life cycle, different social classes or even of every family in the group indicated. Even more important, the weights used are standard for long periods of time. A decade or more may pass from one base period to another. (The last two base periods were 1960-1961 and 1972-1973.) The CPI thus takes no account of any consumption shifts which occur as a result of the very price changes it depicts. Per capita beef consumption may and does decrease as the price of beef goes up, as it did in 1974, and it may continue to decline after the price drops, as it did in 1975. But the weekly amount of beef "bought" by the CPI's fictional family remains absolutely steady.

These are not criticisms of the BLS officials and the CPI index--they are the necessary facts of life of index construction and have been spelled out by the Bureau in its own publications. In order to furnish any kind of measure within the budgetary limits which are allocated (or even conceivably would be worth allocating) only one improvement seems possible: the construction of several such indexes for families with different compositions and consumption patterns. No Congress has yet been willing to finance even this much improvement.

Even within the limits of what they do define, indexes must make allowance for some facts of life to be even reasonably realistic. Because such indexes are used to follow trends, they are expressed in terms of annual purchases. Some provision must be made for the phenomenon of seasonality. Potatoes are normally scarce in May every year in the United States because potatoes are not a crop subject to extremely long storage. At some point there is a minor gap between the old crop and the first of the new. Employment, likewise, has seasonal factors and these must be adjusted for.

The factors used for adjusting for these seasonals cannot take into account all of the possible variations that occur from year to year. Thus the adjustments themselves may cause some distortion. In the late spring and early summer of 1975, for example, the seasonal adjustments used on the unemployment index portrayed a monthly change from April to May and from May to June which the compilers of this index had to warn the public represented a distorted picture. In May the index seasonally adjusted indicated an unemployment rate of 9.2%. In June the seasonally adjusted index showed a drop to 8.6% unemployment in the labor force. In the opinion of the compilers, both figures were incorrect. When corrected for seasonal adjustment and what happens to this seasonal adjustment during low periods of employment the May and June averages should both probably have been close to 8.9%, and thus have shown no monthly change at all between May and June.

Another problem of indexes is that many of them must be reported in dollar figures. Thus the industrial inventory data released by the United States Department of Commerce must be expressed in dollar figures initially, since it is impossible to add pounds of copper to yards of cloth, etc. However, during periods of rapid price movements, price induced distortions arise between commodities and across the board. These distortions are compounded by the effect of the method of valuing inventories, which from the accountanting standpoint, is usually either last-in--first-out or first-in-first-out.

The purpose of collecting these inventory figures is not to collect the value but to indicate some degree of the level of units and inventory. It is possible to do some degree of deflating in terms of the prices, but this can never be accurate. One of the problems, of course, is that most of the companies who were surveyed to get these data do not keep accurate month by month records of inventories. Even to the extent that they do, each plant uses a different method of accounting for these inventories, even between plants within the companies, and some companies will change their method of valuing the inventories from time to time. All of these led to a grave problem in the middle of 1974 when the Commerce Department found it necessary to revise the last quarter of 1973 inventory figures and the first quarter of 1974 upward by $11 billion, suddenly revealing a pile up of goods in plants which had not been realized up until that point, and uncovering a recession which officials had not been aware of up until then.

It was also the necessity to use dollar figures for many of the other series concerned which led officials astray in the matter of the use of so-called leading indicators--that is, various series which tend to move out ahead of turns in the economy. As a result, a new series was chosen which contained less dollar figures and more of physical units.

Another weakness of series is getting actual data rather than formal data. For example, the wholesale price index used by the U.S. Department of Commerce is based largely on list prices rather than the prices at which transactions actually take place. The latter is not an easy figure to obtain, especially in industrial transactions, where many kinds of considerations may enter in addition to the quoted price. Consider the case of steel service centers, which sell relatively small quantities of steel to smaller industrial users (an average of 3/4 ton per user, for example, rather than a minimum of 10 tons per item required by the mills) frequently make strip steel (narrow widths of sheet) out of wider sheets that they buy from the mills, since their customers use quite a diversity of widths. They often will buy over-runs of various nonstandard sheets left over in the mill from an order of a big customer and get these at a discount. Sometimes these are made to special specifications that, if they were bought because of these specifications, the warehouse would pay a premium. In times of steel shortages, the mills are very likely to charge them exactly this premium rather than give a discount, and thus the price actually goes up. But the quoted price for that grade of steel and special specifications does not change. Another case is that of the steel used in making ordinary carbon steel bolts and nuts. This steel must have a special quality known as cold heading. Cold heading specifications calls for an extra charge per ton of steel of the same general grade. However, bolts and nuts, rivets, and similar industrial fasteners are an important outlet for steel companies, since they are bought in volume. In times when steel mills are scrambling for orders the tendency is not to bill for the extra but to sell the steel as though it did not have this extra charge. The order blank does not show a discount, it simply shows the regular price for 1038 steel. However, when a sellers market arises, the industrial fastener companies' cost goes up. The order invoice then shows the extra cost. But the index does not record this change. A final and very important aspect of the problem of indexes is the problem of how individual prices should be weighted in the total (as already mentioned with respect to the CPI). The proportions bought change, in fact vary from day to day. In the case of some items, the total volume can be measured. In the case of others relative volumes in the daily changes are unknown.

In the stock market, for example, we do know, at least so far as the listed exchanges are concerned, the total volumes of transactions in each of the stocks sold or bought on a given day. But the volume in any one given stock can vary so much that it may for a period be one of the 10 most active on the exchange. A year or two later it may have so little volume in trade that it becomes necessary to delist the stock, that is, eliminate from the exchange as not being active enough. So the indexes must be constructed of stocks that have a relatively steady volume of trade on the one hand, or alternatively, be composed of all listed stock, an alternative which has been possible only since the computer came into being. But even if you take the total of the list, how do you weight the stocks? Some stocks have a very wide volume of issue but a very narrow volume of daily trade. Other stocks, which have relatively narrow base of issue may have a substantial trading volume, at least for long periods. If the stocks are weighted equally regardless of this volume (as does the Dow-Jones Industrials) then no account is taken of where the volume of interest is in the trade on the exchange. Either in this case or in the case in which they are listed by volume of issue the movements in the high price stocks will tend to dominate the changes in the index itself. A change of a 1/2 point on a stock selling for $5.00 a share is just as important to the investor holding that stock as a change of $10.00 a share in a $100.00 stock, since in both cases it is 10% of the total. But the averages of 20 stocks in which one of them changed $5.00 would show a change of .25 whereas a change of 1/2 point in one of those stocks would show up as a change of .0025. The problem is that no matter what form of weighting is used, some degree of bias will be introduced into the index. As a result the wise market follower compares all of the various indexes. He looks at the movement of the Dow-Jones Industrial, and from that infers the movement of the higher priced, so-called blue chips. He may compare that with the relative figures on the Standard and Poors and the New York Stock Exchange Index to see whether or not the relative movement is different in somewhat lower priced stocks. If he is interested in what has happened to the speculative side of the market he tends to look at a different index--that of the American Stock Exchange, which lists many low price and more speculative stocks. And because the interest of each investor

148

and each analyst may differ, not only from that of other analysts, but at different period of times, there is no way of constructing a single index that will give each what he needs all of the time under every circumstance.

All averages of any sort share one common problem. They do not indicate how widespread the different measurements may be, how typical they are of the total distribution. To determine this we usually turn to another set of summary figures--measures of dispersion.

With all of their limitations, averages do such a good job of giving us a general idea of the major tendencies of the statistical series with which we must deal that we could not do without them. Generally speaking, however, we need to supplement our knowledge of the average of whatever type used with another kind of summary which tells us how typical or untypical the average may be of the total distribution.

MEASURES OF DISPERSION: SUMMARIZING THE SPREAD OF A DISTRIBUTION

No two items in the universe with which we have direct experience, at least, are identical. The average, therefore, is not a measure of the individual items but only some kind of central point around which the individual items are grouped. The average may indeed not be representative of a single item within a distribution, although there are times when the grouping is so close that, for any important purpose, the average is a good measure. This latter is likely to be true, however only when some artificial restraint is made on the distribution, as in an inspection system which throws out all items which vary more than a certain degree from the average. To evaluate any distribution therefore, we nearly always need some measure of the degree to which the other items diverge from this single measure which we have taken to represent the group. The simplest measure is the range of variation, the value of the two extremes. Quite often this tells us all we need to know. More usually, however, we need to know more than this simple range. We need to take some account of the size of the items between the average and these two extremes, which may be far distant from the rest of the items.

Another simple measure of dispersion is the average deviation -- the average of the absolute values (the values

149

without regard to whether they are minus or plus) from what-ever average is taken. This measure is not as widely used as another one which gives proportionately heaviest weights to the items farthest from the average, the standard deviation.

Standard deviation, as already indicated in discussion of confidence limits in Chapter 3, is the square root of the average of the sum of the squares of the deviations from the mean. Taking the squares of the deviation rather than their simple value serves two purposes. First, it negates the plus and minuses, since the square of a minus and the square of a plus are always both positive values. Second, it gives heaviest weights to the items that are furthest from the mean. Another advantage of the standard deviation is that it is an integral part of the calculation of the area covered by a distribution and thus can be used as a measure of how much of the distribution lies at any given distance from the average, as indicated in Figure 3-1 earlier. The standard deviation is also an integral part of the calculation of any correlation prooefficient.

One problem with the standard deviation is that the measures it gives of the area are true only of distributions that are bell-shaped. Furthermore, it can be calculated only with reference to the mean.

In measuring distribution from median, the usual measures are either to take percentiles or quartiles. Quartiles divide the ranked distribution into quarters, as the name im-plies, and the usual measure of dispersion is to consider the interval between the first and the second quartile as compared with the interval between the third and fourth quartile. This inter-quartile dispersion, which always covers exactly 1/2 of the distribution, by definition, can be very useful. In addition to which, the quartiles themselves are often used as a means of analysis of the data, comparing the top quartile, for example, with the bottom quartile within one distribution or between dif-ferent distributions. Percentiles simply go one step further and divide the total distribution into percentage groups. Per-centiles are usually used to indicate the relative position of an item within a distribution. One use of the percentile distribu-tion is seen in the so-called 70-30 principle which indicates that 70% of the orders for a firm come from the top 30% of its customers and other similar common events in the social and economic worlds.

Percentiles and quartiles thus go one more step then some of the other methods of dispersion by giving us a means of analyzing the nature of the distribution and the analytical aspect is often more important than the possession of a single figure.

One of the weaknesses of averages is that they tend to conceal too many details and sometimes their averages are quite disparate universes. The average income of two men, one a millionaire and one a pauper, turns out to be a very comfortable income. But this average conceals the fact that one of them has no dependable income. The use of averages covering disparate universes is a trap which many people and commentators quite often fall into. One excellent example occurred during the fuel crisis during 1974 and 1975. To help conserve fuel, Congress mandated a highway apeed limit of 55 m. p. h. , and in order to control the shortage situation, the administration allocated the shorter oil supplies on some historical basis. Unfortunately, when people are forced to conserve, their pattern of consumption changes. By allocating supplies on a geographical basis, supplies were distributed in the same fashion as though people's driving habits had not changed. In fact, it soon became apparent people continued to drive almost as much locally as they had before, but eliminated many of their longer trips. This meant that out in the open country there were more than adequate supplies of gasoline but in the cities shortages became andemic. When these shortages were cleared up by greater supplies of oil later, some of the driving habit changes remained because of the much higher prices of the fuel involved. Very little attention was given to this fact. Instead, much publicity was given to a decrease in the overall average speed. Moreover, this decrease was widely credited with a decline in accident and fatality rate, ignoring the effects of less traffic density and less driving away from familiar roads.

Unfortunately for the commentators, the actual average of the speed of any particular kind of trip did not seem, to unbiased unofficial observers, to have changed very much. What had changed was a difference in the amount of driving of two quite different types, short distance and long distance. Any experienced driver trying to make time soon learns to try to avoid situations in which a great deal of local traffic is using the road. Any driver drives much slower when going a short distance than a long distance. There is no point in driving 60 m. p. h. to go a 1/2 mile to the grocery store. For one thing, the average over that distance is still going to be quite low, because of the need to accelerate and to slow down. In fact there is very little to be gained by going 60 m. p. h. rather than 40 m. p. h. if the distance is only 30 miles. The time saved is hardly noticeable. But for the driver on a day long trip, a difference of 5 m. p. h. can mean the difference of an hour in arrival, if he is driving as much as 10 hours. In point of fact, none of the objective observers found very much change in driving speeds on the open highway. Some of the toll authorities discovered, as did the Oklahoma authorities, that the decrease in local driving recovered early but the long distance losses in business were not so quick to disappear. This was still true in the summer of 1975, as was evidenced by the ease with which motel rooms were available at any hour of the evening in almost any area that was more than 100 miles from a major city.

The difference in fatality rates was easily explainable by another factor: the loss in traffic density. It takes no great deal of experimentation to show that the denser the traffic, the higher the number of accidents. In fact, at the extreme of a single car on the road, no possibility for a collision between cars exists. The gain in average speed between the summer of 1974 and 1975 indicated a gain in long distance traffic density, because the average was now an average of a somewhat higher rate of long distance travel compared with the rate of short distance travel.

This is only one of many instances in which a single average figure is really concealing an attempt to represent two quite different universes with a single measure. For this reason, when indexes of any sort are used for decision purposes, it is well to use some form of component analysis to determine whether or not the average really represents anything at all. In scrutinizing various government economic series, for example, it is common to look at the components as well as at the total. One example is in the use of an index of the total value of 12 leading economic indicators to forecast turns in the business cycle. All knowledgeable users of this index pay more attention to how many of the 12 have gone up or down and which ones are responsible for the measure movement. Similarly, in looking at wholesale and retail price indexes, it is usually much more meaningful to consider which prices are responsible for the major movements in the series. Such component analysis also highlights the items which need more careful and more thorough investigation. Thus, economists were led to overlook the signs which indicated an economic downturn as early as the first quarter of 1974, because they did not take enough account of the fact that some of the major indicators then being used were being strongly effected by price movements.

One of the single figures quite often used and misused is that of the "majority." Majorities are important to anybody who hopes to get elected or who hopes to get a measure passed by any voting body, but almost no majority is ever achieved without a great deal of compromise between a lot of otherwise somewhat dissident groups. There are few things in the world which appeal to a single majority. One of the greatest fallacies in marketing, for example, is to try to determine what a majority of consumers desire. In point of fact, seldom does any seller have a true majority of any market. When he does, it is because some of his competitors have been rather lacking in understanding of that market. The tastes and wants of too many consumers diverge far too much for that. One top executive recalls how, in his early days as a marketing research analyst, he advised a client to drop a prospective product because "only 23%" of the prospective customers were interested in this particular formulation. At that time, no single brand had as much as a 23% share of market.

Component analysis sometimes requires only a breakdown into two or three added figures. At other times, a certain amount of summary tabulation is needed, or more often, summary cross tabulation. Simplified summary tables are another means of compressing the important aspects of a situation into a brief enough form that specific trends and relationships can be perceived at a glance.

SIMPLIFIED SUMMARY TABLES TO EMPHASIZE
RELATIONSHIPS AND TRENDS

Some form of data tabulation is a prior step before any computation of an average or measure of dispersion. As the term tabulation implies, the result is in the form of a table, is arranged in columns and rows of figures. Tables can generally be characterized as either reference types or summary types. Reference tables, such as those in the body of the Census, for example, are long, mind-numbing presentations in which every minor detail of possible interest to anybody is recorded. It is normally the form of the original general tabulations, prior to analysis. Such a table is, of course, itself a set of summary figures. Each figure in it represents some degree of classification into groups of items which are unlikely to be exactly

identical. The detail is usually far too voluminous for comprehension without further analysis and summarization. The information must be condensed into a far smaller set of numbers
if its meaning is to be clear. It needs digestion.

The digesting process should result in a much simplified summary table. Such a table combines the detailed classifications of the reference table into a much smaller compass,
in order to reveal some particular facet of the relationships between two types of classifications, or between some one classification and time (which we call a trend). Ideally, such a summary table should be no more than three columns by three rows,
although the dimensions may go up to 5 x 5 without too much
loss in ease of quick comprehension. Although consisting of
from 12 to 25 separate numbers, such a summary table is,
visually, a method of arriving at a single numerical expression
giving the basic outline of the important facts we need. However, even a summary table does not always convey the information on relationships as well as do simple charts and graphs.

All of these single figure summaries are very useful,
yet all lack some of the dimensions we need to fully comprehend the meaning and the hidden relationships in much of the
data we gather. Visual analysis in the forms of charts and
graphs are an indispensable adjunct of any understanding.

SUMMARY

1. Even when numbers are really summarizes of whole
classes of objects and events, the quantity of them may be too
large for comprehension. For this reason the discipline of
statistics has devised a number of standard forms of extreme
summarization to facilitate understanding: averages, indexes,
measures of dispersion and summary tables.

2. All such devices attempt to compress the essential
point of a series of measurements into, preferably, a single
numerical statement, or at most, two or a very few numbers.

3. The most commonly used summary numbers are
the averages, of which three are widely used: the arithmetic
mean, the median, and the mode. These measure, respectively,
the three characteristics generally associated with the idea of
an average: the center of gravity (mean), the mid-point (median) and the most common (mode).

4. However, three averages are equal only when the data are distributed in the form of the bell-shaped "normal curve" of error. This so-called normal curve is not typical of business, economic, or social measurement, all of which, tend to exhibit a strongly unbalanced, or "skewed" tendency.

5. The greatest value of the arithmetic mean is that it is based on the size and frequency of every item in the distribution, and is useful in projecting or comparing totals. It is a true rate. Forgetting that is only a rate, however, misleads the user who does not also note the totals underlying two averages under comparison.

6. Both the median and the mode are choices of single items as representative of typicality: the median as the midpoint item, the mode as the most common. Since they are not calculated, they cannot be used to determine the total value of all items in the distribution.

7. Indexes are widely used averages of a small sample of possible measures. The term "index" indicates their purpose--to point out general trends. What they indicate is approximate direction, not the precise level. At times, even the direction indicated can be temporarily incorrect due to the problems of composition, weighting, and indirect measurement.

8. Normally, any average or index, by iteself, does not give enough information. It needs to be supplemented by some measure of the nature of the whole distribution of measurements.

9. The most commonly used indicators of the nature of the distribution around the mean are standard measures of dispersion: the range (value of the two extreme items), average absolute deviation, and the standard deviation (square root of the average of the squares of the deviation).

10. The standard deviation is the most preferred by statisticians because it is the key element in the measurement of the area bounded by the distribution and thus of probability of any given item. It is also an element in the calculation of correlation coefficients.

11. Distribution around the median can also be indicated by the range, but the preferred measures are the quartiles and percentiles.

12. By compressing all of the detail into a single figure, any average may conceal important detail. This is especially true of the mean. Because the mean can be easily calculated from any set of numbers, it may actually be meaningless

because it is derived from two or more disparate universes and thus represents neither or none of them.

13. As a result, it is wise, in studying trends, to long slightly beyond the average itself, and analyze the trends of major components of the average or index.

14. Numbers of any kind gain more meaningful dimensions when we translate then by the visual devices of graphs and charts.

7

VISUAL SUMMARIZATION: PICTURING DATA TO BRING OUT THE COMPARISONS

Simple numerical representation is seldom adequate for analysis. Numbers tend to be one-dimensional. Any attempt to add more numbers in order to show much in the way of detail or added dimensions tends to confuse rather than to add to perception. For insight into relationships between the numbers, there is no adequate substitute for the use of simple charting techniques. Charts permit the eye to take in, at a glance, details, comparisons, and trends which no method of tabulation, computation or presentation reveals quite so well.

Graphic presentation methods have two sound purposes. The first is purely personal, to enable the analyst to see added dimensions not easily visualized in the figures themselves. Second, because graphic methods do such a good job of visualizing comparisons and trends when properly used, they also are the best method of presenting quantitative results to other people.

All charting methods are basically variations of six simple types:

Line charts--charts connecting the plotted points representing various quantitites in the data when arranged in some specific sequence. When the points are arranged in point of time such charts reveal trends. When arranged in order of size they reveal the shape of the frequency distribution. Their primary use is in the revelation of time trends. Frequency distributions normally are in terms of size classes, and for this purpose bar charts are superior.

Bar charts-- data in which the individual classes are represented by some form of bar. Quite usually these are simple rectangular representations or histograms. However, it is sometimes worthwhile, for presentational purposes, to lend interest to these bars by putting them in the form of people, for example, or of repeated units of whatever is represented. Bars represent relative size in a form in which the eye can catch the relationship without any computation. They also permit the presentation of differences in composition at the same time--percentage distributions for example.

Area charts-- charts in which the relationship is expressed in relative area. These again may be simple rectangles or they may be shapes representing the items being measured. In this case the relationship is between the total area being represented rather than the individual lengths. There are some problems involved in using area charts if this representation is not carefully used, but area charts can dramatize some aspects of differences better than bars.

Map charts-- charts in which the data is plotted on a map, sometimes in the form of figures and sometimes in the form of cross-hatching of one kind or another, sometimes in the form of dots to indicate density. At times, placing the actual numbers on the map is useful for analysts. Such maps enable the kind of multimentional comparisons that a table cannot show--for example, the relationship of the measures in one state of a country compared with those of surrounding areas. They can highlight densities or intensities of various kinds better than any other relative densities or relative intensities better than any other method.

One other form, the scatter chart, is generally an auxiliary to line charts, but sometimes can be used separately. In a scatter chart, each individual point is plotted on ordinary rectangular coordinates on a graph, to see how the data itself distributes. This is an especially useful type of chart when investigating suspected correlations. While the scatter plot does not give the kind of figure which is easy to quote, it reveals the extent to which the data really does group along some form of line and the extent to which there are obviously wide variations from this line. Primarily valuable for personal analysis, the scatter plot also has some presentational values. Many relationships are not linear, as the standard calculation assumes. In such a case, the numerical coefficient understates the correlation. (A

perfectly circular relationship has a zero correlation coefficient, for example.) The scatter plot does what no mere
number can: it reveals the character of the relationship
and highlights any significant clusters or deviations.

Flow charts-- charts which indicate how a system or
procedure really works in practice and what the most critical points in this system or procedure are. This type of
chart enables us to visualize the flow of any operation and
also, in the case of complex operations in which several
flows are taking place simultaneously, what the critical
points in that flow are, what the critical paths which must
be monitored if a schedule is to be met. Use of such charts
in network analysis and critical path analysis is important
enough that it is discussed at greater length in a later chapter.

CHARTING FOR PERSONAL ANALYSIS

The quickest and most certain way to spot the exceptions and observe the constant aspects of any situation is to look
literally at a picture of the whole--to draw a simple chart.

It is unfortunate that many who must regularly make
choices based on quantitative data do not automatically draw
simple charts of that information. No other form of presentation of numerical information can reveal so clearly the basic
regularities hidden in the fog of individual variations. No other
device can so dramatize and make obvious the unexpected comparisons and exceptions. Furthermore, no tool is easier to
use, for the best charts are the simplest line charts, bar
charts, maps, and scatter plots which require no artistic skill.
Their interpretation, when properly planned, is nearly automatic, needing little more than a conception of what might be
expected. As with all pictures, statistical charts use the detailed information only to represent the whole, to shift attention
from the confusing details to reveal the pattern of relationships.

Charts can draw attention to five different kinds of
relationships:

1. How values cluster and how they vary. What the
principle values are which are obscured by the variations
and how dominant these principle values are.

2. How quantities or sets of measurements compare.
It takes a little mental gymnastics to see that 72 is three

times 24. When translated into bars on a chart, the relationship is obvious without the calculation. Again, our interest in Miss America's dimensions are better satisfied with a single snapshot than by the numbers 36-26-40.

3. How values vary and are related in space--revealed by graphic maps.

4. How relationships vary over time and what the trends and regularities in those relationships are.

5. How the steps in any system or procedure are related.

One of the most useful habits we can acquire is to always draw a rough chart or picture of our quantitative information. Simple sketch charts can furnish important leads to basic forces otherwise overlooked in the underbrush of specific detail. Of all charts, the simplest is the frequency distribution chart: a line or bar representing the total account of each classification such as the number of buyers of a product by age group.

INVESTIGATING THE SHAPE OF THINGS: FREQUENCY DISTRIBUTION ANALYSIS

Even the most intimate familiarity with a set of figures may not reveal the basic relationships. Indeed, too much familiarity with and concentration on individual numbers can blind us to the underlying factors shaping them. A buyer for women's sportwear, for example, was aware that he did not carry as complete a size selection in his casual items as did the buyers of better dresses in his mail order firm. His only answer as to "Why?" was to point to past practice. An analyst, with whom the problem was discussed, drew a graph, Figure 7-1, based on sales figures taken from the buyer's own working copy of the catalog. Clearly, larger sizes of his items did not sell--sales volume dropped off rapidly as sizes increased. In his concentration on the trees and bushes of the numbers which he consulted every day in planning his orders, the buyer missed the shape of the forest revealed when the graph subordinated this detail to show the picture as a whole.

Likewise, firms using standard costing and cost variances are prone to look at the individual variances and attempt to find explanations for each one. In so doing, they are very likely to overlook the clues to quite different and more basic cost problems which only the graphs of the distribution of variances are likely to reveal. The shape and the character of the whole is determined by more fundamental and usually quite different forces from those shaping the individual variations from the standard. Both the forecasts of costs and their improvement depend more on locating and understanding these underlying forces, whose <u>presence</u> a simple frequency chart can reveal, than on the less significant factors which cause the smaller temporary variations.

FIGURE 7-1. A Simple Frequency Bar Chart: Number of Ladies Slacks Sold, by Size

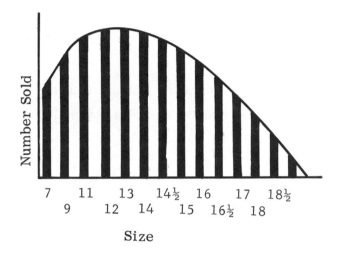

Cost variances, like all other measurement variations, are sure to fluctuate around some central point--the average. The important facts are the location of this average, the extent of the scatter around it, and the change in this location, if any, over time. If we wish to evaluate and control costs, we have a simple model with which to compare the frequency distribution of our cost variances, and alerting us to any possible need for further digging: the bell-shaped normal curve. (For the trend over time, we must use some other model, discussed below.)

What can comparison of any frequency distribution with the normal curve tell us? First, we have learned from the long history of measurement that if the set of measurements all come from the source "universe"--if they all measure the same thing with no significant disturbing or conflicting factors--the fluctuations should assume the shape of the well-behaved normal curve, the pleasantly bell-shaped distribution with a clearly marked mode and a limited, but not too limited, dispersion, as in Figure 7-2A. If this is the way our data plot, then our cost variances, or product quality, or whatever, are under control. But if the distribution, while still bell-shaped, has acquired a middle-aged spread like that of Figure 7-2B, we have begun to lose control of costs or product quality, or whatever we are measuring, and we better start looking for the "how" and "why." On the other hand if our bell assumes that pinched-in corsetted look seen in Figure 7-2C, control has become artificially tight--too tight. If this were output per worker in a piece-rate operation, for example, we might suspect a tacit agreement on some norm which nearly every worker can meet. Any such tight bell needs investigation to see if some artificial constriction is not exacting some cost of its own.

FIGURE 7-2. Some Variations of the Normal Curve

A. The Normal-Normal B. The Flat Normal

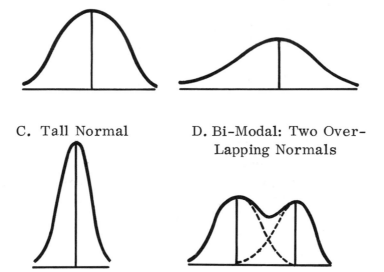

C. Tall Normal   D. Bi-Modal: Two Over-
                          Lapping Normals

Not all frequency distributions look like bells, with their single peaks, or modes. Some are two humped, like the Bactrian camel, which can result from adding two sets of measurements from two different universes, resulting in over-lapping bells (Figure 7-2D). Two machines in the production line may be set up so as to produce to slightly different mean dimensions. A frequency distribution of their combined output would be bimodal. Again, if we are interested in selling trips

162

to Europe, we might find that the ages of the adults in the families who take such trips follows a bimodal distribution: they tend to go before children come along, or after they are fairly well grown. (There may be still a third hump, of course, representing families who wait till after the young are established on their own.)

Many distributions will have no recognizable kinship to the normal bell. Some have the lumpy shapelessness of the person who likes his food too well--the rectangular distribution that results from complete lack of control, as in Figure 7-3A. When costs or product quality exhibit this kind of distribution, production procedures, control measures, or whatever is reflected obviously need a fundamental and drastic overhaul. If this is a market preference pattern, the smart product policy would seem to be that of well-selected custom production for some part of the total, rather than mass production. Such a distribution is the result of mixing several universes simultaneously.

FIGURE 7-3.   Some Common Non-Normal Distributions

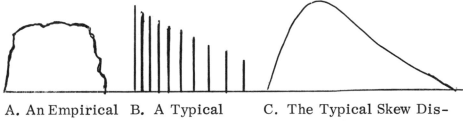

A. An Empirical   B. A Typical   C. The Typical Skew Dis-
   Rectangular   Price Line   tribution of Economic
   Distribution   Distribution   and Social Data

Again, we may find we have nothing like a continuous frequency distribution, but a series of tightly defined, clearly separated values like those shown in Figure 7-3B, typical of prices of major garments of any sort--the price line phenomenon. (In some other context, this might be the distribution of acceptable quality grades.) In such a situation, production must be "engineered" to meet the accepted price line points, and quite exactly. In cases like this, both buyers and merchants have built up expectations and habits around such price line points, and woe to the seller who tries to buck the pattern. A clothier of the author's acquaintance pointed to a suit in his store which did not fit the current price line structure. It was

made to sell at a price in between two price lines. "It really
is one of the best values we have in the store," he said, "but
we can't sell very many. Its price is higher than one class of
our buyers normally pays, and lower than the other group
thinks they must pay."

The highly skewed characteristic social curve of Figure 7-3C has already been discussed. The profits lie in the
interpretation and use of this curve--in the concentrated sales
and dollar volume attributable to the handful of heavy buyers at
the right end of this distribution.

Simple frequency charts can take on many other forms,
of course. A not uncommon form is the U-shaped distribution
which may result from the mixture of measurements from two
quite opposite universes--such as taste preferences we might
find in relation to grits-and-gravy for breakfast, in an Army
outfit made up of equal parts of men from Albany, New York,
and Albany, Georgia.

FIGURE 7-4. A Hypothetical U-Shaped Distribution of the
Probable Taste Reactions of a Mixed Army Unit to Grits-and-
Gravy

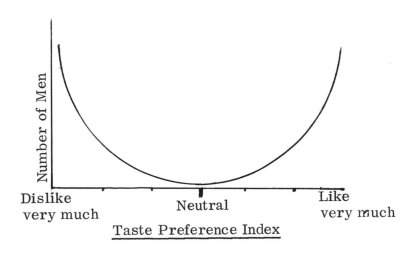

Whatever the shape of the distribution we find,
charting it can furnish valuable leads to the factors which are
likely to exert a major influence on any action we contemplate.
Charting can help our mental eyes cut through the haze of abun-
dant and confusing detail, to reveal the clear outlines of the
true shape of the matter under consideration. It is then up to
us to reason out what these forces may be. Neither our charts

nor any other mathematical tools can, by themselves, do this for us.

Even in charting, we should go beyond the straight frequency distribution to plots which show the relationship to other distributions, to space, or to time.

COMPARISON CHARTS TO REVEAL RELATIONSHIPS

The sportswear buyer already mentioned had called in the analyst to find out why attempts to expand his rather modest volume by expanding offerings had failed. The answer came rather quickly when the size distribution of sportwear items sold were plotted against the corresponding distribution of dresses by size. The resulting chart looked something like Figure 7-5, revealing that only a minority of the firm's clothing customers had the slim builds of the women who buy slacks and similar items. Other types of comparisons then corroborated the conclusion indicated by this comparison: the firm's clientele did not offer a potential target for the volume sales of many kinds of sportwear.

The clustering that a plot reveals is a better guide to the underlying truth than any individual item, as any range rifleman knows. When the marksman wants to know whether his gunsights are set correctly, he aims a few shots very carefully from the steady prone position, then checks how they "group." That is, he looks at where the center of the group of shots (the average, again) is located in reference to the bull's-eye. If he finds the center high and to the right, he will aim lower and to the left by an equal amount, even if one of his "zeroing" shots actually was in the bull's-eye.

Similarly, if a firm has been underbid by its competitors on too many occasions it might do well to chart a comparison of its estimate history with actual cost experience on jobs landed. Such a comparison, would indeed be a sound routine procedure even when no trouble is visible. Such a charted comparison (see Figure 7-6) revealed to one firm why it was being consistently underbid by an average of approximately 5%. On bids it did win, the grouping of its actual costs averaged 5% lower than the grouping of its estimates.

The scatter diagram can yield a quick picture of the degree of relationship between two factors without lengthy calculations and without any of the necessary assumptions about

FIGURE 7-5. A Charted Comparison of the Sales of Ladies Sportswear with the Sales of Ladies Better Dresses

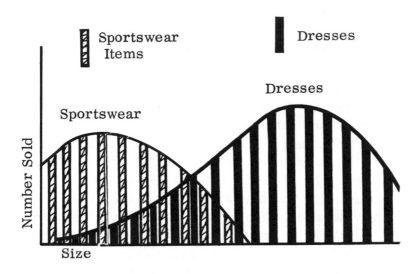

FIGURE 7-6. A Charted Comparison of the Relative Distribution of Cost Estimates and Realized Costs Which Revealed to One Company Why It Was Being Underbid

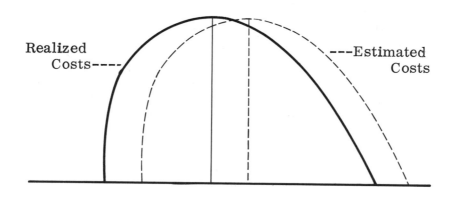

FIGURE 7-7. Hypothetical Scatter Charts

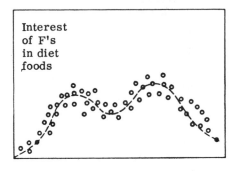

A. Close correlation

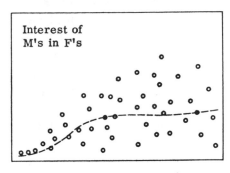

B. No significant correlation over
most of the observations

the nature of the relationship between the factors and the nature
of the regression curve which underlie correlation calculations.
We need only plot our pairs of observations on graph paper and
observe the degree of tightness with which plotted points cling
to the path of some kind of curve. If we get a close coincidence
of paired values of, say, the age of women and their interest in
diet foods, as in Figure 7-7A, we can suspect that there may be
a possible cause and effect of some sort. On the other hand, if
plotting the ages of males against solid evidence of interest in
the opposite sex gave us a correlation chart of the kind shown
in Figure 7-7B, we might conclude that after a certain age,
there are widespread differences in the level of interest.

Such a chart reveals close coincidence of any sort
without regard to the shape of the regression line, whether
straight or curving. It does not yield a number, of course, and
if you need a number to convince someone else (nothing is more
impressive), you will still have to do some calculating. By
drawing a scatter diagram first, you will learn what to expect,
what kind of regression curve it is appropriate to assume, if
any, and much other relevant information about your data. It
can reveal the one or a few "wild shots" which, if present,
could have a decisive influence on any calculations. Data which
are grouped quite closely about a regression line, but which also include several "wild" ones far from the line, can yield the

same numerical value for a correlation coefficient as data much more loosely grouped, but including no exceptional values. The phenomena which produced such divergent series are quite different, but the numerical calculation alone will conceal the fine differences a plot will reveal. Moreover, in the case of the tightly grouped data with a few wild deviants, critical examination of the exceptional values may yield the greatest illumination on the forces at work, and they should be carefully examined, not ignored. It is, then, a good general rule to plot all regression and correlation data whether or not calculations are conducted.

AREA CHARTS

Area charts serve much the same purpose as do bar charts and are really a form of two-dimensional bars in most cases. However, the form of them may not be simple rectangles. For example, one widely used version is to use a distorted area chart. They compare actual areas of countries, for example, with the area they would have relative to their production of oil or coal or some other resource. Or such a distorted area chart may be used to represent the difference between the size of the state as shown on the map, and the relative size of the state with respect to its population or industrial production or some other quantity.

Another form of chart, the pie chart, is essentially an area chart using angles to highlight the differences, maintaining a constant diameter circle. In this case the comparison is between the angles dividing up the total dollar or circle in some manner. The pie chart is usually employed to dramatize the percentage distribution, quite normally of some dollar total. A bar chart may be similarly proportioned, and while more pro saic, may show comparisons more clearly. (See Figure 7-8.) tween the angles dividing up the total dollar or circle in some manner. The pie chart is usually employed to dramatize the percentage distribution, quite normally of some dollar total.

One form of area chart is used to misrepresent data rather than to properly present it. For example, the standing armies of two different countries might be represented as two soldiers in which a single dimension, the height, is propor-

FIGURE 7-8. Two Ways to Present Proportions: Pie Charts
and Divided Bars

Where the Direct Government Farm Payments Went, 1960
and 1971, by Size of Farm Operation, in Annual Gross
Receipts

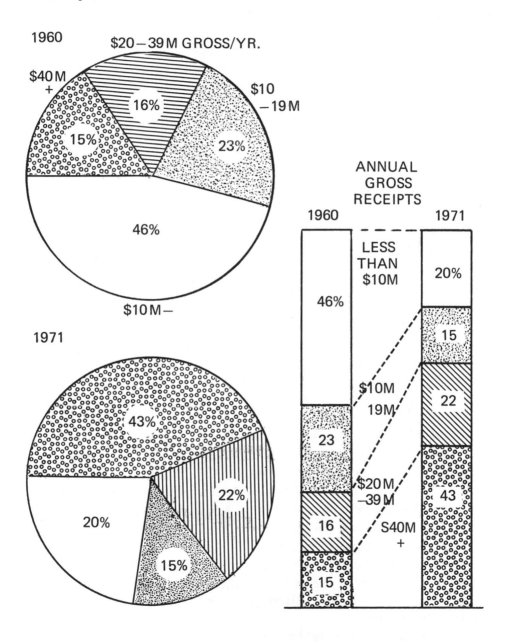

tionate to the totals involved, but the width is also given the same relative proportion as the height. In this way, a figure that is twice another actually is shown as 4 times another because it is given 4 times the area. Even more misleading, from the standpoint of human perception, is such a graph really showing one figure as 8 times the other, because the human perceives such a picture in 3 dimensions and the volume is the cube of the relative dimension.

Area charts are not as widely used as graphic maps which have assumed increasing importance in recent years in a number of areas, for analytical purposes. In medical research, for example, a plot of the incidence of multiple sclerosis has furnished what seems to be the first useful lead to understanding the probable cause of this mysterious malady.

GRAPHIC CHARTS TO REVEAL THE IMPORTANCE OF WHERE

Knowing the "where", geographically, of our profit opportunities, cost, sales, product problems or other matters of interest can be valuable in itself. Information revealed by relative concentrations on a geographic plot usually must be combined with other knowledge to tell us the "why." Geography is more than landscape. It is people and culture patterns; it is occupation, diet and all sorts of tastes; and it is climatic conditions. When a mail order seller became interested in the substantial profits from the sale of his garden tractor line, a simple plot of recent orders on a map pinpointed more than just the shipment destinations. The location plot revealed to him that sales were predominantly in areas with heavy concentrations of part-time farming. This information, in turn, indicated something about design needs.

A geographic plot of complaints about electrical equipment breakdown might point to humid areas as the problem, leading to an inference that some materials needed changing to give greater humidity tolerance.

Even tabulations made by geographic breakdowns are often more revealing if the numbers themselves are actually themselves entered on an outline map, permitting multi-directional comparisons.

Figure 7-9 furnishes one example of how useful a simple spot map can be in revealing salient facts.

FIGURE 7-9. A Graphic Chart Highlighting the Concentrated Nature of Changes

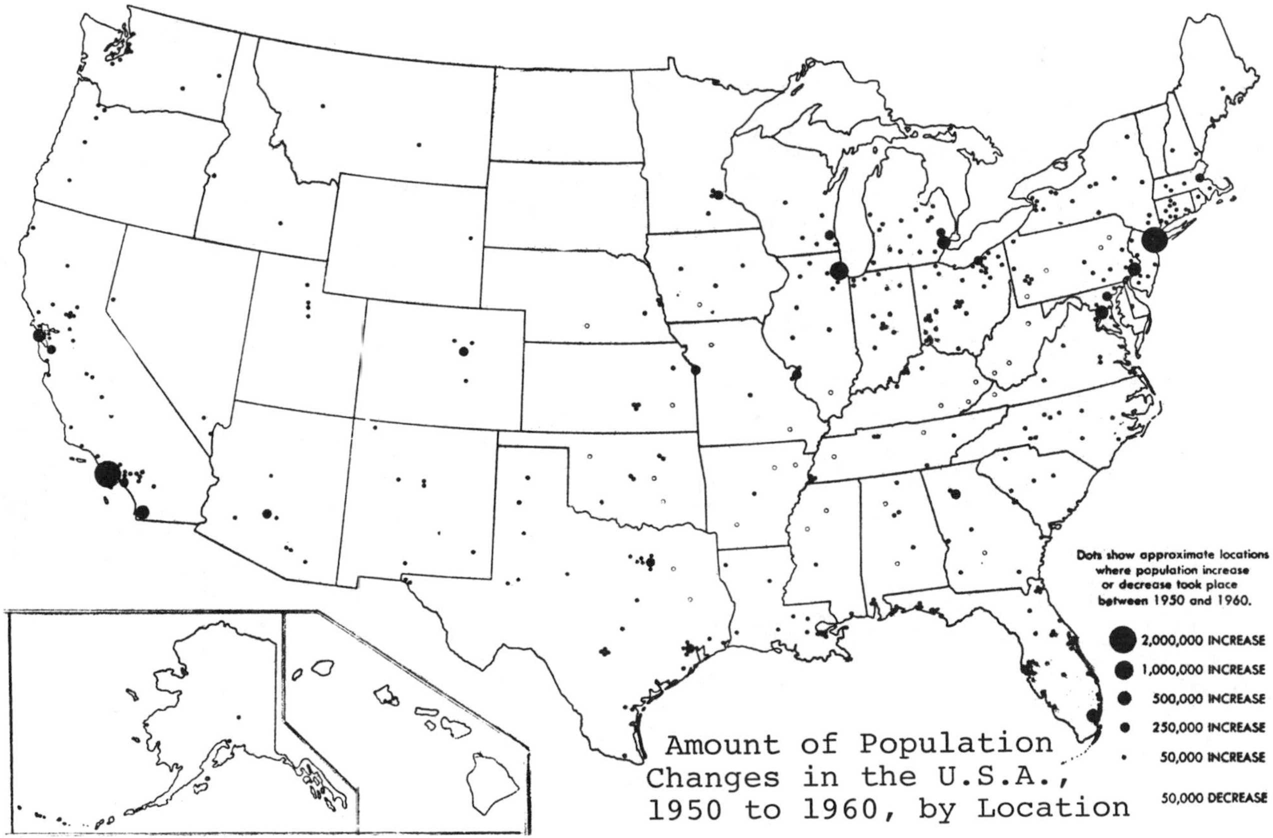

Amount of Population Changes in the U.S.A., 1950 to 1960, by Location

Dots show approximate locations where population increase or decrease took place between 1950 and 1960.

2,000,000 INCREASE
1,000,000 INCREASE
500,000 INCREASE
250,000 INCREASE
50,000 INCREASE

50,000 DECREASE

FIGURE 7-10. A Graphic Chart Highlighting the Impact of Population Changes

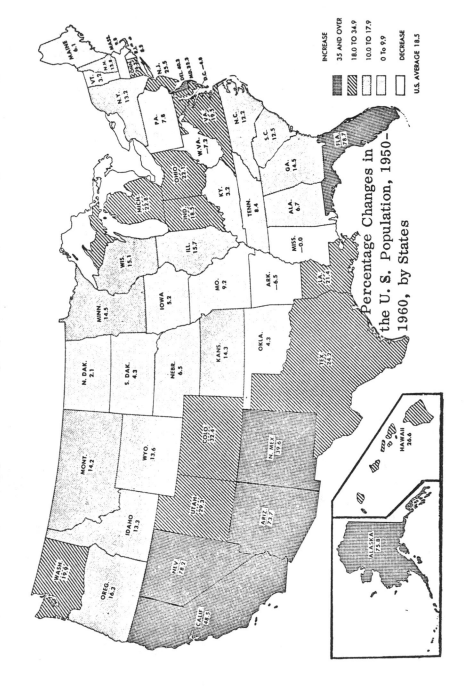

Percentage Changes in
the U. S. Population, 1950–
1960, by States

INCREASE

35 AND OVER
18.0 TO 34.9
10.0 TO 17.9
0 To 9.9

DECREASE

U.S. AVERAGE 18.5

MAINE 6.1
VT. 3.2
N.H. 13.8
MASS. 9.8
CONN. 26.3
R.I. 8.5
N.Y. 13.2
N.J. 25.5
PA. 7.8
DEL. 40.3
MD. 32.3
D.C. -4.8
W.VA. -7.2
VA. 19.5
N.C. 12.2
S.C. 12.5
OHIO 22.1
KY. 3.2
TENN. 8.4
GA. 14.5
ALA. 6.7
MICH. 22.8
IND. 18.5
ILL. 15.7
MISS. -0.0
FLA. 78.7
WIS. 15.1
MO. 9.2
ARK. -6.5
LA. 21.4
MINN. 14.5
IOWA 5.2
KANS. 14.3
OKLA. 4.3
TEX. 24.2
N. DAK. 2.1
S. DAK. 4.3
NEBR. 6.5
COLO. 32.4
N. MEX. 39.6
MONT. 14.2
WYO. 13.6
UTAH 29.3
ARIZ. 73.7
IDAHO 13.3
NEV. 78.2
WASH. 19.9
OREG. 16.3
CALIF. 48.5

ALASKA 75.8
HAWAII 26.6

172

TAKING A LOOK AT WHAT HAS HAPPENED WHEN: TREND CHARTS

If your individual cost variances have been staying within a reasonably narrow range for a considerable period, can you sit back and worry about something else? Maybe, but again, maybe not. It would be wise to see first what they look like when plotted in chronological sequence. If Glamor Industries stock, which was selling for 75-1/2 last week dips to 66-1/4, is it a good buy if you find no reason to believe the company's financial position has not changed? Maybe, and again, maybe not. Better look at the trend, both absolutely, and in relation to other stock prices. In either of these situations, the ability of a chart to cut through detail to show underlying forces can reveal opportunities or warn of dangers.

Although your cost variances may all have been within what looks like reasonable limits, there may have been larger plusses than minuses on net recently. This may mean some new factor has entered which has tended to push up your costs, or happily, the minuses may be overbalancing the plus fluctuations. Even such good news is worth an investigation to see the why of the trend, and what advantage can be taken of it.

And with respect to Glamor Industries (GI on the Big Board), any trader in the market knows that a dip of 9 points in one week is not unusual for this volatile issue. The sophisticated trader will consult his chart to see if this is a new low point in which successive high points have each been lower, and successive lows progressively lower. If so, he may decide he better sell GI, no matter how good the financial news about the company. His chart suggests to him that the wild gyrations of this issue have hit a downslide in public favor, a fact that the naïve investor who looks only at individual quotations (see Table 7-1) may easily have missed, but shows up clearly in the chart (see Figure 7-11).

One important trend that has received increasing attention in industry is the so-called experience curve or learning curve. Because it takes time for habits to be established among workers and management--habits of thought as well as habits of action--and because shortcuts and innovations in the process are developed as time passes, there seems to be a general tendency for costs to decline with accumulated production experience, and efficiency in production to increase, with any new process. This observed relationship is generalized

173

TABLE 7-1. Daily Price Changes in Glamor Industries Common

-2.37	-.37	-1.63	+.88
-.50	-.63	+.63	-1.88
+1.00	-1.00	-1.88	-.37
+.25	-.50	+1.50	-2.37
-.88	+1.25	+.88	+1.88
+.62	-1.37	+.25	-.37
-.62	-2.00	-1.12	+.37
-.37	+1.88	+1.00	-.50
+1.50	-1.50	-1.50	+2.12
-1.25	-1.63	-3.00	-1.63
+1.12	+3.50	-1.00	-.88
+1.00	+1.00	+1.50	+.37
-1.88	+.37	+.88	+1.12
-.50	+1.25	-.88	+.25

FIGURE 7-11. Daily Price Changes in Glamor Industries Common

Price

Date

174

as a principle: for any new process or product, each doubling
of the accumulated production experience should yield a constant
percentage decrease in cost per unit. When plotted on ordinary
rectangular coordinate graph paper, the trend should approximate a downward sloping curve of constantly decreasing slope
similar to Figure 7-12B. Plotting on double logarithmic paper
should approximate a straight line as in Figure 7-12A. Within
any one organization, the slope of the curve seems to remain
stable for any process change. One corollary of this principle
is that management should expect any new process will exhibit
this declining cost characteristic with experience, and price
accordingly.

One of the problems of paying too much attention to such
a single process or product experience curve is that it leads to
the pursuit of continuingly diminishing cost advantages. (Note
that each added increment takes a new <u>doubling</u> of the accumulated production.) It also leads to ignoring another learning curve:
the learning-to-learn curve. The continual exposure to innovation and process change leads to a steepening of the experience
curve. Also, the initial gains with any new process are far
greater than the diminishing gains from an old one.

FIGURE 7-12. The Experience or Learning Curve

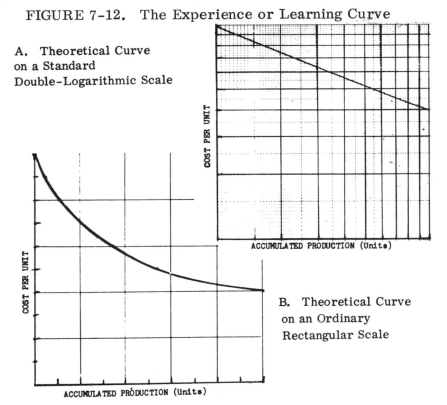

A. Theoretical Curve
on a Standard
Double-Logarithmic Scale

COST PER UNIT

ACCUMULATED PRODUCTION (Units)

COST PER UNIT

B. Theoretical Curve
on an Ordinary
Rectangular Scale

ACCUMULATED PRODUCTION (Units)

FLOW CHARTS FOR VISUALIZATION OF SYSTEMS, PROCEDURES AND PROCESSES

The flow chart is basically a simple, commonsense device for analyzing any actual or proposed system, procedure or process. The relatively recent wide use of such charts seems to have developed as a byproduct of computer training. They are an excellent means of visualizing the essentials of program construction. Computer training use, however, is one small fraction of their utility. There is no better method of analyzing any system, and the valuable planning and control methods known as PERT and Critical Path Method are basically flow chart analyses, although they use a different symbolic structure.

A flow chart is a conventionalized step-by-step graph of a procedure, using four standard symbols, normally:

Broken rectangles to label the start
and finish (terminals) of the process ⌐START⌐ ⌐END⌐

Labelled solid rectangles to show
action steps

Insert key in lock

Arrows to indicate the sequence between steps, and their direction →

Ovals to indicate queries on tests
to be made, or choices

(Does it fit?)

Any answer to a query results in a branched sequence, which may be either a return to a previous step (a looped sequence), or lead on to two or more additional sequences, the path to be taken depending on the answer to the query. Of course, some sequences involve no queries, in which case, there is no branching. Figure 7-13 illustrates a simple looped sequence and an ordinary branched one.

Flow charts are used to analyze existing systems and procedures, to spotlight possible improvements. They are especially valuable for simulating planned systems, to study the effects of such plans as the change in an order processing procedure, the redesign of an assembly line, or the impact of a change to a new process.

Wasson has shown how the probable ease or difficulty

FIGURE 7-13. Examples of a Simple Branched Sequence and of a Looped Circuit Branched Sequence

A. A simple branched sequence

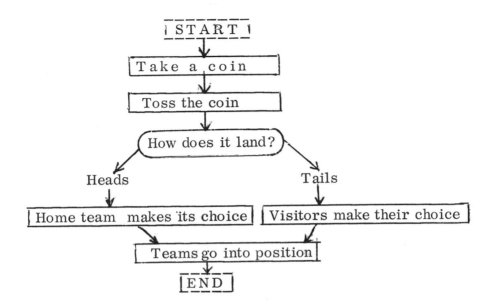

B. A simple looped circuit sequence

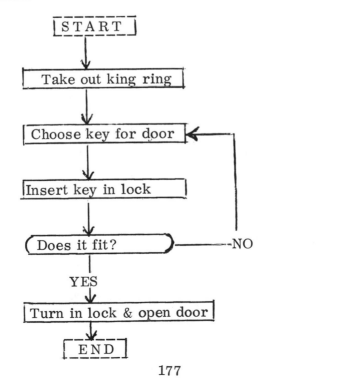

in gaining acceptance for a possible new product can be predicted as early as the concept stage by use of flow chart analysis.*
Flow charts of the use-system involved in the acceptance of the
proposed product and of the use-system of the product to be dis-
placed are compared. Any change in this habitual use-system
signals a possible learning requirement barrier to ready acceptance. He has noted how such a comparison of flow charts
could have saved two large soup companies from disastrous
parallel attempts to introduce quality dehydrated soup mixes.
(See Figure 7-14 for the comparison) The venture cost one of
the processors an admitted $10,000,000 and the other a reputed
$15,000,000 before the failure was admitted. As the charts
quite clearly show, the preparation process for the new mixes
required many more steps and the expenditure of much more
time and energy than does the use of canned soups, which they
were intended to replace. Such a time and energy cost took the
new soups entirely out of the convenience context in which soup
is used in the United States cuisine. To develop a mass market
for such a product would have required a long and extensive
campaign to change American meal habits, and would be unlikely to succeed.

As with all useful tools, graphic methods are not fool-
proof. They can be misused, and all graphs need to be read
with care and understanding.

CAUTION: READ THE FINE PRINT

Even though a chart may be read at a glance, the reading cannot always safely stop with that one glance. Mention
has already been made of the misuse of dimensions in area
charts. It is always wise to read the accompanying figures,
and particularly the scales in any chart, to see if they start
out from zero. It is a far too common practice to magnify
comparative changes by cutting off the bottom of the scale.
Sometimes this is done for a legitimate purpose, but even in such
cases, the zero line should at least be indicated by using the
device of a broken scale (a true zero line, with a jagged break
to indicate a missing segment of scale in the middle, such as:
0 1   30   35).

* Chester R. Wasson, DYNAMIC COMPETITIVE STRATEGY &
PRODUCT LIFE CYCLES, Challenge Books (St. Charles, IL)
1974

FIGURE 7-14. A Comparison of the Consumer Use-System Flow Charts for Quality Dehydrated Soups and for Canned Soup Which Might Have Averted A Product Introduction Fiasco

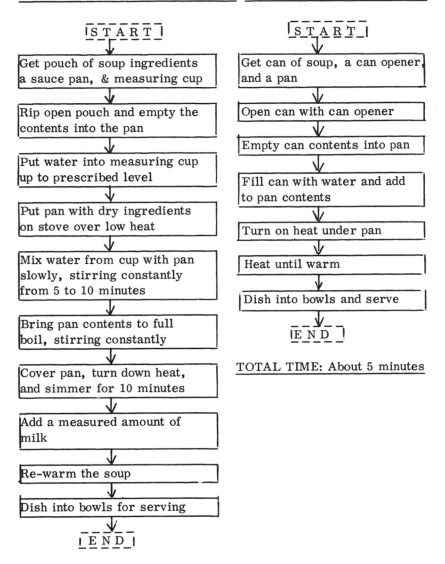

DEHYDRATED SOUP USE-SYSTEM   CANNED SOUP USE-SYSTEM

START

Get pouch of soup ingredients a sauce pan, & measuring cup

Rip open pouch and empty the contents into the pan

Put water into measuring cup up to prescribed level

Put pan with dry ingredients on stove over low heat

Mix water from cup with pan slowly, stirring constantly from 5 to 10 minutes

Bring pan contents to full boil, stirring constantly

Cover pan, turn down heat, and simmer for 10 minutes

Add a measured amount of milk

Re-warm the soup

Dish into bowls for serving

END

TOTAL TIME: About 35 minutes

START

Get can of soup, a can opener, and a pan

Open can with can opener

Empty can contents into pan

Fill can with water and add to pan contents

Turn on heat under pan

Heat until warm

Dish into bowls and serve

END

TOTAL TIME: About 5 minutes

In Figure 7-15 we have two illustrations of a truncated presentation of employment figures to emphasize the depth of the recession. Read without attention to this scale distortion, the changes depicted seem to be truly spectacular. Read with close attention to the scaling, it is still obvious that unemployment has risen painfully, but has only doubled, not skyrocketed. Furthermore, in the accompanying chart showing the number of people unemployed and the total employed, the bars would give you the impression that the quantities involved are quite similar. Looking closer we note that the scale for the total unemployed starts at 4 million and goes up to a little over 7 million, whereas the total employed bar starts at 83 million and reaches a top of something over 86 million. At the low point, the latter is still 84 million. If the total bars were shown, the change would not appear to be nearly as dramatic.

Another trap, which those who use graphs for personal analysis often fall into, is to assume that trends will always continue in a single direction. If a price of stock is rising, you assume the price will continue to rise. If sales are going up, the sales can continue to go up at the same rate. In point of fact, neither of these things can possibly ever be true. There is a limit to how much customers can spend in total and how much they are willing to spend on any particular element of consumption. There is a resource limit to the changes. It was just such an error that led supposedly professional investment advisors to continue to buy so-called "first tier" stocks far beyond the point at which any possible future gain in the companies' business would justify during the early 1970's.

A chart can highlight the trend that has been. What the chart does not show is what is behind a trend and the degree to which the forces involved can continue to cause the trend to go in a given direction. This is a separate analysis and one that cannot easily be dismissed. No amount of quantitative analysis will help in solving this problem of projection. Only a knowledge of the forces which shape the trend will tell us where any plot is going past the last point for which we have a measurement.

SUMMARY

1. Graphic analysis adds a dimension which numbers lack, both to personal analysis and presentation.

2. All charting methods are some variant of one of

FIGURE 7-15. An Example of the Use of Truncated Scales to Magnify Differences

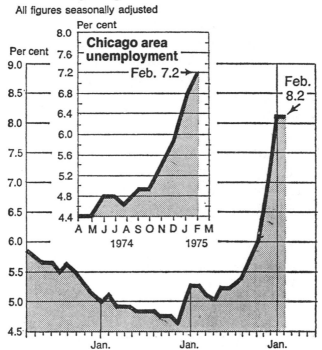

Unemployment in the U.S.

All figures seasonally adjusted

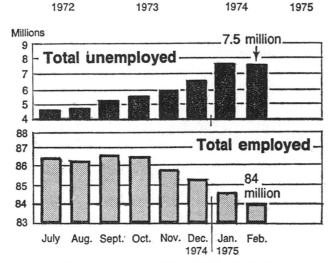

Sources: Illinois Bureau of Employment Security, Bureau of Labor Statistics

six types: line charts, bar charts, area charts, map charts, flow charts, scatter plots.

  3. Graphic methods speed and improve personal analysis. Graphics can reveal unsuspected clustering, dramatize comparisons, show spatial relationships, highlight trends, and aid perception of a system or procedure.

  4. Charting the frequency distribution gives a view of the whole easily lost in the multitude of individual figures. It can give clues to basic underlying forces and structures.

  5. Graphics can sharpen comparisons and reveal otherwise unsuspected forces.

  6. The scatter plot is an almost essential adjacent to any correlation analysis. The use of such a plot can reveal the type of regression involved and the existence of untypical deviation. As a location plot, a scatter diagram can suggest such things as the nature of markets.

  7. Trend charts are particularly useful in investigating fluctuating data, such as variances and stock price trends.

  8. Charts have their dangers. Truncated graphs and implied multi-dimensional representations can impart incorrect impressions. Trends do not continue forever.

A NOTE ON GRAPHIC SCALES, RECTANGULAR AND LOGARITHMIC

  For most graphic purposes, the ordinary rectangular scale of typical cross-section paper is the choice. With this scale, are spaces represent quantities in direct proportion. On them, 100 is 10 times 10. On some occasions, however, the use of paper which is scaled logarithmically in one direction-- semi-log paper--or in both (double logarithmic paper) has real graphic advantages. A particular value of the logarithmic scale is that it measures constant rates of change as a straight line. As already noted in the discussion of the experience curve, such a constant rate of change, an exponential curve, plots as an increasingly steep curve on rectangular coordinates. The logarithmic scale thus reveals how constant the rate of change is, and what its rate of climb is. For this reason, semilog scales are favored by stock market technicians, for example.

  Logarithmic papers also have another legitimate use. They enable us to compress a scale which would otherwise be too extended to graph easily or even comprehensively. For instance, any attempt to show the growth of the automobile in-dustry from its start in 1895 to recent years would be difficult on ordinary rectangular coordinates, since the rise, although steep, was measured in the thousands in the first decades, and into the millions in more recent times. By using semilog paper, the scale can be flattened so that we get a more balanced picture of the whole trend over its history.

PART III. STATISTICAL CALCULATIONS OF VARYING COMPLEXITY

The simpler traditional tools of statistics still bear most of the brunt of the analytical task, and probably always will. Recent attention, however, has focussed on several groups of tools which are computationally more complex, usually to carry out specialized tasks.

Most of the newly fashionable techniques, like most women's fashions, are far from new historically, but have lain largely dormant until resurrected by the easy availability of the computer. Until the advent of the digital computer, their computation was normally too burdensome in relation to the average payout, which in any analytical situation normally produces more disappointments than spectacular successes. With the computer slave, what was complex has become simple and quickly available.

One set of these resurrected tools is composed mainly of variants of correlation and regression methods. In the form of simple two factor regression and correlation, this was once the fashion in the behavioral field. Usage had declined, however, because most events we observe or seek to bring about result from the combined effect of a number of factors. The calculations required to sort out the relative effects of each factor were too complex to be attractive with previous calculator equipment. With the computer, this barrier to use has been hurdled, and recent emphasis has been on the various multivariate and cluster forms of analysis. These aim at the evaluation of the relative effect of a number of factors thought to be operating. As with all computational techniques, the value of the resulting measurement can be only as good as, no better than the quality of the insight which entered into the planning, collection and analysis of the original data.

Bayesian analysis, resurrected after two centuries of neglect, is a second set of tools owing its newly found utility to computer assistance, although the calculations are not always laborious. In one sense, the basic concept of judgmental probability has always been practiced to some degree by the more skilled in any line of research. But the formal computational aspects are recent, and have added a number of decision aids of proven value to the managerial tool chest, when used with understanding of the limitations imposed by any numerical result.

A new form of algebraic notation--matrix algebra-- forms the connecting link between a number of other statistical tools which have risen to prominence in the last couple of decades. Game theory, one of the earliest to gain public acclaim, has yet to prove of any substantial value. Other forms, such as Markov chains and linear programming, have demonstrated value for planning. The calculations are much too tedious without the use of a computer.

No very complex calculations are involved in the PERT and Critical Path Method forms of network analysis, both of thoroughly proven value for planning and control of many kinds of processes with deadline problems. However, the number of computations required for most networks of tasks to be coordinated is often too voluminous without computer assistance.

Finally, the computer's gargantuan capacity for computation has facilitated a more sophisticated version of the old trial-and-error system of getting answers, under the banner of simulation.

8

COMPUTER AIDED ANALYSIS OF
MULTIVARIATE INFLUENCES

The forces with which business decision and prediction must deal, and the various means of competition available to the businessman and his competitors, are far from the simple picture of the elementary economics text. It is seldom that one single factor alone is responsible for any given business result. Furthermore, the factors that succeed best for one business almost invariably must be different from the factors which will enable a competitor to succeed or invade the market. One has only to witness the number of department stores in any main shopping district of any big city, and the differences between these stores, all of them usually profitable, to realize the problems involved. Not only do businesses differ but the customers differ in what they wish. Thus, businesses and all other organizations hoping to attract public support of any kind inevitably welcome any method which will promise to measure the combined effect and the individual importance of the various factors which the executive can hope to manipulate and the various segments of the market to which he can hope to appeal.

A number of such mathematical tools do exist but until the ready availability of computer service, their usefulness was drastically limited by the cumbersomeness of the calculations involved. Most of these methods have been known for long periods of time and some have an extensive history of use in the psychological field, by psychometricians in the development of their various standardized tests. It should be noted that there are usually variations of any of these various methods, but there are basically six forms of so-called multivariate analysis: cluster analysis, factor analysis, canonical analysis, multiple discriminant analysis, conjoint analysis and perceptual mapping. Computer programs exist for the handling of the computation of each of these methods, and any person seriously considering handling any part of the calculations should refer to the standard texts available for discussion of the computations involved.

While all of these systems promise to measure the simultaneous relative effect of a number of factors, all of them depend to a great degree on the judgment that goes into collection of the data and interpretation of the future stability of the answers received. In the field of psychometrics, where they have received the longest use, the factors involved are not usually subject to the changing whims of time as are the factors of market operation results. Even so, the tests built from their results are far from perfect, although they have proved extremely useful. All of these tools have one thing in common. They try to use some technique to so group the information that the resulting grouping has a smaller variation than is true of the measurements for the total population from which this particular grouping is abstracted. That is, they attempt to measure the effect of the factor by showing that consideration of this factor decreases the range of error in a prediction.

CLUSTER ANALYSIS

The simplest of these tools is that of cluster analysis, and it has proved relatively useful in the analysis of markets. The purpose of cluster analysis is to group data or responses that are available into some classification system which will highlight opportunities of some sort or another.

For example, consider the problem of a soft drink manufacturer who has developed a new product and has given a taste test to a group of 100 possible teen-age consumers from four sections of the country--the east, the midwest, the south and the far-west section. In each area the respondents are chosen from three income classes--low, medium, and high. They are asked to score the taste of the new soft drink from their point of view on a scale of from 1 to 5, with 1 representing relatively unacceptable and 5 being highly acceptable. When the results are obtained from all 100 respondents, the average score given by all 100 respondents is 3.2. This would indicate that, on the average, the drink tastes only a little better than mediocre. If accepted on its face, this average figure raises real doubts as to the value of introducing this new product.

If we simply classify the ratings we receive by geography or income, however, we get a somewhat different picture. When we divide them on a geographical basis into 4 regions tested, for example, we find a significant variation between the scores of the 4 areas, with the south showing a stronger preference than any of the other regions, and the far-west essentially rejecting the flavor. Similarly, when we divide all of the respondents into their income classes, we find that the higher we go in the income scale, the higher the average rating. (See Table 8-1). In each of these geography categories taken by themselves, or on the basis of income taken by itself, the average score does not present a really attractive level of acceptance. But when we analyze the two factors together-- geography plus income--we get average scores of 4.1 and 4.6 respectively for the south and midwest portions of the country among those with high and medium income classes--scores which indicate we have a possibility of very real success in this particular set of market segments.

Table 8-1. Clustering by Geography and by Income
           Separately

Item	Number of Respondents	Average Score
Geographical location		
A – East	25	3.64
B – Midwest	25	3.72
C – South	25	3.84
D – Far West	25	2.40
Income level		
Low	40	2.65
Medium	40	3.55
High	20	3.80

This initial analysis shows the southern region to be most receptive to the new soft drink, but by a disappointingly small margin. In fact, normal statistical tests indicate that the margin is too small to be statistically significant.

Consider a somewhat different problem, the problem of advertising themes for a new hair shampoo. We want to test consumer attitude toward descriptive terms that might be applied to the shampoo (and, of course, thus towards characteristics that might be built into the product as well as mere advertising). We administer a psychological test consisting of eight different relevant stimulus words to which we ask for their free association of terms connected with it. In the process we may find that some of the terms in our stimulus group also evoke a free association response of other words in that same list. In this case, we find that some of the stimulus words with which they are associated are considered very similar. Other words have a more distant similarity to each other. From this knowledge we can build an advertising theme which should suggest the most attractive results from product use.

The results of a cluster analysis can be visualized in terms of tree diagram, such as Table 8-2 with respect to the soft drink case. Technically, of course, where only a few respondents are involved and only a very small number of characteristics are concerned, this process can be carried out by a means of hand tabulation. Generally speaking, however, the volume of data often requires the use of a computer program. One that is quite standard--the MCA (Multiple Classification Analysis) is available from the University of Chicago. In using the program, the analyst must decide how much variation he will accept within a group before the clustering itself stops. The purpose, of course, is to produce clusters that have relative homogeneity with very little variation within them.

Cluster analysis is thus really an extension of the widely used and widely useful method of cross-tabulation of data. It has the advantage that the categories within each box in the cross-tabulation are measured for the degree of homogeneity in terms of the variation involved--a step not usually carried out with cross-tabulation. Also, it can be carried out with a computer when the volume of data and the complexity of it becomes quite large. The value of the results, as in all forms of cross-tabulation, depends on the insight of the analyst in choosing the categories into which he intends to cluster his data. If he does not pick good categories, he may miss the

TABLE 8-2. Clustering of Consumer Panel Rating Response Averages by Geographic Region and by Income Level (n = number of respondents in the cluster)

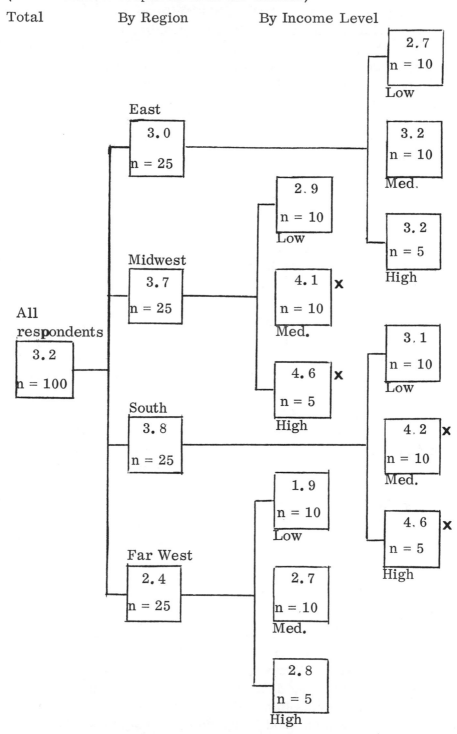

particular factors that are highly associated with whatever it is desired to accomplish. The value of the results are thus highly dependent on the judgment and insight of the analyst. As with any tool, the validity of the results of cluster analysis is no better than the validity of the figures on which it is based, the assumptions underlying the choice of sample, and the accuracy with which the sample is drawn from the intended universe.

Those seeking to understand the technique involved should refer to the following publications:

Green, et. al. Management Science, 13, April, 1967, pp. 387-400.

Yankelovich, D. Harvard Business Review, Vol. 43, Mar., 1964, pp. 83-90.

Armstrong, J. S. et al. Journal of Marketing Research, 7, Nov., 1970, pp. 487-492.

Gatty, Ronald. Applied Statistics, 15, Nov., 1966, pp. 146-158.

Sheth, J. N. Journal of Advertising Research, 10, Feb., 1970, pp. 29-39.

FACTOR ANALYSIS

Factor analysis has long been used by psychological test makers to choose the items in their tests, even before the advent of computers. The computational process, however, is exceedingly tedious without the use of a computer, and thus the technique was not widely used until the 1960's. In test construction, factor analysis is used to determine the extent to which various kinds of possible test items measure the same thing. It is by no means an automatic technique. A considerable degree of analyst's judgment is involved in the selection of grouping of variables to generate the so-called factors into which the variables are grouped. The object is to reduce the number of factors to an important few and to try to identify what these factors really are.

Consider first a simple problem which every sales manager must face--that of evaluating the efforts of the indi-

viduals in his salesforce. Some managers can and do use
sales dollars generated. But this single variable is hardly
sufficient to provide a clear picture of the value of the individual's effort to the firm's prosperity. There are differences
in territory size and potential sales, in the number of new
account calls, in the time of the salesman in the territory and
his previous training, in the degree of competition, etc. While
each of these could be evaluated as a separate variable, it is
probably more effective to group some of these variables into
factors which they have in common. Thus territory geography
and territory potential might be combined into one factor--the
effects of territory. These combination factors could in turn
be weighted in importance to evaluate each individual. The
weights themselves, unfortunately, often have to be arbitrary.
In the sort of situation which we are talking about here, work
is usually done by hand calculation and represents one of the
more simple uses of factor analysis.

A more complex problem of factor analysis, really
necessitating the help of a computer, could be that of corporate
planning and evaluation. Quite often an outside party is used
to interview consumers of a specific industry, insuring the con-
fidentiality of the company having the study performed. In an
instance of this sort it is known beforehand what "factors" are
to be tested. Market factors such as product offerings, low
price, and prompt delivery can be tested for a variety of companies supplying the industry. Assuming that there were 20
questions (which is about as many as can be answered) and 50
respondents, we would have a matrix of 20 times 50, or 1000
answers. This matrix is then fed into a computer having a
program capable of doing factor analysis. Out of this computer run should come a pattern of relationships between individual questions and answers, perhaps in a form of a co-
variance matrix. Whenever a high degree of correlation is
found between two different questions, the underlying base of
the question is combined into another "factor," invariably using
linear weighting. This new factor is then considered as a
principal component of the analysis. Collapsing and condens-
ing the 20 factors into a smaller number continues until additional principal components no longer reduce the residual variance of the matrix. It is important, in addition, that each
principal component should be independent of all the other
principal components, allowing usage of each of the derived
factors as an independent variable in explaining the desired

characteristics of the answers. The factors finally chosen are
then plotted on two dimensional axis at right angles, after rotation of the axis of each of the factors being shown. (The method
of rotation is known as orthogonal rotation. This is the method
of keeping the data for each principal component in a separate
plane.) The computer program used can rotate the axis in
many directions until obtaining the maximum polarization between factors. The end result of our particular example of factor analysis in corporate planning may show, for example, that
economics and service are the two most important factors in
the judgment of the customer firms. Such a plot of five companies, all in the same industry, against their ratings for economics and service, might turn out as shown in Figure 8-1.

Figure 8-1. Factor Analysis of Average Respondent Ratings
of Five Supplier Firms' Images on 20 Items

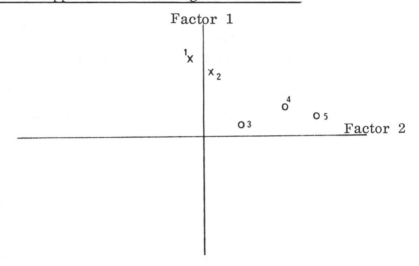

This interpretation shows that some companies, 3 of them, emphasize service (as seen by the customers) while two of them
seem to be more attuned to economic factors such as price,
quantity discounts, and the like. The construction of a new
strategy therefore, would depend on interpreting the results in
terms of where the best combination of economics and of service is most needed by considerable numbers of customers.

One of the problems of factor analysis is that the
choice of attributes which are to be initially measured are at
the discretion of the researcher. The value of the results obtained is thus limited by the insight of the researcher as to
which attributes might be important. This means that factor

analysis itself is of little value until more fundamental research is obtained as to the reactions of consumers or whatever else is being measured.

The answer obtained is far from perfect under the best circumstances, however, even when the data being measured are much more stable than those of the competitive business world. This is evidenced by the experience of the psychological test field out of which the tool itself has been borrowed. Perhaps no series of data have been more analyzed and more revised than the various series of so-called general intelligence tests. There can be no question that the resulting tests are more efficient in measuring whatever they do measure. But it is not always entirely clear what it is that they measure. Psychologists long ago became so doubtful as to the exact nature of the resulting principal components that they define IQ as "whatever the test measures."

College experience has long shown that, at best, the results of intelligence tests, even on a mass basis, only predict about half of what happens to students in college. On an individual basis, none of the tests are nearly as predictive as anybody would like. Some students do badly on the test, yet turn out autstanding work in college. Others score well on the tests, yet flunk out in college.

On one type of professional school admissions test, for example, a prominent school which carefully monitored its own experience over a five-year period found that the test results did moderately well, on the average, in predicting scholastic attainment, but showed no relation between the test results and the subsequent career success of the students, although the scholastic attainment itself did correlate fairly well with school experience. This school also found that many of those who fell in the upper third in the tests were in the lower third of the class, while some of those who were in the lower third of the test ended up in the upper third of their class. Yet the psychological test situation is dealing with relatively stable physical factors in the makeup of the individual. The factor they seek to measure--ease of learning--is objectively observable in practice. In business on the other hand, many of the factors with which business must deal are only partly predictable, at best, and some of them wholly unpredictable and not clearly known ahead of time. One of the major factors in almost any sales situation is the action of competitors, and there is no lack of recognizable examples in which the competitors' actions turned out to be quite different from what was expected and quite influential on the success or failure of the enterprise. Thus this tool, like most others, simply gives us a basis for evaluating the current situation and more insight into what might happen under certain circumstances. As a basis of clear prediction, it is little better than any other crystal ball.

References:

Green, Paul E. and Wind, Yoram, "New Way to Measure Consumer's Judgments," Harvard Business Review, July-Aug., 1975, pp. 107-117.

Harmon, Harry H., Modern Factor Analysis, 2nd ed. University of Chicago Press, 1967.

Kaiser, Henry F., "The Application of Electronic Computers to Factor Analysis," Educational and Psychological Measurement, 21 Spring 1960, pp. 141-151.

Thurstone, Louis L., Multiple Factor Analysis. University of Chicago Press, 1947.

CANONICAL ANALYSIS

One of the most advanced multivariate techniques is canonical analysis, essentially a variation of regression analysis. Canonical analysis uses a combination of multiple independent and multiple dependent variables to attempt a usable explanation of some event, and also to predict possible future results.

Canonical analysis is often combined with another multivariate technique to provide the "best picture." For instance, canonical analysis and factor analysis are frequently used in tandom. Most calculations are run on a computer using a canned program. The following discussions will center on the use of canonical analysis rather than the actual calculations.

Consider again the evaluation of a salesman in the field, a problem no sales manager can escape. As already mentioned, a simple way would be to take total sales and perform a simple ranking upon the entire sales force. However, most sales managers are aware that no salesperson is in complete control of his or her sales. Many uncontrollable factors affect performance and even controllable factors are numerous. There is more to selling than annual sales. For instance, the number of new accounts opened, goodwill generated, expenses used, trade shows attended, etc. all can affect future results and must be taken into account when evaluating any individual sales person. The analyst must first choose two sets of variables considered important, dividing them into predicting variables and resultant variables. Some of the predictors of successful salesmanship might include number of calls, age, geography covered, and spending of expense money. Some of the resultant variables might include gross sales, goodwill generated, number of new accounts, and trade shows attended. The calculation itself might be carried out as indicated below.

Canonical Correlation Analysis

First, values must be assigned for each of the predicting and resultant variables. Some of these values will be obtained from actual experience such as sales, new accounts opened, etc. Others, however, such as goodwill and geography, must be adjusted on some other basis. In the case of geography, it could be a number of miles of roads available or the number of square miles of areas as a measurement. It is often very useful to assign an index number to some variables, such as geography, rather than use values expressed in concrete measurement units.

Step 1 - Assign Values

Salesmen - Able

Factor No.	Predictors		Factor No.	Resultants	
1	# of calls	2.4	5	Sales	1.4
2	Age	34.0	6	New acct's	2.6
3	Geography	6.1	7	Goodwill	4.3
4	Expenses	12.4	8	Trade shows	.7

Second, a correlation matrix is then prepared from all of the predicting and resultant variables. It is imperative that only a very minimum of correlation be present between the variables themselves. Values above or in excess of $\pm$ .3

are usually significant enough to be discarded in this type of analysis, since we are interested in finding independent factors.

Step 2 - Calculate Correlation Matrix - All Sales Staff

Factors	1	2	3	4	5	6	7	8
1	1.0	.3	.28	.62	etc.			
2		1.0	.14	.31	etc.			
3			1.0	.10	etc.			
4				1.0	-.20	etc.		
5					1.0			
6						1.0		
7							1.0	
8								1.0

Third, after the correlation matrix has been prepared and evaluated, the canonical coefficients are obtained. A computer program is most useful in preparing these canonical coefficients.

Step 3 - Obtain Canonical Correlation Coefficients

Predictors		Resultants	
1.	.43	5.	.82
2.	etc.	6.	etc.
3.	etc.	7.	etc.
4.	etc.	8.	etc.

4. The cononical coeeficients obtained are multiplied by the assigned values obtained in paragraph no. 1. The variables are then grouped by either predictor variables or resultant variables. The result of the multiplication of each one of the factors is then summed to obtain a total contributing value for predictor and resultant variables.

<u>Step 4 - Combine (linear) Canonical Coefficients with Assigned</u>
    <u>Values</u>

	<u>Predictors</u>	<u>Canonical</u>	<u>Value</u>	<u>Total (X)</u>
1.	No. of calls	(.43)	2.4	1.032
2.				
3.				
4.				

$$2x = 3.4$$

<u>Resultants</u>

5.
6.
7.
8.

$$Ey = 2.1$$

     5. The predictor variables and resultant variable are
then plotted on an <u>xy</u> plot with one point resulting from each individual sales person. In general the predicting variable occu-
pies the x axis while the resultant variable is the y axis.

<u>Step 5 - Prepare Plot</u>

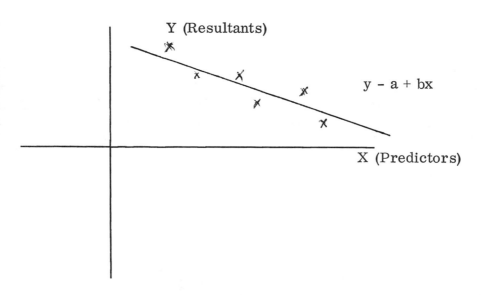

     6. After preparing a plot as described in paragraph 5,
a regression equation can be prepared from the data used to

obtain the plot. This regression coefficient should be useful in predicting future performance of salesmen. Likewise, a correlation coefficient can be obtained to indicate the degree of fit for the regression line. In fact, all standard tests, such as are used in testing of the coefficients, can also be carried out.

Step 6 - Calculate Regression Equation

$$y = a + bx$$

$$y = o + 3x$$

Step 7 - Predict total sales effectiveness and evaluate sales person based on plot of variables.

Canonical correlation analysis can be used for other analyses such as answering the question as to why certain consumers buy certain products. For example, a consumer's total measurable characteristics, such as age, social class, and geography could be combined in a canonical correlation analysis to predict consumption of various meats and vegetables.

It should be obvious that this, like many other tools, depend a great deal on the judgment of the analyst--in this case, the choice of weights for his predictor and resultant factors, and in the choice of these variables themselves. Such a choice may be purely arbitrary, in which case the value of the results may not be very meaningful. At other times it can be based on prior research and experience and furnish a great deal of insight into the value of the measure used.

MULTIPLE DISCRIMINANT ANALYSIS

Discriminant analysis can be considered as closely similar to multiple regression, since several independent variable are used to predict some dependent variable, such as a buying pattern or a brand selection. Similar to regression analysis, discriminant analysis can also predict what would be expected from behavior of the groups being examined.

The basic underlying assumptions of discriminant analysis must be kept in mind if the analysis is to be workable and sound. These are that the value of each predicting variable are normally distributed and have a similar variance, and that the independent variables are grouped and have a similar impact upon the dependent variable.

Take, for instance, the selection of a college by a high school graduate (dependent variable). The independent variables are thought to include the cost of tuition, style of dormitories, and the curriculum. If some measurement could be made of potential student attitudes regarding these independent variables, the admitting officials would have a better idea as to how to shape the schools' promotional efforts. The procedure would then be as follows.

Discriminant Analysis--An Example

A major marketing problem for any organization is the identification of those segments of the population who are potential customers. Consider the selection of Ivy Hall College by potential students. All individuals considering the school are asked to rank (from 1 to 5) certain perceived characteristics of the school. For discussion purposes, results from only six people are shown and on three factors. (The complete analysis would include all recipients, of course.)

Action	Low Tuition Cost	Dormitories	Desirable Curriculum
Selected School	(X_1)	(X_2)	(X_3)
	5	5	3
	5	4	5
	4	4	5
$\bar{X}_A$	4.66	4.33	4.33
Rejected School	3	3	5
	3	1	4
	5	5	3
$\bar{X}_B$	4.33	3.0	4.0

$D (X_1) = 4.66 - 4.33 = .33$

$D (X_2) = 4.33 - 3.00 = 1.33$

$D (X_3) = 4.33 - 4.0 = .33$

Note that these differences, by themselves, are not very great. Consideration of this data on differences is held in abeyance until the linear coefficients for X_1, X_2, and X_3 are calculated. This is accomplished by use of three simultaneous equations which produce the required coefficients. For example the coefficients might be as follows:

Variable	Coefficient	Value
X_1	A =	.34
X_2	B =	.84
X_3	C =	.10

A discriminatory value can then be calculated by using these coefficients and the average values, that is, $\overline{X}_{1A}$.

For the individuals who selected the college, they would be:

D selection = .34(4.66) + .84(4.33) + .10(4.33)

D selection = 1.584 + 5.17 + .433

D selection = 7.187

and for the individuals who rejected, the discriminatory value would be:

D reject = .34(4.33) + .84(3.00) + .10(4.00)

D reject = 1.47 + 2.52 + .40

D reject + 4.392

Note now that the combined factors do have a substantial difference. Assuming the two populations have a similar variance, the following is a picture of the above problem.

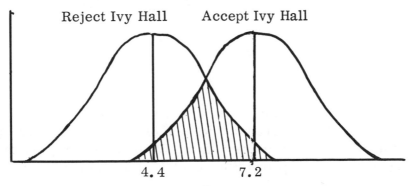

Reject Ivy Hall   Accept Ivy Hall

4.4   7.2

Note the substantial overlap in the scores of those in the reject and accept populations. The individuals represented in this overlap are fringe prospects. Some proportion can obviously be won over with the right appeals.

Since the scores represented in the graph above represent a composite of the reactions of prospects to a number of factors in the Ivy Hall offering, the distributions can be viewed as a cross-section of a 3- or more dimensional distribution of population ratings, as below, with a horizontal cross-section as indicated in the projection:

This visualization of the results tells us more than we are likely to learn from knowledge of the average score and a simple tabulation of the raw data. We now have a quantitative picture of the target promotion population and of opportunities.

The calculated variances now make it possible to measure a potential student's response to Ivy Hall's promotion, and make some prediction whether or not he or she will attend (in other words, make a desirable decision as far as the Ivy Hall's administration is concerned).

Several points should be considered in looking back at the analysis. First, the differences between individuals who selected Ivy Hall and those who rejected it are not very large, nor are curriculaum evaluation differences very great. Second, dormitory life appears to have a great impact between the two populations. The complete analysis shows that the coefficients of the independent variables is heavily weighted towards the dormitories. Third, the weights accorded to the tuition costs and the desireability of the curriculum tend to be much lower in addition to exhibiting very small differences.

The values of the variances can now be used in estimating the probability that a person will attend the school after taking a small questionnaire in evaluating tuition, dormitories, and the curriculum. It also indicates that dormitories is the predominant difference in the group from the population deciding to attend this school. Tuition costs and desireability of curriculum are lesser factors that do have an effect. Discriminant analysis takes account of the combined effect of all factors to project the effects of the independent variables and the resultant probability of some future action. It can show, for example, not only who is the most likely prospect, but how many they are, and it can yield an estimate of the probability that a fringe candidate will "buy." By zeroing in on the best potential, it gives guidance to both the media and message aspects of promotion, as well as some indication of product design features to emphasize or pricing tactics to be considered.

References:

Harmon, Harry. Modern Factor Analysis, 2nd ed. University of Chicago Press, 1967.

Thurstone, Louis L. Multiple Factor Analysis, University of Chicago Press, 1947.

Tatsuoka, M. M. Multivariate Analysis, John Wiley and Sons, 1971.

Press, S. J. Applied Multivariate Analysis, Holt, Rinehart and Winston, 1972.

Gatty, Ronald. "Multivariate Analysis for Marketing Research: An Evaluation," Applied Statistics, Vol. 15, Nov. 1966, pp. 146-58.

CONJOINT MEASUREMENT

The technique of conjoint measurement has been suggested primarily for measurement of consumer attitudes in matters of product design and corporate strategy. Unlike some of the other techniques listed so far, this technique does not require the data be in the form of measured data, but simply relative rankings by respondents of verbal statements or descriptions given to them. (The descriptions may not always be merely verbal. In some cases, for example, they may be in the form of samples of the product if the product is simple enough, such as that of a cake of soap.) The purpose is that of some of the other methods already discussed above--to measure the relative importance to the consumer of the various characteristics or attributes presented in the statements he was asked to give.

Consider, for example, the problem of an automobile manufacturer planning his strategy for the design of a mini-compact car he expects to add to his line three years from now (the normal time span needed to engineer a new model). He wishes to know what aspects of the design to emphasize in order to set up guidelines for his designers and engineers. He knows from other studies that consumers do consider such matters as handling characteristics or nimbleness (which include matters such as steering ease, cornering and traction). They also consider price. To some degree he has reason to believe that mileage is becoming increasingly important. He feels that the ease of servicing or serviceability has become of greater importance in recent years. They would like to know to what extent potential buyers are willing to trade off performance characteristics such acceleration or speed against some of these other items, and how they judge spaciousnes and how important it is to the small car buyer.   We have thus seven different characteristics all of which are not completely compatible with each other. Performance and mileage, for example, do not go together. Some of the other characteristics will influence the cost of the car and thus the price which must be charged for it.

Thus even if we limit the number of choices for each factor to no more then three, we could have nearly 700 combinations to which to confront the respondents--an impossible task. However, it is possible to use a very much smaller number of combinations in such a way that each of the choices for each factor are presented in combinations with other characteristics in an independent manner. One method of doing this is known as the orthogenal array which might, for example, pick out no more than 30 possible combinations such that the independent effect of each of the seven factors are balanced. Another method would be to use the factors two at a time. In either case, the respondent would simply be asked to give a relative ranking of the choices with which he was faced. The results of these rankings would be fed into a computer program (see references) to get a utility scale for each attribute measure. The computer would search for a set of scale values for each factor in the design. Scale values assigned to each level of each factor would be chosen so that when added together the total utility of each of the combinations actually presented to the respondents would correspond to the original ranks, at least approximately. On a graphical basis we might come up with a set of utility graphs as shown in Figure 8-4 (assuming 28 items are rated). The relative importance of each of the seven factors measured would be determined by the range of utilities of the choices presented by that factor against the total range of all utilities. In this case, we might find that mileage, handling characteristics and spaciousness were most important, that price was of medium importance and serviceability only a minor utility.

The technique of conjoint measurement has not been widely used as yet, nor the results of the few uses thoroughly validated against later experience, although writers claim some success for the tool. It is obvious that it should have a great deal of value as guidance as to what items are really important and which are not, at least, and probably would have even more value used on a time series basis to determine trends and consumer preferences. The weaknesses are those of any attempt to get at consumer decisions by verbal responses. In addition to which, if used for purposes of product design, it must contend with the problem of design lead time and the inevitable

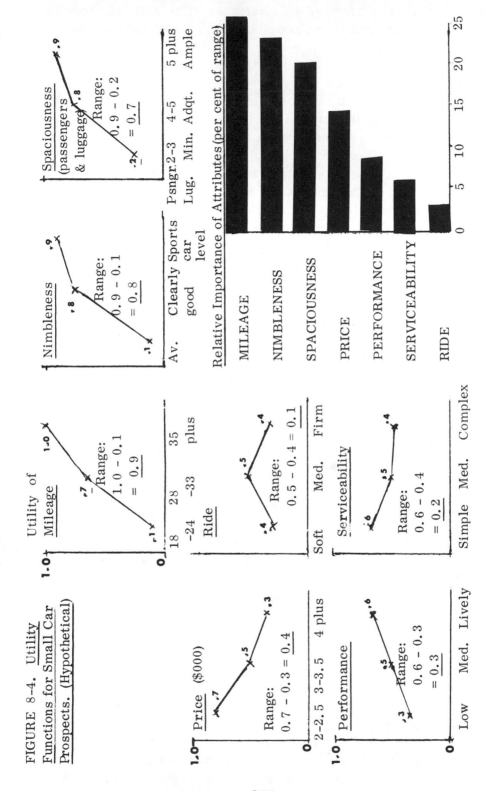

FIGURE 8-4. Utility Functions for Small Car Prospects. (Hypothetical)

206

changes in taste that occur over a period of time. Also, what is obtained is solely the <u>relative</u> importance of those factors which the analyst has chosen. It is possible to miss even more important factors and thus overrate the values of those that are picked out as important.

References:

Green, Paul E. and Wind, Yoram. "New Way to Measure Consumers' Judgment," <u>Harvard Business Review</u>, July-Aug., 1975, pp. 107-117.

Luce, R. Duncan and Tukey, John W. "Simultaneous Conjoint Measurement: A New Type of Fundamental Measurement," <u>Journal of Mathematical Psychology</u>, Feb., 1964, p. 1.

PERCEPTUAL MAPPING

Most of the techniques above assume that the researcher sets out with a list of attributes and then gains some measure of the value of each. By contrast, the technique of perceptual mapping does not assume any attribute list at all, but simply asks that the consumer make judgments as to the similarity of pairs of possible products, models, or whatever is being investigated. In this technique, consumers are simply presented with a series of pair combinations of the series of choices in which the researcher is interested in, such as car models or airline services. He is asked simply to rate and divide the groups into those that are relatively similar and those that are very dissimilar, and next to make a second sort of those that are relatively similar into those that are less similar than the others and those that are less dissimilar than the others. We thus get four sectors of a possible "perceptual map." By feeding these ratings into a computer, we can get an average rating by all respondents for each of the classes involved. (See Figure 8-5.) And we can, of course, ask about the similarity between each of the makes and the ideal for the particular individual, and thus get some sort of density grouping of various products on the market relative to the ideals of various segments of consumers. Working from what is known about the general perception of the products involved on the market, the four sectors into which the chosen models or items

are listed may be given labels. For example, in cars: economical, utility, sporty, luxurious, or whatever the make suggests. These labels, however, do not come from the study itself but from the analyst's inferences as to the way consumers
are reacting in pairing up the products. Figure 8-5 shows a
two-dimensional map, but a three-dimensional form is also
sometimes used, with relative value or intensity of each item
shown.

Figure 8-5. Hypothetical Perceptual Map of Panel Respondents'
Judgments of the Relative Similarity of 10 Imported and Domestic
Compact and Subcompact Automobiles.

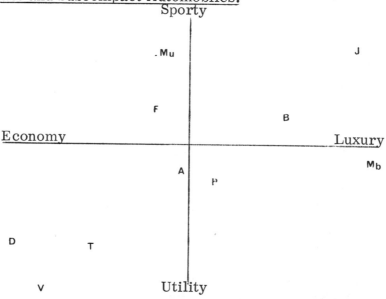

Again, this tool, like all the others, has some obvious values
in terms of gaining insight into possible consumer reactions.
However, testimony from some clients of one service that uses
this method indicate that if too much weight is put on the specific results, the actions taken may not live up to expectation.
Even though the analyst's own judgment does not seem to be as
much a part of this technique as of the others, interpretation
and insight are just as much involved. The labels he gives the
sectors are his. They are not direct results of either the respondent judgments nor of the computer analysis.

SUMMARY

1. The computer's ravenous capacity for computation has made available a number of related tools for estimating the relative importance of a complexity of influences in a business situation. The six most common are cluster analysis, factor analysis, canonical analysis, multiple discriminant analysis, conjoint analysis, and perceptual mapping.

2. The first four of these require input data in the form of a count or a measure. Conjoint analysis needs only respondent rankings, and perceptual mapping simply asks the respondent to separate paired data into the similar and dissimilar.

3. All of these tools except perceptual mapping start with a list of variables or attributes chosen in advance by the analyst. The quality of the results are thus highly subject to the analyst's judgment, and insight and the quality of the information underlying these.

4. The genesis of these tools was in the field of psychological test construction where factor analysis, particularly, has long been used. The history of the resulting tests indicates that the tools work, but the results are far short of perfect.

9

PASTOR BAYES' CONCEPT
OF JUDGMENTAL PROBABILITIES

What has become known as the neo-Bayesian, or simply the Bayesian approach to decision making has been defined as the attitude that " . . . it is legitimate to quantify our feelings about uncertainty in terms of objectively assessed numerical probabilities, even when confronted by a single unique decision and when there is no extensive past history on which to base the assessment of probabilities."*

Bayesian probabilities take their name from the theorem and postulate advanced by an English clergyman, Thomas Bayes, in the 18th century but largely ignored by traditional statistics. The theorem gives a formula for modifying an original estimate of the likelihood of an event through the use of a small amount of new information, and is applicable to traditional statistical data. But Bayes considered subjective, or personalistic probabilities as useful as the objective probabilities to which the orthodox statistician has confined his attention, and was willing to admit experience which objective statistics ignores, even a simple estimate in a situation of total ignorance. Most neo-Bayesians would stop somewhat short of this radical postulate and insist on some kind of experiential basis for the prior probability estimate. It is the use of such much less rigidly defined probabilities which has made the Bayesian approach such a useful decision tool.

---

*Harry V. Roberts, "Bayesian Statistics in Marketing,"
Journal of Marketing, Vol. 27, No. 1 (January 1963), pp. 1-4.

TWO KINDS OF PROBABILITIES

The need to make a decision implies some degree of uncertainty about the outcome of each of the proposed alternatives. Thus the decision itself must rest on some kind of assumption about the likelihood of success of the alternatives being considered. Traditional statistics was formulated to deal with decisions in situations which could be viewed as parts of a history and a future of similar events repeated over and over. The model was that of the gambling situation with honest dice or cards and an honest dealer. The expectation of future decisions with the same choices converts the short-run uncertainty of the individual outcome to a long-run certainty, expressible in terms of an objective probability statement. The latter can be defined as the limiting value approached by the ratio of occurrences of the given outcome to the total opportunities for its occurrence, as the chances for occurrence become extremely large. It is always a ratio, a fraction between 0 and 1, and is never a prediction applicable to a single event, only the long run.

Some of our most important decisions, however, are in the context of situations in which we lack any background of experiences which can be objectively described as similar enough to the current one to meet ordinary statistical standards of comparability. Faced with this kind of unknown outcome, we can make a reasoned choice between alternatives only when we make some judgment about the relative likelihood of occurrence of each outcome perceived as possible. Such a subjective probability is also expressible as a fraction between 0 and 1 which does not represent any kind of ratio but is a statement of our degree of belief in a specific outcome. Generally, too, this fraction derives from some kind of experience, but experience which cannot be described as objectively comparable to the current situation.

Thus we can have either of two kinds of probability fractions, both expressed as some value between 0 and 1: objective probability and subjective probability. To avoid confusion, subjective probabilities are often referred to as likelihood. The term personalistic probability is also often used to emphasize the judgmental character of subjective probabilities. Objective probability is so designated because competent observers analyzing the same information would norm-

211

ally arrive at the same probability statement, and would also generally agree on what evidence was admissable in its determination. By contrast, in the case of really unique decision situation, equally competent observers might well disagree as to both the admissability of the kinds of evidence being used and to the numerical value each would assign to the alternative outcomes. Objective and personalistic probabilities can be viewed either as different attitudes towards the admissability of evidence on the probability of an outcome, or as tools for different kinds of decisions.

The Viewpoint of the Objectivist

The objectivist views probability as the long run relative frequency of occurrence of an event, applicable only to a long series of events that can be repeated again and again under much the same describable set of circumstances. He would obtain the value of this frequency ratio either from an inference about an observable physical situation--such as the probable behavior of a six-sided die--or from observation of the actual number of times the event took place in a series of trials. He does not feel he should make predictions about unique events, situations which are not repeated and therefore can have no long run ratio. Nor does he like to bring to bear on his inference any evidence other than his original observations of repeated events or physical structure. To him, any single event is unknowable, there are no degrees of truth short of the absolute, and degrees of belief are not a subject for measurement.

The Viewpoint of the Personalist

The personalist, on the other hand, is interested less in what will happen in some kind of long run than in what will happen the next time, and thus views probability as a measure of his degree of belief in a particular proposition. To him, truth can be a variable, and the question of "how true is an event?" can have meaning. He will take into account all the problems and all of the evidence accepted by the objectivist, but much more besides. His main interest, however, is in unique events and those which may occur only a few times, or which have no prior history. He will therefore seek guidance from past experience of his own or of others with what seem to him to be similar but not identical situations. And he will use techniques such as Bayes Theorem which enable him to change his judgment by systematically taking experimental evidence into account. The objectivist and the personalist usually get similar answers when the amount of data is large. The two approaches may yield substantially different results, however, when dealing with small samples of data and short runs.

How the Different Viewpoints Lead to Different Decisions

At the beginning of a dice game, both types of probabilists are likely to use the same estimate of the chance of a 7 appearing on the first throw of two dice--6/36, based on an examination of the physical structure of the cubes and on experience with long series of throws of similar pairs. If no 7 has appeared by the end of the 15th pass, both men would agree that if the initial estimate was correct, something rather unusual has occurred. The probability of $(30/36)^{15}$, that is, the probability of no 7, is approximately .06. Each might then inspect the dice more closely, pay extra attention to the dice-handling, recheck his first presupposition that the dice were unbiased. Each might begin to question his original assumption that this one game was part of a long series of "fair" games. But the reactions of the objectivist and of the personalist would then tend to diverge. After considering the evidence, the objectivist would then either continue to estimate the probability of a 7 appearing as 6/36 or would conclude that, based on the collected evidence of the 15 throws, it is unlikely that this game is part of a long series of games where the probability of getting a 7 is 6/36. But he also considers the available evidence too slim for him to make a new estimate of the probability of a 7 on the 16th throw in this particular and unique game, and he lacks any tools for arriving at such a modified estimate. He would probably just quit the game.

The subjectivist, however, may feel that since this is the only game in town, it must continue, and the 16th roll must be evaluated. He simply sees a need to make a revised estimate of probability based upon the observed properties of this particular set of throws. He will therefore employ Bayes Theorem to calculate an estimate of the probability of a 7 on the 16th throw conditioned by the nonappearance of a 7 on the previous 15 throws.

Thus the subjectivist is prepared to address himself more directly to problems such as estimating defect rates in a new production process on which no manufacturing experience exists or projecting the sales of a new style appearing in a women's dress line for the first time. Since many such decisions cannot be avoided, he attempts to bring to them some form of systematic analysis and, in particular, a numerical evaluation of whatever he had available in the way of previous experience, business judgment, feelings, hunches and the like.

How the Problems Solvable by Each Approach Differ

The insurance business provides the classic illustration of the values of objective probability. If I desire to buy $10,000 worth of life insurance protection, the agent will quote the same firm rate to me as to any other applicant of the same sex, age, occupation and apparent condition of good health. His rate is based on a table summarizing the mortality experience for tens of thousands of men of the same general description. With enough policyholders, the insurance actuary can calculate how much premium to charge. This premium represents a financial risk in my individual case, but a virtually certain profit when spread over a large number of policyholders. This premium, however, is not based on any individual evaluation as to my own specific chance of survival during the next year, but on the fraction of all policyholders presently living who may be expected to die during that year. Such an inability to pinpoint the survival chances of the next individual case is intrinsic to the definition of probability as a long-term relative frequency ratio.

The objective probabilities of the insurance actuary are obviously correct bases for the decisions about many of the activities of individuals, businesses, and other institutions, particularly at the routine operating level. Indeed one of the more useful developments in industrial production in this generation has been the adoption of statistical quality control to replace 100 percent inspection. This method of quality control is based on the recognition that each item produced is not a unique event but can be perceived of as one of a series of repeated events subject to minor chance variations. Without question, a great many of the routine operating aspects of

214

business can be made more efficient, and operational prediction can be improved, by recognizing that the particular situation, for the purpose for which a decision must be made, can be perceived as one of a series of repeated events.

But at the policy level in particular, and at nearly every other phase of management at times, decisions must be made and the probability estimated for events that are truly unique because of the constant need to change competitive tactics and to innovate. To place an order for his beginning inventory, the fashion buyer must estimate the probability of a given volume of sales for a given dress of the newest fashion. To develop his production schedule, the factory superintendent must estimate the probable reject rate for a new part never before produced. The contractor must estimate the probability of landing a job with a specific bid. The Board of Directors must estimate the probability that the radical new plastic resin will sell profitably, and in what quantity, before approving the appropriation for the new plant. The bases for all such probability estimates can only be subjective, whether unconscious and intuitive, or formalized and the result of some degree of calculation. The formal methods, called Bayesian analysis by some, permit a more thorough and more reasoned analysis of the assumptions and better integration of information sources.

The use of Bayes Theorem on conditional probabilities to modify subjective probability judgments makes possible an effective combination of experience with experimental data. The technique economizes in the use of available data, extracting the maximum amount of information from each bit. By making formal provision for the blending of past experience, seasoned subjective judgment, and empirical data, the Bayesian approach to decision brings the executive, the practical experimenter, and the statistician into a closer working relationship than is likely with other methods.

BASIC BAYESIAN ANALYTICAL CONCEPTS

The term Bayesian analysis is frequently used to refer to the various procedures growing out of the use in decision making of subjective probabilities and Bayes Theorem. The use of this tool for dealing with economic decisions in the face of true uncertainty involves several basic component concepts. There is an underlying (random) process whose outcome is conceived of as a random variable--the percent defective in production runs of the new process or the actual number of dresses which will be sold if they are stocked. That is, even though only one outcome will occur in actuality, this single outcome is conceived of as variable. In objective probability, the single outcome is considered as fixed but unknown, only the frequency of occurrence thought of as variable. Second, for each value of the variable, there is a known set of decisions related to it. For example, if we knew we would sell exactly 100 dresses or other items, we would know exactly how many to order or to schedule for a production run. Third, a loss function can be constructed which gives the loss or gain which would follow from any difference between the quantity decided upon and the true values which result. Thus, if we estimate and prepare for a sale of 100 items, but experience sales either greater or less than 100, we may incur out-of-pocket losses due to overstock or opportunity losses due to an inability to fill orders. Fourth, our knowledge about the random variable can be summarized in a probability distribution, a frequency distribution of possible values of the random variable. Such a probability distribution is constructed on the basis of some kind of previous experience or personal judgment deemed to be relevant to the specific problem at hand. This prior distribution is modified after the collection of experimental evidence and a new posterior probability distribution calculated, conditional upon the experimental data at hand. The result of weighting the losses by the probability of their occurrence (expected loss or expected profit) are summarized in pay off tables (or pay off matrices) which reveal the estimated profit positions of each proposed action or decision.

Human judgment being fallible, it is usually wise to test the importance of possible error. A sensitivity analysis can be conducted using several alternative possible prior probability distributions, or other parameters involved in the calculations, and observing the effect on the payoff matrices and profit positions. Such a step is particularly valuable whenever the amount of experimental data possible is severely limited and the prior probability estimates particularly important.

Expected value and profit position are both the result of the same kind of computation: the estimate of the payoff of a successful decision is multiplied by an estimate of the probability that such will be the outcome. Whenever the decision is one of a substantially repetitive long-run series under essen-

216

tially the same type of circumstances, then the result is always called an expected value. Since the probability estimate is an objective one, such an expected value is an estimate of one kind of real outcome: it is the average payoff per decision of a long series of decisions.

Expected value is sometimes also used to denote what many refer to as a profit position--a very unreal but exceedingly useful management tool. Profit position is preferred by many to denote the estimate which results when the predicted event is unique and the probability estimate therefore subjective. Such an estimate is never a prediction of any recognizable real outcome. Since the situation is a one-time one, the only outcome is either failure or some anticipated degree of success. The payoff in the event of success will always be the total connected with that degree of success, not some fraction of it. The profit position (or the expected value of a unique event) is thus not a prediction but a means of discounting various alternative courses of action by the degree of the relative uncertainty of each.

A decision tree can be used to visualize the process of estimating profit positions if the number of possible choices and outcomes is small. Consider, for example, the buying decision being faced by (fictional) George Smilson, fur department buyer for a nationally famous Texas store.

ESTIMATING THE PAYOFF IN A FUR-BUYING SITUATION

George's customers include the wives of some very wealthy Texas cattle and oil men, and they always expect him to stock the latest in the most expensive and exotic furs, although, of course, the sales of the top-priced items are not in any real volume. One fur he knows he will have to stock for the coming winter season is a brand new mutation mink shade-- pastel blue-green--made up into stoles he buys for $5500 and sells for $10,000 each. From past experience, George knows he must stock it and will be certain to sell at least one, perhaps as many as three, but no more. Thus his estimate of sales is a random variable between 1 and 3. Whether he sells 1, 2, or 3 depends partly on the prices of cattle and of oil and on the conditions of the high plains pastures, and also, when the season opens, on what the women choose as their current hair color and whether they feel that the new mutation will complement their choice. He also knows that he will sell to each customer only if he has the stole in stock. The customer must try it on and get a chance to fall in love with it enough to loosen her husband's bankroll. Thus an out-of-stock condition means a missed sale. Every such missed sale is a missed profit (opportunity loss) of $4500, the amount he realizes on each sale. All sales will be made early in the season. If he buys more than he is able to sell, however, he will have to un-load any overstock to a jobber at a mere $1,000 at the season's end--a loss of $4500 on each one unsold. We can show the situation facing George in the graphic form of the act-event decision tree of Figure 9-1.

Any decision situation can be put in the form of a de-cision tree such as this, but the method is obviously too cum-bersome if many alternatives are involved. A much more con-venient way to represent the same situation is by means of a payoff table. Table 9-1 outlines both the calculations and the final summary payoff matrix in the case of George Smilson.

On the face of this, it might seem that if George were a cautious man, he would buy 2 stoles, because in this way he would, at worst, break even and might make as much as $9000. But the three possible outcomes of selling 1, 2, or 3 stoles may not be equally likely. For this reason, a question mark has been placed in the profit position blank for each act shown in the decision tree. Since this is a first time for this item, and there never really is a comparable second time for a fashion item, George has no identical experience that will tell him how many pastel blue-green mink stoles he may sell. But he has gone over his experience with other exotic purchases over the last 10 years and has come up with 40 situations in which he feels the customer appeal was comparable. Only 10 of these were mink stoles--a different style and mutation in each case. The rest were fur capes and ultra-high-priced accessories of different kinds. In every case he sold at least 1, in no case more than 3. His tabulations are shown in Table 9-2. Using this experience as his best estimate of the prob-ability distribution of the random variable (the number of stoles he could sell) he can complete his decision tree by computing the profit position (or expected value) for each alternative buying decision. These are calculated by taking each of the payoffs arrived at in the previous computation and multiplying them by the estimated probability of their occurrence. These

FIGURE 9-1. Decision Paths Faced by George Smilson in the Purchase of Mink Stoles

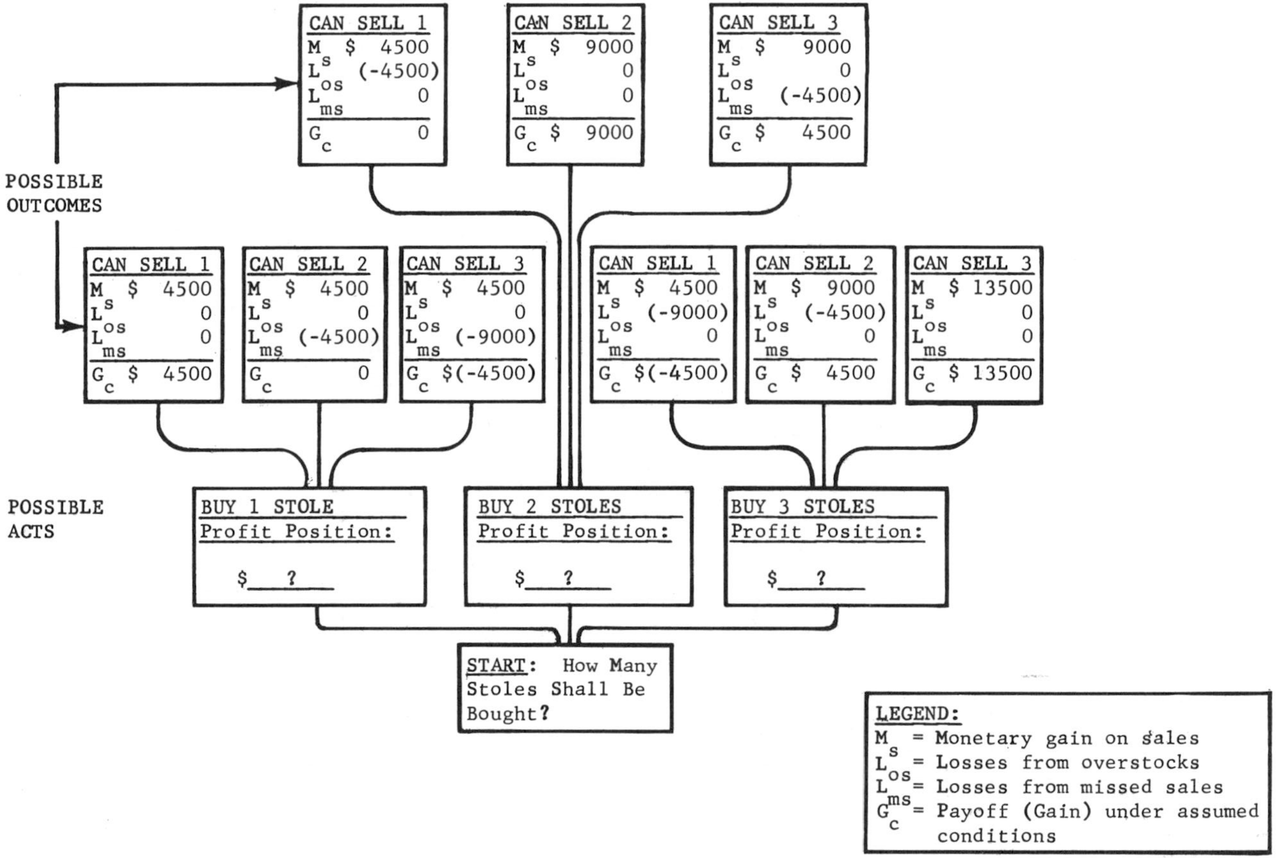

POSSIBLE OUTCOMES

CAN SELL 1		CAN SELL 2		CAN SELL 3
M_s \$ 4500		M_s \$ 9000		M_s \$ 9000
L_{os} (-4500)		L_{os} 0		L_{os} 0
L_{ms} 0		L_{ms} 0		L_{ms} (-4500)
G_c 0		G_c \$ 9000		G_c \$ 4500

CAN SELL 1	CAN SELL 2	CAN SELL 3
M_s \$ 4500	M_s \$ 4500	M_s \$ 4500
L_{os} 0	L_{os} 0	L_{os} 0
L_{ms} 0	L_{ms} (-4500)	L_{ms} (-9000)
G_c \$ 4500	G_c 0	G_c \$(-4500)

CAN SELL 1	CAN SELL 2	CAN SELL 3
M_s \$ 4500	M_s \$ 9000	M_s \$ 13500
L_{os} (-9000)	L_{os} (-4500)	L_{os} 0
L_{ms} 0	L_{ms} 0	L_{ms} 0
G_c \$(-4500)	G_c \$ 4500	G_c \$ 13500

POSSIBLE ACTS

BUY 1 STOLE	BUY 2 STOLES	BUY 3 STOLES
Profit Position:	Profit Position:	Profit Position:
\$?	\$?	\$?

START: How Many Stoles Shall Be Bought?

LEGEND:
M_s = Monetary gain on sales
L_{os} = Losses from overstocks
L_{ms} = Losses from missed sales
G_c^{ms} = Payoff (Gain) under assumed conditions

TABLE 9-1. Payoff Calculations and Summary Matrix In The Mutation Mink Buying Problem

A. Payoff Calculations

Decision	Demand Condition Could Sell:	Monetary Gain On Sales M_s	Possible Overstock Losses L_{os}	Missed Sale Opportunity Losses L_{ms}	Net Payoff Under Assumed Contingencies $G_c = M_s - L_{os} - L_{ms}$
Buy 1 stole	1 stole	$4500	$ 0	$	$ 4500
	2 stoles	4500	0	(−4500)	0
	3 stoles	4500	0	(−9000)	(−4500)
Buy 2 stoles	1 stole	4500	(−4500)	0	0
	2 stoles	9000	0	0	9000
	3 stoles	9000	0	(−4500)	4500
Buy 3 stoles	1 stole	4500	(−9000)	0	(−4500)
	2 stoles	9000	(−4500)	0	4500
	3 stoles	13500	0	0	13500

B. Summary Payoff Matrix

Decision	Net Payoff In the Situation In Which The Demand Is For:		
	1 Stole	2 Stoles	3 Stoles
Buy 1 stole	$ 4500	$ 0	$ (−4500)
	0	9000	4500
	(−4500)	4500	13500

Note: Net monetary gain on an individual sale = $4500
Actual Loss on each overstock item at season's end = $4500 (That is, it is the actual cost of $5500 less the realizable salvage of $1000)
Opportunity loss if sale is missed because item is not in stock = $4500 (That is, this is the amount of the profit opportunity which could not be realized.)

TABLE 9-2. Sales Experience With Presumably Analogous
Items In The Mink Mutation Situation

Number Of Items Sold		Number Of Situations	Per Cent Of Total Experience	Corresponding Probability
Total		40	100	1.0
Sold	1	4	10	0.1
	2	16	40	0.4
	3	20	50	0.5

are then summed to get the average or expected payoff for each
of the alternative buying decisions (Figure 9-2).

By exactly the same process, we can apply these same
probabilities to the payoff matrix of Table 9-1, but the calculations can be visualized more easily. For example, if George
decided to buy only 1 stole and his subsequent sales demand
was also for only 1 stole, then his gain would be $4500. But the
past experience summarized in Table 9-2 indicates that he can
expect a demand for only 1 just once in 10 times. In 4 out of
10 times, he can expect 2 customers to be ready to buy. Under
these conditions, he will be out of stock when the second customer comes in and suffer an opportunity loss of $4500, off-
setting a gain of the same amount on the first sale and thus
breaking even on the decision to buy only 1 stole. Furthermore,
half the time (probability 0.5) he estimates that he would be
able to sell 3 stoles if he had them in stock, and the buy-only-1
decision would cost him an additional opportunity loss of $4500,
for a net loss value for the decision of the same amount. To
estimate the most likely effect of the decision to "buy 1" he
must weight each of these possible outcomes by the estimated
chance it will happen (payoff x probability). The algebraic sum
of these three computations represents what the longrun effect
of a series of similar conservative decisions would be. Table
9-3 summarizes the profit positions (expected profits) for each
of the three possible decisions.

From this it would appear that "buy 2" is indeed a profitable decision, but that "buy 3" is much better. If his

FIGURE 9-2. Profit positions of the Decision Paths in the Smilson Mink Stole Case

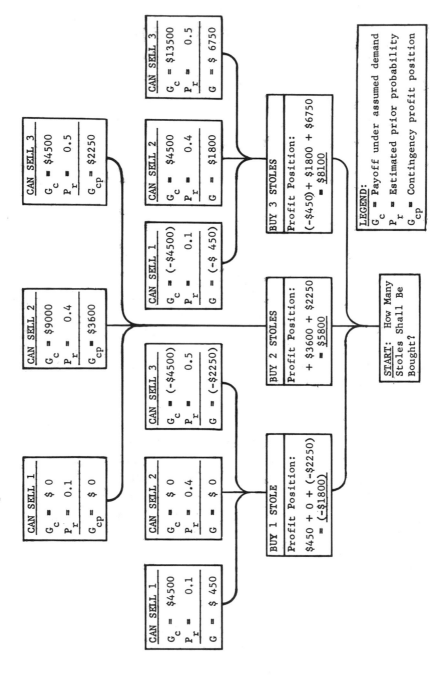

| CAN SELL 1 |
| G_c = $4500 |
| P_r = 0.1 |
| G = $ 450 |

| CAN SELL 1 |
| G_c = $ 0 |
| P_r = 0.1 |
| G_{cp} = $ 0 |

| CAN SELL 2 |
| G_c = $9000 |
| P_r = 0.4 |
| G_{cp} = $3600 |

| CAN SELL 3 |
| G_c = $4500 |
| P_r = 0.5 |
| G_{cp} = $2250 |

| CAN SELL 2 |
| G_c = $ 0 |
| P_r = 0.4 |
| G = $ 0 |

| CAN SELL 3 |
| G_c = (-$4500) |
| P_r = 0.5 |
| G = (-$2250) |

| CAN SELL 1 |
| G_c = (-$4500) |
| P_r = 0.1 |
| G = (-$ 450) |

| CAN SELL 2 |
| G_c = $4500 |
| P_r = 0.4 |
| G = $1800 |

| CAN SELL 3 |
| G_c = $13500 |
| P_r = 0.5 |
| G = $ 6750 |

| BUY 1 STOLE |
| Profit Position: |
| $450 + 0 + (-$2250) |
| = (-$1800) |

| BUY 2 STOLES |
| Profit Position: |
| + $3600 + $2250 |
| = $5800 |

| BUY 3 STOLES |
| Profit Position: |
| (-$450) + $1800 + $6750 |
| = $8100 |

| START: How Many Stoles Shall Be Bought? |

| LEGEND: |
| G_c = Payoff under assumed demand |
| P_r = Estimated prior probability |
| G_{cp} = Contingency profit position |

222

TABLE 9-3. Profit Position Calculations And Summary,
Mutation Mink Purchase Decision

A. Calculations:

Deci-sion	Demand Contin-gency, Could Sell:	Net Payoff Under Assumed Demand G_c	Estimate Of Prior Proba-bility Of Demand Level P_r	Contingent Profit Position $G_{cp}=G_c \times P_r$
Buy 1 stole	1 stole	$ 4500	0.1	$ 450
	2 stoles	0	0.4	0
	3 stoles	(–4500)	0.5	(–2250)
Total				(–1800)
Buy 2 stoles	1 stole	0	0.1	0
	2 stoles	9000	0.4	3600
	3 stoles	4500	0.5	2250
Total				5850
Buy 3 stoles	1 stole	(–4500)	0.1	(– 450)
	2 stoles	4500	0.4	1800
	3 stoles	13500	0.5	6750
Total				8100

B. Summary Profit Position Matrix:

Number Of Stoles Bought	Profit Position Assuming That The Demand Will Be For			Total Profit Position For The Decision
	1 stole	2 stoles	3 stoles	
1	$ 450	$ 0	(–$2250)	(–$1800)
2	0	3600	2250	5850
3	(–450)	1800	6750	8100

estimates of probabilities and overstock costs are correct, his department profit will be better in the long run if he consistently bases his decisions of this type of analysis. But the long run expectation does not protect him from making the wrong decision in the situation immediately before him. Unfortunately, if he does buy 3 stoles, he could still sell only one and sustain a real net loss of $4500. For this reason he certainly would like to have some reading on customer preference for this particular mutation shade so as to narrow the risk in both directions--from possible overstocks and from opportunity losses incurred by an out-of-stock condition. For such an exotic item with such limited demand, it is doubtful if any research could help him much. But there are many instances where data can be gathered about the situation at hand and incorporated into the analysis. The procedure for making use of such supporting data employs Bayes Theorem.

SMALL SAMPLES TO IMPROVE PROBABILITY ESTIMATES

The economy in the collection of new information which Bayes Theorem makes possible can be illustrated by a typical production scheduling problem facing the production manager of Eastern Corporation who is set to start up a new production line for transistors. The layout includes provision for automatic testing of all completed product coming off the line, but if the percentage of defectives is high, other checks will be instituted earlier in the process to lower the percentage of poor product and to assist in pinpointing the causes. Such interim testing entails a substantial expense, however, and is resorted to only in the case of proven necessity. On the other hand, omitting it also involves risking delay in discovery of a higher than acceptable defect rate and thus in tracing its causes. The resulting scrap loss could be a substantial cost also. Since this is a new and untried production line, he has to base his decision on experience with prior production of other similar transistor types. Checking the extensive records of the Quality Control Department, he secures the following information thought to be applicable:

| Process Defective Level | | Portion Of |
Group	Proportion defective	Past Production
A_1	.005	.30
A_2	.01	.30
A_3	.02	.20
A_4	.03	.13
A_5	.04	.06
A_6	.05	.01

This information is reasonably reassuring; since it indicates that if it is a good basis for estimate, he has an 80% chance that the rate of defectives will be less than 3% (.03), the level at which he would institute the additional inspections immediately. Even were the rate as high as .02, he would simply keep a close watch on the line initially in order to detect quickly any tendency toward an increase in the defective rate. However, he would prefer not to risk omission of the additional inspection if the probability of the .03 defect rate should really be estimated to be as high as the indicated 20%, and so he seeks a little information about the probability of the defect rate on this particular new production line. The PM therefore requests that a sample of 20 be taken and the test result reported as soon as it is felt that the line is "running." This done, it was found that none of the 20 samples were defective.

The PM now has two sets of information--a probability distribution of defects in a set of production processes (A_1, A_2, . . . A_6) which he believes are similar to the new and untried one, and a single event indicating 0 defects in a run of 20 transistors in the new process, an event we shall designate as B for convenience. He does not know the probability of B (the probability that any run of 20 in the new process will have no defects), but he can estimate a new or posterior probability distribution by the use of Bayes Theorem, a formula which permits the calculation of the conditional probability Pr (A/B), which means the probability of the prior probability, A, given the new event or information B. The Theorem is stated in set notation, in which the expression Pr ($A_1 \cap B$) is shorthand to mean "the probability that A and B will both occur," that is, in this case, the probability of obtaining an observation of 0 defective in a lot of 20 whose process level defective is A_1.

Bayes Theorem would give us a new posterior probability distribution of six items--$\Pr(A_1/B)$, $\Pr(A_2/B)$, ... $\Pr(A_6/B)$ --according to the following formula for $\Pr(A_1/B)$:

$$\Pr(A_1/B) = \frac{\Pr(A_1 \cap B)}{\Pr(A_1 \cap B) + \Pr(A_2 \cap B) + \ldots \ldots \Pr(A_6 \cap B)}$$

By means of 5 other similar calculations--from $\Pr(A_2/B)$ through $\Pr(A_6/B)$ --the PM will have his new, posterior probability distribution providing an amended estimate of the probable defect level in the new process. To make the estimate, the PM must have someone make four basic calculations for each of the six values $\Pr(A_i)$ in his prior probability distribution, illustrated below for the one value, $\Pr(A_1)$:

(1) The probability $\Pr(B/A_1)$, the probability that if A_1 were the true process experience, he would have obtained 0 defects in a lot of 20. Since the probability of a single defect occurring was actually .005 for process A_1, the probability any given part would be perfect is the complement of this, or .995. From the usual rule for the repetition of any event, the probability of getting 20 perfect transistors in a row in process A_1 would then be $(.995)^{20}$, or approximately .905, calculated to the third significant figure, similarly for the other five values of $\Pr(B/A_1)$.

(2) The combined probability $\Pr(A_1 \cap B)$, the probability that both the process A_1 is the true experience to be expected and that 0 defects would occur in a lot of 20. This is obtained by multiplying the prior estimate of probability, $\Pr(A_1)$, which is .30, by $\Pr(B/A_1)$, which is .905, as shown above. This multiplication, $(.905) \cdot (.3)$ gives us .272.

(3) The sum of the six values of $\Pr(A_i)$ $\Pr(B/A_i)$ as obtained by five additional calculations similar to the two steps above, for each of the values A_2 through A_6, giving us a total estimate of $\Pr(B)$, which is .753, as shown in Table 9-3.

(4) The dividend $\frac{\Pr(A_1 \cap B)}{.753}$, which is $\frac{.272}{.753} = .6$, the posterior probability estimate that our defect rate

will be that of process A_1, or .005.

Table 9-4 outlines the complete calculation the PM has had someone do for him, giving him a new estimate of his probability distribution in the last column. Inspecting it, the PM finds that his posterior probability estimate of a really bad lot (4 to 5% defective) is now only 4% instead of the 7% estimated before he took his new sample, and his estimate of a defect rate of 3% or more has been reduced from 20% to 13% by use of the new information. He decides that this is an acceptable risk, and to start up the line on the assumption that the defect rate will actually be 2% or less. He orders inspection for the end of the line only, with instruction to watch the results very closely--just in case.

However, the objectivist statistician from the Quality Control Group, who carried out the calculations, protests. "How much information did you expect to get from a sample of merely 20?" The production manager admits that 20 is a pretty small sample, but points out that by using the informa - tion from prior processes and the Bayes Theorem, the new information did reduce his estimate of a high defect rate sub- stantially. The statistician, however, does not like the use of information from these previous processes. They do not meet his standard of homogeneity, and he feels the estimate of prob- ability rests on the sample of 20 only. On the basis of his reasoning, there is nearly a 1 in 10 chance that the defect rate will be as high as 10%. The PM, however, feels that the ex- perience from these previous processes is valid information, although he concedes that he probably should use a slightly larger sample the next time in order to narrow still his pos- terior probability distribution. At least, he is going to base his sample size on an initial calculation as to the effect and value of added information.

Just how useful Bayes Theorem can be in estimating the value of added information before getting it can be seen in the case of Jim Walmer, the fashion buyer for Rural Mail Order, who has the problem of estimating the demand for each of 6 dresses he is stocking in his $19.98 line for the coming season.

HOW MUCH IS ADDITIONAL INFORMATION WORTH?

Jim has the complex problem of estimating in detail the demand for each size, each dress, and for each line of better

TABLE 9-4. Calculation Of New Estimate Of Probability Of Defectives In New Process To Be Used By Eastern Corporation

Process Defect Level Group	Proportion Defective	Prior Probability Estimate $Pr(A_i)$	Probability of 0 Defects Given This Estimate $Pr(B/A_i)$	Probability That Original Estimate Is Correct & That Defects Would Be 0 $Pr(A_i \cap B)^* = Pr(A_i) \cdot Pr(B/A_i)$	New Estimate, Given This Initial Information Posterior Probability, ** $Pr(A_i \cap B)/PR(B)$
A_1	.005	.30	$(.995)^{20}$ .905	$(.905)(.3) = .272$	$.272/.753 = .36$
A_2	.01	.30	$(.99)^{20}$ .818	$(.818)(.3) = .245$	$.245/.753 = .33$
A_3	.02	.20	$(.98)^{20}$ .668	$(.668)(.2) = .134$	$.134/.753 = .18$
A_4	.03	.13	$(.97)^{20}$ .544	$(.544)(.13) = .071$	$.071/.753 = .09$
A_5	.04	.06	$(.96)^{20}$ .442	$(.442)(.06) = .027$	$.027/.753 = .035$
A_6	.05	.01	$(.95)^{20}$ .358	$(.358)(.01) = .004$	$.004/.753 = .005$
				$Pr(B) = .753$	Total $= 1.00$

*$Pr(A_i \cap B)$ = the probability of observing 0 defects AND having the observation come from a lot whose process defective level was A_i.

**$Pr(A_1/B) = \dfrac{Pr(A_1 \cap B)}{Pr(A_1 \cap B) + Pr(A_2 \cap B) + \ldots + Pr(A_6 \cap B)} = \dfrac{Pr(A_1 \cap B)}{Pr(B)}$ = the probability that the lot proportion defective is A_1, given that a particular sampling result is B.

228

dresses sold in volume by Rural Mail Order. The estimate for the proportion of each size to order is not difficult because past experience can be relied on to be reasonably well duplicated, although there has been a trend toward the larger sizes over the last decade. The proportion of orders received for each of the price lines has also proved reasonably stable. But total sales have varied from season to season, and the proportion sold of each dress in any given line has fluctuated widely from one season to the next. He needs a reasonably good forecast of the relative demand for each individual number: for example, dress 3293 in the 6-dress $19.98 line. Jim's estimating problem is both simpler and more complex than that of George Smilson and his mutation mink stoles. It is simpler in that he buys--is in fact permitted to buy--only one-fourth of his total season's estimated requirements in advance, and then will make rebuys on the basis of initial sales. He thus has considerable latitude for error in his original estimate of demand-- a situation typical of most business decisions. If his estimate is no more than 4 times too large, he can work off the excess initial purchase before the end of the season. Anything beyond that, of course, has to be jobbed off at a loss, usually for less than half his initial purchase cost. He has some latitude on the underestimate side, too, but not nearly as much, because any reorder during his six-month season takes 6 weeks to fill. He can back order out-of-stock items, but house policy does not permit a back order period of more than 10 days. He can estimate sales of the total line fairly well in advance. In making his estimate of sales of 7500 for the line of six $19.98 dresses, he feels quite sure that, depending on general economic conditions, the total will not be less than 6000 or more than 9000.

But Jim's problem is complicated by the fact that the popularity of the 6 dresses in the line is interdependent: a heavy demand for any 1 number is at the expense of the demand for each of the other 5. On occasion, 1 or 2 of the numbers catalogued prove to be more than ordinarily popular. There have been times when a full half of the orders for the line have concentrated on a single number, with the result that 1 or 2 of the other numbers in the line had sold as few as 3 percent of the total. In those circumstances he sustained substantial end-of-season jobbing losses for unsold dresses of about $6.50 each plus excess inventory-carrying costs of $.50, a full loss of $7.00 for each dress in overstock. In the event of understocks, he has a direct out-of-pocket cost of $1.00 for the handling of any cancelled orders, plus the opportunity loss of the $5.00 profit he would have made on each one, for a total missed sale loss of $6.00.

Jim's real decision concerns the distribution of orders among the 6 dresses within the line, since his total order is limited by the 25% rule and his forecast for the line. To summarize his present knowledge:

For the total line:
    Projected sales:
        Minimum, 6000   Maximum, 9000
    Permissible initial order for
    the line:
        Minimum, $6000/4 = 1500$ Maximum, $9000/4 = 2500$

For the single style, #3923:
    Permissible initial order if allocated equally among all 6 styles:
        Minimum, $1500/6 = 250$ Maximum: $2250/6 = 375$

Knowledge of the extremes of demand for a single style:

Minimum, 3% of the sales of the entire line. Would indicate a total demand of only 180 in a 6000-dress season ($.03 \times 6000 = 180$) and an initial order of $180/4 = 45$, in the poorest season.

Maximum, 50% of the sales of the line. Would indicate a total demand of $.50 \times 6600 = 3000$, and a minimum initial order of $3000/4 = 750$ in the poorest season, or a possible $.50 \times 9000 \times 1/4 = 1125$ if the season turns out to be one of the best.

Jim's range of choice between an initial order of 45 for the single style 3923 and 1125 is pretty wide, so he does some more figuring. He considers the range of various order choice and sales combinations for this one number, and gets the results shown in Table 9-5. By defining a period in which 25% of the customer orders are received and matching it with his initial order period, Jim can calculate losses from overstocks or understocks which would be incurred for various initial order/sales combinations, as in Table 9-6. When the initial

230

TABLE 9-5. Net Actual Profits On Sales Made. For Each Possible Sales Level And Each Initial Order Quantity. In The Period Before The Receipt Of The First Possible Reorder.

Number of Dresses Ordered	Profits On Sales If The Initial Orders Received Total:						
	50	100	200	400	600	800	1100
50	$250	$250	$250	$250	$250	$250	$250
100	250	500	500	500	500	500	500
200	250	500	1000	1000	1000	1000	1000
400	250	500	1000	2000	2000	2000	2000
600	250	500	1000	2000	3000	3000	3000
800	250	500	1000	2000	3000	4000	4000
1100	250	500	1000	2000	3000	4000	5500

TABLE 9-6. Losses Incurred By Unintended Overstocks And Through Stock Shortages As A Result Of Various Initial Order Quantities On Dress 3923.

Initial Order Quantity (1/4 Of Season Estimate)	Seasonal Losses On Sales If Customers' Initial Orders Received Total:						
	50	100	200	400	600	800	1100
50	$ 0	$300	$900	$2100	$3300	$4500	$6300
100	*	0	600	1800	3000	4200	6000
200	*	*	0	1200	2400	3600	5400
400	1400	*	*	0	1200	2400	4200
600	2800	1400	*	*	0	1200	3000
800	4200	2800	*	*	*	0	1800
1100	6300	4900	2100	*	*	*	0

* Initial order will be in excess of enough for the initial period, but will be sold during the season.

TABLE 9-7. Net Contingency Payoff For The Initial Decision
For Each Act-event Combination, Purchase
Decision On Dress No. 3923.

Initial Order Quantity (1/4 Of Estimated Sales)	50	100	200	400	600	800	1100
50	$250	-$50	-$650	-$1850	-$3050	-$4250	-$6050
100	250	500	-100	-1300	-2500	-3700	-5500
200	250	500	1000	-200	-1400	-2600	-4400
400	-1150	500	1000	2000	800	-400	-2200
600	-2550	-900	1000	2000	3000	1800	0
800	-3950	-2300	1000	2000	4000	4000	2200
1100	-6050	-4400	-1100	2000	3000	4000	5500

profits indicated in Table 9-5 are combined with the losses
indicated by Table 9-6, Jim arrives at the contingent payoff
matrix of Table 9-7 for the various combinations of initial
sales and orders. In order to estimate the profit position for
each decision quantity alternative, Jim needs a probability distribution of the various estimates of initial customer demand.
He reviews his experience over the past several years and
decides that, since style changes are no more radical than for
any of the past 5 years, he can use the distribution of relative
demand in the line for 60 similar types of dresses which have
been sold over this period, as shown in Table 9-8.

Jim can now estimate his profit position for each of the
decision quantity alternatives by weighting each contingency
payoff as shown in Table 9-7 by the probability of its occurrence, as estimated in Table 9-8, multiplying each column in
Table 9-7 by the appropriate value of P_i as estimated in Table
9-8. This yields an estimate of the average profit position for
each alternative order decision as shown in Table 9-9.

Using the information available to him, Table 9-9 would
indicate that Jim should purchase between 600 and 800 dresses
for his initial order of 3923, provided the sales behave as have
the average of similar styles in the past 5 years. But it gives
him no assurance that 3923, or any of the other 5 numbers in
the line, will have average sales experience. Furthermore,

232

TABLE 9-8. Estimated Probability Distribution Of Demand Per Number In The 6-Dress $19.98 Line, Based On Experience In The Last 5 Years

Total Seasonal Sales (Number of Dresses)	Average Sales Model	Corresponding Initial Period Order (Approx. 25% of Average)	Number Of Models	Per Cent Of Models	P_i (Probability)
180–199	190	50	3	5	.05
200–599	400	100	9	15	.15
600–999	800	200	15	25	.25
1000–2199	1600	400	15	25	.25
2200–2500	2400	600	10	17	.17
2600–3799	3200	800	7	12	.12
3800–3799	4500	1100	1	2	.02

TABLE 9-9. Profit Position Values For Each Act-Event Combination In The Purchase Decision On Dress 3923.

Jim's Initial Order Quantity	Profit Positions Of The Sales Returns If Customers' Initial Period Orders Are For:							Net Profit Position For All Sales Possibilities
	50	100	200	400	600	800	100	
$P_i =$	.015	.15	.25	.25	.17	.12	.02	
50	$ 12.5	$ -7.5	$-162.5	$-462.5	$-518.5	$-510.5	$-121.0	$-1769.5
100	12.5	75.0	-25.0	-325.0	-425.0	-444.0	-110.0	-1241.5
200	12.5	75.0	250.0	-50.0	-238.0	-312.0	-88.0	-350.5
400	-57.5	75.0	250.0	500.0	136.0	-48.0	-44.0	811.5
600	-127.5	-135.0	250.0	500.0	510.0	216.0	.0	1213.5
800	-197.5	-345.0	250.0	500.0	510.0	480.0	44.0	1241.5
1100	-302.5	-660.0	-275.0	500.0	510.0	480.0	110.0	362.5

with no more information than is available to him, he must estimate the sales of all the numbers as equal. An initial purchase of 600 to 800 each would greatly exceed his maximum allowable initial order quantity of each. (600 x 6 = 3600, 800 x 6 = 4800). The potential demand for one of the 6 styles may well justify an order of this magnitude, but if so, he does not know which of the 6, and the potential for the full line definitely would not justify 6 such orders. Reviewing the frequency distribution, Jim can note that 30% of the styles had initial sales of 600 or more, but that 20% had sales of 100 or less, and the popularity of styles within the line, as noted in the beginning, is interdependent. What Jim needs is some indication of the probable popularity of each style within his current line, and past experience cannot give this to him. As did the Production Manager of Eastern, he feels he needs added information which applies to his current situation, but he cannot get it as simply as did the PM. Whatever he collects will cost substantially, and he needs to weigh carefully the kinds of information he will seek and its value to him.

Jim reasons that the variations in his past sales, and thus in his present estimates, stemmed from two major sources: the effects of general economic affairs, and the relative attractiveness of each style as perceived by his regular customers. His estimating and planning ability would benefit by improved estimates concerning either. Which information would be the more valuable? While the influences of economic conditions and tastes are thoroughly mixed together and confounded, Jim reasons that the economic factors affect primarily the overall level of dress sales and that relative attractiveness is responsible for most of the variation in sales of individual numbers in each line, as measured in Table 9-9. The fluctuation in overall sales is between 6000 and 9000, a factor of about 1-1/2. By contrast, relative sales of individual numbers in the line have fluctuated between 3% and 50%, for a factor of nearly 17. It seems to him that style appeal is by far a more critical factor in his uncertainty than are economic conditions, and that it would be more valuable to try for information on relative appeal. So he approached the marketing research director to discuss with him the possibility of getting information about the relative demand within his current line of 6 dresses. The research director might well tell him something like the following:

"We can devise a small sample mailing to our customers that will cost you about $600 for this one line alone, if you can furnish us with advance copies of your catalog pages, just as they will appear in the catalog. From somewhat analogous tests we and others have run, we feel sure that sampling variation in cultural matters of taste such as fashion is minimal, so we will not need a very big sample so long as we know that our respondents are our own customers, drawn from our own files. A questionnaire return of 200 should be enough.

"But we can expect some considerable bias in the answers, whatever technique we use to obtain them. The expressed preferences will have some tendency to favor somewhat conservative styles. That is, acceptable models which lag slightly behind the coming style trend will test out a little more popular, relatively, than they will be during the coming buying season. Likewise, styles which are in the vanguard of the coming trend will prove slightly less popular in the survey than they will be a few weeks later at the time of buying. The differences will not be great, but you will have to exercise some judgment in using the answers. On the other hand, we have always found in any study of this sort that an item earning a really low preference rating (which gets, for example only 6% of the choices in a line of 6 dresses) will be a dog and sales will not exceed the sample rating.

"Your problem will be in judging the accuracy of the high preference ratings. If dress 3923, for instance, should obtain a relative preference rating of 30%, and 3923 proves to be conservative in relation to the developing style trend, it will sell well, but may not get more than 20% of the volume of the entire line. If it proves to be right in the groove of the developing trend, however, it may actually garner 40% of the demand for your $19.98 line. There may also be some appreciable variation between ratings and sales for those with moderately good ratings--say those in the range between 10% and 20% of a 6-dress line--but the variation will not exceed the adjustments you automatically make when placing your reorders, within permissible back ordering policy."

Should Jim order the survey, at a cost of $600 for this one line alone? Let us look at what the new information could do to the two sides of the payoff table, and the net result, assuming Jim decides to order purely on the basis of the survey results without adjustment on the basis of his own expert knowledge of style trends, using his original estimate of total sales of 7500 for the line, and assuming the total could vary between 6000 and 9000.

First, sales in the two low brackets in our table can be predicted as certainties, if we interpret the research director correctly. A preference rating of 6% of the line translates into a seasonal sales estimate of 450, and an initial order period coverage of just over 100 dresses. Allowing for the economic forecast variation, this works out to a range of 90 to 135 dresses for the initial period, or quantities well within the buyer's ability to adjust. There should be no lost sales costs, since the research director has indicated that sales would not exceed the forecast percentage, and the 25% rule would prevent any overordering.

Similarly, preferences in the middle range would provide perfect information within the procedures open to the buyer--preferences up to 20%, or a total season demand of 1500, for example, on all of the brackets for initial orders up to 400. However, for this group, a surge of better-than-average total demand due to better-than-expected consumer demand could result in some underages at the level of initial orders of 400 or more, and thus some opportunity losses in the 400, 600, and 800 decision columns.

Initial orders of 600 and 800, and of course, of 1100, also presume a very high relative demand, under the 25 percent rule. In each case, however, any overestimate could be absorbed in diminished reorder quantities, since the error has been indicated by the research director as no more than a 50 percent over-estimate. So the only possible losses for this group would be missed sales due to underestimate of both relative demand and economic influences together.

We can see in Table 9-10 that the loss function would be narrowed by this new information to the demand columns between 400 and 800 in the initial order period, and to a narrow diagonal band within this table. The loss table would include only missed-sale opportunities.

The research director gave Jim no probabilities for the possible variations, although he might be interpreted to have meant that the possible losses are less than .5 probable. But Jim can evaluate the value of the survey information by assuming minimum accuracy, comparing the expected values of Table 9-12 with the minimum profit made when using the survey, as shown in Table 9-11.

TABLE 9-10. Losses Possible Through Missed Sales As A
Result Of Inaccurate Economic Forecasts And
Biased Preference Ratings

Initial Order Quantity	Missed-Sales Losses If Initial Orders Are:			
	400	600	800	1100
400	0	$1200	*	*
600	0	0	$1200	$3000
800	*	0	0	$1800
1100	*	*	0	0

* Does not apply, since this combination is prevented by use
of survey information.

The net payoff table now becomes:

TABLE 9-11. Net Contingent Payoff For The Initial Purchase
Decision For Each Purchase-Actual-Sales
Combination, If Survey Is Followed

Initial Order Quantity	Net Initial Period Payoff On Sales If Orders Received Total						
	50	100	200	400	600	800	1100
50	$250	*	*	*	*	*	*
100	250	$500	*	*	*	*	*
200	*	*	$1000	*	*	*	*
400	*	*	*	$2000	$800	*	*
600	*	*	*	2000	3000	$1800	*
800	*	*	*	*	3000	4000	$2200
1100	*	*	*	*	*	4000	5500

* Not a possible act-event combination.

Since the $10,000 indicated savings applies to only one
dress in the line of 6, and there will be comparable savings
from use of the new information in ordering the other dresses
in the line. Jim would have difficulty, in this instance, in
finding a better investment for his funds.

TABLE 9-12. Pessimistic Evaluation Of Survey Worth,
Results For A Single Dress In The Line

Initial Order Quantity	Expected Value Without Survey	Minimum Profit Using Survey	Survey Contribution To Expected Profit
50	-$1769.5	$250	$2019.5
100	-1241.5	250	1491.5
200	-350.5	1000	1350.5
400	811.5	800	11.5
600	1213.5	1800	586.5
800	1241.5	2200	959.5
1100	362.5	4000	3637.5
		Total	$10,056.5

Jim is fortunate, of course, in being able to get useful
information at such a low cost, and in having knowledge of the
kind of information which would be most helpful. Often, however, we do not know exactly which information needs are most
crucial, nor can we always fill them when we do know. Sensitivity analysis is a simple method for pinpointing our needs,
and determining how critical the assumptions we are making
about some of the parameters in our decision.

SENSITIVITY ANALYSIS: PINPOINTING THE CRUCIAL
DECISION FACTORS

Not every decision situation permits the collection of
added information relevant to the choices to be made. Whether
or not such information can be obtained we can learn, through
sensitivity analysis, which of our assumptions and which information needs are most critical to our proper choice. We
must still start out by carefully translating the inescapable
judgments we make into the quantitative statement of a probability distribution. But once we have thus expressed our
prior information in quantitative form, we may vary the values
assigned to the prior distribution and observe the effect on our
average profit position and optimal decision. By this means

we obtain a measure of how much the best decision depends on the assumptions we are making about the values in this prior distribution.

Suppose we, as part of the Frantic Machine Works management team faced with a strike, have to decide whether to settle for the 25-cent-per-hour package the union is asking for, or let the men strike in the belief that we can thus get a better settlement. We have no way of taking a strike settlement "sample" of any sort, but we think we know everything any opinion poll could tell us about the temper of the men and about the politics inside the union. We believe we are as well in touch with worker sentiment as anyone ever is, and as a result of years of dealing with this union and its leadership we think we have a pretty good idea of the probabilities in the situation. We also have reason to feel that the estimated added cost of the 25¢ package, $1 million per year, will put us in an awkward competitive position.

We are convinced that the workers could be induced to settle for a 15¢ package after a relatively short strike, probably 4 to 5 weeks, possibly as short as 1 week, maybe as long as 8 weeks. We also believe that we could get a settlement for a 12-1/2¢ package if we let the strike go twice as long--our best estimate is 9 to 10 weeks. Because of our precarious market position, we feel we ought to rule out the 25¢ package with its $1 million cost and seriously consider taking a strike to get the 15¢ package (estimated cost $600 thousand, estimated savings in comparison with the 25¢ settlement, $400 thousand) or the 12-1/2¢ package (estimated cost $500 thousand, estimated savings $500 thousand). The strike itself, of course, will involve substantial costs offsetting some of the savings: $50 thousand per week in plant maintenance costs and lost markets. Also, we cannot be certain of the exact length of the strike in either case. Table 9-13 lists our best estimates of the probability distributions of each of the two packages, in the columns labelled $\underline{W}_{15}$ and $\underline{W}_{12.5}$, respectively.

These calculations--cost times the probability of incurring them--gives us an expected or average cost of $245 thousand for the 15¢ package and $475 thousand for the 12-1/2¢ package. When these are offset against the estimated savings, we obtain an expected profit position of $400 thousand less $245 thousand, or $155 thousand for the 15¢ package, and $500 thousand less $475 thousand, or $25 thousand for the 12-1/2¢

240

package. If we have sized up the temper of the men correctly, only the 15¢ package is worth trying for. We also note that a strike of 8 weeks duration for the 15¢ package would leave us no better off than an immediate settlement for 25¢ (cost of 8 weeks, $400 thousand, savings on 15¢ package, $400 thousand). Clearly, we should check carefully our assumptions about the temper of the men.

TABLE 9-13.   Original Estimates Of The Expected Costs Of Taking A Strike For A 15¢ Package, And Of Taking One For A 12-1/2¢ Package

If Settled At End Of Week	Total Cost	Probability Of Settlement For 15¢: $\underline{W}_{15}$	$\underline{K} \times \underline{W}_{15}$	Probability Of Settlement For 12.5¢: $\underline{W}_{12.5}$	$\underline{K} \times \underline{W}_{12.5}$
	($000)		($000)		($000)
1	50	.05	2.5	--	--
2	100	.10	19	--	--
3	150	.15	22.5	--	--
4	200	.20	40	--	--
5	250	.20	50	--	--
6	300	.15	45	.05	15
7	350	.10	35	.10	35
8	400	.05	20	.15	60
9	450	--	--	.20	90
10	500	--	--	.20	100
11	500	--	--	.15	82.5
12	600	--	--	.10	60
13	650	--	--	.05	32.5
Total expected cost			245		475

But first, what is the significance of this profit position value of $155 thousand? It is the long run average of a series of similar decisions, our best estimate of what might happen averaged over all similar likely events. Only by rare coincidence will this be the actual net effect of this particular strike, even if our cost and loss estimates are accurate, which is not likely. In addition, there is no long run of strikes--every one is different. Nor have we in any sense a prediction of the duration of the strike. We have only a means of ferreting out and analyzing the quantitative implications of all we think we foresee about the possibilities in the situation in order to be able to weigh the policy alternatives--to settle immediately, or to take a strike to force one of two alternate packages we think we might get, assuming we have judged the temper of the men correctly.

How sensitive is our calculation to this particular probability distribution as to the length of the strike? We can find out by using a series of other, less favorable probabilities as to the duration of the strike. (We might also do the same thing with our assumptions about strike costs.) Table 9-14 makes the calculation for one such set: the estimate that the strike will last at least 5 weeks before we can settle for 15¢, and would end not later than the 12th week. This calculation yields a profit position of minus $25 thousand ($400 thousand less $425 thousand), worse than if we settled immediately for the 25¢ package. Thus our position and our optimal decision are very sensitive to our assumptions about the length of the strike. We must be very confident of our probability distribution on the duration of this strike, and in particular of the assumption it will not last longer than 8 weeks.

USES AND LIMITATIONS OF SUBJECTIVE PROBABILITY

It should be clear from all of the above that the principal use and purpose of subjective probability analysis is more than just prediction, which concerns objective probability. The individual event on which one focuses never, in actuality, has a fractional probability: it either is going to take place, with a probability of 1, or it will not, for a probability of 0. The additional uncertainty, (which is what subjective probability estimates), the imprecision it attempts to evaluate, is our foreknowledge of the given event, our degree of belief in its outcome. However imprecise that foreknowledge, we must nevertheless make a relatively precise commitment of resources to whatever action we decide upon, and we need some

TABLE 9-14. Expected Cost Of A Strike Lasting From 5 to 12 Weeks

If Settled At End Of Week Number	Total Cost K ($000)	Probability Of Settlement W	K x W ($000)
5	250	.05	12.5
6	300	.10	30
7	350	.15	52.5
8	400	.20	80
9	450	.20	90
10	500	.15	75
11	550	.10	55
12	600	.05	30
	Total expected cost		425

rational method of evaluating the worth of that commitment. Neo-Bayesian analysis forces us to analyze the quantitative significance of every kind of knowledge we bring to bear on the decision. It seeks to force all of this knowledge, plus all of our assumptions, out into the open and to make us put a hard quantitative tag on each bit rather than falling back on vague and sometimes unconscious formulations. The quantitative results are simply a means of comparison, not a set of predictions, and are, in fact, not likely to coincide with reality. The value of the process is in proportion to the care and thought which goes into the effort to arrive at the quantitative statement and the subsequent analysis. Because once we have taken the initial quantifying step, we can and must proceed to apply careful logical analysis of these probabilities to the alternatives we face and find their implications in the light of the judgments we have made. In the process of the analysis, we can learn how important to our choice each of the assumptions made, and each of the bits of information fed into the calculations, are, pinpointing those assumptions and types of knowledge most crucial to correct decision.

No analysis can be any better than the information on which it is based. Faulty judgments about the relevance of information or incorrect assumptions about the relationships involved can only lead to inaccurate conclusions. But if we do a careful job, we have available a number of formal analytical tools to carry out the rest of the job.

The rather simplified examples we have given so far depict relatively common types of business situations which are often decided reasonably well without recourse to computations such as those indicated (although the latter might well lead to more efficient decisions at times). Even for such situations, formal use of the types of calculations illustrated can probably give substance to experience by creating a record of the judgments made, and their subsequent accuracy. However, many of the uncertainties faced in the complicated and dynamic modern business world contain more dimensions than do these simple illustrations, and the executive who can make really rational choices in such cases without use of subjective probability analysis is exceptional. The next chapter outlines four Bayesian decision models capable of handling complex situations.

SUMMARY

1. Neo-Bayesian statistics is designed to make use of subjective, or personal, probabilities: the personal conviction of the likelihood of unique events in the kind of real world situations in which all observable influences cannot be eliminated. Any such personal probability is a statement of opinion as to the likelihood of an individual event, subject to change with the addition of new information. It is an informed judgment, based on analogous experience, of the type every decision maker has to rely on in cases of true uncertainty.

2. The five central concepts of the Bayesian approach are the payoff table, the probability distribution of a random variable, profit position, opportunity loss, and conditional probability.

    a. The payoff table lists the estimated values for each possible act-event combination.

    b. A random variable is any event which may be the outcome of a given action, subject to some estimated probability distribution of its value.

c. The profit position of any one act-event combination is estimated by multiplying the payoff profit from that combination by its estimated probability.

d. Opportunity losses are those profits that are missed as a result of that particular act-event combination.

e. The conditional probability of a compound event refers to the probability of a specific event, given the occurrence of some other event about which we are able to obtain sample information.

3. The Bayesian approach aims at sharpening our basis for judgment about the likelihood of different outcomes foreseen as possible, and thus assumes that the events flowing from any action can be viewed as variable--that is, can be viewed as uncertain.

4. For the Bayesian, a sample is not simply a measure of some characteristic of the universe, but is additional information against which to evaluate the prior probability distribution of this characteristic which had been arrived at on some judgment basis.

5. The calculations help us to appraise the profit position value of each possible alternative decision and thus furnish a solid basis for judging the value to us of added information that would narrow the range of the prior probability distribution.

6. Even when the situation is such as to preclude collection of new information, sensitivity analysis helps us make full use of subjective judgments about our expectations and facilitates the pinpointing of those factors most crucial to an accurate estimate of the outcome and thus in need of the most careful consideration.

GLOSSARY OF BAYESIAN STATISTICAL TERMS

BAYES: refers to the Rev. Thomas Bayes, an 18th century clergyman who formulated Bayes' Theorem and Bayes' Postulate

BAYES POSTULATE: a personal prior probability estimate should be made in any uncertainty situation before seeking new information, even in the case of complete ignorance.

BAYES' THEOREM: an equation defining conditional probability:

$$P(A_1 / B) = \frac{P(A_1 \cap B)}{P(A_1 \cap B) + P(A_2 \cap B) + \ldots + P(A_i \cap B)}$$

This translates into the prose expression: The probability of event labeled A_1, given the knowledge that another event B has occurred, can be found as the ratio of the probability that both B and A_1 can occur jointly to the probability that B will occur jointly with all possible A_i events (that is, all of the possible variations of A in its prior probability distribution). A_1 might be the specific proportion of the season's sales--20%, for example. In this instance, B might then be a preseason survey preference of 20% among those surveyed.

Bayesian Statistics: The approach to evaluation and analysis of decision alternatives consisting of giving numerical value to the decision maker's personal judgment about the likelihood of possible decision outcomes, and of the payoffs associated with the possible outcomes attached to each act-event combination, then modifying this judgment on the basis of additional information collection if this is feasible.

PROBABILITY AND PROBABILITY DISTRIBUTION: in general, a probability is some statement of the relative likelihood of an event, expressed as a positive fractional value, a number between zero and 1 which represents the ratio of chances favoring the occurrence to the total of all chances for and against. A probability distribution is a statement of the probabilities of all of the expected outcomes of a given act. They must, therefore, add to 1, or certainty. Probabilities are classified as objective or subjective.

Objective probabilities are basically a prediction of the relative frequency with which an event will occur in a very long series of trials, as the number of trials approaches infinity. They are estimated on the basis of either a long history of trials under conditions believed to be the same, or a priori objective evidence of the structure of possibilities (the number of directions a rat has available for choice to move in a maze, and the like).

Subjective probabilities are expressed in the same kind of numbers, but they refer to the degree of belief the estimator has in the likelihood of a single event. Whoever makes the stimate may be using historical data in part, but even when he does, he will not insist that it be obtained from occurrences taking place under the identical conditions.

Conditional probability: the probability of A occurring, given the knowledge that the event B has already occurred. Pr(A/B)

Joint probability: the probability of events A and B occurring together. Pr(A ∩ B)

Personalistic probability: the same as subjective probability.

Posterior probability: the new estimate of probability arrived at on the basis of additional information; often the prior probability conditioned by an observed outcome.

Prior probability: the initial probability estimate made on the basis of whatever belief the decision maker has about the factors favoring a given decision outcome.

PROFIT AND LOSS, PAYOFF

Contingent profit: an estimate of the actual profit to be realized if a given decision outcome materializes.

Contingent opportunity loss: an opportunity loss itself is a profit which might have been made but was not because the decision made resulted in a loss of the opportunity to realize that profit. A contingent opportunity loss is an estimate of the opportunity loss realized because of a specific decision outcome.

Payoff matrix: a table of values of profits and losses under every decision alternative being considered and every outcome foreseen as possible.

Profit position of a decision: the actual profit which would be realized if the outcome is favorable, discounted by the degree of likelihood estimated for that particular outcome.

SENSITIVITY ANALYSIS: an estimate of the importance of precision of the major assumptions about a decision outcome, carried out by recalculating estimates of resulting profits and losses with different values attached to all important factors entering into the estimate.

VALUE OF INFORMATION: the total difference in the profit position values of the payoffs as estimated without the value of new information, and as they would be estimated given this additional information.

10

FOUR BAYESIAN DECISION MODELS

By far the best way to minimize emotional reactions and avoid confusion and personal conflicts which tend to interfere with the rational decision process is to translate the available knowledge, on which a decision has to be based, into numbers. Without the therapy of numbers, emotions can easily override sound judgment, to the detriment of success. The need for quantifying information and judgments becomes especially acute whenever the problem involves a chained series of decisions with different timing of outcomes. Numerical comparisons are also particularly useful when pricing is a critical factor. Any informed observer who has witnessed soul-searching price decisions can testify to the obvious fear which much too frequently deprives sellers of probable legitimate profit. Such is obviously the case in bid pricing situations, whether the bidder be buying or selling. (Any experienced auction fan can give many a story of outrageous bids.) Bayesian probabilities form the basis of four especially useful techniques (or "models") for placing relative values on proposed decision: (1) the sequential decision model, (2) competitive bidding strategy, (3) inventory, (4) production run and scrap loss.

As with many mathematical decision models, these last two have a wider applicability than the convenient labels given them seem to imply. The inventory model is useful in any situation in which a choice can lead to both underages and overages with costs proportional to size. Some production-scheduling situations have such characteristics as much as do most inventory situations. The production-run and scrap-loss model applies to any problem in which the costs of the overage are proportional to its size, but an underage of any size results in the same lump sum loss. In the case of some inventory decisions, this also applies (as when a delayed delivery of any size could result in the loss of a major customer, or the shortage of a part cause the loss of a production run).

SEQUENTIAL DECISION THEORY

Not infrequently, some of the alternatives open to us do not lead to some definite outcome, but to the probability that other sets of alternatives will have to be considered, some of which may in turn lead to a definite outcome, but others may lead to a need for further decisions before the final end can be seen.

It should be clear that in such a situation we need some way of calculating the values of the end result of all possible decision paths if our choice is to be a rational one. Let us consider a simplified example of such a situation. Suppose a man owns some land in the midst of a newly discovered oil field. A new value has now been added to this land; there is a possibility oil could be found under it, but not a certainty. He faces two choices immediately, if he desires to capitalize this new opportunity. He can sell a lease and get an immediate, certain profit. But the other alternative is to take some steps toward establishing the probability of oil, and even of drilling for himself. He can test for geological formation and, if the formation is favorable, sell the lease for a higher immediate return, or take a chance and drill. If he drills, he may find oil, for a greater return than the lease would have brought, or he may hit a dry hole and get nothing. In either case, the outcome is final. Let us look at Figure 10-1, a diagram of this sequence.

Which should the landowner do: sell the lease, test for formation, or drill? He has no means to arrive at a rational decision if this is the only information he has.

On the left hand side, he knows the payouts on the alternatives of selling the lease. But on the extreme right-hand path, the outcome of every decision has some degree of uncertainty. The test for formation may reveal a favorable formation, in which case the lease is worth more without going further, and the chance of getting oil if he himself drills is also better. But if the test is unfavorable, he has lost everything,

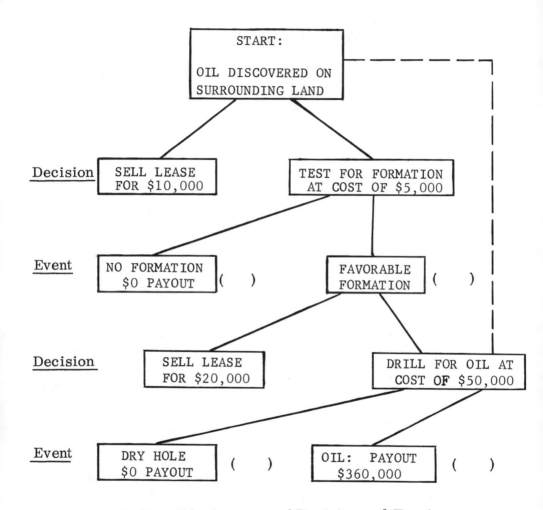

FIGURE 10-1. Possible Sequence of Decision and Event
Alternatives in an Oil Lease Situation

including the added cost of the test. If he does drill himself, he adds another cost for drilling, and he may again lose everything, or get a big payoff. To know whether to test or to drill, he must somehow estimate the probability of finding a favorable formation, and the added probability of striking oil if he does. He thus needs some estimate of associated probabilities to fill in the blank brackets shown on the diagram: the probabilities that a favorable formation will be found, and the probability that oil be struck if he does find formation.

He is not likely to find such information in any objective table. But he should have some data on which he can base a subjective estimate of both probabilities. If there has been any testing in the areas around him, he may be able to find out how these tests have come out and what percentage of the area, in each case, has shown favorable formation. If so, he can make some judgment as to the probability that a test on his land would reveal a favorable formation.

Let us suppose that he thinks these other tests indicate a 3 to 2 probability (p = . 6) that a test would reveal a favorable formation, and that if the test is favorable, the value of a lease rises to $20,000. If he has decided that his finances and other circumstances dictate selling the lease eventually, he can now estimate the value of testing, in comparison with a sale without a test, by discounting the $20,000 sale price by the uncertainty that the outcome would be favorable. Applying the discount (. 6 x $20,000), we find that the expected outcome is only $12,000. Thus a test would increase the payoff only $2,000, but would cost $5,000, and the position value of this alternative is only $7,000, or $3,000 (30 percent) less than the alternative to sell immediately.

Note that the actual payout would be either $15,000 ($20,000 - $5,000 = $15,000), which may happen 3 times in 5, or (-$5,000), which may happen 2 times in 5 when the formation is unfavorable. Since this is a one-time decision, as with most business matters, it will be one or the other; there is no averaging over several identical situations. But the $7,000 can be viewed as the average value of the test drill alternative if one imagines a series of decisions of similar nature, with similar information available and decided by similar rules. If a major oil operator were to make 100 such decisions--as he might well do--and we simplify by assuming that both payout values and costs would be the same in every case, he would receive $1,000,000 net if he sold all such leases before testing. But if he chose to test first in every case, he would incur a cost of $500,000 for a gross return of $1,200,000 (60 x $20,000), or a net of only $700,000.

Either before and after such a test, however, the landowner can decide to do the drilling himself, rather than sell the lease to someone else who would drill. Such a decision would commit him to a further cost of $50,000. Is this option worth the cost, even if he can afford the commitment? To find out, he must have some further information, and make some further judgments as to the probability of success. Since the initial decision arose because of oil strikes on surrounding property, it should be easy to find out how many struck paying quantities of oil. Assume that he finds that 1 out of 4 sunk into the favorable formation were paying wells, and that each such well had a capitalized value of $360,000. If only one or two wells have been drilled in the area, he may look for information on success in older fields that seem to have similar formations.

If our landowner had made a test, and it was favorable, the value of a decision to drill rather than lease may then be estimated as:

$$(.25 \times \$360,000) - \$50,000 = \$90,000 - \$50,000 = \$40,000$$

(The payout discounted for its uncertainty)   - (Cost of drilling)   (Position = value of the alternative to drill, after a favorable test)

Once the test has been made and a favorable formation found, the position value of the alternative to drill is thus worth twice the certain payout of $20,000 from the sale of the lease at that time. Working back to the initial situation, however, we must discount this position value by the risk of an unfavorable test, and the cost of the test itself:

$$(.6 \times \$40,000) - \$5,000 = \$24,000 - \$5,000 = \$19,000$$

With all due allowance for risks and costs, this alternative has a higher position value than the certain $10,000 to be received from the immediate sale of the lease before a test.

To get to this point, however, he spent $5,000 simply to get some information, information on whether the formation was favorable for the presence of oil. As we discovered already, this information was not worth $5,000 if the owner had decided to sell the lease anyway. Would it be worth $5,000 if the ultimate choice would be to drill? After all, the chance of finding formation seems to be better than even, anyway 3 to 5. In this case, the position value of the decision to drill immediately is determined by discounting the value of a well by the product of the two probabilities of finding formation, then of finding a well in a favorable formation, and subtracting the cost of drilling:

$$(.6 \times .25) \times \$360,000 - \$50,000 = .15 \times \$360,000 - \$50,000$$
$$= \$54,000 - \$50,000$$
$$= \$4,000$$

clearly less than the position value of the path test-then-drill information. The information gained from the test thus returns a value of $15,000 over its cost.

Note that in making these calculations, the sequence of calculations starts with the end point of a decision path, and works backward.

Figure 10-2 depicts graphically the three initial decision alternatives and the four decision paths which would result, together with costs and payouts. Comparing the four possible paths, we find that their position values are:

Path	Position Value (000)	Probability of Success
Sell lease right away	$10	1.0
Drill immediately	4	.15
Test—then sell lease	7	.6
Test—then drill if favorable	19	.15

Clearly, the position value of test-then-drill is highest of the alternative decision paths. Is this the decision the landowner should make? Not necessarily. At this point, he must weigh some personal considerations not easily introduced into a mathematical formula (having used the latter to reveal the implications of his available objective information and subjective estimates). The implications thus revealed are very helpful. They show that testing is not worth the cost if the end aim is to sell a lease anyway. On the other hand, the test is worth up to $20,000 in the information it gives, if the decision is to drill (the difference between the $24,000 gross position value of the test-then-drill alternative path, and the $4,000 position

FIGURE 10-2. Completed Decision Tree, with Estimated
Decision costs, Etimated Probabilities of Events, Payouts, and
Expected Values of each Path
(Circled quantities indicate the expected value of the given
decision-path sequence, p is the subjective probability of the
event)

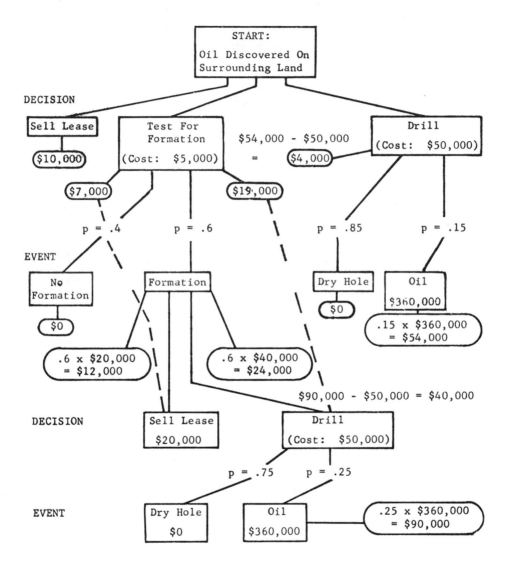

value of drill-immediately). They show that in choosing between the other two alternatives, we choose between a certain $10,000 for immediate sale of the lease, and $19,000, the expected position value for test-then-drill, not between $10,000 and $360,000 for a successful well. And they bring into focus the reason for the difference between the well value of $360,000 and the $19,000: the high risk of failure, and the financial resources committed.

Our landowner must now assess his own risk affordability, financial resources, and the utility of the relative returns to him. The question of financial resources is easily disposed of; either he has available $55,000 of risk capital needed to make a test and drill, or he does not. In the latter case, he must sell the lease immediately. If he does have it available, then more subjective considerations come into play, best illustrated in terms of three different landowners:

1. Alberts is a small landowner, with just this one lease to sell. The $10,000 from the sale of the lease would put him in a position to improve his own operations materially. The loss of the $55,000 in case of a dry hole would mean disaster. Since there is an 85 percent chance that he will lose all, the assured return of $10,000 has much higher utility for him than the $19,000 position value of an alternative with only a 15 percent chance of success, even though the $19,000 result is arrived at by taking objective account of the risk. His risk affordability is too low.

2. Baker is a wealthy neighbor, to whom the loss of $55,000 would be little more than an annoyance, even if the Internal Revenue Service did not bear most of the brunt of it. On the other hand, while the $360,000 from a successful well would probably have relatively low marginal value for him, the excitement of success, if he does bring it in, would probably have considerable personal utility. He would probably test-then-drill.

3. Charleston can scrape together the $55,000, if necessary, although it would take all of his resources. But he needs more than $10,000 or even $55,000; he needs nearly $90,000 to stave off impending family disaster and pay for an operation needed if he is to live more than another year. The $10,000 would have little value to him. The $360,000 would salvage everything and give him a substantial stake in addition. Whatever the risk, he must go for broke. He probably would

drill immediately.

Where Do the Figures Come From?

The mechanics of such a calculation are obviously not exotic. Given the numbers, the computation is elementary arithmetic. The essential problem is assigning something like the correct value to the payouts and their probabilities. (The costs can usually be estimated with adequate accuracy.)

The quantities in our equations will nearly always be rough approximations. They may be based on empirical observations of situations which are only somewhat similar or analogous, adjusted on the basis of the kind of personal feeling or hunch that grows out of the accumulation of minor, usually subconscious, experiences which give us a feel of the market. They may be inferences drawn from various kinds of available objective data--e. g. , in our example, the experience of other testing and drilling operations in the neighborhood or elsewhere--such as census tabulations, trade statistics, or personal observations made by those familiar with the kind of situation with which a decision is concerned.

They should never be arbitrary guesses pulled out of the air, and all adjustments made on any objective base data used should have a supportable logic. Wherever we get our figures, we must check their credibility and their relevance to the kind of decision with which we are confronted.

Seldom will our figures have any high degree of precision. At most, they will usually express some sort of rough maximum or minimum. Our landowner thought that the probability of finding a favorable formation was .6 on the basis of the best information he could get. He probably meant "about .6," and did not imply the figure could not have been as low as .54, for example, or that it could not have been as high as .8. If such an initial statement leaves too high a range of uncertainty to permit a choice, the best decision is probably to seek additional information before acting. Otherwise, we are taking a gamble, not a calculated risk. We are permitting the outcome to be decided by the net effect of an infinity of minor factors that mathematicians sum up under the term random. In the long run, the true gambler always loses out to the certainty of the house percentage.

What Do the Results Tell Us?

Putting down some probability figures and performing the arithmetic confers no particular magic. The process can lead to false confidence if the figures alone are thought to be able to carry the weight of the decision. The real value of the process is often in trying to arrive at as accurate a representation as possible of the quantitative significance of all the data we have which we think is pertinent to the decision, at a specific measure of the kinds of risks we think are involved, and at the size of the payouts we have a right to expect. When you must put down a specific figure and justify it, you are more likely to hone your thinking to a finer edge than when you are allowed to get away with some comfortably vague generalizations.

Calculations carried out with figures arrived at with care can then reveal to us the relative monetary value of different decision sequences and thus help us choose a decision path that will optimize the kinds of results consonant with our objectives, capabilities, and situation.

WHAT SHALL WE BID: COMPETITIVE BIDDING STRATEGY

The decision theory tool of competitive bidding strategy (CBS) can help us put the value of the alternatives in a bidding situation into clearer focus. Like all statistical decision theory techniques, CBS furnishes a means of extracting the best estimate possible of the expected value of a given estimated profit outcome, using normally available information. It helps sharpen our perceptions of the values of possible alternatives and the likelihood of profitable outcomes, if immediate profit is our objective. CBS does not, of course, tell us what our objective should be, but it can help us evaluate the profit position cost of some other objective, to help us decide whether it is worth the price.

Whenever the purchase or the sale is awarded on the basis of competitive bids, the final decision on the proposed price can be an ulcer-creating compromise. When the bid is on the sale side, the objective is presumably to quote a price just low enough to beat out competitors, yet one which, if successful, will lead to as much profit as possible. When the bid is to buy, the aim is the reverse, of course--one just high

257

enough to land the purchase on terms which allow a profit on eventual realization. * The purpose of competitive bidding strategy is to quantify information normally used in arriving at such bids.

The process of any bid preparation is usually built on appraisal of:

1. The number and identity of competitors and some idea of their degree of eagerness to win.

2. Some past history on the bidding performance of each competitor.

3. Some knowledge of the costs of past projects on which competitors' bids are known.

4. The bidder's own cost estimate for the project in the case of sales bids, or the buyer's own estimate of his expected later sales realization in the case of purchase bids.

5. The direct or indirect profit objective sought by the bidder.

CBS is thus a means of getting fuller use of the kind of evaluations commonly made in the usual bidding process. No change is made in the normal bid preparation procedure itself, which might be outlined as follows:

1. Make a careful estimate of the probable cost of doing the job.

2. Evaluate what special abilities or advantages we have for carrying out the task.

3. Take a look at the importance, to us, of landing this bid: judge its significance in terms of getting profitable jobs in the future or of holding together an organization.

4. Decide how anxious possible competitors may be for the success in this competition, in the light of what we know about the current and near future activity of each and of the industry.

5. In the light of these appraisals, redefine what we consider the elements of real cost to be.

6. Decide what information on past bids of probable competitors is relevant: which bids and bid situations represent similar circumstances. When chosen, tabulate the past bids of each competitor, and estimate how each competitor may

---

* An interesting discussion of purchase bidding will be found in Norman E. Taylor, "A Look at Competitive Bidding," Montana Business Quarterly, Spring, 1964, pp. 22-36.

be expected to bid this time.

7. Decide what our objective is to be if we submit a bid: choose whether or not, why, and under what circumstances we would like to win the bid. On this basis, select a specific profit target, usually in terms of a specific percentage of cost.

CBS mainly improves the operation in point 6 above: the estimate of what each competitor may be expected to bid. It consists essentially of four steps:

1. Make an estimate of our cost and of the range of bids we might make, based on this cost, as usual.

2. Construct a probability distribution of the percentage profit targets of each competitor who will be in the competition.

3. Calculate a combined probability distribution of our chance of winning for each bid within the range we are considering.

4. Calculate the profit position distribution of bids in this range.

The heart of CBS is a logical process for making full use of information normally used anyway, to develop a probability distribution for the bids of each competitor. This distribution, in turn, permits a quantitative evaluation of the profit position of a bid.

Calculating the Profit Position of a Bid

The calculations do not directly indicate exactly what bid the firm should enter. This follows from the firm's purpose in making the bid. What competitive bidding strategy comparisons accomplish is to make clear the relative effect of all the possible bids under consideration on the long term profit position of the firm, as nearly as this can be determined from the available information and judgments entering into the computations. The technique does this by producing a set of numbers which combine the estimated profit of each bid if successful with the odds that each particular bid can be successful. The figure calculated for each bid--the profit position of that bid--is the simple product of the estimated actual profit times the odds that it can win. The estimated actual profit, of course, is merely the difference between the proposed bid and the firm's own computations of the project cost. The likelihood of winning is developed through a simple statistical analysis of past bidding strategy, based on several necessary assumptions:

    1. Each bidder tends to follow a consistent pattern in his cost estimating procedure.

    2. Cost estimates made by competing bidders will be similar and reasonably parallel over time.

    3. If only winning bids are directly known, the competition was probably keen enough that the losers' bids were close to those of the winner.

    4. As a result, the profit objective of each bidder can be approximated for any of his past bids if we have either knowledge of or a close estimate of his bid and our own estimate of the project cost. While such an estimate will contain some degree of error, the error in a series of such estimates will be small and consistent.

    5. Each bidder makes his own bid without knowledge of the action of others and competitors' bids are therefore independent of each other. Thus the chance that each will enter a given bid is independent of the odds that others will enter that bid.

    These assumptions would be familiar to anyone who has been making bids, just as the procedure cited earlier would be. All that competitive bidding strategy contributes, therefore, is a quantification of the inferences drawn about competitor behavior, in terms of a distribution of profit position values for all possible bids.

    The profit position value of any given bid is merely the estimated profit <u>times</u> the likelihood of winning <u>successively</u> against each and all competitors likely to enter. (This follows from the assumption of independence of bidders.) Expressed in mathematical symbolism:

Let V_i = the value of the profit position of a given individual bid

    M_i = the estimated value of the actual profit margin of that bid

    L_1, L_2, L_3, ... L_k = the individual likelihoods that the given bid will be better than that of the competing bidders, 1, 2, 3, ... k.

Then $V_i = M_i (L_1 \times L_2 \times L_3 \times \ldots \ldots L_k)$ for $\underline{k}$ number of bidders.

    Since M_i is a known figure, this formula is simple arithmetic once we have an estimate of the L's. To take a concrete example, assume a bid for $275,000 estimated to yield a profit of $25,000. Assume further that our estimate of the likelihoods that each of the three known competitors will bid higher than $275,000 are 0.5, 0.4, and 0.3, respectively. Then:

$$V_{\$275,000} = \$25,000\ (.5 \times .4 \times .3) = 25,000\ (.06) = \$1,500$$

Taken alone, this profit position figure of $1500 has little tangible meaning. It is not an estimate of the actual profit which might be realized. If a bid of $275,000 secures the contract, the firm will get the actual difference between its bid price and the actual cost--a profit already estimated at $25,000. If the bid is not a winner, the firm gets nothing. The profit position values simply permit a rational comparison of the best estimated consequences for the long run financial health of the firm of bidding procedures proposed and of immediate objectives--the effect on average earnings of a series of similar bids, taking into account the number of times the bids might lose.

Clearly, the computation hinges on obtaining as good a distribution of likelihood values as possible for each competitor. How such distributions might be estimated is probably best illustrated in terms of the hypothetical case of STL Fabricators, Inc. This general structural steel fabricating firm has been asked to bid on construction of a set of special purpose Inland Waterways barges whose cost STL estimates at $250,000 each. STL executives are aware that three other familiar contractors (B&R, C&T, and D&Y) will be entering serious bids. STL men are also aware that all 3 competitors have had considerable slack capacity over the last 37 months. During that period, the competitors have been quite eager to land jobs and there is little reason to believe that this attitude has changed. The STL executives have therefore asked for the files on all bids made by STL and these 3 others during the 37 month period, excluding earlier bids made during a more prosperous period. Of the 24 files on hand, they judge 19 to be bids made under circumstances similar to those of the present job. In the other 5 cases, they believe that either special facilities of a competitor or special relationships between some one competitor and the awarding authority made the bidding circumstances noncomparable, even noncompetitive.

Of the 19 cases under review, only 4 had been for

barges or other vessels of any design, and all of these for quite different designs and different kinds of programs. Other projects had been for a variety of other types of construction normal for the industry--for TV towers and microwave installations, for tank farms, pipelines, and other fabrication projects. But all of them were within the competence of all four competitors and all had entered serious bids.

Table 10-1 lists the information yielded by STL's files for the 19 projects considered comparable. In terms of total project value and dollar profit, the 19 were far from alike. However, the important data is not these totals but the estimated profit objectives of the winners, given in the last column. Except when STL won, these estimates are not precise, of course. It is rather unlikely that STL and its competitors arrived at identical cost estimates much of the time. But the difference cannot be substantial, and the figure listed is the best information available. In any event, the main problem is not the accuracy of the known figures, but the size of the missing ones--the bids of the losers in each case. About such bids, STL has one solid bit of knowledge: the losers had bid higher than the winner. How much higher? This, too, can be estimated from past experience. Looking at the difference between STL's bids and those of a winning competitor when STL lost, it appears that the difference has tended to oscillate around 1 per cent. The random distribution of the winners seems to indicate that bids, in general, have been close to each other, and STL officials believe they have done as well as any.

The loser's bid then is estimated by adding a nominal amount, in line with experience, to the winner's profit objective. Proceeding thus, STL has arrived at the profit objective values shown in Table 10-2. It is now ready to develop an estimate of the likelihood distribution of the profit objective of each competing contractor for the barge job.

To apply the likelihood objective estimate to the next contract, STL makes two additional assumptions: (1) for any contractor, each of his past bid objectives is as likely as any other at this point, (2) one additionally likely condition exists-- the possibility that any contractor may bid just outside the range of past experience, might set a profit objective either just above or just below any of the 19 previous ones. STL then must consider each past bid objective as equal to the fractional likelihood of $\frac{1}{19 + 1}$, or $\frac{1}{20}$ of the possible bids.

TABLE 10-1. STL's Information on 19 Contract Lettings in the Last 37 Months

Item Bid No.	Winner	STL Estimate Of Cost (C_s)	Winning Bid (B)	STL Bid	Difference: ($B - C_s$) Amount	Per cent of C_s
1	STL	$ 97,300	$105,110	$105,110	$ 7,710	+8%
2	B&R	120,500	129,030	131,000	8,530	+7
3	D&Y	190,300	196,015	196,700	5,715	+3
4	C&T	75,700	80,248	81,050	4,548	+6
5	B&R	253,200	240,550	243,100	-12,650	-5
6	D&Y	211,800	190,595	192,500	-21,205	-9
7	D&Y	495,600	455,970	460,100	-39,630	-8
8	C&T	136,500	146,055	147,490	9,555	+7
9	C&T	97,400	100,320	101,250	2,920	+3
10	B&R	157,100	136,251	137,600	-18,849	-12
11	STL	64,500	71,560	71,560	7,060	+11
12	C&T	77,900	84,920	85,670	7,020	+9
13	B&R	176,200	193,825	194,494	17,265	+10
14	D&Y	246,700	254,195	256,950	7,395	+3
15	STL	195,100	199,005	199,005	3,905	+2
16	STL	117,400	122,090	122,090	4,690	+4
17	D&Y	195,800	193,950	194,900	-1,950	-1
18	C&T	147,300	142,875	144,300	-4,425	-3
19	B&R	99,475	97,565	98,389	-1,910	-2

TABLE 10-2. STL'S Best Estimate Of The Bid Objective
Distribution For Each Of Its Three Competitors
In 19 Contract Lettings In The Last 37 Months

| Item No. | Estimated Bid Objective As Per Cent Of Cost, For: | | |
	B&R	C&T	D&Y
1	9	9	9
2	7	8	8
3	4	4	3
4	7	6	7
5	-5	-4	-4
6	-9	-10	-9
7	-7	-7	-8
8	8	7	8
9	4	3	4
10	-12	-11	-11
11	12	12	12
12	10	9	10
13	10	11	11
14	4	4	3
15	3	3	3
16	5	5	5
17	0	0	-1
18	-2	-3	-2
19	-2	-1	-1

Table 10-3 gives the initial raw estimates of the cumulative
likelihood distribution for each of the three competitors, and
Figure 10-3 graphs these with a hand-fitted line for each contractor. By interpolating convenient values from each of these
smoothed distributions, we can get an estimate of the cumulative likelihood that all three competitors combined will enter a
bid higher than any given value, that is, the cumulative joint
probability that STL will not be underbid. Table 10-4 shows
the calculated values based on Figure 10-4. These calculated
values are plotted in Figure 10-5 and again smoothed to yield
the final estimate.

TABLE 10-3. STL's Initial Estimate of the Cumulative Bid Objective Likehood Distribution for Each of the 3 Competitors (Each single past bid = 1/20 of total)

B&R Bid Objective (% profit)	L (cum.)	C&T Bid Objective (% profit)	L (cum.)	D&Y Bid Objective (% profit)	L (cum.)
12	.05	12	.05	12	.05
10	.10 } .125	11	.10	11	.10
10	.15 }	9	.15 } .175	10	.15
9	.20	9	.20 }	9	.20
8	.25	8	.25	8	.25 } .275
7	.30 } .325	7	.30	8	.30 }
7	.35 }	6	.35	7	.35
5	.40	5	.40	5	.40
4	.45 }	4	.45 } .475	4	.45
4	.50 } .50	4	.50 }	3	.50 }
4	.55 }	3	.55 } .575	3	.55 } .55
3	.60	3	.60 }	3	.60 }
0	.65	0	.65	-1	.65 }
-2	.70 } .725	-1	.70	-1	.70 } .675
-2	.75 }	-3	.75	-2	.75
-5	.80	-4	.80	-4	.80
-7	.85	-7	.85	-8	.85
-9	.90	-10	.90	-9	.90
-12	.95	-11	.95	-11	.95

FIGURE 10-3.

SMOOTHED DISTRIBUTIONS OF THE ORIGINAL ESTIMATE OF THE LIKELIHOOD THAT EACH OF THE 3 COMPETITORS WILL ENTER A HIGHER BID

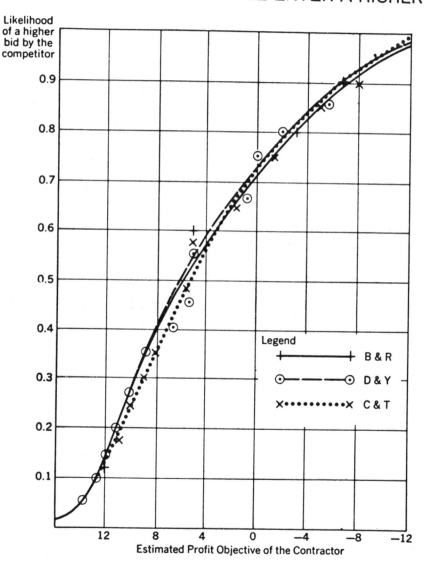

FIGURE 10-4.

SMOOTHED ESTIMATE OF THE DISTRIBUTION
OF THE LIKELIHOOD THAT ALL THREE
CONTRACTORS WILL SUBMIT A HIGHER BID

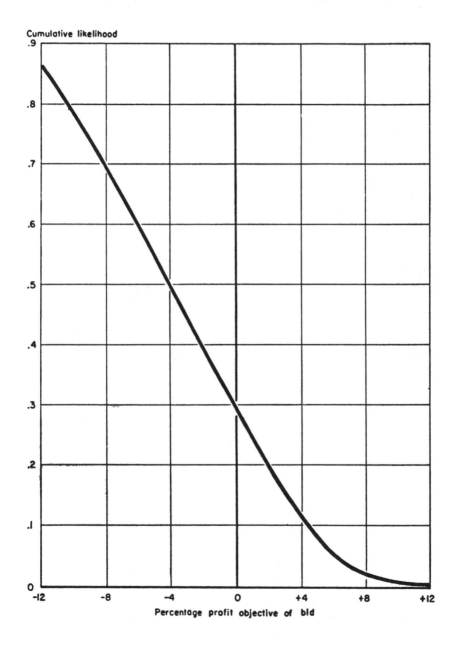

TABLE 10-4. Computation of Profit Position Estimates for a Selected List of Percentage Profit Objectives, Based on Figure 10-4

Profit Objective (per cent)	Estimated likelihood that a higher bid will be entered by:				Estimate of actual profit		Estimated profit position
	B&R	C&T	D&Y	All three			
+12	.05	.05	.05	.000125	x	$30,000 =	$ 4
10	.14	.125	.15	.0026		25,000	65
8	.27	.24	.275	.018		20,000	360
6	.38	.35	.40	.0533		15,000	800
5	.435	.45	.45	.08		12,000	1,000
4	.49	.465	.5	.114		10,000	1,140
3.5	.515	.495	.525	.134		8,750	1,170
3	.535	.52	.55	.154		7,500	1,155
2	.575	.57	.59	.193		5,000	965
0	.655	.66	.67	.29		0	0
-1	.695	.7	.71	.344		-2,500	-860
-4	.78	.795	.8	.495		-10,000	-4,950
-8	.88	.885	.89	.695		-20,000	-13,900
-12	.95	.95	.95	.862		-30,000	-25,960

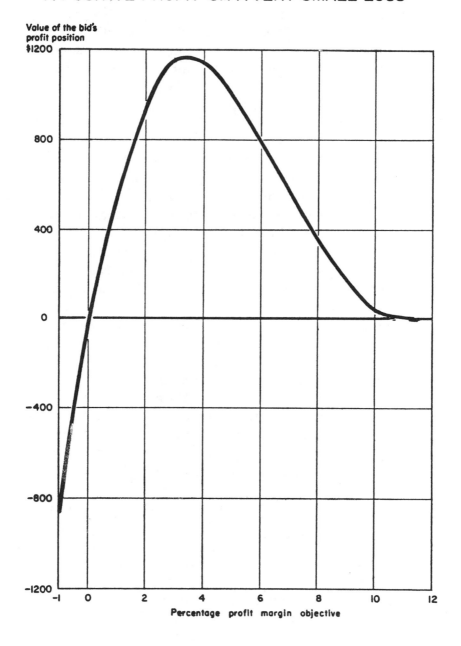

FIGURE 10-5.

FINAL ESTIMATE OF THE PROFIT POSITION DISTRIBUTION FOR ALL BIDS YIELDING EITHER A POSITIVE PROFIT OR A VERY SMALL LOSS

Value of the bid's
profit position

Percentage profit margin objective

Given this final estimate curve, what should STL bid? The curve does not tell directly, only in conjunction with a decision as to the immediate objective of STL officials in trying for the contract. If that immediate objective is the best profit position, then the answer is approximately $258,750 ($250,000 cost + $8,750 profit), corresponding to the optimum profit position value of $1,170.

But the objective of STL and of its competitors is not always optimum immediate profit as is evident from the numerous loss bids submitted in the recent past. Some contracts were for prototype structures where the winner was sure of considerable advantage in bidding on a series of contracts that would follow. In such cases, the objective was frequently to maximize the chances of winning the prototype award. If such were STL's objective in the current job, it would bid with a lower profit objective than any previously submitted by anyone-- lower than the -12% with which B&R landed the contract for item number 10. If, on the other hand, STL decides that it would undertake the project only for significant profit, it might bid $260,000, a little less than the optimum profit position, if willing to accept 4% as reasonable profit in the circumstances, or even $270,000 for an 8% profit but only a 2% chance of winning.

By contrast, STL may realize that in any case, no bid it can make has a very good chance of winning because one of the others--perhaps C&T--has an inside track with the awarding authorities and will be given an opportunity to change its bid to meet that of any other competitor. STL then ponders whether to submit a bid so low as to entail a considerable loss if the "second look" relationship C&T has is broken and would otherwise penalize C&T by forcing it to underbid at a much lower price than intended.

The judgmental computations of competitive bidding strategy are therefore only part of the whole--they simply furnish the prospective bidder with a reasonably objective measure of the likely long run consequences of any proposed bid. Like all Bayesian calculations, those of competitive bidding strategy are only as good as the judgments made as to what kind of past experience is applicable--no better. While they furnish the semblance of objectivity, they are not objective in the sense that traditional statistical measures are. The basic data is derived from merely analogical information, not demonstrable similarities. In competitive bidding strategy, for example, the past bids used to estimate the likelihood distributions are chosen on the basis of a highly personal judgment as to which ones occurred in similar situations. They were for projects so varied that they would not meet traditional statistical tests for homogeneity. Every quantity used contains a large component of judgment.

But the purpose of any such Bayesian approach is to obtain optimum value from the kind of information available, information which will be used in any case, since nothing better can be obtained. By so doing the executive can learn the full import of the information for the decision he must make.

THE INVENTORY MODEL

The inventory model takes its name from an early and still important use, but its applicability is far broader than the logistics of material movement. Any problem is an "inventory" problem which has the following characteristics:

1. There is an appreciable lead-time between an input action and useful output, which lead-time may or may not vary within a predictable range but if it does vary, varies in random fashion. (In the case of an actual inventory problem, this is the lag between placing an order and getting it into stock.)

2. Potential usage of the items during any period of time can vary in a predictable range, but does so in an unpredictable random fashion. (In an actual inventory situation, potential usage means demands for withdrawal from stock.) Whether or not the actual lead-time varies significantly, then, this means that demand in any given lead-time is not fully predictable, and there will be shortages during some lead-times, overages during others (that is, some old items still available when the new inputs arrive).

3. The input timing, or the amount, or both, can be varied at will. (Order quantity or the timing of orders can be varied at will.)

4. There is an associated fixed cost for each act of input or start-up. (The cost of acquisition --ordering, receiving and placing in stock--is relatively constant regardless of the size of order.)

5. The cost of shortages--items not available when demanded--is proportional to the number of items short. The cost of overages is variable and proportional to the number of

old items left on hand. (There is a cost associated with any item not in stock when demanded, proportionate to the unsatisfied demand, and another variable cost associated with any stock left in inventory at the time a new order is put in stock.)

Many kinds of business situations will prove to have these characteristics, if we interpret the conditions above into the proper language. Systematic personnel recruitment and training programs would often fit, for example. The fixed costs of "acquisition" would become the fixed costs of the recruitment and training system; lead-time, the lag between attempt to hire or otherwise recruit and the end of the training period; demand, the positions which have to be filled with trainees during any given period. Shortages would be any jobs which had to be left unfilled until the new training class graduated, and the shortage cost those costs incurred because of the lack of adequate trainees. Overages would be the excess of trainees at the end of a training period who were not immediately needed to fill the positions which opened before a new class was available, the costs, the difference between their pay and the productivity expected from a trainee.

If the inventory is produced in intermittent batches within the firm, rather than purchased, cost of acquisition becomes the start-up costs for the production of each batch. The costs themselves do not have to be expressible directly in money, just so long as some kind of alternative to these costs can be so expressed.

The uncertainty of the demand during the lead-time is, of course, the reason we have a problem at all, whether that uncertainty arises from an uncertainty in the length of the lead-time itself, or results from the variability of the demand during a given period of time, or both. Any order clerk would need only a simple arithmetic calculation if total demand and the demand pattern are known and the lead-time to restock is predictable. In such pleasant circumstances, the minimum order quantity is just enough to carry the demand volume during the lead-time period. The most economical order quantity (Q) will be that which minimizes the total of two costs:

1. the annual cost of carrying inventory such as financing, storage, and deterioration (which increases as the order quantity, and thus the average size of stock, increases).

2. the annual cost of acquisition of stock such as the costs of processing an order (or making a machine setup),

receiving, payment of invoices (which goes down as the lot size increases).

In the case of predictable demand flow and lead-time, the reorder point (R) which will trigger the new order is just the amount of residual stock needed to cover demand during this lead-time. Under such ideal circumstances, of course, inventory is no management problem, but routine clerical work.

In most real life, inventory is a management concern because demand can fluctuate in an unpredictable pattern within reasonably predictable ranges and lead-time between order and receipt cannot always be considered constant. With either demand pattern or lead-time a probability variable, no single values of either the order quantity Q or the reorder point R, and no single combination, can simultaneously prevent both occasional stock shortages (stock-outs) and occasional overages of residual stock at the time of new order receipt. Both stockouts and overages add to inventory cost. Stock-outs can result in lost business, particularly if backordering is not possible or practical. Even with backordering, some customer goodwill is probably lost, and order cancellations are certain as the length of the backorder period is increased. Any stock overage results in an average inventory level higher than under certainty, and thus additional inventory costs.

Minimizing inventory costs thus requires determination of a procedure for routine calculation of two quantities (or parameters): Q, the quantity to be ordered, and R, the stock level at which a reorder will be triggered.

Whatever the form of inventory system, determination of the best procedure and rules for these parameters is a cut-and-try process, aimed at minimizing the net total of three conflicting costs:

1. the cost of carrying inventory
2. stock-out costs
3. the costs of ordering and acquisition.

The mathematical model that is needed is thus some systematic trial-and-error procedure such that each succeeding step gets a better solution until the optimum solution is reached and can be recognized. The mathematician calls such a model or rule an algorithm. There are two main types of inventory systems:

1. The fixed reorder point system, which seeks the best (Q, R) combination in which Q is held constant and the

date of reorder is variable, being triggered by $\underline{R}$, the level of inventory at which a reorder is to be placed

    2. the system with <u>fixed ordering dates</u>, set once and for all, the quantity, Q, being determined by the stock on hand at the time of ordering.

    The latter system has some important applications in cases in which delivery has to be scheduled on the basis of some kind of routine (as with bakery goods on the grocery shelves), or in which recent experience is a valid guide to near future demand. But the fixed reorder point system has more general applicability and will be discussed below. It is the preferable system whenever all of the following hold:

    1. lead-time is relatively constant regardless of the order date
    2. recent history is not a reliable indicator of demand
    3. the cost of placing orders is not significantly affected by irregularity of their dating

Even when lead-time is variable, it is still usually the better system, and it may be preferable when one of the other conditions is violated. The ability to use recent history to partially predict near future demand adds a minor complication in that it requires that we have a family of (Q, R) solutions, rather then one. Such would be the case of the dress reorder situation used as an example earlier. Seasonal demand patterns of known conformation would also require such a family of solutions. Furthermore, when recent history really is a valid guide to future demand, demand patterns are quite likely to approach a definite known pattern, and inventory control is dealing with a narrower range of uncertainty.

Fixed Order Point Inventory Control: Estimating The Probability Distributions
<u>Fixed Order Point Inventory Control: Estimating The</u>
<u>Probability Distributions</u>

    Let us visualize the problem of real-world inventory control in terms of Hectic Fishing Supply, a commercial fisheries distributor that sells, among other items, kippered sardine nets costing Hectic $500 each. Hectic can count on selling close to 365 nets nearly every year, an average of one per day, with no perceptible seasonal variation. But on some days, none are sold at all, and on some, as many as 3. Hectic's experience on getting delivery for stock replacement has been that this can vary from 1 to 3 days. In setting up an inventory system for its nets, then, Hectic starts with the following knowledge:

1. Per item cost to Hectic is $500.

2. The cost of holding inventory is 20% of the average value, per year.

3. Order cost is $20 per order for placement, handling, and receiving, without regard to the number of nets ordered.

4. Hectic can expect to sell 365 nets per year.

In addition, Hectic has a policy of backordering all nets demanded but not available in stock and filling all backorders immediately when stock is received.

Looking over its past experience, Hectic decides that last year's demand and supply patterns were quite typical, and would be as good an estimate of the probability distribution for next year as could be made. Tabulation of the daily demand during last year shows volume fluctuating from no nets to 3 in one day and lead-time to refill stock from one to three days (Tables 10-5 and 10-6).

TABLE 10-5. Daily Demand of Kippered Herring Nets During The Past Year

Nets Demanded During One Day	Percentage of Days
None	40%
1	30
2	20
3	10
	100%

TABLE 10-6. Lead-Time for Restocking Nets During The Past Year

Lead-time Per Order (Days)	Percentage of Orders
1	25%
2	50
3	25
	100%

Careful analysis can detect no predictable pattern of any sort in either the daily demand or the order lead-time; they appear to be purely random variations. Hence there were times when no nets were needed to fill orders from the time stock was exhausted until a new stock was received, and there could have been times when 9 nets were demanded between the time stock was exhausted and a new shipment was received (a DDLT, demand during lead-time, of 9 nets). Hence, if Hectic were really to pursue a policy of never risking an inventory shortage, it would have to set a minimum reorder levels in excess of 9 nets. Such a policy would inevitably result in an excess stock on order receipt most of the time, however. Unless stock-out cost was inordinately high, this policy is unlikely to be as profitable as one which risked an occasional shortage. Hence, Hectic's officials must make the best estimate they can of the cost to them of a stock-out. After calculating the cost of keeping the necessary backorder records and adding to this their best appraisal of the cost of occasional customer illwill caused by backordering and delayed deliveries, these officials put the cost of a stock-out at $40 per item/time. Hectic now has enough information on which to determine a possible inventory policy, first constructing a table of probabilities for each possible demand level during the lead-time, from 0 through 9 nets per lead-time period.

If the demand and lead-time patterns are as simple as those we have assumed for Hectic, we can simply enumerate all of the combinations of demand and lead-time variations that could occur and compute directly the probabilities of each possible combination. One of these combinations would be a lead-time of 3 days and a demand for 7 nets during those 3 days. Such would be the case if the demand on the first day were for 3 nets and on each of the succeeding 2 days was for 2 nets, or any other permutation of 3, 2, 2. This combination of 7 nets and 3 days could also result from a 3 day lead-time and any permutation of demand per day of 3, 3, 1. Table 10-7 lists the 6 possible combinations resulting in a demand of 7 nets per day during a 3 day lead-time.

TABLE 10-7. Probability That Seven Nets Will Be a DDLT of 3 Days

Possible Pattern of Demand on Successive Days	Probability (P) that this will be the Total Demand-Lead-Time Pattern = P(lead-time of 3 days)	x	$\underline{P}$ (daily demands)	x	$\underline{P}$ (this combination)
3 2 2	.25	x	(.10x.20x.20)	=	.001
2 3 2	.25	x	(.20x.10x.20)	=	.001
2 2 3	.25	x	(.20x.20x.10)	=	.001
3 3 1	.25	x	(.10x.10x.30)	=	.00075
3 1 3	.25	x	(.10x.30x.10)	=	.00075
1 3 3	.25	x	(.30x.10x.10)	=	.00075
		TOTAL P (DDLT = 7)			.00525

We could thus proceed to count all the ways in which the various demand and lead-time combinations could occur and to compute their probabilities. The result would be as in Table 10-8.

TABLE 10-8. Probability Distribution of DDLT for Hectic
             Fishing Supply's Kippered Herring Nets

DDLT No. of Nets	Probability of This Demand	Cumulative Probability (Probability That The Demand Will Be Greater Than This)
0	.1960	.8040
1	.2310	.5730
2	.2260	.3470
3	.1797	.1673
4	.0935	.0738
5	.0477	.0261
6	.0190	.0071
7	.0053	.0018
8	.0015	.0003
9	.0003	.0000

The quantities in the last column are simply the sum of the probabilities of all the demands for a quantity greater than the number listed. The value of this at the DDLT level of 9 nets is zero, since Hectic does not anticipate any day with a demand greater than 3 nets, nor any lead-time for restocking of more than 3 days. This cumulative figure is the probability that a reorder level R of the number of nets listed in column 1 will result in a stock-out of at least 1 net. Thus if R is set at 5 nets, Hectic can expect a stock-out during about one reorder period out of 40 (261/10,000). The expected value of the stock-out for each lead-time period using a reorder level of 5-nets can be calculated as:

Probability of a shortage of 4 nets, DDLT: $(9-5) \times .0003 = .0012$

"   " "   "   " 3 "   " : $(8-5) \times .0015 = .0045$

"   " "   "   " 2 "   " : $(7-5) \times .0053 = .0106$

"   " "   "   " 1 "   " : $(6-5) \times .0190 = \underline{.0190}$

Total expected unit shortage when R = 5   .0353

Now, obviously, there is no such thing as .0353 fractional part of a net, but this is the average risk expectation of a shortage over a long period, if the past year's experience can be used as a close approximation of DDLT probability. We shall label all quantities like this value, .0353, as E(DDLT >R), to be translated as "the expected amount by which DDLT exceeds R (the reorder point)," or the expected average stock-out risk per lead-time, in number of nets short. Multiplied by the estimated cost of a stock-out of $40, this tells us what the stock-out cost of an R would be for Hectic; in this case of R = 5, $1.412, per reorder period.

Fixed Order Point Control: Calculating the Optimum Order Quantity and Reorder Point

Our Hectic example chose a very simple case in which the demand quantities and lead-time values were very small. Even here, as can be seen, the total calculation would be rather cumbersome when done by hand. Where total quantities are much larger, as is usual, this system would be too much work to use if we did not have access to a computer and a convenient technique for using it. The technique, in this case, is to use Monte Carlo simulation (discussed later) to construct tables of probability based on known experience.

The starting point and general procedure would remain the same, however: First, an estimate of the probability distributions of unit-time demand and of lead-time variations on the basis of some kind of experience considered to be a valid approximation of the pattern that lies ahead and then construction of the total DDLT probability distribution this experience implies. From this we can use some procedure to calculate the total annual cost (TAC) for each plausible combination of Q and R, on the basis of this experience, starting with the minimum reorder value R needed to cover this average lead-time (2 nets), then trying progressively larger values of Q and R until a combination of Q and R are found for which TAC is less than any preceding value and also less than the next succeeding value.

The basic formulae for the three cost elements are:

1. Annual Ordering Cost =

$$\text{(cost per order)} \times \frac{\text{total estimated annual demand (AD)}}{\text{Number per order (Q)}}$$

$$\text{or, in terms of Hectic,} = \$20 \times \frac{365}{Q}$$

2. Annual Inventory Holding Cost =

$$\text{holding cost rate} \times \text{cost per unit} \times \left(\frac{Q}{2} + R - DDLT\right)$$

As inspection will reveal, the last expression is the average quantity on hand, or, in terms of Hectic, $= \frac{Q}{2} + R - 2$ (since average lead-time is 2 days and average demand per day is 1 net)

3. Annual Stock-Out Cost =

$$\text{(cost per stock-out)} \times \underline{E} \text{ (DDLT} > R) \times \frac{\text{annual demand}}{Q}$$

or, for Hectic, $= \$40 \times \underline{E} \text{ (DDLT} > R) \times \frac{365}{Q}$

How do the minimum values of (Q = 2, R = 2) work out for Hectic?

<u>Cost of holding inventory</u>
       year

$$= .20(\$500) \times (2/2 + 2-2) = .20 \times \$500 \times 1 = \$100$$

<u>Annual ordering cost</u> $= \$20 \times \dfrac{365}{2} = \$3650$

<u>Annual stock-out cost</u> $= \$40 \times .3470 \times \dfrac{365}{2} = \$3430$

Then TAC $= \$100 + \$3650 + \$3430 = \underline{\$6180}$

For Hectic, it is obvious that the company could afford to carry a larger stock in order to reduce the frequency with which orders are placed, and cut down on inventory shortages. Increasing Q substantially, say to 8, would raise holding costs by only another $300 per year, even with (R = 2), but drop ordering cost to only $912.50 and stock-out costs to $857.50. Increasing R to 3 at the same time would increase holding cost by only $100, but cut E (DDLT > R) from .3470 to .1673 and thus further reduce stock-out costs by more than one-half of the $857.50. So, obviously, we must search further. A complete search will reveal that the minimum expected TAC will be $1534 with a Q of 13 nets and an R of 4 nets, if we can rely on our cost estimates.

      But one item in our cost estimate is the roughest of

approximations, if that much: our estimate of stock-out cost. In fact, stock-out cost is probably a volatile value, its level probably depending on the general tightness of supplies and our competitors' delivery policies. Whenever demand tends to out-run current supply, everybody may have trouble making delivery of nets on time, and our fisherman customers may be so aware of the problem that frequent stock-outs may mean the loss of little goodwill, if any. When supplies are plentiful and most competitors vying with each other for service, a single stock-out may cost us a major customer.

So we need to find out how sensitive our policy calculation is to the estimate of stock-out cost. In Table 10-9 are our sensitivity analysis calculations of the differences between estimated TAC and actual TAC if the actual (and to some degree unknowable) stock-out costs were at various points in the wide range from $10 to $80. In the Hectic case, at least, a considerable error in the stock-out cost estimate can be tolerated without serious consequences.

TABLE 10-9. Comparison of Optimum Inventory Policy Costs At Varying Stock-out Costs, Between $10 and $80, and Annual Cost Based on an Estimate of $40 for Stock-Out Cost

Actual Stock-Out Cost Per Unit	Optimum Inventory Policy Q R		Minimum Annual Cost	TAC if Policy Based on Estimate of $40 Stock-Out	Added Inventory Cost of Ignorance of Actual Stock-Out Cost (in per cent)
$10	14	2	$1384	$1442	5.6%
20	14	3	1466	1473	0.5
30	13	4	1503	1503	--
40	13	4	1534	1534	--
50	13	5	1561	1564	0.2
60	13	5	1571	1595	1.5
70	13	5	1581	1625	2.8
80	13	5	1591	1657	4.2

Suppose, however, an abrupt easing in the market supply of nets makes quick delivery almost imperative if the patronage of Hectic's largest customers is to be retained. How many stock-outs are we risking with a (Q = 13, R = 4) policy? Referring back to the cumulative probability column in Table 10-8, we find that the probability of a stock-out of at least 1 net is .0738 with R = 4. In other words, out of about 28 lead-times per year ($\frac{365}{13}$), Hectic will experience stock-outs 7.4% of the time, or about twice a year. If we now run a sensitivity analysis on the values of Q, R combinations, we find that TAC is no more than 10% above the minimum for any of the values of Q between 11 and 16 (11 < Q < 16), and R between 3 and 6 (3 < R < 6). By reordering at R = 6, instead of when R = 4, the stock-out risk is reduced to 0.0071, or about once in five years. (P = 0.0071, 0.0071 x 28 = 0.199/year). By ordering only 12, instead of 13 nets when R = 6, Hectic's total inventory cost per year will rise only about 5% from $1534 to $1619, even without recalculating for a new value for stock-out cost. Hectic might consider this cheap insurance.

Inventory and the Inventory Model

Inventory models neither apply to all kinds of inventory situations, nor to inventory situations alone. They fit any situation, and all those situations, in which both underestimates and overestimates result in cost proportional to the error. Such an "inventory model" might thus apply to the scheduling of a final "lifetime" production run of spare parts for a discontinued engine design if, in case of an underestimate, all additional orders would be filled individually by the model shop without the aid of special tooling, so that all additional parts costs were variable (and, of course, higher than before). And as already indicated, shortages can result in lump-sum losses in some conceivable inventory situations. For the latter, the inventory policy is best optimized by use of the lump-sum loss production scheduling model outlined below.

THE LUMP SUM LOSS PRODUCTION SCHEDULING MODEL

The Basic Approach

When scheduling production runs of special designs or nonstandard dimensions, the percentage of defectives can only be estimated as a probability variable developed on the basis of analogous experience from operations thought to be similar. Over-runs normally result in some loss proportional to the overrun; at the extreme, the excess units must be treated as scrap, or at least unloaded at a substantial discount. Or the product may be unstable and deteriorate before sold or used, and losses suffered in this manner. Overage losses of this sort are the same sort of proportional costs as overages in inventory.

But quite often, if the percentage defective proves to be greater than allowed for, by even as little as one unit, a lump-sum cost will be incurred regardless of the actual size of the shortage (as, for example, when it results in the need for a new machine setup). Such a lump-sum loss situation yields an optimum solution through a simple form of graphic analysis.

To visualize the lump-sum model approach, we need to think of each item scheduled as being one of a series, each with its own serial number, and the decision as being whether or not to schedule a particular numbered item, $\underline{j}$, to be the last one run. The problem is worked out in terms of two pairs of quantities:

Q--the total number of pieces scheduled for production, of which j is the serial number of the last piece run

G--the total number of good pieces actually produced, of which n is the serial number of the last good piece needed to fill the order and n_{ac} is the actual serial number of the last good piece produced.

The aim is to schedule the quantity Q so that the last piece run, j, is equal to n, the last good piece needed, which is equal in turn to Q. With a known process and a repeat run of an item on which a lot of experience has been accumulated, this means only that enough be scheduled to allow for a known number of defectives. But when we have no direct experience with the item, we must make some kind of probability estimate of the percentage of defectives to be expected, basing the estimate, usually, on the analogy between the item being scheduled and other items with production requirements we consider comparable, and whose defect percentages are likely to vary over some kind of range.

In such a situation, we can have 3 possible kinds of outcomes:

1. We may, by luck, schedule just enough production that $j = n = Q$, that is, such that the last piece produced just fills the order.

2. We may produce an over-run, so that $j > n$, in which case we sustain some unit loss k on each piece produced beyond those ordered.

3. We may schedule too few to produce n good pieces-- $j < n$--in which case, however few or many the shortage, we have the same lump-sum loss, K, because of the need for a new machine setup, for example.

In the case of an over-run, our actual total loss is equal to $k(Q - n)$. In the case of any shortfall, it is K. We do not know the value of <u>n</u> (the serial number of the last good piece needed), in advance, so that we must choose the best value of Q to schedule on the basis of our estimate of the expected value of two possible losses. Thus for every individual j, the last piece scheduled, there are two expected loss values:

1. the expected loss from an overage, due to scheduling: $j \times k\, P(n < j)$, that is, (the unit loss from one surplus piece) x (the probability that <u>j</u> will be greater than the serial number of the last piece needed)

2. the expected loss from a shortage if j is not scheduled: $K\, P(n-j)$. <u>In order for it to be profitable</u> to schedule the jth piece, <u>the expected loss from scheduling it must be less than the expected loss of not scheduling it</u>, or

$$kP(n < j < KP(n = j).$$

A transposed form of this inequality is more revealing as to the condition the most profitable decision will meet:

$$\frac{P(n = j)}{P(n < j)} > \frac{k}{K}$$

The value of this form is that $\frac{k}{K}$ is a value known in advance: <u>the ratio of the unit loss incurred for each unwanted piece produced, to the lump-sum loss incurred in the event of any shortage of any size.</u>

We need, then, to make estimates of the two related probability distributions, $P(n = j)$ and $P(n < j)$, prepare some kind of summary of their ratios, and match $\frac{k}{K}$ with one of these ratios.

To take a simple example, assume we require a special production run of 10 good skyhooks, and that past experience with other designs leads us to conclude that the 10 good skyhooks can be any of the pieces from the 10th to the 14th, with individual probabilities as shown in the second column of Table 10-10, under $P(n = j)$.

TABLE 10-10.   Individual and Cumulative Probabilities That $(n_{ac} = j)$ for Different Values of $\underline{j}$, with 10 Good Skyhooks Required

j	$P(n_{ac} = j)$	$P(n_{ac} < \underline{j})$ (cumulative)	$P(=)/P(<)$
10	.20	0	(infinity)
11	.40	.20	2.0
12	.25	.60	.42
13	.10	.85	.12
14	.05	.95	.05
15	0.0	1.00	0

Note that $P(n_{ac} < j)$ is derived from $P(n_{ac} = j)$

Let us assume that $\underline{k}$, the loss occasioned by producing one un-wanted skyhook is $10 and that a setup cost to make a second run is $50. Then

$$\frac{k}{K} = \frac{\$10}{\$50} = .20$$

By inspection of our table, the profitable run to schedule is thus 13 skyhooks.

   To deal with the long production runs of real life, with their large numbers, such a table would be too long, and data not available in such neat form. We use instead a graphic approximation technique that also gives us an answer by in-spection and comparison of the probability ratio

$$\frac{P(n_{ac} = j)}{P(n_{ac} < j)} \quad \text{with} \quad \frac{k}{K} .$$

285

Probability estimates for long production runs must
usually start with information on the gross percentage defectives experienced on a handful of previous runs of other designs
believed to have similar process requirements to the item
being scheduled. Starting with this limited handful of observations, we usually proceed with a 6-step graphic estimating
procedure as follows:

1. Treating each run experience, ranked by percentage
defectives, as a proportional fractile of the total process probability, plot these points on a graph, then fit a smoothed curve
to the plot as an estimate of the continuous probability distribution of the ratios of total produced to good (of Q/G, or n_{ac}/G)

2. Rescale this graph to represent the cumulative
probability $P(n_{ac} <, n)$ on the vertical and of $\underline{n}$ on the horizontal
scale, for the size of run desired.

3. Read off from this graph a set of grouped probability
values of $P(n_{ac} = n)$ and calculate from this the distribution of
$P(n_{ac} = n)$.

4. Use these grouped data estimates to calculate
grouped data estimates of the ratio $P(n_{ac} = n)/P(n_{ac} < n)$.

5. Plot this grouped data ratio on a log-scale graph and
fit a smoothed curve as an estimate of the continuous probability distribution of the ratio $P(=)/P(<)$ with values of n as
the horizontal scale.

6. Locate on this graph the value of the ratio
$P(n_{ac} = n)/P(n_{ac} < n)$ corresponding to the value of k/K, and
read off the corresponding value of n, the serial number of the
last good piece needed to fill the order (that is, Q, the size of
the run needed).

The Graphic Technique, in Terms of an Example

A realistic example of graphic technique might be the
scheduling of 5000 acceptable NG1099 port valves for a special
modification kit for the now obsolescent SN 365 aircraft engine,
a lifetime supply with no expectation of additional sales after
this one order. Each valve made after the 5000th good one
will cost us $5.00 in variable manufacturing cost and unsal-

vageable material loss. If we underestimate the number Q that should be run, a second setup cost of \$1000 will have to be incurred to make up the shortage. We can assume that after the first run, enough will be known about the probability of defective production that the second run can be scheduled rather accurately, but we have never produced the NG1099 before and so must rely on data from other valve production runs which required the same 25 operations, and our experience with which is judged by our engineers to be as comparable as it is possible to be. There were nine such runs, with the variable experience shown in Table 10-11. We wish to use this experience to estimate the value of Q for which $P(n_{ac} = n)/P(n_{ac} < n)$

will be less than \$5/\$1000, or ($< .005$).

TABLE 10-11. Production Experience for 9 Analogous Runs in The Past

Run No.	Total No. of Pieces	Number Good	Number Defective	Fraction Defective	Ratio of Total-To-Good
1	6100	4873	1227	.201	1.25
2	7300	5184	2116	.290	1.41
3	8200	6673	1537	.190	1.23
4	6700	5119	1581	.248	1.33
5	7900	6589	1314	.164	1.20
6	8100	5588	2512	.310	1.45
7	6600	5128	1472	.223	1.28
8	7600	5623	1977	.260	1.35
9	6400	5088	1312	.195	1.24

None of these runs produced exactly 5000 good valves, but we feel that the numbers are large enough that the difference has no significance. We really do not know, either, that the last valve in each run was a good one, but even if as many as 30 defective valves in succession were produced at the end of the run, our ratio of total-to-good would not be changed for any of the runs, within the 3 significant figure precision being used here.

The next step is to rank these Q/G ratios in order of size. Then, since we have no reason to believe any of them is a more applicable experience than any of the others, treat them as fractile points on a continuous probability distribution, each accounting for $1/(9 + 1)$, or 1/10th of the total cumulative probability from 0 to 1.0. Thus the lowest value, 1.20, will be plotted as a $P(n_{ac} < n)$ of .10, the next lowest, 1.23, as .20, etc., as has been done in Figure 10-6. The points thus plotted, we draw the smoothed curve fitting them and then put a second scale label on the horizontal signifying the serial number n, of the last good piece needed to fill the order for 5000, for each value of n_{ac}/G.

From this we can now construct a table of conveniently grouped values of n, showing the total probabilities for each bracket, and derive the average probability of n per unit width within the bracket. For purposes of illustration, Table 10-12 utilized brackets of 100 (except for the initial bracket), but in practice, much narrower brackets would probably be used for slightly greater precision. The total probability of the bracket is estimated by reading the cumulative probabilities at the left and right edges of the bracket, and subtracting the cumulative probability at the left edge from that at the right edge. The probability per unit width is then simply this total divided by the number of units in the bracket, 100 in this case. Then, using this calculation of P(n) and getting $P(n_{ac} < n)$ by referring to the value at the midpoint of each bracket on Figure 10-6 we can construct our final Table 10-13, giving estimates of the value of our probability ratio for each bracket. From this, we plot the points on semilog paper as in Figure 10-7 and smooth the fitted line.

TABLE 10-12. Estimate of Unit Values of P(n), Using
          Grouped Data

n-value Bracket	Cumulative Probability at Left Edge	Total Probability of Bracket	Probability Per Unit Width
5890–5999	0	.120	.0011
6000–6999	.121	.094	.00094
6100–6199	.22	.081	.00081
6200–6299	.292	.072	.00072 etc.

FIGURE 10-6.

ESTIMATING CHART FOR DETERMINATION OF P(n$_{ac}$<n)

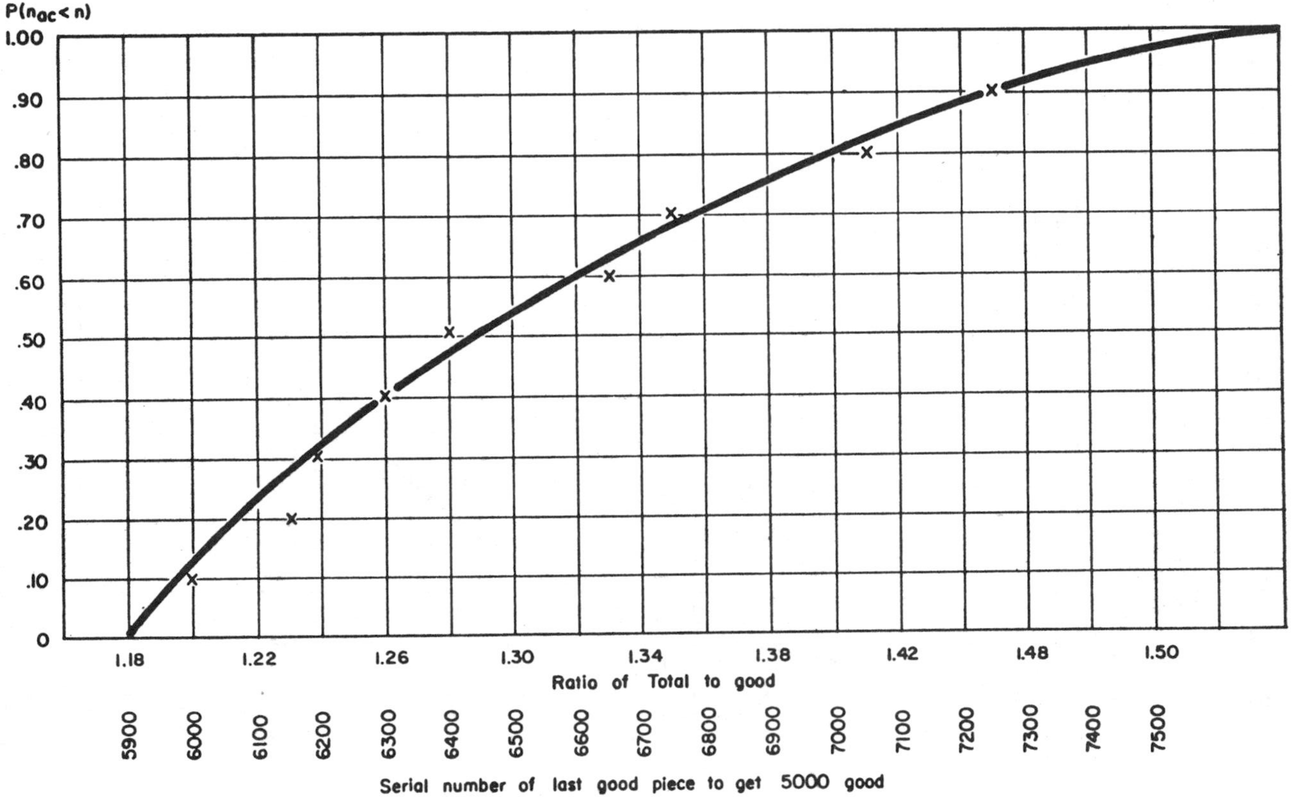

FIGURE 10-7.

ESTIMATING CHART FOR DETERMINATION OF Q,
GIVEN $\dfrac{P(n_{ac}=n)}{P(n_{ac}<n)}$

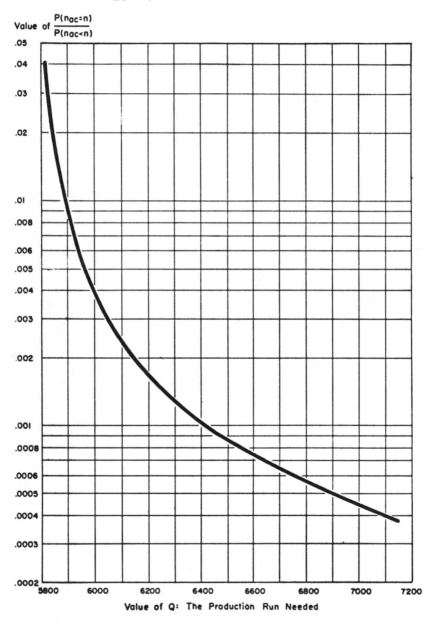

We can now read our optimum value of Q directly from this graph. Recall that for our valve schedule of 5000, the value of $\frac{k}{K}$ was .005. Reading for a value of $\frac{P(n_{ac} = n)}{P(n_{ac} < n)}$ of .005 on our graph we find it equivalent to 6092, the number to be scheduled.

TABLE 10-13. Estimating Work Table for Determining Value of Ratio $\dfrac{P(n_{ac} = n)}{P(n_{ac} < n)}$

n-value Bracket	n	Estimated P(n)	$P(n_{ac} < n)$	$P(=)/P(<)$
5890–5999	5945	.0011	.06	.018
6000–6099	6050	.00094	.18	.0052
6100–6199	6150	.00081	.27	.0030
6200–6299	6250	.00072	.35	.0021
6300–6399	6350	.00065	.44	.0015
6400–6499	6450	.00060	.50	.0012
6500–6599	6550	.00056	.56	.0010
6600–6699 etc.	6650	.000525	.63	.0083

SUMMARY

1. Bayesian analysis furnishes a method of dealing objectively with the quantitative side of subjective judgments and of spelling out the implications of what we deem to be the probabilities for profit expectations. Four very useful Bayesian decision tools are: sequential decision theory, competitive bidding strategy, the inventory model, and the production run and scrap loss model.

2. Sequential decision theory helps us reduce, to an objective statement of comparable present values, each of the decision paths in a situation in which some of the action alter-

natives lead to the need to make further choices in a series of chains of unequal lengths and probability composition.

3. Competitive bidding strategy uses the kind of background experience normally considered in a subjective manner in any competitive bidding situation, to arrive at an objectively stated estimate of the probability of winning at any given bid level, and the consequent profit position value of any given bid.

4. The inventory model helps us minimize costs in any logistics situation in which, (a) there is a lag between ordering an input and having that input available, (b) the usage during this lead-time is not completely predictable, (c) there are fixed costs associated with each acquisition of an input, and (d) there are variable costs associated with any discrepancies between the amount available for use during the lead-time and the amount needed. The model is more widely useful than the label indicates, important as physical inventory problems can be.

5. The production run and scrap loss model is a helpful solution, using graphic methods, for any situation in which the cost of an overage is proportional to its size, but in which an underage of any amount results in a given substantial lump-sum loss.

GLOSSARY OF BAYESIAN MODEL TERMS

SEQUENTIAL DECISION: a decision which can result in the need for additional decisions rather than in a definite outcome for all of the acts.

Profit position of a decision sequence: the final profit which would be realized if every act in the chain of decisions has a favorable outcome, discounted by the cumulative probability of that favorable outcome.

Risk affordability: the ability, psychological and physical, of the decision maker to withstand the kinds of losses inherent in the risks to be taken.

Utility of a profit return: the marginal value which a decision maker might attach to the profit he would realize if successful.

COMPETITIVE BIDDING STRATEGY: an approach to estimating the worth, the profit position, to a potential bidder of each of the bids he might make on a specific contract, given his assessment of the past history of competitor bidding and of the current interest of the industry in this particular contract.

INVENTORY MODEL: an approach to estimating the least cost rule for input action in a system of repeated batch inputs with an appreciable time lag between the act of ordering the inputs and their availability for use, and with uncertainty concerning the output demand during this lead time. The model requires that there be substantial fixed costs associated with the input act, regardless of size of input, and that costs be variable for any shortages or overages resulting from the prescribed input. Applies to any situation meeting these conditions, not just inventory problems.

Cost of acquisition: all costs other than the cost of the items themselves, associated with the input act itself. In the case of an actual inventory problem, this would be such costs as the cost of preparing orders, receiving goods, putting them in stock, and the like.

Cost of carrying inventory: all of the costs associated with maintaining the availability of an input until it is needed as an output. In the case of a physical inventory, the financial cost of carrying the goods, cost of warehouse space, deterioration in value during storage, and the like.

Lead-time and demand during lead-time: lead-time is the time which elapses between the initiation of an act of acquisition of an input and the time such inputs become available as potential outputs. Demand during lead-time is the potential need for output during this lead-time, the potential usage for the items of input.

Order quantity (Q): the quantity to be ordered under the rule as calculated.

Reorder point (R): the stock level (level of available outputs) at which an input acquisition act is to be initiated (an order to be placed).

Stockout cost: the loss associated with the unavailability of an output item would be composed of any opportunity losses from missed sales, for example, plus other costs such as loss of customer goodwill.

PRODUCTION RUN AND SCRAP LOSS MODEL: an approach for the estimation of the least cost rule for scheduling acquisition in any situation in which exact useful output to be obtained is uncertain, there are substantial fixed costs associated with the initiation of the act of acquisition, variable costs associated

293

with any resulting overages, but lump sum fixed costs associated with an underage of any size.

MATRICES AND MATRIX DECISION TOOLS: GAME THEORY, LINEAR PROGRAMMING, QUEUEING THEORY, MARKOV CHAINS

Four quite different decision models share a common computational technique--the modern matrix method of algebraic notation which grew out of the use of the digital computer: game theory, linear programming, and two kind of Markov chains--absorbing and non-absorbing. In the matrix method of notation, the coefficients of an expression are listed in tabular form, separated from the variables which they modify. Traditional notation couples the coefficient with the variable to which it applies--$10x + 3y$, for instance, juxtaposing the 10 to the variable x which it modifies. In matrix notation, the coefficients are listed in rows and the variables which they modify are indicated separately to one side, in a specific format. A matrix appears to be, and is in truth, one particular form of table exactly like those we use all of the time when summarizing numerical data. It is simply a more useful form of notation, to carry out computations identical to those of traditional algebra.

Assume, for example, that we are showing the September sales records of the three salesmen in the Metropolis District of the Industrial Fastener Corp. Industrial has only three classes of products, bolts at $1.50 per gross, nuts at $1.00 per gross, and rivets at $.75 per gross. We would usually summarize the monthly unit sales in some such form as:

TABLE 11-1. September Sales for District 9

Item (gross)	Jim	Joe	Jerry
Bolts	9,372	10,169	8,791
Nuts	7,867	11,243	13,319
Rivets	12,289	3,918	7,913

We would be somewhat astonished if our statistician gave us the table in the same form we have always used for our algebra:

TABLE 11-2. September Sales for District 9

Jim =	Joe =	Jerry =
9,372 gross bolts +	10,169 gross bolts +	8,791 gross bolts
7,867 gross nuts +	11,243 gross nuts +	13,391 gross nuts
12,289 gross rivets +	3,918 gross rivets +	7,913 gross rivets

We would consider the repetition of the item labels (bolts, nuts, and rivets) as superfluous, and mathematicians have come to feel that this does not make sense when those labels are the symbols of algebra. Matrix notation format differs slightly from Table 11-1, and it uses terms which could be unfamiliar. The term vector, for example, denotes any single collection of numbers or symbols written either in a row or in a column. The number or symbol is itself called a component. A combination of row vectors or column vectors in a specific tabular form is called a matrix. Examples of row vectors are:

$$(1, -3, 5) \qquad (x, y, z, -k)$$

If arranged vertically instead of horizontally, these same components would be in the form of column vectors:

$$\begin{pmatrix} 1 \\ -3 \\ 5 \end{pmatrix} \qquad \begin{pmatrix} x \\ y \\ z \\ -k \end{pmatrix}$$

A series of equations is represented as a matrix of their coefficients, with the variables listed as a row vector to the left to designate the label variables in the column. Thus if written in the form of matrix notation, Table 11-1 would look like:

(bolts, nuts, rivets)
$$\begin{vmatrix} 9,372 & 10,169 & 8,791 \\ 7,867 & 11,243 & 13,319 \\ 12,289 & 3,918 & 7,913 \end{vmatrix}$$

If we were to put this in the form of instructions for getting the dollar value of the sales of each salesman, it would be shown as follows:

(1.50, 1.00, .75)
$$\begin{vmatrix} 9,372 & 10,169 & 8,791 \\ 7,867 & 11,243 & 13,319 \\ 12,289 & 3,918 & 7,913 \end{vmatrix}$$

leading to the following result:

$$\begin{vmatrix} 14,058 & 15,253 & 13,186 \\ 7,867 & 11,243 & 13,319 \\ 9,173 & 2,939 & 5,935 \end{vmatrix}$$

If, in addition, the bonus commission rates differed, with Jim receiving 12%, Joe 10%, and Jerry 11%, instructions for computing the commission rates for each class of product sold would be shown as follows, with a column vector listing the amounts by which successive columns would be multiplied:

$$\begin{vmatrix} 14,058 & 15,253 & 13,186 \\ 7,867 & 11,243 & 13,319 \\ 9,173 & 2,939 & 5,935 \end{vmatrix} \begin{pmatrix} .12 \\ .10 \\ .11 \end{pmatrix}$$

This would be read as instructions to obtain the total commissions on bolts by solving the expression:

(14,058 x .12) + (15,253 x .10) + 13,186 x .11)

and similarly for the other two rows, giving commission payouts on nuts and rivets. Note that the symbol + is always understood unless a minus sign is indicated.

Convenience of use in computer input is the main reason for matrix notation. The tedium of the necessary computation involved in each of the four tools to be discussed in this chapter usually requires access to a computer.

Game theory notation clearly illustrates the tabular

nature of a matrix, and makes a good starting point. This tool has been touted so widely that we need to understand the limitations which have disappointed the hopes that were aroused.

THE THEORY OF GAMES: FORESTALLING THE MOVES OF A COMPETITOR

Game theory has had such useful application to strategic military thinking that high hopes have been held for adapting it to competitive business decision. But military conflict is a much simpler type of confrontation than the differentiated competition of business enterprises. The hopes have not been fulfilled, and any expectation that game theory will ever play a major role in the business decision process seems to be wishful thinking. Thus two expert sources have concluded that the theory contains too much simplification for business use:

"It is not surprising that the 13 years that have elapsed since the publication of The Theory of Games have seen no important applications of game theory to concrete economic problems."*

(With reference to nonzero-sum games and proposed solutions:) "The fact that none (of these various solutions) fits every conceivable nonzero-sum game is perhaps an indication that such games do not reveal enough of the richness of real-world situations to provide universally satisfactory answers."**

At least one problem is the very necessary simplification which the use of numbers themselves entails. Although a real source of strength in the normal use of mathematical models, this very simplification becomes a fatal weakness in attempts to estimate the outcome of complex multidirectional competition characteristic of the marketplace.

Nevertheless, the game theory approach does yield qualitative insights into the incentives leading to such various business phenomena as cartels and other coalitions, price leadership, and the emphasis on so-called "nonprice competition",

---

*Robert Dorfman et al., Linear Programming and Economic Analysis, McGraw-Hill (New York, 1958), p. 445.

**Kemeny, et al., Finite Mathematics With Business Applications, Prentice-Hall (Englewood Cliffs, N.J., 1962), pp. 461-462.

more properly designated as product and promotion competition
(see the author's Economics of Managerial Decision, Appleton-
Century-Crofts, 1965). Game models do indicate the kinds of
rational decisions managers will arrive at in the absence of
knowledge of a competitor's plans, and the pressures that may
exist to soften competition.   Basically, there are three types
of game structures:

      1. zero-sum, strictly determined games

      2. zero-sum, nonstrictly determined games

      3. nonzero-sum games.

     Definite solutions exist only for the first category--
zero-sum, strictly determined games--and then only when limited to two players in direct conflict, or to a multiplayer game
reduced in essence to a two-player game by coalitions. Workable probabilistic solutions exist for two-person zero-sum,
nonstrictly determined games. For the nonzero-sum game,
even when limited to two persons, no satisfactory general solutions have been developed. Regardless of game type, no really
satisfactory solutions have been developed for games of more
than two persons.

The Two-Person, Zero-Sum, Strictly-Determined Game

     A two-person zero-sum game is one limited to two
players, and one in which the gains of one just offset the losses
of the other. Let us consider the simplest form of such a game
in terms of two players: Max Row (R) and Min Column (C).
Each has two cards: R has a red 7 and a black 7, C a black 7
and a red 5. The rules of their game call for both to expose
one of their cards on an agreed upon signal. If the cards match
in color, R wins by any amount by which his card is higher than
that of C. If R does not match the color of C's card, then C
wins by the amount of the difference in the card values. The
game can be represented by the payoff table (matrix) for either
one of the players. In this case we will use R's table and look
at it on the assumption that Max Row is trying to maximize his
gain, and Min Column's aim would therefore be, from this representation of R's table, to minimize his losses. A positive
entry means a gain for R and a loss for C; a negative entry, a
loss for R, and a gain for C. (If we were to look at it from the
standpoint of C's payoff table, the values would be reversed.)
Conventionally, R, the maximizing player's strategies are

represented by the horizontal row strategies (thus R for Row), and the minimizing players (since this is not his table), by the vertical columns (thus C for Column). Thus if R chooses to expose his black 7 and C turns up his black 7, then R matches, but wins nothing, while if C turns up his red 5 instead, R loses 2, and thus our table shows a -2 for this event:

Player C
plays

		Black 7	Red 5
Player R plays	Black 7	0	-2
	Red 7	0	2

Obviously, then R would not pick the strategy of turning up his black 7, but expose his red 7 instead. In the latter case, he might still not win anything if C chooses to turn up his black 7, but could win 2 if C exposes his red 5. C, on the other hand, hoping to keep his possible losses down, will choose to expose his black 7, since he will never lose if he does, whereas he can lose 2 if he turns up his red 5 and R chooses to expose his red 7. Thus in this game, there is one clear strategy for each player, one play he would always choose to come out best. R should always play his red 7, since he can thus make certain he never loses, and has a chance to gain the maximum amount. His <u>optimum</u> <u>strategy</u> is thus: play red 7. C will always play black 7, since this way, he achieves his aim of minimum losses: he can never lose (and never win either). His optimum strategy for minimizing losses is thus: play black 7. This particular game is also a <u>fair</u> game, so-called because neither player has either a net gain or a net loss if both play their optimum strategies. The <u>value of this</u> <u>game (v)</u>, is zero, since this is the best either player can make sure of winning. If one of them could assure himself of any particular gain--say 2--then the value of the game would be 2, and the player who could assure himself of that much should pay an entry fee of 2 to get in, if the play is to be fair.

This is a <u>strictly determined game</u> because there is one entry in the matrix, the value designated above as <u>v</u>, which is at one and the same time the <u>minimum</u> for the row designating a strategy of the row, or maximizing, player, and the <u>maximum</u> of the strategy for a column, or minimizing, player.

The table by which we have represented this game is a conventionalized table of gain and loss values for the <u>row (R) player</u>, the one who is viewed as on the offensive (in military terms), or as trying to <u>maximize his gains</u> (in economic language). Each row in the table represents one of his possible strategies by listing the contingent values for each of the <u>defensive</u> strategies of the <u>column</u> (C) player. The latter is assumed to be trying to <u>minimize his losses.</u> The table above has been couched in terms of a specific card gamble, but is really a generalized representation for any situation in which the respective gains and losses for two opponents have the same relative values listed. The situation could be some other kind of gambling game, in which the figures stand for money gains and losses, a military skirmish in which gains might be casualties, or amount of territory gains, or some other strategic objectives. Or, if we could find such an uncomplicated business situation, the values could be business profits and losses, or market share gains and losses of two opponents with identical products seeking the identical market segment, one seeking to take over, the other to hold his position.

We need only the bare bones of the matrix itself to represent any two-person, zero-sum, straight-conflict situation, since each horizontal row is always understood to represent all possible value outcomes of one alternative strategy of the maximizing player (R) and each vertical column represents the results for R of each of the counter-strategies of the opposing minimizing player (C, for column). Like all symbolic abstractions, this convention enables us to strip down and analyze the essentials of the gains and losses involved without concerning ourselves with the details of any given situation (such as the rules of the game) which result in the listed values, or to invent some simplified gambling situation to fit the results.

A conflict situation can be strictly determined without being fair, both in the casino and in textbooks. Any game in which one player can assure himself of a consistent profit is a zero-sum game if the losses of one are equal to the gains of his opponent. The following matrix represents such a game:

	C	
	Strategy C_1	Strategy C_2
R Strategy R_1	9	6
Strategy R_2	-8	-4

Given the knowledge that this is the situation, R will always play strategy R_1, since he will always win whatever C does: 9 if C plays strategy C_1 and 6 if C plays strategy C_2. C, on the other hand, since his objective is to minimize his losses, will always play strategy C_2, since he can lose only 6 this way, whereas with strategy C_1 he could lose 9. The value of this game is thus 6, and it can be made fair only by means of a compensating side payment to C by R on entry into the game.

Nonstrictly Determined, Two-Person Zero-Sum Games

The strictly-determined game has little practical value except as a method of introducing the general principal of game analysis. No one knowingly enters conflict when the outcome is so foreordained. Conflict of any sort usually arises only when both opponents feel there is some uncertainty about the outcome of a given confrontation, and each believes that under some possible moves of his opponent, he can hope to win. When the proper choice of the move hinges on knowing the specific move of the opponent, the game is nonstrictly determined, even if it is also zero-sum. Consider the matrix:

		C	
		Strategy C_1	Strategy C_2
R	Strategy R_1	0	4
	Strategy R_2	6	0

If R plays his bottom row strategy, R_2, he can maximize his gains only if he can know that C will certainly play his left-hand column strategy, C_1. But C would do better, if he plays the right-hand column strategy, C_2, since the maximum possible loss is less in this column. If R foresees that C will play C_2, he would play R_1 to win 4. But if C were to know or guess this would be R's move, he would choose strategy C_1 and come out even. Thus any move either makes depends on his knowledge or estimate of the likely move of the other, and this move is uncertain on both sides.

Note that in the strictly determined games previously discussed, any move made by an opponent could be determined from the structure of the game, and the knowledge of his objectives (to maximize or to minimize). But in the nonstrictly determined game as above, any player needs advance knowledge of the opponent's immediate intentions to determine his best strategy. And knowledge of your own intended play by your opponent can enable him to defeat your hopes. Thus your own play must not be consistent, or the opponent will know what that strategy is. So the optimum strategy would have to be some kind of inconsistent one which would leave the opponent guessing, and thus help you win part of the time, at least: a mixed strategy.

A nonstrictly determined game is characteristized by the fact that all of the payoff values on one diagonal of the matrix are greater than any of the values on the opposite diagonal. Thus in the matrix just above, both the 6 and the 4 on the one diagonal are greater than the 0's on the other. Put in general terms, if we consider only a simple 2 x 2 matrix such as we have been using (there could be more strategies for each player, and thus a larger matrix), a game is nonstrictly determined if in the matrix

a	b
c	d

either: $a > b$, $a > c$, $d > b$, and $d > c$

or: $a < b$, $a < c$, $d < b$, and $d < c$

As already indicated, there cannot be a single optimum strategy in such a game, since this permits the opponent to choose an offsetting strategy which can let him deprive you of the maximum gains or saddle you with more than minimum

losses. Suppose in the matrix

0	4
6	0

, however, R

chooses the top-row strategy four-tenths of the time, and the bottom-row strategy six-tenths of the time, and does so in a completely random manner, so that C never knows what his opponents next move will be, and that C chooses some independent set of mixed strategies, then R can assure himself of some expected value $\underline{v}$ at the least, depending on C's choice. For each there will be an optimum mixed stragegy such that when both play at their optimum, R will get just the expected value, $\underline{v}$, and C will also realize $\underline{v}$ as his minimum loss. If C chooses a strategy with a probability mix of less than the optimum, his losses will be greater than $\underline{v}$, and R's gain greater. If C chooses the optimum probability mix, and R does not pick his, then C will lose less, and R gain less, over the long run. For a two-person, two-strategy game (a 2 x 2 matrix) the following five formulas tell what those strategies are, and the value of

the game, v; in the matrix

a	b
c	d

with R playing rows 1 and 2 in the ratio $\dfrac{r_1}{r_2}$ and C playing

columns 1 and 2 in ratio $\dfrac{c_1}{c_2}$:

$$r_1 = \frac{d - c}{a + d - b - c} \qquad\qquad r_2 = \frac{a - b}{a + d - b - c}$$

$$c_1 = \frac{d - b}{a + d - b - c} \qquad\qquad c_2 = \frac{a - c}{a + d - b - c}$$

$$v = \frac{ad - bc}{a + d - b - c}$$

For larger matrices, the solution is the same calculation as for linear programming, once the problem is expressed in positive numbers, as it can be. The right probability ratio and the inconsistency of individual play sequence are maintained by use of some randomizing device to choose the strategy for each play, such as a table of random numbers.

Nonzero-sum Games and More-Than-Two Person Games

Solutions of the two-person game type have been well-developed both because they yield definite generalized solutions, and because they are applicable to problems of military confrontations. Military showdowns normally tend to become two-sided pure-conflict situations in which what one side gains, the other loses. But business competition is almost never that simple. The number of "players" usually exceeds two, and it is seldom possible to really identify and define the total number of "players." When the number of players is more than two, then competition is not direct conflict, unless coalitions form that reduce the effective number to two. Even when there are only two sides, net losses and net gains are possible to both sides.

Consider a highly simplified situation such as we might have with two gasoline service stations on opposite corners, say the C Oil Co. and R Gas, with just two possible price strategies: a high price strategy, and a low price strategy. Assume also, that no other service stations are close by, and that the total sales possible in any one day are represented by the following matrix in which R's payoff is the first listed, and C's the second in each square. (Note that the payoff must be listed for both in a nonzero-sum game, because they differ in more than just the sign.) Assume that prices must stay at the level fixed when the station opens in the morning, and that fixed costs are the same for both--$20--so that either one loses money if his sales are less than this.

	C prices	
	High	Low
R prices High	(26, 26)	(16, 42)
R prices Low	(42, 16)	(17, 17)

Note one difference between such a matrix and the payoff matrix for the zero-sum games. In the zero-sum game, all payoffs were of the form that the payoff for C was always the negative of that for R. In the nonzero-sum game, some of the payoffs are not complementary. (In the one used, none of them are.)

Note that we now actually have two different matrixes, R's and C's.

R's =	High	Low
High	26	16
Low	42	17

C's =	High	Low
High	26	16
Low	42	17

Each now has a <u>maximin strategy</u>, defined as any optimal strategy for him in his own payoff matrix. In the case above, R's optimum strategy in his matrix is obviously "quote low price." But C's matrix indicates his is also "quote low price." In this case, both will then end up with a payoff of 17, and be operating at a loss. Unfortunately, this "gas war situation" is also an equilibrium point, defined as a pair of strategies such that neither player can increase his payoff by any strategy change, assuming that his opponent does not change his strategy. Thus, if R were to change to a high price strategy while C stayed with his low quotation, R would reduce his payoff to 16. Similarly, if C switches to a high price strategy while R stays at low, he also reduces his payoff from 17 to 16.

Such is not always the outcome of every nonzero-sum game, as can be demonstrated later. But it is a realistic one in cases in which the product sold is, so far as the consumer is concerned, homogeneous as between competitors. Obviously, such a situation cannot go on indefinitely, for either R or C or both will be bankrupted eventually. If one has stronger financial resources than the other, he might be tempted to let this happen--except that in real life, there are antitrust laws which pose the threat of legal penalties to any large competitor which attempts such a solution. Or they both might continue the "war" until the stronger one feels that the other is tired of it, and raises his price first. If he is right in assuming "price leadership" at the opportune moment, the other follows, to the same high price policy, and both are better off.

But neither will be doing nearly as well as he might with a different strategy, with a low price against the other high price. In addition, the matrix indicates that both together would be somewhat better off--that is, combined sales would be higher--if one had a low price and the other a high price. War having failed, what might they do? They might form a cartel, with one agreeing to stick to the high price segment of the market for a side payment which would make up for the business he would lose, plus a share of the additional combined payoff total of 6 resulting when both follow the high price policy (26 + 26 = 52 as compared with 42 + 16 = 58). Or they might actually merge, and new company sell under two labels at the two stations: one station with a low price label, the other with a high price label. Or, if one is very much stronger financially than the other, he might enforce a split giving himself the lion's share of the profits of a high-low policy under the threat of pursuing a low price policy until the other went bankrupt. A solution such as this does give us some insight into the forces which give rise to various non-competitive arrangements in business.

There is another type of strategy not reflected in the matrix which is the most common one followed in business-- remove the core of the problem, the homogeneity of the product.

One station owner may decide to let the other specialize in selling gasoline, at a low price to that part of the market to which price is important. He would go after more business per customer from each one he does reach by offering added services--mechanical work, lubricating services, road conditions information, or other services highly valued by a different market segment. Or he may up his profit margin by differentiating his product in the consumer's mind by intensive, well-planned advertising. Then we no longer have a direct conflict situation, but two stations selling somewhat different products to different market segments, and our game theory is no longer of much help, even in the case of a hardship equilibrium point such as we have hypothesized in the problem above.

Not all nonzero-sum situations lead to hardship equilibrium points. The fact that nearly all business competition is differentiated competition leads to situations in which what looks like competition can often be a direct benefit to both participants, and the maximum strategy leads to the maximum level for both parties. Thus shopping centers have learned that having two department stores in the center will not only increase business for the center, but that both stores will sell more than either would alone. Women's clothing stores nearly always do better if there are at least three in the same shopping district. In such a situation we might have a matrix like this:

		C Store	
		Location 1	Location 2
R Store	Location 1	(33, 31)	(14, 21)
	Location 2	(21, 14)	(20, 26)

In this case, obviously both R and C will choose location 1 by mutual agreement, and this is not the sort of agreement that needs to be hidden from legal view. At other times, both may have somewhat different talents for serving different market segments, and a matrix like the following may result:

		C Mfg. Co.	
		Product Variation 1	Product Variation 2
R Mfg. Co.	Product Var. 1	(26, 20)	(36, 31)
	Product Var. 2	(21, 14)	(20, 26)

In this case, each participant's matrix leads to a maximin strategy that is the same no matter what the other does: R will make the product variation 1 which one market segment desires, and C will make product variation 2, at which he is better, and which has a good demand in a different market segment. The result will be a payoff of 36 for R, and 31 for C.

Thus some nonzero-sum games have profitable equilibrium points, and others do not. Those that do not must have solutions outside the terms of the calculations. Or there may be more than one equilibrium point. Thus, game theory provides some qualitative insight into the general direction in which competitive forces may push business action. But the alternatives lie in so many directions (collusion, market leadership, product differentiation of several kinds, etc.) that general solutions are not likely to be formulated for the really critical situations, nor the calculations to give precise answers on the correct strategies.

LINEAR PROGRAMMING: STRIKING THE RIGHT PROPORTIONS

In linear programming, the operating side of business has gained an invaluable tool for use in those situations in which the problem is to find the least costly mix of alternate components or the most profitably proportioned output mix from limited resources. All of the various kinds of problems that may be solved with linear programming have four elements in common:

1. We have a limited number of resources and of choices, and we wish to sustain the least input cost or obtain the most valuable output mix. (The goal of minimum cost or maximum profit is sometimes referred to as the objective function.)

2. There are certain restraints on the choices we can make--certain conditions of "not more than" or "not less than." A general one for all linear programming problems is that all inputs and outputs must be nonnegative (that is, they must either be positive in value, or zero).

3. Within limits, we are free to vary the proportions of components in such a way as to satisfy the restraints and arrive at an optimum (maximum or minimum) solution or solutions. (There may be more than one solution.) The quantities

we proportion are sometimes referred to as the <u>choice vari-</u>
<u>ables.</u>

   4. Restraints are, or can be, expressed as linear
(straight-line) equations and the objective function can be at-
tained by direct (or linear) proportioning of the choice variables,
or by some mathematical transformation of them into linear
form. A linear equation has the general mathematical form
$y = ax + b$, where a and b are constants.

   Most operating relationships and requirements are
linear in form.* Within plant or shift capacity limits, variable
production costs tend to be linear, and so do many price-
quantity relationships within the narrow range open to decision.
Many decision requirements are in the form of linear restraints, the stipulation that they be "at least" or "no more
than."

   Even when the relationship itself is not linear, transformation into linear form is often easy. Relationships characterized by a constant percentage change--exponential rela-
tionships--become linear when expressed in logarithms. Total
production cost, including both the fixed and variable components, is hyperbolic in form: $y = 1/x + c$ in its simplest form.
By substituting $z = 1/x$, and maximizing z, we can minimize x.
Such usable tricks are familiar to anyone with even a moderate
training in mathematics. For a broad range of middle management decisions, data from repetitive operations is usually
available for linear programming of extremal points, by setting
the relationships up as a series of simultaneous equations which
can be solved by the simplex method. This latter is a version
of the method we learned in high school, except that in linear
programming we usually do not have enough equations to solve
for every variable and must resort to a tedious cut-and-try
approach on a computer. The basic principle can be illustrated
with a highly simplified textbook example.**

---

   *The discussion of method which follows is adapted
from Chester R. Wasson, <u>The Economics of Managerial De-</u>
<u>cision,</u> Appleton-Century-Crofts, New York, 1965, pp. 211-
213.

   **Adapted from Kemeny, Schleifer, Snell, and Thomp-
son, <u>Finite Mathematics with Business Applications</u> (Englewood
Cliffs, N.J.: Prentice-Hall, Inc., 1962), pp. 379-380.

The maker of both passenger cars and trucks has a factory divided into two shops: (1) Assembly Shop 1, which requires 5 man-days for a truck and 2 man-days for each passenger vehicle, and (2) Shop 2, which does the finishing at the rate of 3 man-days per vehicle, whether passenger car or truck. Shop 1 uses 180 man-days per week at capacity operation, Shop 2, 135 man-days per week. Profit on each truck completed is $300, on each passenger car $200. To maximize operating profit, what mix of trucks and passenger cars should be scheduled?

In mathematical notation, the problem is stated as follows:

Let x_1 = no. of trucks, x_2 = no. of cars
Then the values of these two variables must be such that:
$$5x_1 + 2x_2 \leq 180 \quad \text{and} \quad 3x_1 + 3x_2 \leq 135$$

subject to the restrictions that $300x_1 + 200x_2$ has at least one real value, and that $x_1 \geq 0 \leq x_2$ (that is, that some trucks or cars will be built).

Every possible solution to the problem as thus defined lies in the shaded area of the graph in Figure 11-1, on which all of the conditions laid down appear as straight lines. Not all of the infinity of points within this area are at a maximum, of course, and in this case, only one is. The maximum can only be located by comparing all of the points which could be at the maximum profit. Fortunately, we need to consider only those points at the intersection of the lines, as indicated. Were there not some such limit on the number of solutions, even a computer would be useless--the number of possible solution points is truly infinite.

Not all such problems are soluble; sometimes the conditions are incompatible. Sometimes there are two or more solutions meeting all conditions equally, and management will make a choice between them on some other basis.

Linear programming applications are many and varied, because the allocation of scarce resources to get maximum profit is at the heart of all business operations decisions. Indeed, one form was developed before the computer was invented or the general linear programming algorithm discovered. This was the transportation model, originally so designated because its first uses were to find the best shipping plan from a series of points to different receiving points, with differing shipping costs from each shipping point. Certain universal simplicities in this type of problem permit calculation by hand. Though the name transportation model still persists, some of its more useful applications are not concerned with transportation or transportation costs. The model is applicable to any business or economic problem in which we seek a minimum or maximum of some resultant allocation of the inputs subject to restraints on both inputs and outputs. It is, for example, of value in determining the best disposition of a military force or in any other assignment of a limited number of silled personnel of various abilities to varied responsibilities, provided we can arrive at some measure of individual output value. Or it can be used to determine the assignment of various kinds of competing machines or other capital equipment to an assortment of scheduled jobs, to minimize time, or costs, or some other relevant measure.

Figure 11-1. Graphic Representation of Truck-Car Production
            Problem

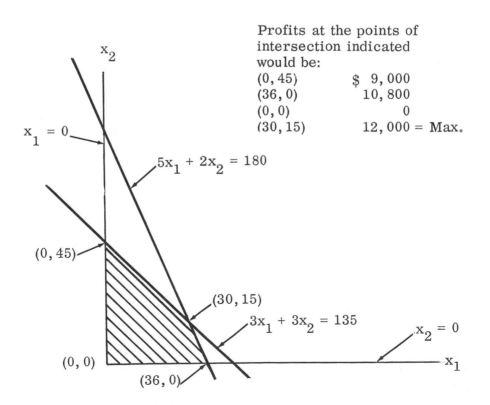

Profits at the points of
intersection indicated
would be:

(0, 45)	$ 9,000
(36, 0)	10,800
(0, 0)	0
(30, 15)	12,000 = Max.

x_2

$x_1 = 0$

$5x_1 + 2x_2 = 180$

(0, 45)

(30, 15)

$3x_1 + 3x_2 = 135$

$x_2 = 0$

(0, 0)

(36, 0)

x_1

The typical transportation problem starts with limits on the inputs of each component, such as the capacity of the individual factories out of which shipments are being made. These limited inputs are usually completely used up to meet and just satisfy numerically limited outputs, such as shipments to designated localities. There are effective restraints on both the inputs and the outputs.

In general, however, linear programming requires only that there be restraints on one or the other, either on the inputs or on the outputs. In one typical linear programming model, the so-called diet, or feed-mix problem, the restraint is on input cost, not quantity. In the kind of problem from which this model takes its name, the aim is to produce a diet meeting certain minimum standards of nutritive composition (protein, fat, carbohydrate, vitamins, minerals, etc.) at least cost, given a set of ingredients containing various proportions of the elements. All "diet" problems are not feed cost problems. Any problem of allocating a freely available output to get a minimum cost can be a diet model problem, so long as the proportions can be combined linearly. The production of a mixed fertilizer fits the model.

In other cases, there may be no effective quantitative restraints on the output, only the objective of getting the most profitable mix within broad limits of proportionality. Oil refinery product mix has been one important application. Processing of the crude oil and other feedstock elements can be so regulated as to yield varying quantities of gasoline, kerosene, diesel fuel, heavy fuel oil, lubricating oils, etc. All of the products can be disposed of at some price, but the price and profit per unit of input will vary between products, and the yield will vary depending on the mix.

Although there is no published account of using linear programming to allocate shelf space in a store, the problem of maximizing profitability of the merchandise mix would seem to be identical, up to a point at least, with that of optimizing the output of an oil refinery. One recent interesting application of linear programming is the development of optimum operating plans for individual farms, given a known mix of land types and capital equipment.

Not all allocation problems can be solved by linear programming, however. After considerable experimentation, the Young and Rubicam advertising agency decided that the optimum decision rules for allocating an advertising campaign be-

tween media did not fit the requirements for linear programming and developed a different computer model which did seem
to be of value. *

MARKOV CHAIN ANALYSIS: PREDICTING THE OUTCOME OF
A DYNAMIC SITUATION

     Most mathematical models postulate a relatively stable
set of relationships. Markov chains (or Markov processes),
by contrast, are useful only when we can assume some underlying force for changes in the relationships between some sets
of universes. A fictional example will illustrate the nature of
the two kinds of Markov chains--absorbing and nonabsorbing,
of which the nonabsorbing is the simpler.
     Consider the mythical Republic of Rurbania (ROR), a
country in which, for the moment, no one dies and no babies
are born. The population of ROR, however, is not static--
there is a constant two-way flow of migrants between city and
the country, as can be seen from the following table:

Residence type at the beginning of the year	Percentage distribution of the same people at year's-end:	
	City	Rural
City	90	10
Rural	30	70

This cross-migratory flow goes on year after year, continuously altering the rural-urban balance until some equilibrium
point is reached--a point at which 10% of the city population
just equals in number the 30% it gains from the rural-to-city
flow, and the residential composition is in dynamic balance.
     In Markov language, the table above would be labelled
a matrix of transitional underlying probabilities. "Residence
type at beginning of the year" denotes the previous state of nature (whether city residence or rural in this case).

---

*William T. Moran, "Practical Media Decisions and
the Computer," Journal of Marketing, Vol. 27, No. 3 (July,
1963), pp. 26-30.

"Residence at year's-end" is the succeeding state of nature. The equilibrium point at which the process will come into dynamic balance (in this case, at the point of 75% city) is known as the fixed point.

All of the states of nature in the above example were nonabsorbing. That is, all were reversible. Those who moved to the country did not necessarily remain, nor did those moving to the city. We need merely bow to the reality of death, however, to convert our ROR example to an illustration of an absorbing chain--of a chain containing one or more states of nature, transition into which is not reversible. Death, of course, is not the only irreversible state in life. Graduation is an absorbing state in a study of school populations, completion of the transaction and bagging of groceries in a supermarket checkout line, etc. Because of this absorbing state, the fixed point of any absorbing chain is zero for all nonabsorbing states. Clearly, the potential values of the two types of Markovian analysis differ. The widest-spread use of the nonabsorbing chain has probably been in the analysis of brand-switching.

Where Are We Heading? The Nonabsorbing Markov Chain

Consider our problem as members of the marketing team of Blue Sky Detergents who are evaluating the effects of our introduction of a new special duty detergent, Orion, formulated to capture parts of the market segments of two established brands, Castor and Pollux. We put Orion into test markets three months ago, with suitable promotional fanfare, and simultaneously commissioned the tabulations of a consumer purchase diary panel to be able to follow consumer buying of ours and competing products. We have met to discuss the significance of the tabulations drawn from the panel purchases in the second and third months and to see if we can divine how well we are doing. Our research analyst informs us we had 18.5 percent of the market in the third month, as compared with 43 percent for Castor and 39.5 percent for Pollux. He interprets the panel data to mean we are going to get an even larger share of the market. The tabulations, he points out, indicate that we hang onto more initial users than either Castor or Pollux do, and gain a larger share of their previous users than they get back from us.

TABLE 11-3. Brand-Switching Pattern During Third Month
After Introduction of Orion Brand Into the
Subopolis Test Market. (The numbers denote
the fraction of those who were purchasers of the
brand listed to the left during the second month.)

Brand bought during the second month	Brand purchased during the third month		
	Castor	Pollux	Orion
Castor	.57	.15	.28
Pollux	.15	.52	.33
Orion	.17	.16	.67

It certainly seems to us that the analyst is right, and
that we have indeed a detergent whose characteristics do meet,
better than either of the competing brands, the desires of a
substantial segment of the market they have been getting. But
we would like a more specific fix on how big that segment is.
It certainly looks like better than one-fifth, but how much better? Just looking at the table as is, it is pretty hard to tell.

But suppose we look at this table as a transitional
probability matrix, as an estimate of what the brand-switching
pattern in any one month may be, at least as long as there is
no change in competitor's products or in their sales promotion
elements. The first state of nature is then the brand purchased
during the second month, the succeeding state of nature is the
brand purchased during the third month, and the fixed point we
calculate from this matrix tells us our ultimate market share
for Orion. The calculation itself is not very intricate, but, for
a 3 x 3 table such as this, could involve quite a few steps.
However, we can simplify the problem by not concerning ourselves with how the segments we do not snare divide up between
Castor and Pollux.

We therefore revamp our tabulations into a simpler
2 x 2 table, as follows:

315

TABLE 11–4. Simplified Brand–Switching Pattern

Purchases in second month	Purchases in third month	
	Orion	Not–Orion
Orion	.67	.33
Not–Orion	.30	.70

Viewed as a transition matrix, each line is viewed as the coefficients of two variables, standing for Orion and Not-Orion, and we make use of the known properties of transition probability matrices that are nonabsorbing: As the process proceeds through successive time periods, it approaches (and usually rather quickly) a limiting value we call a fixed point. This can be demonstrated empirically by trying these switching percentages out over several periods, from any starting point of quantities. At this fixed point, the customers being gained by switching from other brands just compensate for the number of customers being lost to other brands.

The calculation of this simpler 2 x 2 table in terms of traditional algebraic notation is possible if we let:

x be the Orion market share

y be the Not–Orion market share

We then solve for two conditions which must hold at the point of equilibrium:

(1) The Orion and Not-Orion market shares together comprise the whole market, or

$x + y = 1$

(2) The number of Orion purchasers lost to Not-Orion just equals the number of Not-Orion purchasers switching to Orion, or

$$.33x = .30y$$

and thus

$$\frac{.33}{.30}x = y = \frac{11}{10}x$$

Substituting this value of y in the first equation gives:

$$x = \frac{11}{10}x = 1 = \frac{21}{10}x$$

and thus

$$21x = 10$$

$$x = \frac{10}{21}$$

Since

$$x + y = 1$$

then

$$y = 1 - x = \frac{11}{21}$$

Hence our table of brand-switching during the third month implies that Orion will get about 10/21 of the market. Exactly 10/21? Probably not. For a number of reasons, our data for the third month is not a precise estimate of the actual transition probabilities. And we probably cannot assume that the makers of Castor and Pollux are going to stand still as Orion threatens to take over a large part of their market shares. But as of now, we have a product capable of sustaining a differential advantage for perhaps between 40 percent and 60 percent of the market, and can lay out future strategy on this basis.

Note that in none of this calculation were we concerned with what the current market share was. All we needed to know was the estimate of the percentages of brand loyalty and switching, i.e., the transitional probability matrix. The Markov chain might well be dubbed the rumor-mill model. The final result is solely dependent on the built-in bias toward change and is unaffected by state of origin.

The nonabsorbing Markov chain would be a useful but rather specialized model to know if brand-switching problems were its only use. But it would seem a useful technique to determine the possibility of changes that might be taking place in underlying probabilities of other sorts, e. g. , changes in the trend in public taste and fashion, whether they concern clothing, automobile designs, or forms of investment. Any change in basic trend would show up as a significant change in the fixed point.

What Are the Implications of the Dynamics? The Absorbing Chain

In our brand-switching problem, no transition was irreversible. None of the detergents was so completely preferred that none of the users, once they tried it, might not go back to some other brand. The situation simply shifted until a point was reached at which the shifting and shifting back cancelled out. But there are various kinds of changes over time in business and elsewhere in which some of the states are absorbing. Once the change reaches one of these states, there is no reversal. Consider, for instance, the following table, showing the experience of a hypothetical trailer rental agency operating in three cities: A, B, and C. While the majority of the rentals are for local use, trailers are rented on a one-way basis and thus may start in any one of the three cities and end up in any other of the three. But trailers may come to another kind of end, too: They may be stolen or wrecked. Such trailers never return; they reach an absorbing state, as shown in the following table giving a typical month's experience:

TABLE 11-5. Starting Point and Destination of Drivuron
            Trailers Rented During the Month
            (In percentages of those from the designated
            origin)

Place of Origin	Terminal City or Condition			
	A	B	C	Lost or Wrecked (L)
A	58	20	19	3
B	18	63	15	4
C	13	21	62	1
Lost, wrecked (L)	0	0	0	100

Computational Format

	L	A	B	C
L	1	0	0	0
A	.03	.58	.20	.19
B	.04	.18	.63	.15
C	.01	.13	.21	.62

If we change the percentages to decimals, we have a table of transition probabilities, or a Markov matrix, with one absorbing state, lost or wrecked. If no new trailers are purchased, we need no computer to calculate the end result: all trailers will finally end up lost or wrecked. If we had more than one absorbing state--if, for example, trailers were sold on reaching a certain point of service or dilapidation--we would have to make a calculation to determine how many would end up in each of the absorbing states.

But our principal interest is likely to be in the answers to some different questions:

1. How long, on the average, will it be before the process is absorbed? In terms of our illustration, how long will a trailer be in service, on the average?

2. How many periods of time will the process be in each nonabsorbing state? That is, how many months is a trailer likely to be in each of the cities during its term of service?

3. How much input is needed to stabilize the process at some desired point of equilibrium? How many trailers must we buy each month to hold the stock at the current level?

4. At what points in the process should the input be injected to hold the process in some form of desired balance? In this case, where should we have new trailers shipped to start their service, A, B, C, and in what proportion? If we look at the original table, we can see that A loses more to B and C than it gets back from either. Likewise, C ships more to B than it gets in return.

The answers to each of these questions comes from a different calculation, but one that follows a generalized standard and is a simple computer program. Even for a highly simplified illustration such as the one given, the tedium of cal-

319

culation requires a computer, and even a short explanation of the process requires use of matrix notation. Those who are familiar with this form of mathematical symbolism, will find an explanation of nonabsorbing chains and some uses in Kemeny, et al., Finite Mathematics with Business Applications (Prentice-Hall, Inc.,), pages 282-298.

In other types of problems, other questions would be asked, and a calculable answer would be available. For example, one whole branch of Markov analysis deals with waiting-line, or queuing problems. The line at the supermarket can fluctuate erratically in length. The states of nature of interest to the store management would be the various possible lengths of line, and the units of time measurement would be the smallest interval of time in which at least one customer would arrive at the counter. Presumably, management's interest would lie in balancing out two antithetical costs: (1) the costs of checkout clerks, whose number determines the maximum length a line can attain, and (2) loss of good will and patronage from impatient customers. With some empirical observation on line lengths and customer time intervals and service intervals, he can find out how long the line will grow with any counter checkout force. His estimate of the cost of this force is likely to be very accurate, but he will have more difficulty determining the costs and probabilities of patronage loss due to waiting, i.e., just how long, on the average, and at the maximum, a line can get before significant numbers of customers shift at least part of their buying elsewhere, and how much loss this will entail. But there is such a cost, and if he can make a rough estimate, he will know how many counters he should operate and with what personnel.

While the details of the calculations are not particularly intricate, mastering the tedious procedure requires hours of drill and had best be done in a mathematics course. The computer programming needed is standard, and very simple. The important thing, as with all these mathematical implements, is to understand its uses and meaning. Outside of production processes, it is safe to say most of the uses of Markov chains have not even been explored. One interested mathematician has used it to analyze a department store's charge account system, determining what the distribution of delinquency can be expected to approach after a period of time, and in what length of time. (The absorbing states were two here: bad debts turned over for collection and paid-up customers.) He has also experimented with it to project the expected teaching load in a graduate program subject to student turnover due to transfers and other causes and thus to estimate the intake permissible with a given available teaching staff. By analogy, a firm with a large management training program could estimate the needed recruit intake to get the eventual supply of middle and top managers needed.   Although no case has come to public attention, Markov analysis of a mail-order customer file would seem a useful way of predicting how long a customer will remain active.

As with most mathematical calculations, the actual answers that come out of a Markov analysis look very precise. But their true accuracy is no greater than the accuracy of the somewhat limited empirical observations on which the initial probability tables are built. The approximations resulting are, of course, far better than we are likely to use in the absence of such analyses and are normally quite adequate to the needs of business decision.

SUMMARY

1. Four matrix tools have received wide publicity as models for business decision: game theory, linear programming, and two kinds of Markov chains (transitional probability matrixes). All four are usually formulated as algebraic matrixes, and game theory and linear programming use the same method of computation.

2. Game theory has shown some utility in military analysis, apparently, where the two person zero-sum game has proved a reasonable simplification of reality. But business situations are representable only by the more complex multiperson nonzero-sum game for which no satisfactory solutions have been or seem likely to be developed. Construction of such game matrixes have been of value principally in providing qualitative insight, but no quantitative answers, concerning the incentive effect of some aspects of competition.

3. Production functions in business have proven amenable to the allocation help rendered by linear programming. This tool will identify the optimum allocation of scarce resources when: (a) resources, or some of them, are limited, (b) some of our choices are restrained--can be expressed in terms of "not more than" or "not less than," (c) there is some

freedom to vary the quantities of the "choice variables" within the restraints, and (d) restraints are, or can be, expressed as linear equations. It has proven useful in such matters as allocating shipments from several sources to several destinations (the transportation model), assignment of skilled personnel for most efficient use of their abilities in total, calculating the most economical mix of complex components (the diet problem) in such things as feedstuffs, fertilizers, etc., or in getting the most valuable product mix, as for an oil refinery.

4. Markov chains are of two types: (a) the nonabsorbing chain, which permits an estimate of where a dynamic change can be expected to stabilize (such as the market share of a recently introduced new product variation) and (b) the absorbing chain, used in "waiting line theory" to investigate the proper policies of handling any waiting line, backlog, or other situation in which inputs must be or are introduced continually to balance outputs which are not reversible.

GLOSSARY OF MATRIX DECISION MODEL TERMS

MATRIX ALGEBRA: a system of algebraic notation set up in the form of tables of coefficients, with the variables denoted separately.

GAME THEORY MODELS: models designed to reveal optimal strategies in situations of pure conflict. Calculation methods are the same as for linear programming, but the uses are quite different. The model has proven of value for the analysis of military strategy situations, which can be reduced to conditions of pure conflict and tend to be limited to two sets of opposing forces, but has not yet proven to of any real value in giving quantitative answers to problems of business strategy, mainly because business situations are almost never matters of pure conflict, nor are the number of participants reducible to two, or any clearly defined number.

> Games are of two types: zero-sum games, in which the losses of one side are exactly the same as the gains of the other, and nonzero-sum games, in which the combined losses and gains of the two sides do not cancel out.

Strictly-determined games: games in which there is a single clearly defined strategy for each side, which will maximize the gains of one side and minimize the losses of the other.

<u>Nonstrictly determined games</u>: situations in which there is not a single clear strategy for each participant.

<u>Mixed strategy</u>: a strategy in which a player varies his moves in some random manner, according to some previously decided-upon ratio.

<u>LINEAR PROGRAMMING</u>: a method for calculating the best allocation mix of scarce resources in any situation in which the important relationships, cost and otherwise, are either approximately linear in form, or can be transformed into linear expressions. This is a special case of the more general method known as <u>mathematical programming</u> for situations in which some of the relationships cannot be reduced to linear form. However, only the linear form of programming has proved to be of much utility.

<u>Choice variable</u>: any of the factors subject to allocation which we can, if we choose, vary.

<u>Diet model</u>: one form of linear programming in which the physical quantities which may be proportioned are not subject to any limitations, but in which the costs must be carefully proportioned.

<u>Objective function</u>: the goal we hope to achieve with our allocation: minimization of cost, maximization of profit, and the like.

<u>Restraint</u>: any limitation on what can be done, on the supply of a particular resource, on the relationship of resources used, and the like.

<u>Transportation model</u>: the earliest form of linear program developed, so-called because it was initially used to work out the best shipment pattern out of a number of factories or warehouses of limited capacity to a number of different shipping points. It is applicable to any problem in which there are limits on both the inputs and on the outputs, with both being just exactly satisfied. Can often be calculated without the aid of a computer.

<u>MARKOV CHAIN PROCESS MODELS</u>: models for deciding where a dynamic process is heading and how, if desired, the course of events might be modified. In Markov processes, some "system" such as a body of customers (or a group of vehicles on the road, for another example) moves from one <u>state of nature</u>, such as the purchase of one brand of soap, to a different state of nature (purchase of different brands) in the next time period, in some probabilistic manner. This <u>transition</u>

323

from one state to another depends only on the state of nature in the previous time period. A table representing the probabilities of change from each state to each possible succeeding state during one transition period is known as a transitional probabilities table.

Markov absorbing chains: Markov processes in which the transition to certain states is irreversible. If the process is not continuously interfered with by the introduction of new inputs into the nonabsorbing states, the system ends up divided between the absorbing states after some calculable number of time periods (it becomes absorbed).

Markov nonabsorbing chains: Markov chain processes in which all transitions are reversible--in which, for example, the switch from the purchase of one brand to another brand is not permanent. Nonabsorbing processes end up at a calculable fixed point, a stable distribution of the system over all of the states. Each brand of soap, to carry out the original example, would then have a stable market share, gaining as many customers during each time period as it loses to other brands.

Queuing theory or waiting line theory: a variant of the absorbing chain approach aimed at balancing out the costs associated with the buildup of a waiting line (as, for example, the number of cars delayed by a slow moving truck on a two-lane highway, or the number of customers waiting to be checkout out at the supermarket) with the costs of reducing the length of the waiting line (putting in an extra passing lane, or adding more checkout counters in the market).

12

MEETING DEADLINES:
PERT AND CRITICAL PATH

The success or profit of a project often hinges on the meeting of a critical deadline. The technique of network analysis (under the various labels of Critical Path Analysis--CPM-- and PERT--Program Evaluation and Review Technique) furnishes an efficient means for pinpointing those tasks in a process or plan whose timing is critical to scheduling and helps find the most effective means of minimizing completion time economically. As originally used, CPM was developed for the analysis of programs for which reasonably close estimates could be made of task time requirements. PERT was developed to handle complex programs such as R & D in which a really close estimate of time requirements was not feasible. The two terms are often used synonymously, and the variations are matters of detail. Both are as much a part of the control process as of the planning. For simpler jobs, these tools can be handled with a hand-drawn chart, but they can be programmed on a computer, and must be for more complex projects.

The efficiency of the execution of a wide variety of jobs has been greatly improved through scheduling based on network analysis; from the development of the Polaris submarine, for which PERT was perfected, through all sorts of new construction projects, to plant maintenance shutdowns and development of new product marketing operations.

Analysis and control is a nine-step process:

1. Describe the entire job in terms of the simplest component tasks.
2. Estimate the time required to carry out each component task.
3. List the tasks in their technological sequence. This

means determining which tasks must be finished before others which are dependent on their completion can be started. The result is usually the identification of a number of semi-independent sequences.

4. If the job is simple enough to permit it, prepare a project graph with arrows connecting boxes or circles representing each task, ordered in the proper technological sequence and indicating completion time for each task.

5. For each task, as originally sequenced and planned, compute the earliest starting time by counting forward from the project start. Similarly, obtain the latest starting time by counting backward from the "end date" or "due date". Enter both times on the project graph. (On very complex projects, a computer can handle this part by use of a program published by F. K. Levy, G. L. Thompson, and J. D. Wiest as Chapter 22 in Industrial Scheduling, edited by J. F. Muth and G. L. Thompson--Englewood Cliffs, N.J., Prentice-Hall, Inc., 1963.)

6. Sum the times required for each path on the project and identify the path requiring the longest time. For this sequence, the earliest and latest possible starting times will be identical for every component task, and this path is thus the critical one--the path on which any delay in any task will delay the entire job. Any other kind of sequence will contain some slack time, some permissible delays which can occur, as shown by a difference between the earliest and latest possible starting times indicated.

7. Reexamine the original critical path to determine if more tasks can be carried out concurrently, even at some extra cost, and in what way and at what extra cost the time span of individual tasks can be shortened.

8. After these adjustments have been made in the plan, draw up a new project graph or revise the old one and reinspect the whole to determine whether or not another path may now be the bottleneck. If so, decide on new adjustments needed until a satisfactory schedule is arrived at and the final critical path tasks defined.

9. Set up a formal control system to keep a continuous check on the progress being made in the accomplishment of the bottleneck tasks.

To put the mechanics of this process into more concrete terms, let us look at a simplified example. A company which currently sells a product on a limited scale through small specialty stores would like to broaden the market by introducing a variant into supermarkets. Let us see how a critical path analysis of their plan could be used to improve its execution and then consider a more typical and therefore more complex product introduction effort.

A SIMPLE EXAMPLE: PLANNING A NEW PACKAGE AND A NEW CHANNEL OF DISTRIBUTION

Let us say we have decided to broaden the market for a successful pet supply specialty by introducing it into supermarkets, limiting initial expansion plans to three major metropolitan areas. To protect our present sales through pet stores, we shall develop a new label and a new package specifically designed for supermarket display and sale. Sales will be pushed through newly appointed food brokers, and the initial contacts with chain warehouse buyers will be done by the sales manager together with the broker in each area. Production itself will be no problem. We will continue to have the product processed and packaged by a contract supplier. But we will, in addition, have to get a new source of supply for a potentially greater market, and we will have to work with this source in setting up his processing and packaging operations--a relatively simple matter requiring only a little new equipment.

After careful consideration of past experience, we have analyzed the whole project as composed of the following basic steps, with time requirements as indicated on the following page.

Clearly, if we take these steps one at a time, it will be six months before the new label gets on the market. But we know we ought to be on the store shelves by mid-September, when there is a seasonal pick up in sales and we are making the decision to go-ahead at the end of the first week in June. We need to do the job in 14 weeks, not 27. And we see we can do it in this time without any crash program, by carrying on some aspects of the project concurrently with others. Looking at the

Item	Time Required (weeks)	Prerequisite Step
a. Arrange for new manufacturing source	4	--
b. Produce preliminary package copy and label designs	1	--
c. Consumer test preliminary designs	1	b
d. Develop final package design	1	c
e. Consult with package sources and get quotations	3	d
f. Send package copy and get plates made and proofed	2	e
g. Prepare portfolio of sales presentation material	1	d
h. Interview and select brokers	2	g
i. Sales calls on chains	2	h
j. Consideration and acceptance by chain buying committees	3	i
k. Manufacture and deliver packages to source	5	a, f
l. Manufacture product and deliver to stores, get display	2	i, f, k
TOTAL TIME	27 weeks	

list and at the prerequisite tasks, there seems no good reason why we cannot start designing the package at the same time we start arranging for a new source. Nor, once the package copy is frozen, is there any reason not to arrange for the stock of packages at the same time we are setting up our sales organi-

FIGURE 12-1. Project Graph for Introduction of a New Package into a New Channel

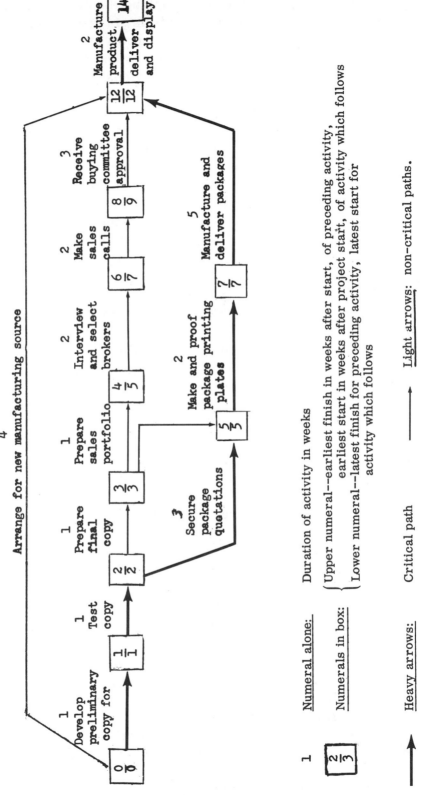

Numeral alone: Duration of activity in weeks

Numerals in box: {Upper numeral—earliest finish in weeks after start, of preceding activity,
                   earliest start in weeks after project start, of activity which follows
                   Lower numeral—latest finish for preceding activity, latest start for
                   activity which follows

Heavy arrows: Critical path   ———▶   Light arrows: non-critical paths.

1

$\frac{2}{3}$

329

zation and getting the orders. Graphing the project in this fashion, we find we can come out at just 14 weeks, with the critical path indicated by the heavy arrows in Figure 12-1.

Normally, of course, in as uncomplicated a project as this, the parallelling of tasks is so obvious that no formal analysis need be made, and the plan is worked out with minimum resort to paper and pencil. But product introductions as well as construction projects can involve so many sequences and subsequences that it becomes impossible to carry all the details in our head, and foolish to try to work out all the needed adjustments without the help of formal graphics and even the computer. Consider the situation which might realistically occur when a radically new office reproducer-copier is introduced by a business machines firm. The machine is sufficiently complex that it requires a new missionary sales force to get industry acceptance rolling.

USING NETWORK ANALYSIS TO REVISE SCHEDULING

Suppose that, as the members of the New Product Committee of the Weuns Office Equipment Company, we are met to make a final decision giving the go-ahead to a complete pilot testing and market introduction program for the Ocoprep, an exciting new office copier and fast multicopy reproducing machine which our laboratory has developed and proved out in internal operation with a hand-built model. In previous meetings and in an individual study of reports on the potential market and on performance tests in our own operations, we have pretty much convinced ourselves that this machine holds promise of a major breakthrough, and have tentatively agreed that a pilot test program in outside companies should be conducted to get the bugs out of the design. Following this, preparations for a full-scale market introduction program should be pushed as rapidly as possible. We are all aware that the ideal time to unveil the Ocoprep to potential customers is the coming OMAC show, to be held in the week following February 29 next, a bare nine months away. We have asked first that an initial project graph be prepared according to our usual introductory procedure of an initial pilot test followed by the development of the program for marketing.

However, both the planning and the preparation for marketing will be unusually elaborate. This will require a different kind of selling from our other machines and the training of a special missionary sales force. The test itself must proceed for a minimum of 10 weeks if the companies in the test are to become accustomed to the machine and learn, both for themselves and us, what its capabilities and problems are in normal office use. We anticipate some minor design changes as a result of the test, as well as important leads both for the instruction manual and for promotion themes. Ten outside firms to be asked will have to be carefully selected to cover a wide variety of office conditions and copier and reproduction needs, and their cooperation will have to be secured for placements.

To our dismay, when our best time estimates are put into our usual new product production procedure and displayed as in Figure 12-2, the time between now and the OMAC show is impossibly short. The normal test sequence alone would eat up 24 of the available 39 weeks, leaving only 15 weeks for the critical initial production and delivery sequence which is estimated at 42 weeks. In addition, even if we were to shorten the initial production sequence by some kind of crash program, we would need 39 weeks to get the distributor training program worked out and train and introduce the salesmen. Even operating instructions, as normally scheduled, would take 31 weeks after completion of the pilot test.

Of course, not all activities form critical paths or near-critical paths. We have adequate time to develop accounting, billing and credit procedures, for sales manual preparation and for at least two of the advertising and publicity sequences. Others can be managed if some adjustments are made in the length of the test cycle. For this reason, only the total estimates for these sequences are indicated on the chart in Figure 12-2. The detailed time estimates are (the first figure indicates time required for that phase, the figure in parentheses indicates the total elapsed time since beginning of the task):

TRADE ADVERTISING SEQUENCE (weeks)			PUBLICITY SEQUENCE (weeks)			DIRECT MAIL ADVTG. SEQUENCE (weeks)		
Choose media	1	(1)	Prepare rough copy	3	(3)	Develop direct mail piece	4	(4)
Rough out advtg. copy & layout	4	(5)	Review	1	(4)	Review	1	(5)

331

FIGURE 12-2. Initial Project Outline for Ocoprep Introduction, Following Normal Procedure

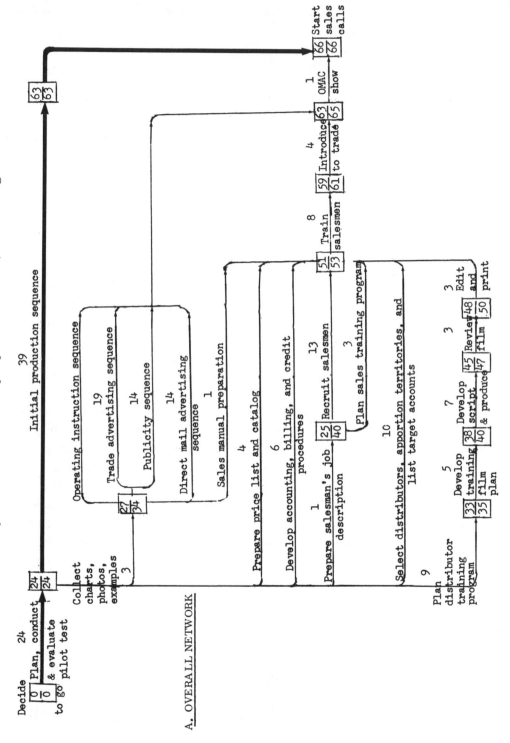

A. OVERALL NETWORK

B. NORMAL PILOT TEST SEQUENCE (Estimated Total: 24 weeks)

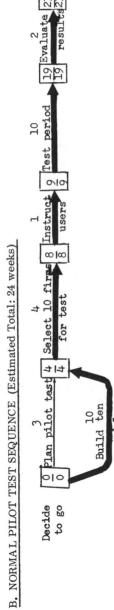

C. NORMAL INITIAL PRODUCTION PROCEDURE DETAIL (Estimated Total: 39 weeks)

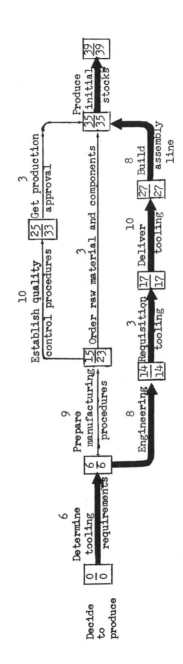

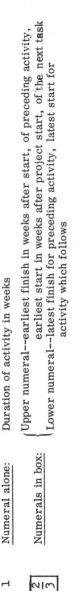

1   Numeral alone: Duration of activity in weeks

$\boxed{\frac{2}{3}}$ Numerals in box: { Upper numeral—earliest finish in weeks after start, of preceding activity, earliest start in weeks after project start, of the next task

Lower numeral—latest finish for preceding activity, latest start for activity which follows }

Heavy arrows: Critical path   ⟶   Light arrows: non-critical paths.

333

	(weeks)			(weeks)			(weeks)
Review	2 (7)	Revise copy	2 (6)	Prepare final copy	4 (9)
Prepare final copy	4 (11)	Print	2 (8)	Approval	1 (10)
Approval	2 (13)	Release for publication	6 (14)	Print & mail	4 (14)
Place with media	6 (19)				

Since the Committee has already been informed that the OMAC show introduction date is a must, justifying abnormal expenditures, we start to look for ways to speed up the process. The obvious first choices are the test sequence and the initial production and delivery sequence.

In looking over the details of the normal test procedure sequence, we see no way to safely reduce the actual 10-week test duration, or to cut down the 4 weeks allotted to hand-build the 10 test models. But someone points out there is no need to wait until we have those models before lining up firms to co-operate in the test, and that if we start immediately on this, we can save the whole 4 weeks. Another member asks why we have to wait until the end of the test to make our evaluations and to gather materials for the instructions and advertising. Why, he wants to know, can't those responsible take time to monitor the tests at least weekly as they proceed, making decisions on any last minute design changes as we go. We decide if we handle things this way, we should be able to make all final evaluations within a week after the end of the test, and revise and freeze the final design within 19 weeks from the go-ahead, instead of 24 weeks.

The 20 weeks remaining would still be far too short for 3 post-test sequences:
1. the manufacturing and initial delivery sequence estimated at 42 weeks
2. the distributor and sales training programs which take 39 weeks as set up

3. preparation of the operating instructions, programmed to take 31 weeks.

Moreover, no further internal concurrence of tasks seems feasible in any of the three tasks. We note no reason, however, why the review process in the development of the distributor program should really require 3 weeks. Everyone agrees to give top priority attention to any reviews, reducing them to a maximum of 1 week each. Planning the distributor training program could also be started concurrently with the pilot test, and if this is done, we should even gain a couple of weeks slack in this sequence.

We find no further ways of shrinking the time requirements without time or cost penalties of some sort, such as diverting executive attention from other important matters, making substantial use of overtime for key personnel, and risking wasted effort by proceeding with some engineering before the design is finally frozen.

If we are willing to accept the costs, we find four manufacturing sequence activities which can be shortened by throwing in more manpower, using overtime, and diverting skilled manpower from less critical projects:

1. determination of tooling requirements can be cut from 6 weeks to 4
2. engineering can be cut from 8 weeks to 4
3. requisitioning the tooling can be reduced from 3 weeks to 2
4. the assembly line can be built in 4 weeks, at a considerably higher cost, rather than 8.

Air shipment would reduce delivery of initial stock to more distant distributors. If we took all of these steps, we could shrink the manufacturing sequence steps to 29 weeks, it seems. But a second look tells us it would still take 31 weeks because the quality control subsequence has now become a bottleneck. So we find ways to shrink this by 2 weeks and are satisfied that 29 weeks is the least we must have from start of the sequence to final delivery of initial distributor stocks. This is still more time than is available before the OMAC show unless we can see a way to telescope the testing and manufacturing operations together in some manner.

Clearly, any attempt to start the manufacturing sequence before firming up the design will cost something in duplication of effort and design change confusion. But it should be equally obvious that the changes in design would be minor at this point and that most of the tooling for the machine could be started even before the testing begins, if necessary. If we wait until the test is half over, changes should not be too disruptive provided we have carefully monitored the test as it proceeds, and evaluated what we observed as we went along. If we start planning the tooling at the midpoint of the test and accept some wasted effort, we can have the Ocoprep machines in stock by the end of the OMAC show without crashing as many of the steps.

Finally, we could very easily pick up the photographs, charts, and work examples we need for the various promotion programs and the operating instruction in the first 6 weeks of the test. We should have nearly all of the information we need for preparation of good operating instructions and a trouble shooting guide, if we continuously monitor progress of the test. So we can get this path within needed time dimensions with only a more intense and compressed review period.

As a result, we draw up the revised project graph of Figure 12-3. To avoid crash operation of too many activities, we settle for three critical paths, all of which will have to be carefully watched and controlled. In the process, however, we have created even more slack in the noncritical activities. The biggest price we have had to pay is in creating more work in the planning of the tooling and the manufacturing procedures, by starting them before the design can be frozen--a necessity in any case if we are to keep within the desired deadline. We have even managed to avoid crashing the development of the assembly line. We now have a tool to help us control execution of our plan--a definite statement of the timing needed for every activity in the plan, and a knowledge of which activities must get constant surveillance to assure success.

CONTROLLING THE NETWORK

Network analysis, like every effective planning tool, includes a built-in management control mechanism. The initial plan makes certain that deadlines will be met if diligently followed. The completed plan should save top management resources by spotlighting the small minority of tasks whose planned progress is critical to meeting these deadlines and must be closely monitored. The control value lies in mini-

336

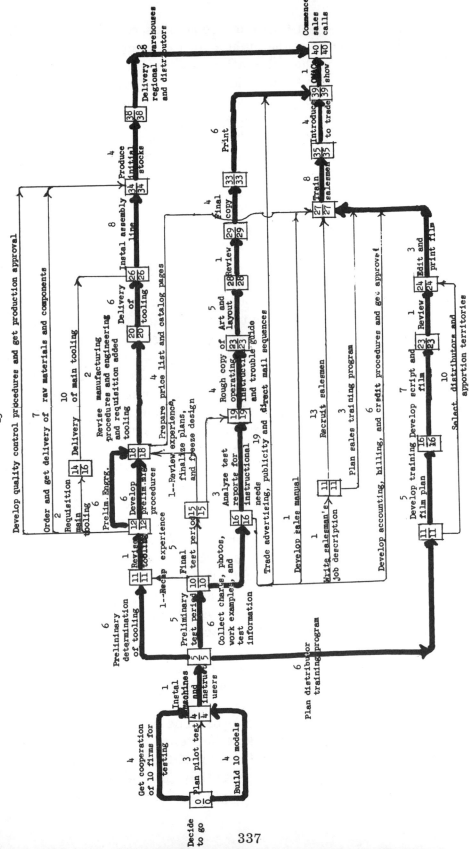

FIGURE 12-3. Final Revised Project Graph for Ocoprep Introduction Program

337

mizing the number of tasks and sequences requiring close observation. However, the number of these must be kept small, and this hinges on the delineation of component task elements themselves and on adequate delegation of details.

By definition, a component task represents an action sequence which, for the purpose of analysis and control, is indivisible, and would be carried out without interruption and close oversight. The indivisibility and freedom from close supervision are thus dependent, like all quantitative methods, on human judgment and on the needs and objectives in the situation.

Every one of the steps in our first simple example of a new package introduction clearly involved whole sequences of component tasks themselves, each of which had some degree of elasticity of time requirement. "Arranging for a new manufacturing source" calls for numerous telephone calls, letters, personal visits, and contract preparations. Similarly, production of a series of preliminary package and label designs is not something done with a few strokes of a pen. These actions can be considered indivisible components for planning purposes only if we can be assured that those responsible for the sequences can be relied upon to complete the task in the allotted time without prodding and oversight. We must, however, be sure that those to whom we delegate such responsibilities both understand what their deadlines are, and can be trusted to meet them.

The alternative to such delegation is continual checks on a myriad of details of task performance. At the extreme, this alternative could mean an attempt to foresee each necessary phone call and each tentative sketch of a label design, to count them and insist on reports and checks on them. To even state the problem in this manner is to sketch the problem at its most absurd extreme, of course, and we need not undertake it to realize that the administrative burden would defeat the very purpose of planning. But it is easy to attempt too detailed a breakdown unless the necessity of delegating responsibility and minimizing supervision is kept as clearly in view as the need to meet the deadline.

Maintaining that correct balance in practice means that management will delegate whole sequence deadlines to lower levels, and that such lower levels will themselves set up such production control procedures as they find necessary--preferably informal procedures, but conscious ones. If this is done, network planning will achieve its real aim--limiting top management concern to just those details which are really crucial, and making certain management concentrates on performance in these areas.

SUMMARY

1. Network analysis, critical path method and PERT are terms for similar graphic and computer methods for breaking down the time requirement of parts of a project in such a way as to reveal the bottleneck component tasks and thus finding least costly ways to minimize the time between project start and completion.

2. CPM methods require reasonably firm estimates of the time requirements of component tasks, PERT systems were developed to analyze tasks with major components whose time requirements were less predictable. The general procedure is the same in both methods.

3. Analysis starts with a careful breakdown and listing of stages of the project into simple component tasks, an estimate of the time requirements for each such component, and a listing of related tasks in their technological sequence. The whole is then charted as the tasks would normally proceed, or so programmed on a computer, the cumulative time requirements calculated, and the result analyzed for task sequences which are critical in the sense that any delay in their performance will cause similar delay in the completion of the project.

4. Attention is then focused on such critical paths only, to determine whether and how some of the included tasks might be made concurrent (paralleled) or their time requirements reduced, and at what cost.

5. The entire new project plan is then reanalyzed to determine if other task sequences have not now become critical paths, and further adjustments made until a plan with a satisfactory job schedule and completion date is achieved.

6. The critical paths in this final plan will then be earmarked for special attention to make sure that they are carried out on schedule. The analysis thus also serves as a way of minimizing the executive attention needed to follow meaningful progress, focusing attention on only those details essential to

successful performance.

7. The principal problem is to maintain the proper balance between detailed specification of tasks and timing and delegation of responsibility for the less critical detail. Too much fineness of detailing can defeat the very purpose of network analysis.

NETWORK ANALYSIS: GLOSSARY OF TERMS

Component task: a stage of the project which can be considered indivisible for the purpose of analysis and control and would be carried out without interruption and need for close supervision.

CPM (Critical Path Method): the form of network analysis used when the time requirements of all important tasks are subject to relatively firm estimate.

Crashing a task: putting more than the normal optimum effort and expense into a task to gain substantial time in its completion.

Critical path: any sequence of tasks between the start and completion of a project, all of whose earliest possible finish times coincide with the latest finish time necessary if the project as a whole is to be completed on schedule; sequences in which there is no slack for any component task. Any delay in even one of the component tasks in such a sequence thus means a corresponding delay in the completion of the total project unless specific provision is made to shorten the time of some subsequent task.

Earliest finish time: the earliest point in the project time schedule at which, under the scheduled sequence charted, a task can be completed, taking into account the minimum time estimated for this task and all preceding tasks in its sequence.

Early starting time: the earliest point in the project schedule at which a task can be initiated, based on the minimum estimated time required for all preceding tasks in the same task sequence.

Late finish time: the latest time at which a task can be completed without delaying completion of the project.

Late start time: the latest point of time at which a task can be started and still leave enough time available to meet its estimated requirement without delaying the project.

Paralleling: scheduling independent tasks or independent task sequences so that they will be carried out concurrently.

PERT (Program Evaluation and Review Technique): a group of variations of network analysis designed for projects having components whose completion time requirements cannot be firmly predicted, and thus must be estimated on a probability basis.

Slack: any difference between the early finish time estimated for a task and its late finish time. All tasks on a critical path have zero slack.

Technological sequence: the specific sequence in which tasks must be carried out because of their physical interrelationship. For example, if we are putting in a concrete foundation for a building, we would have the following five component tasks in the technological sequence as follows:

1. Excavate for foundation
2. Build forms for the concrete
3. Pour concrete
4. Allow concrete to set
5. Strip off forms

We could not put the forms in place until the excavation is complete, pour the concrete until the forms are in place, etc.

13

COMPUTER SIMULATION: BARGAIN BASEMENT TRIAL AND ERROR

Most of the tools and techniques discussed in the previous chapters concerned the use of predetermined models. That is, they assumed advance knowledge of the nature of some orderly and relatively simple and direct structure of relationship between action and consequences. Unfortunately, a great many of the decisions we have to make deal with situations in which the relationships are not only unknown, but even unknowable. What we do know about them reveals something nearer anarchy than order, and a great deal of complexity and even chance. Even when we do have what seems to be a useful theoretical model, the disorderly or ambiguous character of the needed available data may render it useless. A valid mathematical model would tell us what we always wish to know: precisely how much input will be needed to obtain the desired output quantity (that to get X million dollars of extra profit we must spend exactly 1 million more dollars for advertising, for example). Such a model assumes verifiable knowledge of a one-to-one functional relationship, and a simple relatively constant and continuous relationship. Few relationships of this character can be found in our disorderly, complex world of innovative differentiated competition. Even when we find a seemingly usable model, the relationships are frequently too chaotic and discontinuous to permit of use.

Thus linear programming is conceptually an ideal model for solution of warehousing and inventory problems. In practice, however, the constraints on which the solution depends are frequently not even approximately continuous functions. Transportation rates, an important variable in location problems, are a complex mixture of discontinuous functions.

342

The rates change abruptly at the margin of arbitrary quantity boundaries (such as carload and less-than-carload). Moreover, there is a maze of special commodity rates and other special considerations.

Whenever we have no applicable model and whenever what should be an applicable model cannot be used, we can, thanks to the computer, fall back on trials of a number of suggested rule-of-thumb solutions--we can simulate.

WHAT IS SIMULATION?

Simulation is nothing new. The dictionary definition includes the terms "imitation" and "pretense". The Army's "dry runs" are simulations. It means going through the motions without incurring the expense, trying out the essentials without duplicating the less essential details. The architects, preliminary sketches, and even his final blueprints are simulations--the elements of the basic plan, on paper where they cost little.

What is new is the computer and its capacity for trying out suggested or possible solutions electronically at relatively little cost in time or finances.

THE COMPUTER AND SIMULATION

Because the computer permits the ultimate in mathematical abstraction, it can be used to approximate all kinds of possible experience without the pain and cost in time and money of actually trying things out. The only input, output, and storage actually involved are simply electrical impulses and charges which, because they are devoid of any kind of meaning, can be made to represent and actually read or produce and compare numbers, real words, sentences (in English, Swahili, or any other language), or geometric patterns or maps--all at the option of the programmer and operator, with suitable auxiliary machinery and equipment. Moreover, whatever the computer is instructed to do, in the infinitely detailed painstaking language we call a program, it carries out in the millionths of a second, giving rise to a new term in business, real time, to indicate practically instantaneous availability of stored or processed information output in more than adequate time to use it for decision or action.

The functions of a computer are simply stated. First, it carries out the same basic operation that every mechanical computation device has ever performed: it adds quantities. This means it can also be used to subtract (negative addition), multiply (repetitive addition), and divide (repetitive negative addition). The computer can also store data, instructions, and results and can retrieve the stored information for internal calculations or for output. Because of its storage capability, it can make predetermined comparisons. Because it can make predetermined comparisons, it can make predetermined choices. Most important, each operation is performed in millionths of a second because the whole internal process is carried out by electrical currents and charges. Thus it can store whatever important data we have, and carry out any set of rules we construct about meeting a specific type of situation, such as setting up a warehouse distribution plan.

Programming is a tedious operation requiring tremendous patience in the preparation of minutely detailed instructions. But once we prepare a generalized program, we can use it over and over with new parameters and data. Time consuming as the programming process frequently is, computational time savings in even a single use can be enormous. Assuming no errors in the programming itself, the utility of the answers depends only on two factors which the data user himself must evaluate:

1. the applicability of the general procedure programmed to the kind of decision to be made

2. the quality and meaning of the input data for the purposes of the decision. Since both are matters of personal judgment, not mathematics, it is always well to consider how well the answer corresponds with experience.

The computer performs two major types of service for the decision maker:

1. the purely computational service of assuming the tedium of multitudinous and prolonged calculations, such as those required by more complex linear programming solutions, Markov chain analyses, network solutions, and statistical decision computations, when alternatives are many and complex.

2. simulation: that is, a cut-and-try process for determining what the resulting patterns or quantities would be if

344

a given procedural rule, policy, or course of action were adopted.

In one sense, the solutions of linear program or network algorithms are forms of simulation: the carrying out of successive trial solutions in an iterative operation which gets progressively closer to an optimum solution. But this is properly considered a simple calculation process. Simulation is more often applied to somewhat less structured trial-and-error procedures of four types:

1. Experimental application of accepted rules and relationships to discover their pertinence and meaning in specific circumstances and to compare the results with known experience, in the hope of arriving at better analytical formulas, or to develop designs. Thus a computer has been used to simulate wind tunnel fluid dynamics, revealing important details difficult to obtain in physical experiments. Pictures were produced on a cathode ray tube giving a "remarkably faithful impression of the behavior of smoke or dye filaments" in a wind tunnel experiment. The purpose of the experimental simulation was to try "to discover workable approximations that will simplify the mathematics needed to solve complicated problems," in a situation in which the needed mathematical techniques for complete solutions have not yet been developed. * Such uses are not likely to have direct business decision application in the near future, but have great possibilities in physical sciences and in engineering.

2. Monte Carlo simulation of a probability distribution, to construct a prolonged random synthetic experience, based on limited observation data.

3. Heuristic programming or simulation, a pure cut-and-try procedure according to some arbitrary or intuitive rules, comparing the results obtained from the use of such rules when applied to situations with a known structure.

4. Simulation of population distributions in miniature and testing the effect of proposed actions in terms of its effects on these simulated populations.

Monte Carlo simulation is a very useful auxiliary device for developing a more prolonged series of experiences than

---

*Francis H. Harlow and Jacob E. Fromm, "Computer Experiments in Fluid Dynamics." Scientific American, Vol. 212, No. 3 (March, 1965), pp. 104-110.

would be economical through direct observation, when the variability of quantities is thought to be of a random character, within specified limits and under a given probability distribution.

Heuristic programming offers promising possibilities as a really cheap substitute for extensive practical trial-and-error in many business decision situations for which we have no very satisfactory mathematical models capable of yielding optimum solutions.

Population simulation has already proved its worth as a device for projecting the interacting results of planned political campaign efforts and commercial advertising media programs, and would seem to have more extensive possibilities for forecasting the results of other kinds of planned action when we have data on the impact of individual actions on various parts of the population.

MONTE CARLO SIMULATION

Some kind of probability distribution is a basic assumption in the solution of many types of mathematical decision models--in inventory problems, in waiting line problems, and in some kinds of network analyses, for example. It is, of course, possible to fall back on an extended series of actual observations as an approximation to such a probability distribution, if such an extensive series is available. But often only limited observation is available, enough to indicate the extent of variation, and something as to its shape, but not quite enough by itself. The alternative is to generate an approximation by random selection, or the so-called Monte Carlo method.

In its essentials, Monte Carlo simulation consists of nothing more than production of a series of random numbers, according to some previously determined probability distributions, in order to develop the kind of unpredictable individual variations which might be expected in practice, with the distribution governed by previous probability experience. If the number needed is small, this is exactly what is done by hand.

Consider a previous example: the Hectic Fisheries Supply inventory control problem. To start with, Hectic had the frequency distributions of nets demanded per day and of the number of days lead-time per order. They might have simply programmed a computer with this daily experience, as it occurred, and compared various combination of $\underline{Q}$ (order quantity) and $\underline{R}$ (reorder level) with this one year's experience. But all possible combinations of 0-to-3 nets per day demand, and 1-to-3 days lead-time would not occur within 1 year, in the proportions to be expected. (Remember that one possible policy tested would result in a shortage only twice in 5 years, according to our calculations.) So we chose instead to calculate the probability of every possible combination of demand per day and lead-time and to compute the costs and risks of each possible policy of $\underline{Q}$, $\underline{R}$ combinations until our computations indicated we had found the optimum one.

Even this simplified problem involved a rather burdensome series of hand calculations. Had the maximum demand - per-day been not a mere three items, but hundreds or thousands with comparable variability, counting and calculating would have been more work than most would feel is justified. Without a computer, we would certainly have tried a Monte Carlo approach to sample the possible combinations instead of trying to enumerate all of them. Even this would have been no spare-time task if carried out by hand. A computer would have shortcut the tedium of Monte Carlo methods or allowed us to evaluate more samples. If we had a long enough back series of experiential information, it would even have permitted us to consider enumerating all of the actual combinations of lead-time and demand-per-day and calculate the values directly.

If we chose the Monte Carlo approach, let us see how this would work in Hectic's case, starting with the tabulated frequency of demand-per-day and of lead-time per order, which were as follows:

Nets Demanded During Day	Percentage of Days	Lead-time per Order (Days)	Percentage of Orders
None	40	1	25
1	30	2	50
2	20	3	25
3	10		

For each period, we would draw two sets of numbers from our random number table:

    1. a number to represent the reorder lead-time for that period, to tell us whether the lead-time is

1, 2, or 3 days.

2.   a number for each of the lead-time days, to tell us whether demand on that day is 0, 1, 2, or 3 kippered herring nets.

For the lead-time number, using some arbitrary sequence for successive drawings, we will read off a 2-digit number from our table and interpret it as follows:

1 day's lead-time if number is between 1 and 25

2 day's lead-time if number is between 26 and 75

3 day's lead-time if number is between 76 and 00

Then for each of these lead-time days, we will read off a 1-digit number in the same way, interpreting it thusly:

0, 1, 2, or 3 means $\underline{0}$ demand

4, 5, or 6 means $\underline{1}$ net demand

7 or 8 means $\underline{2}$ nets demanded

9 means $\underline{3}$ nets demanded

If a computer is available, we can instruct it (program it) to do the same thing, no matter how large the series is likely to be (within reasonable limits), and then tabulate the results in a combined probability table as we did for the Hectic case. If we have the computer run the simulation for a large number of order periods, the results are the same as though the probabilities were calculated directly.

PURE CUT-AND-TRY: HEURISTIC PROGRAMMING

Suppose you were the head of a large food processing firm--say H. J. Heinz--and you realized the time had come to modernize and streamline your complex processing, shipping, warehousing and selling system. * You have production plants scattered all over the country, each with a different product-mix capability, a complex of warehouses and shipping points handling scores of different products to serve literally thousands of customers of many sizes and differing demand patterns and ordering habits, you have the choice of shipping by rail or

---

*The example which follows is based on the report of a study which H. J. Heinz made, as printed in Harvey N. Shycon and Richard B. Maffei, "Simulation--Tool for Distribution," <u>Harvard Business Review</u>, Vol. 38, No. 6 (Nov.-Dec., 1960) pp. 65-84.

by truck, in full carloads or truckloads, or less than carload or truckload, under a complex rate structure whose costs are not linear nor representable by any simple equations. The nature of the relationships rules out any simple linear programming solutions. Two factors need optimizing: service time and overall cost. In studying any suggested distribution configuration, customers would have to be defined in terms of at least four variables (geographical location, order size and frequency, volume of purchases, variety requirements), and producing factories in terms of three variables (geographical location, production capability by product line, and product mix, both actual and potential). The distribution system would have to be represented by a model expressed in the following terms:

1. How frequently each customer orders, how much, which products and sizes, where located, and how they prefer to take delivery.
2. The kinds of goods which can be shipped from each specific factory point, in what quantities, and the location.
3. For truck and rail, the relationship between shipping rates and points of origin and destination, for different types and sizes of orders.
4. The relationship between total volume handled at warehouse and mixing points and total costs.
5. Knowledge of where these relationships differ, so that adjustments could be made in cost and volume estimates. (For example, at some given volume, direct shipping would be better than warehousing.)

Hand calculation would require 75 million computations for only one suggested configuration with this model; or about the output of 100 clerks working for a year, just to estimate the overall cost and service time results for a single set of assumptions as to the product mix at each factory, the warehousing points and mixing points to be used, and the transportation arrangements. Moreover, quite a number of such configurations would have to be tested. But once a computer is properly programmed, it could handle the calculations for any one configuration in one hour. To test the results of some variation in the detail of a configuration, such as the change of the product mix at any one plant, even less computer time is needed. This makes possible a form of dry-run experimentation which can add knowledge about the importance and effect of individual factors through systematic variation, one at a time. Some of the plans tested could thus be suggested by interim computer results. At the end you should know more than merely which of the plausible plans tested gives the best estimated combination of cost and service, but also why, and how sensitive the choice of a given configuration would be.

Carefully thought out computer simulation can be used to evaluate many kinds of business operating plans and procedures. Various studies have shown, for example, that a large part of any salesman's time is spent in travelling from one customer to another, and that an easy way to lower sales cost is to reduce this time by proper routing. The problem is made more complex by customer classification systems which vary the number of calls scheduled over time, between classifications, in order to optimize the sales per call. No known mathematical model is guaranteed to give an optimum answer to the routing problem, but various plausible routings can be tried and compared with each other. One such plausible rule might be to direct the salesman to the next nearest point in a clockwise direction, avoiding any backtracking, another to divide the territory into a number of subterritories, each with a focal point out of which all calls in the subterritory would be routed according to some specific rule of direction and sequence. The computer output might be available not only in numbers, but as a map on a graphic display terminal, which could be reproduced for study and use.

Some rough mental model is needed to gain insight into alternatives of course. Pure blind simulation is unlikely to produce a usable result.

Even when no definitive model is available which yields an optimum answer, we can find the best of any at several suggested alternatives through computer simulation, if we can express the factors influencing outcomes in some kind of quantitative terms (such as cost, distance, direction, time, and the like). In most such cases of heuristic simulation, the program against which we test our arbitrary rules are relatively simple static relationships: the geographical relationships of stops in a salesman's territory, the freight cost schedules and location of producing areas in customers for Heinz, the equations expressing the physical laws of aerodynamics when we want to try out alternate wing section designs for an airplane. Little or no actual statistical experience data is needed because the meaningful influences on the outcome are the statically simple relationships of the physical world.

But some kinds of usable simulation are concerned mainly with the dynamic and complex socioeconomic relationships of human behavior. The computer program we need for such simulations is not only many times more complex, but so dependent on meaningful statistical experience in the input and so in need of constant updating as to be a really different sort of simulation.

POPULATION BEHAVIOR SIMULATION

When we wish to simulate the design of an airplane, we can program the computer with a few mathematical equations, representing such things as the behavior of structural materials under stress and of a wing surface under air flow. When we wish to simulate the response of the electorate to a potential campaign appeal, or test the possible impact of a given selection of advertising media on the national market, we have no equations, but only piles of more or less meaningful statistical tabulation from various surveys, in constant need of updating, classified by various socioeconomic groupings and geographical segments. The detail involved in the analysis of this mountain of tabulations, however incomplete at times, was far too much for computation before the computer became available, and would tax the capacity of the largest computers available if we tried to cover the full population. Fortunately, both in politics and in advertising, (in both of which population behavior simulation has proved useful), we are interested in significant segments of the population, rather than in individuals as such.

Computer capacity is adequate to permit us to develop a replica of the total population, representing what we can know about its composition socially and economically, by major market areas, and about major market reactions and exposure to advertising communications of various types. In politics, the method proved useful in the 1960 campaign as a means of testing how various subgroups would react to different candidates and statements of issues. The technique has begun to find use in the advertising area, particularly in the testing of possible advertising media choices. Each developer of such a program has put his own trademarked label on it, but the title at the head of this section appears to be as good a designation of the type of simulation as any the author can think of. In writing of their trademarked Data Breeder Model, the Young and Rubicam advertising agency has indicated:

"This model is an 18,000-sample simulation of consumer behavior. It takes as its data input what information is available about a brand's customers or media audience, and then produces estimates of the information that is missing. In the bank of information from which the model may draw are considerable data from the United States Census, from survey sources, and from syndicated services. The computer draws on these data as they are needed, to produce the best estimates of missing information.

"The Data Breeder Model also has the capability of analyzing reach and frequency patterns of existing and proposed media schedules among the entire population, or among a wide variety of different prospect groups."*

Obviously, such population behavioral simulations are of little value if they are static. They would soon be made obsolete by the changes constantly taking place in various aspects of population composition and in public tastes and attitudes. But one of the virtues of the computer is that stored data can be automatically updated by programming trends into the model, and by input corrections, both of which can be carried out with very little effort.

SUMMARY

1. The computer is simply a fantastically fast, automatically instructed electronic device which can store information and process it as instructed. Its flexibility and capacity are making it a major aid in the use of mathematical decision tools because the electrical impulses it generates can be designated and come out as numbers, other symbols, words, sentences, or diagrams.

2. The computer is often needed to carry out the lengthy calculation needed for solution of most of the quantitative tools discussed in previous chapters, but it has also given us a virtually new way of finding out how suggested plans might

---

*William T. Moran, "Practical Media Decisions and the Computer," Journal of Marketing, Vol. 27, No. 3 (July, 1963), pp. 26-30.

work: computer simulation.

   3. The most common forms of computer simulation
are:

   (a) Experimental application of accepted rules and
   relationships to learn more about the results of
   their application and to develop more accurate
   knowledge. Largely limited to investigation in the
   physical sciences so far.

   (b) Monte Carlo simulation for the construction of
   an extended synthetic experience series where the
   variations are thought to be random and actual experience data limited. Primarily an auxiliary
   tool in the solution of such problems as inventory
   and waiting line.

   (c) Heuristic programming, or the calculation of
   the results of arbitrary rules and procedures and
   the comparison of these results with those obtained from variations in these rules and from alternative sets of rules. Very promising in the
   solution of business decision problems where no
   known form of quantitative analysis yields an optimum answer.

   (d) Population behavioral simulation: the creation
   of sample populations and their known behavior
   patterns relative to those characteristics in a
   given problem situation, against which we can try
   various planned actions to get an estimate of the
   net effect of complex interactions which may result. Has already proved its value in estimating
   the effect of political campaign actions, and in the
   handling of media mix problems in advertising.

GLOSSARY OF SIMULATION TERMS

ALGORITHM: a rule for carrying out a series of iterative
(repeated trial solutions for a problem) in which each attempt
gets progressively closer to an optimum solution until it is
reached, and includes a means of identifying that optimum
solution.
COMPUTER PROGRAM: data and instructions stored in a computer for the purpose of producing a solution to a series of
problems, or occasionally for a single problem.

CUT-AND-TRY: not an orthodox technical computer term, but the common sense elliptical form of saying "cut and try to see if it works," familiar to anyone whoever carried out a non-routine mechanical task. Used here because it is an apt description of many of the values of a computer--its ability to go through the tedium of numerous successive trial-and-error calculations speedily and cheaply, whether the calculation is an iterative algorithm such as in linear programming, or the calculation of arbitrary heuristic solution rules, as in pure simulation.

HEURISTIC PROGRAM: more understandably, and just as accurately, labelled "rule of thumb" programming. Use of the same kind of arbitrary rules for decision used by human problem solvers when standard analytical methods are not available, and calculating the effect of different variations of the quantities in the situation against these rules.

ITERATIVE SOLUTION: one in which the same mathematical procedure is repeated over and over again in reaching a solution.

MONTE CARLO SIMULATION: generation of a synthetic chance experience series by some variation of a random numbers system, to represent probable actual experience over a long period of time, in a situation in which such experience is thought to be subject to chance variation, within known limits.

POPULATION BEHAVIOR SIMULATION: the author's own label for a class of trademarked programs which provide a computer with large quantities of available statistical information about a given human population and its behavior in matters relevant to various advertising, marketing, political or other types of decision. The population is usually a scaled down simulated simplification of the actual population. The factors programmed are usually subject to continual change and must be kept currently updated, a characteristic not generally true of most kinds of heuristic programming.

PART IV. MAKING USE OF STAFF-PRO-DUCED CALCULATIONS AND FINDINGS: ACCOUNTANTS, MARKET RESEARCHERS

Most of the quantitative data any executive uses are produced, digested and summarized by someone else, for his use--usually by a staff member or department. Quite often, the report does and even should include recommendations for action. This is especially true of staff reports in two major areas which lead to major planning decisions: accounting and market research. The line between such recommendations and actual decision is often a thin one. Nevertheless, there is a difference. The staff preparing the report is not accountable for decision results. The administrator deciding on the appropriate action of accepting, rejecting, or modifying the recommendations is accountable for what happens. He must therefore always make his own interpretation of the information presented to him, in the light of the decision alternatives he knows he faces.

14

BOOKKEEPING COSTS AND VALUE VS. OPPORTUNITY COST AND VALUE

A key staff operation in any organization is that of accounting. The central work of any accounting operation really revolves around two related matters: cost and value. Profits and earnings are residuals between one relatively objective set of facts--receipts--and another set which is not nearly as objective as it appears: cost and/or expenses.

It is true that the historical record of expenses the accountant produces is, as history, reasonably objective. They serve a real purpose in reporting to the tax collector and the stockholders. But for purposes of planning, few economic concepts have a more slippery content. Even as history, they must take into consideration the question of accountability. When used for forward planning, many items may be irrelevant, and some important aspects omitted. When new process costs are involved, the historical cost may be a multiple of what can be expected as volume and experience improve.

PERFORMANCE, ACCOUNTABILITY, AND COST

Even as history, the accountant's statement of cost may not be correct for the purposes of management. When a single department of a business is being judged, the evaluation must omit costs beyond the control of that department. Thus, if a department is arbitrarily charged with materials bought from another department with no choice as to source, it cannot be held accountable for cost variations due to acceptance of these materials. Neither can it be held accountable for any allocation of the general company overhead. Thus we find reference in management literature to controllable and uncontrollable costs. Clearly, no executive should be charged with responsibility for costs over which he has no jurisdiction. Such distinctions are primarily a subject of personnel and organizational management and control, however, not of economic decision.

ECONOMIC DECISION COSTS

The economic decision commonly concerns itself with the use of past costs as a major basis for the estimation of probable future costs. The length of time to be covered by the effect of the decision then becomes the major determinant as to which expenditures are cost and which not relevant to the decision.

Those costs will include both actual expenditures and unseen ones. Take the case of a firm contemplating the construction of a plant to make a new product. There are visible elements of cost in every item connected with the planning, construction, and eventual utilization of this plant and the marketing operation involved. All such expenses should be counted in the total cost. But the total must also include other elements of real economic cost that will not appear on the books of account.

Adoption of this project means foregoing alternate opportunities for profit through use of the funds appropriated for its realization. Its prosecution will preempt some resources already on hand such as land, buildings, equipment, and organization talent. Some of these real costs will not show in the accountant's figures. They are hidden, or imputed costs, and we must add into the estimate some sacrifices of income or opportunity involved in this decision and perhaps subtract some imputed losses that would be incurred by failure to proceed.

For such costs of not doing can be either positive or negative. Failure to introduce a new product may jeopardize the market position of the company and adversely affect profits. The estimated profit loss would be a cost subtraction for such a long-term project.

At the other extreme are such short-term decisions as one to make a one-time sale of some standard product of ours to a market to which we do not normally have access and which does not overlap some of our other market segments and, in so doing, utilize idle resources such as idle plant capcity and labor or otherwise worthless by-product materials. For such an extreme short-run decision, the only relevant costs are those actual cash outlays that would be added by going ahead with the filling of this one order, such as cost of added raw materials that would not otherwise be bought and cost of such labor as would not otherwise be on the payroll. Any revenue obtained over and above these directly attributable added expenses is a contribution to overhead and thus to eventual profit. The by-product raw material used may be costless if it has no alternative use. Labor force that would otherwise have been kept on at any kind of task just to hold it intact is also costless even though the books show wages actually paid out.

In other words, in any decision involving only such short-run considerations at this one, the only relevant costs are those that are incremental, those incurred as a direct result of the decision that would not otherwise have to be met.

The two simplified illustrations above highlight some of the more important relationships between decision needs and cost allocation. They involve most of the concepts used in discussing economic cost. Let us consider some of these concepts.

OUTLAY VERSUS ALTERNATIVE OPPORTUNITY COSTS

Books of account usually carry only those costs resulting from actual cash outlays and include all such costs without regard to those directly attributable to this one decision. But many decisions involve real costs that do not show up as any kind of cash transaction, and some of the actual cash outlays incurred are not true economic costs, relative to that decision.

Depreciation reserves a firm has may be used in undertaking an expansion, for example. This money, although on hand and not borrowed, has a real cost. It costs whatever return it could bring in the next best alternate use. Or we could charge its use with the interest the firm would have to pay to borrow the money--the alternative source of funds. In deciding to use the funds on hand for this expansion, the firm is sacrificing--spending, in other words--income it would otherwise receive from this money in some other profit venture, or saving the cost of the borrowing for this purpose (and probably incur-

358

ring an interest cost for some other purpose).

Similarly, the new plant may occupy land bought many years before, at a price much lower than it could now be sold for. The cost of the land for this project is no longer the original cost, but the cost the land would bring if put on the market. If the firm did not already own the property, it would have to buy it at the current market price. The latter is the real cost, even though the books may show a different figure.

Labor that would be kept on in any event to hold a skilled workforce intact obviously results in a cash payroll outlay. But this outlay is no part of the real cost of a job taken on simply to keep the force busy. Nor can any of the plant overhead outlays be charged against such a job. They would go on without reference to the decision to take or reject such an order. Only the difference in cost between doing and not doing is an economic cost.

Most cost decisions are between the extremes of long-run and short-run. Regardless of the length of time affected, the true economic cost and the real economic profit of a decision are measured in relation to the opportunity costs involved. Good opportunity cost estimates require care in uncovering all of the available facts determining the alternate opportunities (one of which is always the opportunity of not doing). The last illustration was carefully limited to a one-time order from a market to which the firm did not normally have access, and which did not overlap its normal market segment, i. e., a completely sealed-off market segment. Such completely sealed-off segments are rare; some overlap is more common. If an overlap is present, consideration of the relative losses and the effect on the rest of the marketing operation would have to enter into cost estimates and be judged in comparison with the alternate costs involved.

Whatever the basis, all costs must be evaluated with regard to the decision's effects on the entire system involved in the firm's operations--its full marketing operation as well as the entire production operation. It may be profitable to assume added costs in production if this is offset by greater savings in shipping costs, materials purchasing, handling costs, marketing expense, or costs in any other part of the operation. Costs far outside the sphere ordinarily considered parts of production are real costs of any production decision.

ESCAPABLE, UNAVOIDABLE, SHUTDOWN, AND STANDBY COSTS

When we use the term incremental costs, we usually imply increases in the firm's activity. But contraction has also to be faced at times. The same logic determines what costs are relevant as when the decision concerns activity changes in the positive direction, except that we now refer to escapable or unavoidable costs.

Hence, at the end of 1963, when the Studebaker board of directors learned that the automobile end of the business was continuing to lose money on the basis of the best accounting information, they had to go beyond these accounting calculations. Losses now had to be recalculated to determine which of the figures were mere accounting conventions and which costs the company could hope to escape if it ceased making automobiles. The problem was to estimate which alternative form of reduced activity carried the lowest cost of not doing. For an operating plant, labor cost was a true variable in the sense that a cut in the force brought a proportionate cut in cost. But a complete shutdown involved a real added outlay--severance pay. Production equipment of real value to a going plant and of real sales value when sold one piece at a time, might have a much lesser value in terms of complete plant liquidation. Had it been decided to close down only part of the operation and hold the plant involved as a standby for some other purpose, certain standby costs would have been required, e.g., watchmen, equipment maintenance, and water service. The correct standard, again, is the cost of the alternate opportunities open--complete shutdown, or various levels of partial suspension--in contrast to trying to continue.

URGENT VERSUS POSTPONABLE COSTS

Sometimes it may seem that revenues and even sources of borrowed funds are so limited that all costs not absolutely necessary to keep the firm in business must be eliminated or postponed. Costs then tend to be grouped into those which are urgent and those which are postponable.

Certain of the costs may appear temporarily at the discretion of management without many obvious unacceptable immediate effects. These are discretionary expenditures.

Thus research and development funds and advertising appropriations may be cut and postponed at management discretion without effect on the revenues for the current year. Proper costing of such changes in discretionary expenditures must include the best possible estimate of the hidden costs of such cuts. Cutting its research and development expense in half may reduce the company's outgo by a half million dollars, for example. But the end cost may be 10 million dollars in lost profit if a less economy-minded competitor pushes ahead regardless of cash stringency and grabs a share of the firm's market segment with his own improved product. The inertia of the market is such that advertising and selling expense cuts seldom have an immediately visible effect, even when the cuts are deep. But the momentum sacrificed may enable some competitor or some competing type of product to gain a foothold otherwise denied him. In both cases, the net cost of the reduction would be far higher than the immediate reduction in outgo. Such outlay reductions are in no sense the equivalent of economic cost savings.

Estimate of the possible losses is hard, of course, and never will be precise. But the costs of the opportunities foregone must be estimated when evaluating such cutback alternatives. In a dynamic economy such as ours, ignoring the ultimate cost can prove costly indeed.

SUNK COSTS

We call expenditures that have actually been incurred, but which cannot be recovered whichever way a decision goes, sunk costs. Consider the example of a cattle feeder who has paid $30 per hundredweight for lean steers he has bought to fatten for market. Suppose that during the time he is feeding them the livestock market declines drastically to $24 per hundredweight, and he decides to cut feeding early and sell in the belief the market will go down further, at least to $22 per hundredweight, if he waits any longer. If his estimate is correct, and the market does drop by another $2, his decision to sell at that time earned him a profit of $2 per hundredweight, even though he sustained a real loss on the total operation of $6 per hundredweight, plus the cost of the feed used up. This loss of $6 and the feed is not relevant to the profitability of the decision to sell at this particular time. The money is already paid out and cannot be recovered. All that is relevant is the prospect of future prices, and by selling now, the feeder is $2 per hundred-weight ahead of where he will be if he waits. The $30 originally paid, like most past expenditures, is sunk.

DEPRECIATION: OBSOLESCENCE AND WEAR-AND-TEAR

Part of the depreciation we carry on our books is a form of sunk cost, i.e., that part due to pure time, or obsolescence. When you drive the new family chariot off the show-room floor, it immediately loses value and continues to lose value with each passing day even if you park it in your garage and never move it again. It is being superseded in style and newness by other shiny new models. You can do nothing about this part of depreciation cost--it is sunk.

But other parts of the losses we charge to depreciation may have nothing to do with time. They are incurred by your decision to use the car, to subject it to ordinary wear-and-tear. Some items of wear-and-tear become due quite regularly and we class them as current expenses, e.g., periodic lubrication and purchases of spark plugs. Other use costs occur at relatively infrequent periods and can be treated as semitime charges. The tires, for example, may last over fifty thousand miles if you keep the car that long. Under normal circumstances, you may very well trade in the car before you need either tires or a major engine overhaul. In such a case, the overhaul and new tire costs become part of the depreciation expressed as the difference between original price and trade-in value. But if you were a salesman with a territory requiring a hundred thousand miles of travel per year, both might be charged off to a separate wear-and-tear account. Such wear-and-tear can be an incremental cost.

DIRECT COST AND INDIRECT COST

The accounting profession has given some attention to a costing procedure similar to the economist's division of costs into fixed and variable. It is labeled direct costing. In some presentations, there appears to be no difference between the concept of direct cost and the economist's variable cost. The economist will define variable costs as those varying directly with the volume of an item produced, and the accountant will define direct cost, in much the same terms, as costs such as raw materials, direct labor, and direct supplies, plus costs that vary closely with production and can be allocated to it, such as electric power and foremen's wages.

Other writers, however, seem to include in direct costs any that are directly traceable to a given item of production, which could include some costs the economist considers as fixed or even sunk costs. One problem is that the accountant must follow the same rules all of the time in making his cost allocations. What may well be variable cost in terms of one kind of decision may be a fixed cost in terms of another. For example, a decision requiring the doubling of near-capacity production must treat supervisory salaries and warehousing as variable costs. By contrast, a decision, when production is at a low level, to make a modest 5 percent increase, may treat all supervisory and inventory costs as fixed.

STANDARD COSTS

Any firm must consider costs of some sort in any pricing decision, if only using them to decide whether or not it is worthwhile entering the market at the existing price level. But if the industry is one with a relatively volatile demand from year to year, prices cannot be raised in years when demand is short simply because expenses per unit sold are up, and low earnings in such years need to be offset with extra earned margins in years when demand is high and average costs down. Basically, this requires the allocation of estimated fixed costs under some estimated long-run average level of production. These fixed cost allocations are then combined with estimated variable costs to give a "standard" cost for a "standard" level of product volume. The price decision is then based on this standard cost, which is seldom the actual cost for any one given year.

Under the standard costing procedure, fixed costs are not fully allocated each year. Instead the fixed cost allocated to each unit of production is that amount which would be incurred at some fixed production level which is less than capacity. Generally speaking, the production level chosen is the estimated average level over a long period of time. General Motors, for example, is believed to use 80 percent of capacity as its allocation level. The estimated cost of any planned model design is then the estimated variable cost of the model plus a fixed cost allocation assuming the standard level of production activity.

Such a standard costing procedure is a necessity in any operation which, like that of the auto industry, must design to a cost and price three years away from current market conditions and demand leads. It is just as necessary to any industry which must make cost-related price quotations under widely varying levels of demand (as in job-shop foundry operation, for example).

COSTS IN A MULTIPLE PRODUCT SITUATION

The previous discussion has centered around the costing of a product. The single product firm is the exception, however, not the rule, and the multiproduct firm has a very real problem in allocating joint costs. Any firm selling more than one product uses some resources and facilities jointly for different products, and such joint costs must be allocated by some rule. Accountants tend to use some arbitrary variable cost to apportion allocated costs, e. g., the amount of direct labor involved, the amount of floor space required, or some combination of similar variable measures.

Such accounting allocations are usually quite arbitrary and should be recognized as such. No base can always take into account all of the possible alternatives involved in different kinds of decisions. A cost that is invariable within the area of the decision sought may be treated as variable under the costing procedure. For example, doubling a product's sales volume by reason of some decision will not necessarily double the sales and administrative costs of handling it. In some instances, total sales cost may actually be lowered and administrative costs not affected at all. No rule-of-thumb costing procedure can substitute for a careful determination of exactly which costs are opportunity costs in relation to any major decision.

Exactly in what direction the opportunity costs lie will depend on the basis for the decision that puts the product into the company's line. From the standpoint of production decision, products can be classified into three types:

1. Products that must be produced jointly. The smelter of copper ore must inevitably produce not only copper, but some sulphur dioxide. He can throw this sulphur dioxide away

by letting it float into the atmosphere, or he can transform it into sulphuric acid. The refiner of crude petroleum must produce heavy fuel oils and lubricating oils as well as gasoline and kerosene.

2. Products that can be produced partly or wholly at the expense of each other. The petroleum refiner we just mentioned can vary the amount of light fuel oils and kerosene produced at the expense of gasoline volume, and vice versa, and his demand for the products varies at different times of the year (fortunately, in a complementary manner).

3. Products produced relatively independently of each other. The automobile manufacturer, for example, can produce not only passenger cars, but trucks and even tractors. While some of the same equipment can be used for all three, the decision to produce trucks usually requires addition of new facilities. Market demand, and the skill of the firm in serving it, determines the additions of products to such product lines.

Inseparable Joint Products

Relative market demand and relative price margin obtainable should determine cost allocation for products that must be produced together. If any are true by-product production, the only costs of any sort that can be allocated against them are the added ones necessary to put them into forms desired by customers and to sell them. If the copper smelter decides to go into the sulphuric acid business, the sulphur dioxide obtained from the smelter operation would not be a cost for the acid operation unless the possible profit from the acid were one of the considerations that made the whole operation economically feasible. In the latter case, some of the overhead costs must be assessed against the acid operation, how much depending on the market demand for the acid as compared with the blister copper.

Development of by-product production may even have a negative cost at times. Discard of the by-product materials may be so obnoxious to the surrounding community that some acceptable provision must be made for their disposal, or the facility will be outlawed. The cost of moving the facility then becomes one of the decision alternatives, and the gain from not moving becomes a contribution to the cost of transformation of the by-product into a saleable commodity.

Joint Products Producible in Variable Proportions

With valuable products that are necessarily joint, but with variable relative quantities (such as gasoline and kerosene), the production decision will not usually hinge on the cost allocation. Instead, the latter will hinge on the relative strength of market demand for the various products, to which production will be attuned. Fixed cost allocation should be a reflection of profit in such cases, rather than relative profit a reflection of cost allocation.

Products Produced Relatively Independently

Most multiple product lines have been developed for market reasons rather than production necessity. In such cases, the nature of the market demand that occasioned their inclusion in the line must be a major element in the relative costs. From the market standpoint, such product lines are of four general types:

1. multiple products with a relatively independent market demand, brought together because they contribute to production efficiencies, or for financial reasons such as combined automobile and truck production
2. products that supplement each other such as spare parts along with the total automobile, a service network along with a sales operation, or a number of model types of automobiles
3. products combined into a line because customers desire an assortment of goods and insist on limitation of the number of sources of supply, such as sugar the grocer must carry whether or not it is profitable, the ladies' hosiery the department store must carry, top coats and slacks the men's clothing store must carry as well as suits, or aluminum sheets and shapes the steel warehouse must carry as well as steel items
4. products combined in order to lower the average sales cost per item sold and included in the desired assortment bought by customers such as adding machines and office supplies handled along with typewriters, not because customers require

it, but because the same customers will buy them, thus lowering overall sales cost per dollar of volume.

Presumably, in the case of products with an independent market demand, some kind of incremental analysis entered into the decision to include each in the line, and the reasoning in back of this inclusion would be the first basis of allocation. Later reappraisals might allocate joint costs on some basis such as the amount of key resources and executive attention required in their successful production and sale.

Supplementary products are really different aspects of the same single product package and comparative costs would be irrelevant to business decision.

In the case of items that must be carried in the line because the market demands a limited number of supply sources, the seller cannot choose to drop them and thus eliminate costs. The line itself is his product, and his only choice is between the kind and amount of costs he will incur in making it available. If he can choose to get it manufactured outside his own organization, then the cost of the outside purchase is one opportunity cost for an item. If he can produce it for less himself, then he makes a profit even though he may sell the individual item for less than his production cost. On the other hand, if he chooses to make it himself even if he could buy for less, then the sales operation may be properly charged only its possible purchase price. Any additional cost must be charged against whatever purpose led to the decision to make rather than buy (such as the desire to level out a seasonal production cycle).

Traffic-building items included in such a line in order to gain or maintain some important profitable portion of the business are really part of the sales promotion effort for the main profitable items. Cost for such sales-supporting items must be compared not with revenues and profits of the individual items, but with the total revenue and profit brought in with the item compared with that obtainable without it. The grocer may make no money on the sugar he sells, but if he does not always have it in stock, the total traffic in his store will be so much less and the sales of other really profitable items will suffer so much that his total profit will diminish drastically.

In all joint cost problems of this sort, the concept of contribution to overhead must be the primary consideration.

This is simply the difference between the total added revenues secured with the inclusion of the item, and those costs that could have been avoided by not carrying the item. The allocation of costs to traffic-building items should be a function of the margin obtained, not the reverse. This is, indeed, the practice of every merchant, when he uses a variable margin to determine his price structure, expecting a low margin from those products that will not bear a higher one, and a high margin from other products to offset his major fixed costs.

When items are carried in order to lower the total percentage of sales cost, this contribution of each item to overhead and sales and administrative cost is the only relevant cost measure, after allowance for the variable cost of handling and producing each and for directly attributable programmed costs.

SOME SPECIAL PROBLEMS OF COST DETERMINATION

Costs are of many kinds. Some of them are a direct function of production. They vary with the number of units produced. The amount of raw material used up in making the product and the wages of the men on the assembly line are good examples.

Other costs have a stairstep formation and are sometimes called semivariable costs by economists. That is, they are fixed costs over certain ranges of the production level, but must increase abruptly when that production level is exceeded. A production department must have at least one foreman to operate at all, and perhaps only one will be needed to run the department at full tilt on a single shift basis. But if a second shift is added, another foreman must be appointed regardless of the size of the second shift operation.

Some costs probably have some kind of relationship to volume, but the extent is not determinable, and their size is determined by executive decision. Among such programmed costs would be the size of the advertising budget, frequently a matter of arbitrary decision. The volume of sales the firm gets is related in some manner, presumably, to this appropriation, or at least to some of the appropriations in the past. But the exact relationship is seldom knowable, and the size of the cost is determined by executive fiat. So also, frequently, is the size of the sales force and the costs of supervising, training, and operating that sales force.

Some costs have no direct relationship to production at all as long as the firm operates at all; they are inescapable. The rent that must be charged, whether paid directly or imputed to the cost of property owned by the firm, is such an inescapable cost, as is usually the president's salary. As already indicated, that part of the depreciation charge due solely to time and obsolescence is unrelated to production and is also inescapable.

Costs and the Learning, or Experience Curve

Evaluation of future cost can be both crucial and difficult in the case of new product or new process introduction. The historical cost of a pilot run or initial commercial run can never be accepted as even an approximation of the eventual cost. It will always be too high, and not by a fraction, but usually by a multiple of what the cost will be later. The reason is the learning, or experience curve.

The phenomenon that industry has come to call the learning curve or the experience curve grew out of the experience of the airframe industry in World War II, with its continual emphasis on model change and also on volume production. This experience demonstrated that as cumulative unit production grew, labor costs declined at a relatively constant rate for each doubling of the cumulative units produced. Later studies showed that all costs tended to so decline, even when labor was a minor factor. As noted earlier, when plotted on rectangular coordinates, the curve is a typical logarithmic curve of constantly diminishing cost at a constantly diminishing absolute value for each additional unit produced. When plotted on double-logarithmic scale, cost declines seem to vary around a straight line relationship between the logarithmic of cost and the logarithm of total cumulative production. The slope of this line can be expressed as a constant percentage decline for each doubling of the number of units produced. The percentage itself differs from firm to firm. It generally has the same characteristic slope for any new product within a given firm, so long as the firm is working within the bounds of familiar processes. (With any major process change, the slope is much slower.)

Although most business literature treats this as purely an empirical observation, the experience curve is an inevitable result of a principle known to psychologists, since the turn of the century, as the learning curve for individual skill and habit formation. As workers gain experience with a given production task, their actions become habitual and thus more efficient. Where their accomplishment of that task permits some personal leeway, they also may introduce innovations in method. As supervisors and management become more familiar with the task, they also develop innovations. Even the sales force gains from experience, or should. They learn to know what to emphasize, what customers to approach, what circumstances improve sales success.

Since the learning curve is an exponential curve, it can, with time, lead to very large decreases in cost, whatever its slope. Just how large is illustrated by Boeing's experience with the 707 airliner. It is generally known that the initial unit cost on this model was about $12 million. But Boeing foresaw a strong demand and was quite familiar with its own experience curve. The price was set at $5 million, and it is no secret that the 707 was a very profitable introduction.

Thus, one costing corollary of the learning curve is that new product price decisions, or even product entry decisions, should not be based on the level of costs shown by initial runs. These cost estimates will always be too high. Those making the decision need to evaluate these initial cost estimates on the basis of two factors:

(a) How familiar is the process and thus what kind of learning curve slope will be involved?

(b) How large is the market potential, and thus at what level will costs tend to reach by the end of the initial introductory period?

A second corollary of the learning curve is that new process changes will introduce greater potential cost savings than minor process improvements. The minor process improvements will be down at the bottom of the curve where the absolute cost gains are flattening out. The new process will be at the beginning of its experience curve, where costs decrease rapidly with relatively smaller absolute numbers of units made.

A third corollary is that the curve serves as a warning standard: if costs do not decline with experience, some factor is operating to inhibit innovation and restrain the possible gains. These need to be discovered and overcome.

Thus our knowledge of the learning phenomenon warns us that historical cost accounting figures can not be taken at

370

face value at any time. Those making decisions must look beyond the mere history to the meaning of that history for future plans.

VALUE, PROFITS AND EARNINGS

As can be seen, measurable expenses cannot be taken for granted. Much less dependable are those estimated evaluations of the worth of plant, equipment, inventories and other goods-in-being which we call assets. To one degree or another, these, too affect our measures of earnings and profits, and through them, our decision choices.

Part of the reason for confusion regarding these figures is that tax laws often mandate, or at least encourage, specific formulas. However, operating and marketing plan decisions should never be based on the tax collector's arbitrary definitions. The proper rule is the same as for expenses: the worth of an asset is the value of the next best alternative for its use.

The tax collector may permit, even encourage or require, that equipment be valued at its historical cost. Historical cost, however, may be a fraction of its replacement value, and if only enough depreciation reserves are set aside at this level, the firm may be out of business when the equipment wears out. On the other hand, tax laws may encourage use of a higher value depreciation than is occurring purely from physical depreciation and technological obsolescence. Decisions on depreciation reserves and even retention and use of the equipment must also, in this case, be based on the use value of the equipment, or its possible resale value.

Indeed, equipment in the best of condition, and even relatively new, may be valueless if technological changes have made it thus in terms of profit production. In the case of real estate, one alternative which must always be considered is the sales value, quite often much higher than cost.

The opportunity cost approach to value is extremely sensitive to decision alternatives. One firm, for example, had built a large clerical facility (located in a manufacturing area) to such low floor load standards that it could not be used even with heavy filing equipment. Realizing that the building would be worthless to anyone else, the firm wisely eventually "wrote down" the building value to the nominal asset value of $1.00.

The sudden spurt of inflation in the middle 1970's obviously educated industry to the importance of inventory valuation methods. Companies which had been using FIFO (first-in-first-out) valuations suddenly discovered that "earnings" were based on this method included the phantom profits of inventory gains. The latter were certain to become losses when the inventory had to be replaced. As a result, there was a massive industry-wide shift to LIFO (last-in-first-out) valuation of inventories. It should be noted that LIFO is the closest the accountant's historical record comes to the true alternate opportunity value--the current cost of replacing the entire inventory. It is still, however, not quite the same.

SUMMARY

1. Cost is not a fixed value. The term can have meaning only in relation to the decision purpose for which the cost figure is to be used. As a result, there are a number of ways of classifying costs. In addition, for the purpose of decision, actual past costs, however calculated, serve only as bases for estimation of probable future costs.

2. When used for evaluating managerial performance, the only relevant costs are those for which the manager can be held accountable.

3. The most important distinction is between outlay costs, representing real cash expenditures as they appear on the books, and opportunity costs, representing the actual economic sacrifice attributable to a given decision. Not all cash outlays are economic costs in the sense that the decision made would have affected their incurrence, and not all real economic costs show up on the books as cash outlays (the rent that could be obtained from the building the firm owns and uses, for example). Which costs, including cash outlays, should be charged against a decision will depend on the opportunity afforded of avoiding them, on the time span involved, and on other considerations.

4. When the decision involves an increase, expansion, or change that is not a decrease in scale, we usually charge off the added or incremental costs resulting from that decision, i.e., the added cost of doing as compared with the costs of not

doing. When special costs are incurred because of a decrease in scale or a complete shutdown, we refer to the added costs incurred as inescapable, unavoidable, shutdown, or standby costs.

5. Expenditures for activities that can be curtailed because of emergency decisions may be divided into urgent and postponable costs. When arriving at such a classification, recognition must be given to possible future losses that may far outweigh possible current savings from the reduction in such easily postponed costs as research and development and advertising appropriations.

6. Sunk costs are actual past cash outlays the incidence or recovery of which will not be affected by a given decision and therefore are not costs for the purpose of that decision.

7. Direct cost has recently been added to the accountant's vocabulary. Some seem to use the term synonymously with the economist's variable cost. Some seem to mean any cost traceable to the operation, whether or not variable in terms of a proposed decision. In any event, no rigid classification can hope to be used as an all-purpose measure of costs for every kind of decision.

8. Standard costs are estimates of what the long-run average equivalent of present cost functions would be. The main use of this calculation is the appraisal of the possible price structure for products whose demand is highly cyclical (such as automobiles), and for which fixed costs are an important part of the whole.

9. Costing is complicated by the fact that most firms make multiple products for which many costs are incurred jointly. Such joint costs must be allocated to each of the products on the basis of some kind of formula.

10. Accounting practice generally uses some directly attributable variable cost as an arbitrary basis for allocation of joint costs, e. g. , direct labor required or the floor space occupied. Such arbitrary standards seldom measure correctly the opportunity costs of many of the necessary decisions. The only accurate method is to compare the cost opportunities involved in the reason for the joint production.

11. Some joint products are joint by necessity, platinum produced in mining for nickel, for example. If some of the joint products are true by-products in the sense that pro-

duction would proceed in their absence, then only those incremental costs necessary to rendering the by-products marketable and selling them can be charged to them as cost.

12. In other cases, such as the joint production of gasoline and kerosene, joint production cannot be avoided, but the proportions can be varied and will be proportioned to expected demand. In such a case, cost allocation to the individual product is without point. Excess of return over variable costs should simply be credited to joint costs and profit. No decision will hinge on any joint cost allocation.

13. Most joint production is of assortments of items produced together for convenience and to meet marketing requirements. The nature of the marketing decision leading to their inclusion in the line should determine the cost allocation. Quite frequently, the allocation should be determined by the relative profit, rather than the reverse.

14. In appraising the cost estimates for new models and new product introductions, account must be taken of the learning curve phenomenon--the tendency of costs to decrease at a constant ratio with each doubling of cumulative production volume. These decreases tend to become quite large over time.

15. The rule for valuation of assets is the same as for expenses: an asset has the value of its next best alternative use. This is not related to its historical cost.

15

MARKETING RESEARCH:
WHAT QUESTIONS NEED TO BE RAISED?

For forward planning of external strategy, the executive is as dependent on the information produced by his marketing research analyst as he is on the accounting data for internal control. However, the jobs of these two staff operations are at opposite poles. In a sense, both types of staff operators produce data out of the past, because that is the only kind available. But the accountant's information is largely used to appraise that history. By contrast, the historical aspect of most of the market analyst's information has little value or interest except as a basis for projecting future market reaction.

Within the limits of his precise definitions of the classifications the accountant uses, his figures are usually quite accurate (unless someone is keeping false records). With accounting data, the executive's problem is simply whether or not those definitions and classifications are the correct ones for any unique decision purposes he has in mind. Even the collection of accounting data is highly structured, requires only a little judgment, given the fact that it is collected primarily for routine control purposes, not generally for the solution of unique problems.

Very little of the market analyst's job, on the other hand, is structured. The only data generally gathered for routine control purposes is that of sales and market analysis. Even this, even for purposes of control, must be subject to interpretation in the light of ever-changing external market influences. When the accountant finds costs of one item, or profit from it, are higher than those from another, he is correct, at least historically. But when the sales analyst discovers one salesman's efforts result in higher dollar volume than those of another, it is well known that we do not necessarily have a measure of the relative profitability of the efforts of the two men.

Moreover, the great bulk of the output of any useful marketing research operation is concerned with the solution of unique problems. The purpose is to furnish data which can be used to compare alternatives for future competitive moves, matters always fraught with uncertainty. The analyst's task is to interpret whatever measures he finds in terms of what can be expected in that unknown future--never, even theoretically, a mechanical task.

In addition, the measures the market analyst comes up with are not nicely structured like accounting procedures. There are no universally applicable forms for their collection and analysts. They do not necessarily mean what they seem to say on the surface as dollars usually do. In fact, it is often not clear in the beginning what kind of data needs to be collected, or in what form.

The real job of the market analyst involves more judgment than technique at every step. The validity of his conclusions and recommendations depend wholly on that judgment. Marketing research figures do not speak for themselves. Much of the expertise which the accountant has is in data collection and in highly structured methods of classification, to meet intricate legal and internal needs, neither of which change frequently.

By contrast, data collection is a small part of any well designed marketing research project. What is collected must fit a different need with each project, since the external forces with which the marketing executive must contend are always changing. Nevertheless, it is so obvious that many executives respond best to research service sales presentations which are based on some currently fashionable technique label that it is worth getting some perspective on the extent to which a degree of pure fashion element is involved in such waves of popularity.

FASHIONS IN RESEARCH DATA COLLECTION

Any survey of marketing and advertising periodals over any lengthy period of years will reveal clear waves of fashion in market research data collection emphasis and techniques. Figure 15-1 shows the results of one such study,

FIGURE 15-1. The Swings in Research Techniques Fashions

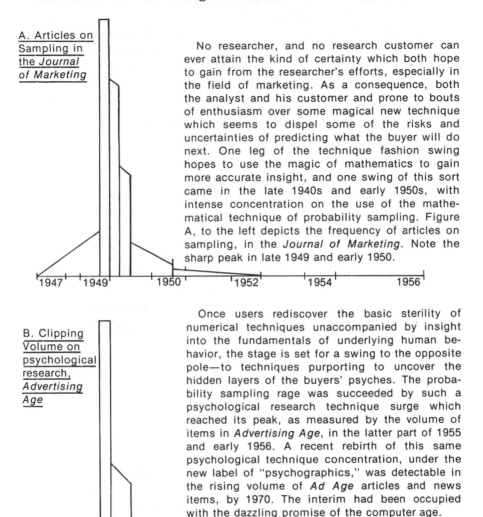

A. Articles on Sampling in the *Journal of Marketing*

No researcher, and no research customer can ever attain the kind of certainty which both hope to gain from the researcher's efforts, especially in the field of marketing. As a consequence, both the analyst and his customer and prone to bouts of enthusiasm over some magical new technique which seems to dispel some of the risks and uncertainties of predicting what the buyer will do next. One leg of the technique fashion swing hopes to use the magic of mathematics to gain more accurate insight, and one swing of this sort came in the late 1940s and early 1950s, with intense concentration on the use of the mathematical technique of probability sampling. Figure A, to the left depicts the frequency of articles on sampling, in the *Journal of Marketing*. Note the sharp peak in late 1949 and early 1950.

B. Clipping Volume on psychological research, *Advertising Age*

Once users rediscover the basic sterility of numerical techniques unaccompanied by insight into the fundamentals of underlying human behavior, the stage is set for a swing to the opposite pole—to techniques purporting to uncover the hidden layers of the buyers' psyches. The probability sampling rage was succeeded by such a psychological research technique surge which reached its peak, as measured by the volume of items in *Advertising Age*, in the latter part of 1955 and early 1956. A recent rebirth of this same psychological technique concentration, under the new label of "psychographics," was detectable in the rising volume of *Ad Age* articles and news items, by 1970. The interim had been occupied with the dazzling promise of the computer age.

From Chester R. Wasson, *Dynamic Competitive Strategy & Product Life Cycles*, Challenge Books, St. Charles, Ill., 1974.

tracing two full cycles and the start of a third one. As with fashion of any kind, public interest starts out slowly, rises to a clear peak, then fades away.

As with any fashion, interest usually arises because of the promise of some element of real value in the fashionable item. As is also true of many other kinds of fashion, the peak acceptance marks a period of excessive over-expectations, causing interest to ebb rather rapidly. In general, the fading signifies, not a disappearance, but incorporation of whatever residual value the fashion had into its proper place in the research process.

Thus the enthusiasm for probability sampling designs soon subsided when it became obvious that the content of the study was of greater importance than the design for data collection. Psychological techniques and concepts do have value, but only to the extent that something other than the objective physical attributes of the offering dominate the demand picture. Even then, their greatest value is for the advertising, and there must be some way to identify those who possess the motive or prefer the "life style" in question. The results have very limited value otherwise.

As with most fashions, the waves tend to be somewhat repetitive--old styles dressed up in new labels, as has been the case with the reincarnation of the "motivation research" of the 1950's in the guise of "psychographics" in the 1970's.

The promotional push of most such fashions comes from the need of research services for a handy sales tool. Technique gives the seller something solid to talk about, and something that can also be made to sound mysterious or arcane and new. It is much easier to sell a client on a novel technique in which the presenter claims expertise, than on reliance on the seller's experience and judgment. Yet in fact, the latter is all the buyer really gets in any case.

No technique negates the importance of judgment in planning what kind of data is needed, nor in interpreting the meaning of the information collected. In fact, even the wisdom of using a given technique is itself a matter of judgment. Just how much personal judgment is involved in interpretation of results is well illustrated by two different psychological studies made for the prune industry during the 1950's "motivation research" boom. The two studies, by different firms, discovered similar customer attitudes toward prunes--largely a feeling that they were a medicine--a laxative. But one firm interpreted this to mean that the advertising should emphasize this aspect, the other firm that the advertising should seek to build a different attitude!

As this indicates, in marketing research, the answer does not come out of the technique, but out of the analyst's own judgment. Any analyst, whether consultant or full-time member, is delivering far more than a knowledge of a few simple techniques. (And, stripped of their mystical labels, all techniques of any kind are, in their essentials, simple, as we have already shown with respect to the mathematical ones.)

The specific technique is a useful sales label, but in no sense critical to even the collection process. One analyst may measure attitudes with a few simple questions. (One famous researcher measured the morale of World War II army units by simply observing the kinds of answers he got by asking unit members "How is the chow!") Another may use intricate scales. Quite often this is a matter of taste (and what seems most likely to sell). One careful piece of psychological research tested seven different methods for checking consumer preferences, from a simple ordering of items to a supposedly sophisticated scaling device. They found no substantial difference in results. * In other words, the technique used is often of very minor importance relative to the skill in analyzing the results.

If data collection techniques are not the principal tools of the market analyst, what should we expect from him, and how must we interpret what he does for us? Let us look at his job to see.

THE MARKET ANALYST'S TASK

Generally speaking, the main job of the market analyst is to plan studies which will help the executive decide on future competitive moves. Although he may have some continuing duties of a semi-accounting nature (such as sales analysis), his major purpose is the answering of specific management questions with respect to the consequences of possible

---

*Harold H. Kassarjian and Masao Nakanishi, "A Comparative Study of Selected Marketing Research Techniques," a paper presented at the 1966 Annual Meetings of the American Psychological Association.

future actions in the matters of product development, product introduction and sales support, advertising and selling plans, pricing, and distribution and logistics. The most frequently asked questions are probably product and communications oriented. Given an action-oriented management question, the analyst must generally develop his reply through the following steps:

1. Formulation of the underlying research information question.
2. Developing an economical plan to gather just the amount of information needed to solve the research question, involving
   (a) use of readily available information from both published trade and internal sources
   (b) development of a plan for any field research, if any, needed to supplement the available information.
3. Collection and assembly of planned data.
4. Analysis and summarization of data.
5. Interpretation of the analysis in terms of market action.
6. Development of a presentation which can reveal the alternatives open to management and show why, in terms the specific management understands.

FORMULATING THE UNDERLYING RESEARCH QUESTION

Although the original management question may appear to be an information question, it is nearly always really action-oriented, not pointed toward the underlying issue. When management asks "Why is our . . . (item) not selling well?", it is really asking "What can we do to sell this?" The research question may very well be, as it was in one case, "Who is in the market for this item, and is she our kind of customer?" Management may ask "How many branch warehouses should we have, where, and how well will they do?" The answer may be in the question "What determines our sales potential?" Management may ask "How shall we advertise and promote (. . .)?" The proper question may be "What is this product, in the buyers' eyes, and is this our kind of product?"

Again, management may ask "How big is the market for this instrument be in the (-------) industry, (a new mar-

380

ket for us)?" The researcher may need to ask "How is this bought, under what circumstances, and which buyers are likely to be receptive at all to a new supplier, for how many, and for what kind of design?"

Any research question is necessarily related to the management question, and it is easy to see how it follows, once stated. But getting to that statement is not an easy process. Instead, developing the research question is a diagnostic skill which, like all good diagnosis, comes only after long experience and requires the best of judgment. Once well done, the research is more than one-half finished. A really good question focusses on the kind of information needed in the next step and thus predetermines the general nature of the data collection process, although by no means the technique or the details.

PLANNING THE DATA COLLECTION: ASSEMBLING THE INFORMATION--READILY AVAILABLE DATA

Newly collected field data of whatever kind is seldom the principal basis for any marketing study. Indeed, any study is tremendously handicapped at the start if no kind of background data is available. Results will be costly, and the study quite likely a prolonged exploration. Such is rarely the situation, and the content of most studies, implicitly or explicitly, rests heavily on two kinds of data already available in some form:

(a) Base or background data which gives meaning and measurement, such as the volumes of available governmental and private censuses and statistical series, as well as internally-generated information.

(b) Directly applicable data from both external and internal sources which may or may not need supplementation.

The first step in any sound research is to explore the volumes, indeed full libraries, of information available in the United States Census and other official governmental reports, in trade association statistics, published research, directories, and other publicly available sources, and in internal studies and regular internal reports. In some cases, by no means rare, careful analysis of this information will eliminate the need for any substantial added data collection. More usually, some additional information may be needed, but the initial search will limit that amount drastically, and permit a sharper focus on that need. In nearly any situation, census and trade statistics form the benchmarks which permit measurement and interpretation of field study results. It does little good to know that the potential market for widgimatics consists of machine shops with sales of $20 million per year or more unless we know how many such there are, and how distributed geographically. The latter is normally in some available statistical collection.

Available data is cheap--often requiring no more than the cost of a few hours in the library. Field studies, at the best, are always expensive relative to the information obtained. The time saved is one very important aspect of the use of available material. Field research normally is very time consuming, since it requires advance planning, and quite often some pretesting, even before it can get under way, as well as digesting after it is done.

Marketing decisions seldom leave much room for time, and research has to be evaluated in terms of its cost as well as its output. Thus search and thorough analysis of available information is a major element in any good research plan.

ASSEMBLING THE INFORMATION: PLANNING AND CONDUCTING PRIMARY RESEARCH

Planning for and conduct of the field research can start once the research question is formulated and the survey of available information completed and digested. At this point, the analyst must decide whether the research question is as clearly defined as he desires, and also whether or not he can foresee clearly which respondents would be most useful, and what kind of answers he might get from them, in what form. If he believes either that the research question needs clearer definition, or that more information is needed to structure the field work, he may conduct some exploratory surveys. If possible, he will probably pretest his survey instruments in any case where personal responses are part of the plan.

Only when he has settled such matters to his own satisfaction is he ready to start the visible part of the research--data collection. Close supervision of this is important, and field workers do need some training. But this aspect of the job

requires the least judgment and skill. Indeed, whenever extensive interviewing is needed, the field work is often delegated to
an organization with an established field staff. Such organizations can also often provide a useful second look at the proposed
interview instruments. It is not necessarily wise to delegate
all of the field operation, however. There is much to be said
for some personal participation by the project director. Some
potentially important sidelights turn up which could prove very
valuable in re-directing the research, and in the very important
next step--analyzing the results in relation to management's
action questions. Moreover, many such agencies are skilled in
handling a relative type of field research and may tend to try to
make the plan fit their special tools rather than develop tools to
fit the special situation. The field plan must be formulated by
those who will conduct the analysis. The nature of this plan
will depend on how much is already known about the market and
its reactions, and on the character of the added information
needed.

THE FIELD RESEARCH PLAN

There are very few really cut-and-dried field research
plans. In reality nearly every plan has to be custom made and
the variety could be almost infinite. However, there are several general classes of plan, each of which can be made to fit the
particular situation. In general, data gathering instruments
are either structured or unstructured. Primary field data can
be gathered either by observation or by some form of personal
response instrument or it may be experimental in character.
Personal response surveys may deal directly with potential
customers or consumers or it may draw on the experience of
people who deal with such customers or consumers. If the research involves personal response the contact may be by direct
personal interview, it may be by telephone, or it may be by
mail. The responses may be obtained by direct questions or by
indirect questions or by symbolic stimulus presentations. Experimental methods may involve some form of simulation of the
situation in which the customer normally makes a decision or
it may involve a test marketing operation. Finally, parts of the
plan may and quite often do involve some form of exploratory
surveys to be followed up by some kind of definitive data
gathering.

Any problem-solving research requires some preliminary exploration before more formalized work can be undertaken. For some problems, this exploration is a project itself. Starting with information available in personal experiences of various people, or in print, or both, the analyst searches first for ideas--ideas about what to observe and measure, about possible information resources, about the best data collection techniques for his purpose, about the best place to begin. Data collection cannot be safely structured until these points are very clearly defined. Until you know what to sample, you cannot determine how.

The analyst must use relatively flexible techniques and research design until this exploration has developed a reasonably clear picture of the real problem and its setting. The investigation must be kept loose, ready to proceed in any promising direction. Four of the more general types of data sources have the flexibility and breadth of data coverage needed. The first three might be classed as available summarizations of information collected for other purposes:

1. experience data--the mentally stored, summarized impressions of people working in the area in which the phenomenon occurs
2. routine data collected in the normal process of running a business
3. library or other secondary material--both formal studies and published experiences.

The fourth does require specially collected data. It is the detailed study of insight-stimulating examples.

Some of the resulting information may well be in statistical form. But the priority aim of exploratory research is to get ideas that can lead to the right kinds of measurements later, not to get the statistics and measurements themselves.

THE EXPERIENCE SURVEY AND OTHER EXPLORATORY FORMS OF INTERVIEW

Much human knowledge--especially in the business world--is never recorded. A lot of it consists solely of observations made, filtered through whatever personal biases the observer has, and stored in his memory. The effects of business actions and decisions are observed by business executives, salesmen, trade paper editors and reporters, dealers, customers, and others in contact with a given area of action. Somewhere among each of these groups will be some who are truly observant and mentally curious. They summarize what occurs within their observation and draw conclusions therefrom. The aim of the experience survey is to gather and collate such summarized experience from the more observant and thus obtain ideas as to the best direction for more definitive research.

Choice of Respondents

Only a minority of those exposed to possible experience gain it, at least in the sense of developing a rationalized summary they can articulate. Fortunately, these individuals are usually known to their associates, who can point them out and save much searching on the investigator's part. For example, a sales manager who worked through a score of manufacturer's agents was able to point out five who gave a very clear picture of a potential market not then being covered by the manufacturer in question. As a result of their comments, the potential market was shown to be in four major industries, permitting the analyst to focus his attention on these without further waste motion.

On another occasion, a few pilot interviews with a half dozen assorted individuals not only narrowed down the area for a descriptive study of a component market, but indicated the sources for further interviews and opened up unsuspected market possibilities. The half dozen included a small manufacturer, two distributors, managers of branch sales offices of potential customers, and the purchasing agent for a company buying equipment such as that on which the component would be installed.

Editors and reporters for trade papers are observers by profession and thus nearly always valuable sources of information about people and trends inside the industry covered. They can also tell much about the best way to approach other people who must be contacted.

Interviewing Respondents

The interview form used for the exploratory project is the generalized exploratory interview, sometimes called the unstructured interview or depth interview. In essence, this is the ancient journalistic technique of the reporter. After some preliminary discussion with those initiating the project, a list of points that seem relevant is prepared, and a list of generalized probing questions developed from these. These questions are as open-ended as possible, designed to uncover a wide variety of responses and perhaps open the way to comments not directly foreseen. The order is not fixed and will probably be varied from interview to interview, as may also the exact wording. The aim is to get the respondent to unload every aspect of what he may feel and know about the subject. Although the questions are general, the respondent is encouraged to talk in specifics, to give examples whenever possible. Only in this way can the analyst get meaningful summaries out of the kind of discursive conversation he gets.

The kind of outline used by an investigator, and the methods used in drawing out respondents are illustrated in the appendix to this chapter.

Group Interviews Versus Individual Interviews

"Respondent" has been used in the singular in the above. However, the exploratory interview can be with two or more persons simultaneously. There are real advantages in such group interviewing, especially in the case of consumer research. In the first place, there is considerable economy of time. It does not take six times as long to interview six people at once as to interview one of the six. More important, group interaction can bring to the surface points that the individuals talking separately might all forget to mention. This same group interaction can lend interest to the interview and cut down on the fatigue factor. Most of these same advantages hold for exploratory interviews in industrial marketing. Of course, it is not easy to get a group of executives together as it is to get some housewives into a coffee klatsch. But two or three partners in a manufacturer's representative firm can often meet together with the interviewer, and even two or three officials of a manufacturing firm may do so if the proper arrangements are made.

Size of Sample

The number of exploratory interviews will usually be quite small. A half dozen can be enough at times. Anything more than two dozen becomes quite unwieldy from the standpoint of analysis. The universe being sampled is not the number of potential respondents, but the number of possible ideas, and a very untypical sample is often drawn on purpose. When new ideas of value in problem formulation dry up, it is usually time to take stock to determine whether all suspected types of sources have been tapped, and to quit if this is so. The analyst will first make sure, of course, that all necessary types of ideas have been covered--possible hypotheses for developing models, the kinds of market descriptions that seem to be worth specific development, the kinds of respondent or data sources worth more intensive study, the best means of contacting these data sources, the degree of homogeneity in the universe to be sampled, and even at times a rough idea of the kind of numerical values to be expected.

THE DETAILED STUDY OF EXAMPLES

Available information and experience studies will not always clarify the research problem. The only way to gain the necessary insight may then be a detailed study of carefully selected examples. Even the most experienced observers may have missed the key elements of significance in events and prove to be the persons seeking help concerning their meaning.

Such was the case encountered by Dick, the new research director at Ajax Chemical. Ajax employed a large force of salesmen to contact professionals who determined the choice of, but did not directly buy, its products. At the first sales meeting after Dick came on the job, some district supervisors complained that they had trouble picking salesmen, asked for help. The sales manager talked it over with Dick after the meeting--suggested that he dig into it. He had not been able to find an answer either. Dick decided he needed to know more

387

about what happened in the selling situation before he could work toward any kind of answer. He hired some professional psychologists to travel with the salesmen and observe. Out of these observations came leads that finally resulted not in a change in selection procedures, but in a changed training program.

The examples selected for detailed study may be specific market situations rather than people, and the study can be indirect study through recorded information as well as through direct observation. Or selected individuals or groups may be surveyed and the results analyzed. Available recorded information about selected individual customers or markets may be an adequate basis. The essence of the technique lies in the intensity of study of a few selected examples. These are chosen to produce the greatest yield in insight, not for their degree of typicality. Indeed, one common type of choice is to shun the presumably typical in favor of deviant extremes. Which methods are chosen depends on the kinds of insights desired; it would be difficult to list all of the possibilities that may be considered at various times. Some useful types are:

1. Top and bottom types, for contrast--usually chosen in terms of members of the top and bottom quartile' of whatever distribution interests the analyst, e.g., the top and bottom salesmen groups in a firm, the top and bottom customers in order of size or frequency, top and bottom markets, etc.

2. Birth and death types--those just entering a classification compared with those who have just dropped out, e.g., new customers compared with customers recently become inactive. The characteristics studied might be objectively measurable items such as age, stage in the family life cycle, occupation, size of firm, nature of business, etc. Or a characteristic might be purchase motivation, more easily distinguishable in the marginal groups of customers than in the generality.

3. Coming generation types--in determining the acceptability of long-leadtime new designs, for example, it has often proved more valuable to analyze the reactions of the next wave of potential buyers than the reactions of recent purchasers, e.g., in the case of automobiles, college upperclassmen.

4. Other marginal types--the brash, rising competitors in an industry may be more indicative of sales trends or distribution methods than the experience of established organizations.

5. Key individuals--in the market or in the adoption process. The opinion leaders or tastemakers, for one such group, may be the only accurate indicators of changes in demand.

6. The analyst himself, his family and friends--provided they are valid members of the market involved. There is much to be said for taking an introspective look at yourself and interpreting this observation in terms of your own position in the market spectrum. To be sure, there is much unavoidable bias in this procedure, especially in your concept of the degree to which others are like or unlike you. But nobody is more accessible to close detailed observation of his actions and thoughts than you are, and your family and friends are only relatively less accessible. So long as you recognize the bias and your aim is to secure ideas, not some measure of typicality, this can be a fruitful source of ideas.

The intense exploration of selected examples has three special values:

1. The attitude of the investigator can be that of flexibly alert receptivity.
2. Study of each individual case can be both broad and deep.
3. The ability of the analyst to integrate diverse bits of information as he gathers them can be utilized to the utmost, permitting him to draw them together into a unified interpretation as he proceeds.

Because he has only a few cases to study, and because his only aim is better insight, the investigator can concentrate on the hunt for ideas without being inhibited by the need to test immediately any hypothetical models conceived. He can be guided into new directions of attention by any ideas his observations trigger, reformulating such ideas as new information is collected, changing the kind of data sought or even the criteria for case selection as he goes along.

DESCRIPTIVE RESEARCH: USING THE OBSERVATIONAL AND SURVEY TOOLS

Systematic observation and properly designed surveys are the main tools of descriptive research. The aim of such description is to develop a precise enough tentative picture or pictures of the way events take place and the relationship between individuals involved in these events to permit the construction of models which permit sufficiently accurate predictions of the expected outcomes of decisions for the purposes at hand. Whether we can rely on systematic observation or must design a survey, the design of the study must be sufficiently structured to yield adequate quantitative relationships while maintaining a wide degree of coverage of the kind of information that can be collected and of the universe being studied.

SYSTEMATIC OBSERVATION

Most of the knowledge we possess comes from unplanned observation, both conscious and unconscious. In one sense, every form of data collection involves some degree of observation. Surveys that make no provision for collecting observations of the way people answer as well as their actual answers are lacking in vital details needed to properly interpret the answers received. Informal observation, however, usually lacks three requirements for systematic observation when used as the central tool of investigation:
1. systematic planning focusing on specific propositions for study and making provisions for every detail that is expected to be observed
2. systematic recording of all events related to this observation and provided for in the plan
3. carefully planned checks and controls to assure the completeness and reliability of the observation and the validity of the data obtained.

Advantages and Disadvantages of the Observational Technique

When it can be used, observation is a powerful tool of investigation with three major advantages:
1. It permits the recording of actual behavior as it really occurs under natural conditions.
2. It often can be carried out in such a way that neither the willingness nor the ability of the subject under observation is necessary.
3. It does not require that individuals being observed be conscious of their behavior.

The data obtained is, thus, more likely to be valid than that which can be had by survey methods, for which none of these three points can be completely true. The survey must rely largely on the ability of the respondent to report what he might do under circumstances not currently present, or what he had done in the past. Or, on the other hand, he must report his actions to certain hypothetical stimuli that must be somewhat different from those he would face in an actual situation. We must thus depend on the respondent's recollection of his own or others actions in the past or on his verbal anticipation of choices he would make to a stimulus he is not at the moment facing.

Much data open directly or indirectly to observation is not available through survey methods. The comparison shopper can discover information about a competitor's product specifications, and even his degree of quality control, which the competitor himself would never suspect as important. A well-designed time and duty study of a salesman's effort will reveal details the salesman might not only be unwilling to report, but about which he would be completely unaware.

On the other hand, a great deal of badly needed information is not directly open to observation. In addition, the elements of time and timing constitute a weakness of this tool. To be easily observable, an event must cover a relatively brief time span and must either be frequent in occurrence, occur at predictable times, or be announced in advance. Events may be closed to observation either because they take place in the privacy of the family or because they involve the subjective mental reactions of those in whom we are interested. For example, we seldom have access to the family councils that take place when the purchase of a house or car is being considered. We may be able to observe the kind of bargaining that takes place between the buyer and the car salesman but can only speculate concerning the reaction of the buyer to the salesman's presentation. By the use of mechanical recording devices we can sometimes invade the privacy of the home in a limited way, as we do when we record television tune-in by means of a recording device, or with the cooperation of the respondent mount some sort of inconspicuous camera to see who is in front of the set at the time of the tune-in. We cannot determine whether or not the individual is really listening and what his reaction is to what he is hearing.

We may be able to extend our reach by means of the self-observation method of the diary, but at the expense of sample bias due to the necessity of getting cooperating individuals who will meticulously follow directions.

Making Use of Observation

Formulation of a systematic observational plan requires the determination of:
1. who or what and what characteristics shall be observed
2. whether the observer shall be a participant in the group being observed or be an acknowledged outsider.
3. what kind of safeguards are necessary to be sure that the results will be accurate and valid for the purposes of decision contemplated
4. whether preliminary investigation or other knowledge has been sufficient to permit of relatively structured observation or whether further unstructured observation must be made before an efficient research plan can be developed.

Establishment and clear definition of the categories and people to be observed is no less important than careful wording of questions in direct interview surveys. Data that does not contribute significantly to the making of some future business decision not only wastes time and resources in its gathering, but can dilute the value of the effort expended by diverting attention from those points that are important. One of the major problems in many kinds of observation is determining what is important. In comparison shopping for example, it is relatively easy to lay too much stress on comparison of items the expert thinks are important in the construction of a product, but which may be of no importance in the consumer's mind or may even be of negative importance.

One problem in the use of observation is that the known presence of an outside observer can change the course of action of people being observed. If the subject of observation is that behavior, then it is often wise for the observer to become a member of a group in which the action is taking place. One interesting example is that of a food firm which decided, on the basis of interviews and other information, that the ruinous turnover then being experienced in its processing plant was due to the fact that those who took jobs in the factory had an erroneous impression of the kind of work they would be doing. As a result, officials hired an industrial film company to produce a set of film strips about the work, which could be shown to applicants. Before making the film, the producer sent his scriptwriter into the plant to determine the kinds of points that must be covered and the manner in which they should be covered. The scriptwriter went to work through the regular personnel channels of the company as a manicurist. As such, she worked directly with all of the employees (because clean fingernails were important in the work of this plant). After six weeks, she had the information around which she could develop the kind of film needed. The validity of her unstructured observational research was confirmed by the subsequent experience of the company. Every applicant was made to view the film about the job before filling out a formal application. The turnover dropped from a level on the order of a hundred percent in three months (with many people staying only six weeks) to a level that is considered normal for the class of employee concerned.

Participant observation is not always feasible, however. The subject of the observation might well be a salesman concerning whose routine a time-and-duty study is required. When the subject is such a lone individual, there is no choice but to use an acknowledged outsider and there is no real possibility of hiding the purpose of this outsider's presence. In such cases, some other method must be used to ensure the validity and accuracy of the observation as a sample of the occurrences in the universe under study. If the observer is reasonably skilled, however, he can establish a considerable degree of rapport with the individual being observed after a period of time. After a short initial period, the old habits of routine should reassert themselves and the results be reasonably valid.

The unstructured observational plan is best when there is insufficient knowledge to start research above the exploratory phase. In some cases, no more may be needed if the conclusions are based on analysis made by highly skilled professionals.

This was the course of events in the case of Ajax Chemicals mentioned earlier. The research director who was asked to find a better way to select salesmen for Ajax decided he did not know enough about what occurred in the selling situation to make a definitive study of selection processes, or even that the selection process was the problem involved. Accordingly, he hired a group of professional psychologists who traveled with the salesmen, observed what happened at the receptionist's desk when the salesmen first went in, and also what happened in the interchange between the salesmen and the professional buying influences they interviewed. These psychologists were, of course, first thoroughly indoctrinated into the nature of the management problem involved so that they could focus their attention on those aspects of what occurred that might reveal the kind of information on which management decision could be taken. Analysis of their unstructured observation reports led directly to a conclusion that the problem lay in insufficient sales training of the representatives. Accordingly, the whole training program and its management was revamped. The problem, which had first appeared to many to be a personnel selection problem, was eliminated by an adequate sales training program.

SURVEY TECHNIQUES

Surveys fall into three main groups of techniques: (1) relatively unstructured open-ended exploratory forms, (2) highly structured, detailed lists of direct questions asking for the answer sought, or (3) indirect psychological questions and stimuli presented to respondents in order to get a response not obviously sought in the question asked.

The exploratory interview has some value in descriptive studies concerned with extremely small universes, universes involving a handful of firms and respondents, for example, particularly where the aim is to carry out both exploratory and descriptive phases at the same time. Otherwise it has little real value. The possible sample is so limited that if the universe is of any size at all it lacks significance. The answers obtained are highly unstructured. Tabulation is extremely difficult and involves a great deal of interpretation which may not always be valid.

The direct question technique is most widely used because of the ease of covering a large sample, the simplicity with which it can be administered by a large staff of inter-viewers with limited training, and the ease of tabulation of the final results. Fortunately, a great many of the questions to which we wish answers can be properly answered by this

method. In fact, every questionnaire of any sort contains
some direct questions about the characteristics of the respondents themselves, e.g., their sex, age class, income level, or
occupation. The direct question is the shortest path to answer
but not always the best. Use of a direct question involves at
least four assumptions that cannot be taken for granted:

1. that the words used mean the same thing to all re-
    spondents. (This must always be checked inde-
    pendently.)
2. that the answers received are to the words in the
    questions asked. (Triggered responses do exist.)
3. that human reactions can always be fitted into neat
    categories, and that the proper categories have
    been chosen. (People do have ambivalent feelings
    about some things, e.g., the feeling that B might
    be a good idea, but, at the same time, having
    doubts about B.)
4. that the market reactions sought can be ascertained
    by rational, conscious, verbalized responses. (In
    some cases, the real answers might meet social
    disapproval. In others, people have never given
    conscious consideration to their feelings in a parti-
    cular matter, and cannot articulate an answer.)

Words are symbols which carry different meanings to
different people depending on their background, their ambitions,
and their current attitudes. To the communist, the word democratic means a one-party system in which the individual has no
choice whatsoever. To the senator, filibustering to block a
bill on which he knows he cannot win, it means the right of a
minority to talk freely and attempt to block action of another
minority or even of the majority. To the economist, the term
free enterprise means the freedom of entry for new firms into
an industry and the absence of any price or cartel agreements
between those enterprises. To many businessmen, on the
other hand, as the statement of one of the defendants in the
heavy electrical industry equipment conspiracy case showed,
the term free enterprise may mean collusive agreements between producers and aggressive attempts to bar new entrants
from the industry. While these examples are extreme, word
meanings have many subtle differences which may be far from
obvious but cannot be safely ignored.

Even when the words themselves seem to be free of
possible misinterpretation, the response obtained may not be to

395

the question as worded. Anyone who has ever done extensive polling, on controversial political matters in particular, has observed that, when feeling really runs deeply, a question touching on the controversial matter does little more than trigger a ready response--a response that is pretty much the same no matter how the question is worded. The same kind of triggered response may indicate quite an opposite type of reaction, a reaction about which the respondent does not feel at all deeply but one which is imbedded in the mores of the group of which he is a part.

Ease in tabulation, which comes from fitting questions into neat specific categories, carries with it the disadvantage that the complete reactions of people do not always fit neatly into such tight categories. "Yes" is usually "Yes, but" or "Yes, under certain circumstances," and the circumstances as well as the buts may vary considerably between correspondents. Some of these sources of error can be corrected by the participation of the skilled project director in some part of the questioning, enabling him to observe the tone, emotional depth, and circumstances under which answers are given (provided, of course that the method of contact is personal and not by mail or telephone).

Finally, the straight question technique assumes that all important market reactions concerned in the particular study can be ascertained by rational, conscious, and verbalized responses to such direct questions. Use of the technique assumes that the respondents are able to articulate the proper answer, and if honest, in the conventional sense, they will give this correct answer.

For the great bulk of subjects investigated and for a great many people, these assumptions are accurate enough for the purpose in hand. But, like all research assumptions, they cannot be taken for granted and must always be subjected to test. For a great many marketing situations, these assumptions can easily be at least partly wrong. Especially where the marketing situation involves a choice of no great consequence to the consumer (as he sees it), people are seldom aware of the basic motives for their decisions. Few individuals are sophisticated enough to admit to themselves that many of their marketing actions are culturally motivated. Taught throughout their lives that certain motives are improper, they will deny to themselves the possibility that the banned motives could be the operational ones in making purchasing decisions.

As one researcher phrased it, "If you want to know what people want, don't ask them." This is especially true in matters of product design and pricing.

Indirect questioning techniques have arisen to get around these difficulties. The more able practitioners of marketing research long ago came to look upon some of their questions as _stimuli_ to which the answer is in the fullest social sense _a response_ subject to careful analysis. Psychological indirect questioning techniques are usually more time consuming than those of direct questioning techniques and, thus, are somewhat more limiting in the amount of sampling that can be done with the same amount of money. Some of them are just as easily tabulated, however, as are the answers from direct question techniques, while others require a great deal of interpretation and coding before being adapted to statistical tabulation.

Indirect Question Techniques

Most respondents are honest and cooperative with the investigator, at times perhaps even too cooperative, attempting to give the answer they think the investigator would like rather than searching their own consciousness. The straight question is likely to lead to distorted answers in at least three types of circumstances:

1. questions touching on an action or event some alternatives of which are subject to custom or other reference group influence
2. questions concerning matters about which the correspondent may never have seriously given conscious thought, either because the decisions so made were not considered to be of major importance, or because the reaction invoked was almost entirely emotional in origin.
3. questions which involve details of product design, or pricing. These are matters concerning which the consumer must often make hard choices, and cannot tell specifically what those choices will be in advance.

In the first case, the attention of the respondent must be diverted from the intent of the survey and in the other he must be offered stimuli that permit him to act out his attitudes and impressions in some manner. The same indirect tools will accomplish either of these aims. Some tools, of course, are better at aiding articulation of a response while others are better at revealing possibly hidden motives and attitudes.

The simplest form of indirect question, and the hardest to develop and formulate, is the indirect question that looks like a direct one. When one investigator was asked by the War Department in World War II to determine which outfits were most ready to be sent to the front and had the highest morale and faith in their officers, the investigator questioned the men regarding the quality of food in their outfit. In this case he was relying on an inference that men in outfits whose morale was low would be more inclined to complain to an outsider about internal matters than those in an outfit in which morale was high. Use of this type of questioning obviously requires a high degree of accurate insight into the kinds of replies that will be highly correlated with the kinds of information sought. Few investigators are good enough social psychologists for this, and in too many areas our knowledge of social psychology itself is much too skimpy to permit a widespread use of this type of technique.

A more easily formulated type of indirect question relies on what psychologists call projection--a tendency of people to ascribe to others motives that in the situation given apply to themselves. Thus, when cars were being redesigned in the early 1950's, one manufacturer asked customers what they would like. He was told that potential customers desired cars that were easy to park and maneuver and comfortable in their seating arrangements. He then designed cars with squarish compact lines to meet these specifications only to suffer considerable loss of market share as a result. Another asked potential customers what kind of cars their neighbors would like and was told that neighbors liked cars heavy in chrome and long and racy. This design sold well.

A second type of projective technique depends not so much on another form of question as on the use of a vague generalized cartoon-like picture called the Thematic Apperception Test (TAT) (see appendix). The respondent is faced with a cartoon-like sketch, usually centering about some situation supposed to elicit some responses of the type sought. Participants pictured are usually expressionless people and the situation itself is unbiased in the sense that it does not lead to any particular response--only the one which the respondent reads into it out of his own attitudes or observations. Since he is telling a story about somebody else under some hypothetical circumstance, the respondent presumably is not subject to the same taboos he would be if he were answering the question directly. He is under no pressure to give a socially acceptable response.

Both in the case of the questions about other people and in the cartoons, the responses obtained are often quite different in their distribution from those obtained from a direct question which presumably parallels the indirect question. Many analysts assume that the answer obtained under the indirect question is, thus, more valid. This is, however, an assumption and some comparative tests have indicated that it might not always be true. In fact, the respondent who is also a good observer may be quite aware that his own tastes are quite different from those of his neighbors and report tastes that do not reflect his own at all quite accurately. In addition, it is extremely difficult to completely parallel a pictured situation with a direct question that seems to be the same. Engel and Wales have reported regarding a series of questions about doctor-patient relationships. * Their results seem to indicate that, in some cases at least, the difference in the answers is due to the fact that the questions themselves really are different in content. Use of a projective technique does not necessarily assure that the answer we get is a projection or is any more valid than the answer to a direct question would be. The validity must be checked by independent means or must rest on the investigator's skill and efforts, not on the type of question.

The TAT form of test, however, has another aspect-- its ability to help respondents to articulate their feelings or expressions about a given kind of situation. However, even here care must be taken because the type of stimulus presented is not one to which people are normally accustomed to reacting-- the telling of stories about a picture. The object of the study is to determine attitudes in which the respondent may have no very deep-seated reactions. It is not difficult for the interviewer to unconsciously bias the response received--if only in response to a question for enlightenment as to what is asked. Westfall has shown how a minor suggestion can lead to an acci-

*James F. Engel and Hugh Wales, "Spoken versus Pictured Questions on Taboo Topics," Journal of Advertising Research, Vol. 2, No. 1 (March, 1962), pp. 11-17.

dental bias of considerable proportions.* The tabulability of the answers from such a cartoon test, of course, is far from simple. Since the responses are bound to be unstructured, there must be a great deal of interpretation and inference as to the categories in which they should be cast.

Two final sets of indirect questions are more adapted to aiding articulation than to revealing tabooed responses: word association and sentence completion tests, and rating scales. Word association tests are of two types: (1) attempts to get at the words freely associated with the object itself and (2) guided association, which asks respondents to pick out of a list of attributes those they feel apply to the object. Exhibit 6 contains examples of both types. The conventional free association test seeks to discern attitudes toward bus travel by asking for "the first word" that comes to mind in relation to each of the different kinds of travel. (In this appendix example, note the intermixture of irrelevant words added to the list to divert attention in part: grass, electric, house.)

Sentence completion is really another form of word association test, asking for the response to the beginning of some such sentence as, "When I get a headache, I . . . ." The respondent is asked to complete the sentence with the first thought it suggests to him. Both free word association and sentence completion end up with a tabulation of different kinds of responses listed by frequency--in the first case, of words listed; in the other, of ideas categorizing   or actions. Originally designed to delve into the psychological unconscious, their primary value in marketing studies is in the help they give respondents in the articulation of feelings and impressions to which they have never given conscious thought. For example, college business students asked directly why they were not interested in the job of salesman gave rather vague answers. But when asked to designate the occupation of two kinds of persons below, they listed salesman for the first and engineer for the second.

1. Bachelor, lives in a penthouse, extremely well dressed, drives a Jag, has lots of glamorous girl friends.

*Ralph Westfall, "Student Involvement," Advancing Marketing Efficiency, (American Marketing Association, 1959), p. 512.

2. Married, has two small kids, owns a new Chevy
and an older station wagon, lives in the suburbs.

No special insight is required to see that the second represents the usual aspiration of the normal low-middle-income student and the unlikelihood that he can fit the first description to himself.

Rating scales are of a number of different types, but all have a similar structure and a similar purpose--to get away from forcing the respondent to make a sharp choice between two extremes, and to get some indication of the degree of feeling behind the respondent's choice. One popular form, the semantic differential, offers him the choice of a number of steps between two polar extremes such as hot-cold, gentle-harsh, masculine-feminine, and the like. The scale may be designated as from 1 to 5, from −2 to +2 with a zero neutral position, or can be designated as COLD, COLD, cold, neutral, hot, HOT, HOT. One variation used in comparing brands presents the respondent with a folder in which the extreme point labels are in pockets at each end of a series of pockets into which he may slip some pictures of brand packages given him, ranking them as he feels they should be, between light and strong, for example. Others develop groups of statements reflecting various aspects of attitude, each statement having a scale-value.

Such rating scales can be analyzed numerically, but it should be recognized that the difference between two rating point numbers is in no sense necessarily the equivalent of the values given. It is impossible to know whether a rating of 4 is psychologically equal to twice that of 2, half again as much, or ten times as much, either for the individual or the group as a whole. And within the group, one man's 4 may in fact be equal to another individual's 1 in terms of the emotional incentive to action being sought. As convenient as a numerical result may be for manipulation, such numbers do not necessarily constitute a measure in any sense of the term, "measure".

METHOD OF CONTACTING RESPONDENTS

Most projective methods require personal interview in order to carry them out, although some of the simpler and more objective forms can be handled in other ways. Of course, seemingly direct questions that are a disguised indirect approach can be administered by mail or by telephone as well as in person. With the direct question, all three methods of contact are feasible: in person, by mail, or by telephone.

Personal Interview

No one method is best for all purposes. The direct personal approach has the great advantage that the interviewer can observe directly the conditions under which information is being given and can make note of the tone and manner in which answers are made as well as any side comments likely to be volunteered by the respondent. In addition, any apparent misunderstandings can be cleared up by rephrasing of the question and any side explanations that might be called for can be made.

However, some people are reluctant to tell another person directly about matters which they will enter on a written report under the guise of anonymity. Where it is advisable to consult records, the respondent is much more likely to do so if given the latitude of time available on a written questionnaire to be mailed back. Where interviews are scattered widely over space, direct personal interviewing can involve unexceptably high costs. There are even times when the respondent is difficult to contact directly in person but can be reached by telephone. If the type of respondent involved is frequently away from home or absent from his office, personal interview may require a higher number of callbacks than is economically feasible.

Mail Surveys

Mail interviews often permit the respondent to hide under a cloak of anonymity and there are types of questions many respondents consider too personal to answer in person, but to which they will given an accurate report on a written questionnaire. The mail questionnaire has no limitations on time or space, especially in terms of cost. On the other hand, returns from a one-time mailing are usually a minor fraction of the total mailing and this can be a source of bias in the returns received. In general, for example, the higher the economic and educational status of the respondents, the more likely they are to answer a mailed request for information.

The bias involved, however, is not automatic. Where the group being contacted is, for the purpose of the survey, a relatively homogeneous one, there may be no response bias. In an extensive test some years ago, Time Magazine proved by making a subsequent personal interview check that the responses of their subscribers returning a questionnaire did not differ materially from those who did not return.

When using a mail questionnaire, therefore, it is important to assess the degree of homogeneity in the population being sampled with respect to the characteristic being measured. And it is also well to make provision for some degree of internal check on bias in the return. Further, there are certain types of respondents who, for one reason or another, will not give a good return to a mail questionnaire under any form of incentive. The author ran into this situation, for example, with oil field superintendents, who spend very little time in their office.

The problem of return, however, often can be cancelled out by the use of various forms of incentive to return the questionnaire. The incentive may be in the form of nominal payment (a dime or a quarter), in cash, or in the form of a suitable premium. This may either accompany the questionnaire or be sent subsequent to its return. The incentive may also take the form of some kind of follow-up of those who did not return the questionnaires. A great many analysts have found that nothing much more is needed than some form of flattery or mark of special attention (in the form, for instance, of special postage--air mail or special delivery--on the questionnaire sent out).

One of the major problems in the mail approach is getting a properly tailored, up-to-date, mailing list. Where all respondents must come from actual current users of a product, one interesting variant is to bypass the mails entirely and use the product itself as the carrier. One company seeking out the possibility of a rare reaction to its product succeeded in getting the needed return of several thousand by use of a self-mailer form in packages, coupled with an attractive premium offer for the return of the filled-in questionnaire.

One real weakness of the mailed questionnaire is the uncertainty concerning the extent to which respondents all understand the questions in the sense intended. Many simple words carry widely different connotations in different parts of

the country and to different individuals in each part. There is
no way of making certain that responses are all uniform in
meaning.

Telephone Interviewing

To a great degree, the telephone shares with the personal interview the flexibility of approach permitting explanation of meaning whenever the respondent obviously does not
clearly understand the intent of a question. In addition, no
other type of interview is the equal of the telephone in attaining
complete coverage of the intended sample. The callbacks are
relatively inexpensive and can therefore be made in whatever
frequency is required. While distance does add to cost, the
additional amount can be relatively moderate even where there
is a rather considerable distance between respondents. The
telephone call has a way of getting directly to the person being
called and, at times, is far more insistent than the personal
presence of the interviewer. This insistence factor can be increased where advisable by transforming the call to a long distance call where a local does not succeed. On the other hand,
the telephone interview does often impose a somewhat more
stringent time limit on the interview, or in the number of questions asked, than either the direct interview of the mail interview. This time limit is somewhat flexible, since people who
are being interviewed on a subject in which they have a great
deal of interest will sometimes be willing to answer at length.
And quite obviously where visual stimuli are important to the
answers, the telephone interview is not a possible technique.

EXPERIMENTAL TECHNIQUES

The use of the various kinds of survey techniques has
been so widespread and so fruitful that it is often assumed that
no other methods are possible or necessary in the field of marketing and business research. Certainly the results of a great
deal of this survey work have justified the amount of attention
and care put into developing survey techniques. Furthermore,
accurate description of the actual market situation often con-
firms a model. Finally, the probability of an inferred model
of the market reaction is sometimes so great that further test-

ing does not justify either the time or cost that would be involved in developing an experiment.

Nevertheless, it must be recognized that the information developed out of descriptive types of research such as the survey method is purely inferential and frequently needs testing for its validity. In addition, the survey can seldom answer the question of "how much?" accurately enough when the analyst is dealing with such problems as advertising expenditures and pricing, or the intensity of consumer reaction that might be expected from a given type of sales appeal. Whatever the survey technique, results give only a stronger or weaker basis for inferring the direction of consumer reaction to be expected in an actual market situation. Observation, surveys, and available collected data can yield information only on:

1. past actions or characteristics of past consumers
2. what people say they like or what they say they would do under specified circumstances
3. what they say is their reaction to certain words or pictured or described situations.

No survey response measures the depth of reaction in the only sense that is important to marketing--the depth they will reach into their pocket to pay.

Respondents can, of course, be asked whether they would purchase something under a specified set of circumstances, but the response obtained is purely verbal. Experience has shown that only under very limited circumstances can it ever be considered even an approximation of the actual purchase response to be expected under the actual market conditions at the time the decision being considered is implemented. One of these limited circumstances is the reporting of intentions to buy major items in the very near future. But this kind of information is valid only for items that are carefully considered purchases. It loses validity fast as the future is stretched out, becoming very unreliable when projected beyond a six-month period. When valid, such reporting of intentions is, in effect, a reporting of decisions already virtually made.

In addition, where product or price decisions to be made by the consumer do not present any really new types of decisions for him or her, the indirect inferences from survey data may be enough to supplement the marketing experience of executives. Where the decision to be made involves subjecting the consumer to a new experience, such as a really new type of product or a new form of sales approach, no kind of survey

405

data furnishes a trustworthy guide. In almost every case where the question of relative sales appeal is concerned, there is no real substitute for the purchase situation, or a valid direct simulation of it.

The purchase decision is a complex one, the vector of a multitude of stimuli--some personal, some external, some strong, many weak. There is no way the consumer can predict how he can make it until he is placed under the necessity of making such a decision, or some decision closely akin to it. That is, there is no substitute for actual experimentation for getting the kind of data needed for a great range of marketing decisions.

Basic Requirements for Good Experimental Technique

True experimentation is not at all the same thing as "trying something." Use of the experimental method requires careful provision for controlled observation and adequate cognizance of the requirements of good experimental design. Such design makes thorough provision for observation and control of all factors expected to be significant. The existence of a hypothetical model to be tested is an absolute prerequisite for all true experimentation. Experimental design cannot be constructed until it is known what factors are significant. In addition, the ideal experimental design makes provision for substantial acceleration of the time factor. The right kind of design would be conducted on a small and relatively inexpensive scale. It would be so set up that the experiment can be conducted and results known before any major investment is made in production of product or advertising. To the extent that these three conditions are not met, the value of the method is greatly compromised.

It is possible for the true experiment to look like a survey. In one such case a manufacturer desired to test the value of an alternate form of packaging for a product already on sale--a toy being distributed through variety stores. The organization conducting the test surveyed a great many families with children. They spent the great part of the survey discussing how people bought toys, how they used them, conditions under which and where they bought them. After ostensibly completing the survey interview, respondents were told that for their effort in cooperating with the interviewer they would be given a toy. They were shown both packages and told that both of them contained exactly the same toy and exactly the same quality, that the only difference was the package. They could have whichever one they wished. When the great bulk of respondents chose the new package, the manufacturer's uncertainty as to the wisdom of changing the package was greatly reduced.

Such a research design can be experimental even though the "laboratory" is on the doorstep or in the respondent's home. Control would have been more adequate, of course, if some respondents had been told, or led to infer, that the products were different in some vague way.

TYPES OF EXPERIMENTAL DESIGN

There are three basic types of experimental design used in marketing research: (1) market tests, (2) laboratory techniques, and (3) disguised surveys.

Market Tests

The market test is by far the most widely known and most widely used. In any week of the year, the trade press takes note of hundreds of tests being conducted in scores of cities across the country. Most of them are in the packaged consumer goods field, with the volatile toiletries and cosmetic category the most common.

Results from such market testing have not been uniformly useful. Products that seem to sell well in test cities have flopped later, and some that did not seem to do too well have succeeded when put on the national market. Part of the trouble has been the tendency to try to test too many variables at once, and to leave jobs for market testing which should have been done earlier by simpler methods. The market or sales test is too expensive and cumbersome a device for trying out the basic product concept. To get a test under way requires too much commitment to production and extensive marketing costs to make it a useful tool during the development of packaging, labeling, and promotional approaches. But experienced observers agree that there is no substitute for the market test when making a final trial of promotional, distribution, and product concepts before launching a full-scale national promotion. The market test, in other words, serves the same purpose in marketing plan development that the semiworks scale plant does in production process development. When well designed, it locates and permits the elimination of bugs in an otherwise workable plan.

Laboratory Techniques

Some form of laboratory technique is essential if we are to measure the acceptability of a product idea before that product idea has been translated into a specific manufacturable design, and certainly before any production equipment has been ordered to carry out the design. Similarly, for packaging we need some way of testing packaging ideas before printing plates and press runs must be undertaken. The testing of alternative prices in the market place is cumbersome at best and frequently completely impossible on a practical scale. For known products on the market, the dynamic effects of a price change may mask the effect of both increases and cuts. In general, whenever alternatives must be sifted to a smaller number, we should first look for some form of simplified laboratory test to screen out the less likely choices. In addition, such things as the appeal of a copy layout or an advertising theme cannot be measured easily in advance, or even at all, under actual market conditions and only some form of laboratory simulation can do the job.

The two most widely used laboratory techniques are consumer jury tests of taste or other use tests of projected new products, and laboratory tests of packaging. In use and taste tests, a group of potential consumers are furnished with different alternate versions of the product to be tested, usually together with some types of control products, such as competitive products or a previous formulation. After a sufficient period has passed for them to get used to the product and its characteristics, panel members are interviewed or otherwise asked to give a report on their experiences and reactions to the product. Packaging is kept as neutral as possible and care is taken in assigning symbols to designate the different types so that no psychological predisposition to one or the other of the products is likely to be present.

Of course, there are many variations of the carrying

out of this type of test. The consumer may try one version one month and a different, or a presumedly different, version the next period. (In some phases, this "different" product ought always to be the same version given as a presumedly different one.) Or a customer may be given two or three versions at the same time and then asked to compare them.

One of the problems of use tests is that the decision made by the customer is sometimes more heavily influenced in actuality by the kind of package in which the product is purchased, or by the label on the package, than by the actual reaction to the product itself. In one startling case some years ago a meat packing firm blind-tested a mutton product with customers. The reaction to the taste was almost uniformly favorable, but in reporting the findings on their test, the researchers involved predicted that the product itself would fail because of the fact that it would have to be labeled as mutton. Subsequent introduction of the product on the market amply fulfilled the forebodings of the researchers.

Certain types of packaging characteristics are frequently tested under laboratory conditions in the meaning in which laboratory is normally understood. Thus, the apparent size of two packages sitting together on the shelf may be rated by subjects who are given a fixed, very brief, time to look at them. The attractiveness of alternate designs may also be so judged.

Again, one of the problems is to be sure the laboratory situation is not so different from the total situation that important factors are omitted. It is entirely possible for a package design, for example, to prove outstandingly attractive in isolation, but when placed on the shelf be so similar to the designs of competing packages that it is, in effect, invisible. At the very least, the design of such experiments should include some realistic tests of the attention-getting effect of various designs in a setting so similar to that in which they will be placed in the actual marketing situation.

The lottery purchase simulation has been developed to measure purchase incentive and has proved valid in a number of cases. When this technique is used, the respondent is given a list of choices which he is asked to make with the understanding that his name will be among those who may get whatever choice they decide to make, based on some form of drawing. One of the earliest known uses of this technique was that of the Opinion Research Corporation, nearly forty years ago, in making a study of rug designs. Respondents were brought into a showroom where a lot of possible rug designs were exhibited. They were told that somebody would be given a door prize of one of these designs, the design indicated as his own choice after looking over the patterns. After a number of showings in a number of cities, 120 such customers were awarded either the rug chosen or (if that was not available) a closely similar pattern. When the winner called for the rug, each was told that he could change his mind if he so chose. The validity of the original choice is clearly indicated by the fact that only 2 of the 120 made such a change. One woman had changed her plans, replacing the bedroom rug instead of the one in her living room. Another had turned her winning number over to her daughter, whose tastes differed.

The same device of the lottery was used to test price variations in a laboratory test reported by Pessemier. Participants were "sent" on a simulated shopping trip. Each was told how much money he had to spend, the assortment of brands available in each class of goods for which he was "shopping," and the price of each item. He marked his choices on the questionnaire in front of him, and then one "shopper," selected on a random basis, was given the actual items called for by the selections made during one of his shopping trips, together with any change from the money he was to "spend."*

Accelerated Purchase Experiments

Dik Twedt has outlined an interesting controlled experimental technique using an accelerated purchase incentive in ordinary food stores.** Two observers are stationed full-time in each cooperating store. One passes out a coupon good for a substantial cash discount on any brand in the product category that includes the test item, e.g., any cake mix. The other is stationed near the display containing the item, to keep a tally

---

*Edgar A. Pessemier, "A New Way to Determine Buying Decisions," Journal of Marketing, Vol. 24, No. 2 (October, 1959), p. 41.

** Dik Twedt, "A Cash Register Test of Sales Effectiveness," Journal of Marketing, Vol. 26, No. 2 (April, 1962), pp. 41-42.

of movement of every brand. Where package design is being tested, through the use of sample mock-up packages, the second man also intercepts the customer after she has made her choice and gives her the standard package in trade for the sample.

Since the coupon is good for any brand, sales by brand are not biased, but sales of all brands speeded up. The degree of acceleration is regulated by the size of the discount offered. Since only a small stock of mock-up packages is required, an experimental package design can be tested before any investment in printing plates and press runs needs to be made. And since an observer is right on the spot, displays, pricing, and all other merchandising variables can be kept under close control. Coupons turned in also may give the user a chance at a drawing (say for twenty-five dollars cash), giving a further purchase acceleration effect, and also making the customer furnish name and address. The latter could be used as a basis for a follow up survey to get useful analystical detail about purchasers.

Interpretation of Experimental Results

Just because a good type of research design was used does not mean that the results as they are can be evaluated. The data must be assembled and broken down into its component parts, and these parts interpreted in terms of their meaning with regard to the model used. The analyst can never be sure that he has considered all of the important alternatives. He must always carefully check to be sure that some unexpected factor did not enter into and contaminate the results. Since the essence of experimental technique is a great deal of simplification of the actual situation, he must always be wary of assuming that he has come sufficiently close to the actual situation to ensure a valid response. Finally, he must always remember that the results he has are measurements of the present and near past, and that conditions may have changed between the time that the experiment was conducted and the time at which the decision resulting from it will go into effect. This, in itself, is no minor problem where matters of fashion, style, and taste are involved--as they nearly always are in marketing problems. Research technique does not itself produce recommendations for action. It simply produces the raw materials with which the analyst must work in producing a useful business recommendation.

STRUCTURED VERSUS UNSTRUCTURED INSTRUMENTS

There really is no such thing as an unstructured survey or observation. If the observation is going to have any value at all the observer must have in mind some kind of outline of materials that he intends to observe in the situation--some types of actions, incidents, or reactions which he considers as relevant and worth observing. Similarly an exploratory interview must also be conducted as some sort of formal outline in mind. One such outline is included in the appendix to this chapter. The difference is really in whether the answers are structured or not. The outline that the observer or the person conducting an exploratory interview has is not necessarily followed in sequence. It does not call for any particular set of answers and leaves the observer or the interviewer free to follow up leads based on the responses he gets. Thus the unstructured form is best in those instances in which the person gathering the information is not exactly sure of what kind of responses are possible. The kind of responses he does get are bound to be rather diverse in form and rather difficult to tabulate. The result is seldom a result which can be arranged in neat tables of numbers with any validity. To get the kind of quantitative measures we need, we need instruments giving structured responses. However, structuring of responses limits the kind of information to the types of responses that the person planning the research can foresee. It is quite possible for him to lack insight into the most crucial aspect of possible consumer reaction and thus the research itself may lead to a false conclusion. There is no fool-proof means of avoiding this except the use of analysts with both extended experience and insight in the planning end of the research.

LIMITATIONS ON FIELD RESEARCH

Any research which depends on the reactions of people to direct questions or indirect stimuli of any kind must build on materials that are within the experience of the respondents. Much marketing research, however, involves materials that may be somewhat beyond that experience. If the difference is not great, then the problem may not be substantial. Thus concept testing for new products, using purely literary descriptions, will work for a new brand of soap of a different color or a new beer advertising theme, for example. If the matter involves some sort of taste or feel sensation, then the customer will have to be given this taste or feel experience. Even then the result can not always be trusted. A major food processor, for example, that has never been able to gain on the No. 1 company in the field, for years developed new soup brands that tested well with women's panels coming through their laboratory, but failed to sell when they reached the market. The problem was simply that adults are not the primary users of soup, but children. The products they were testing were highly spiced, which children do not like. It is not possible to get a good answer about any product, however, that would make a major change in people's habits. Such research must make use a combination of methods to find out the trend in which taste is moving. This is a difficult problem and is not easily solved within the laboratory dealing purely with literary description. Most product research has demonstrated that asking people what they want always gets a reply that is close to what they have, especially in matters of design where the relatively long lead times that any new product development involves, this answer is always behind the times, often by years. Nevertheless some studies have been successful in discovering the directions in which people's satisfactions and dissatisfactions are moving.

ANALYSIS OF RESULTS

The common title of "analyst" is quite appropriate for those directing marketing research studies. Analysis is the key skill involved in every step of the research, the key to the quality of any results, and the nature of the most important steps, especially those following the data assembly process.

It is a gross error to view analysis, as is sometimes done, as a mere arrangement of tabulations in neat standardized tables, much as the accountant presents his income and expense summaries and his balance sheets. If the analyst does no more than simple tabulation, and if he uses a standardized structure of presentation, he has not earned his pay. The initial tabulations are a mere clerical operation, although even the planning of these must vary from project to project. The analysis step should involve the development of revealing inter-relationships between the various kinds of information to show probable market opportunities and trends. Without such measures of inter-relationships, the research effort is wasted.

It does no good to find out, for example, that 65 percent of the golfers interviewed like a proposed golfing gadget, that 20 percent are indifferent, and 15 percent definitely dislike it. Such figures do not tell who would be in the market. They do not hint at what kinds of satisfactions would form the motives for purchase. Nor do they help decide how it should be priced and distributed. What we need to know is what kinds of golfers make up the 65 percent and what kinds the opposite 15 percent. Once this is pinpointed by cross-tabulation of replies with characteristics of the respondents, the analyst should go further and look for other relationships.

In searching the relationships, the simplest tools are also the most widely used and useful: charts, graphs, and cross-tabulation (relating answers to one question to those elicited by another question, by the same persons), as already noted. Overall averages are seldom of value, since they tend to conceal the differences which reveal the real market opportunities, but averages typical of individual market segments make useful comparisons.

At times, of course, more complex calculations can be valuable, as already noted.

The skills involved in carrying out the work of cross-tabulations themselves, or even more complex calculations, are not great. The quality of that work is measured by the insight into what comparisons to make, and this is where prolonged experience in analysis of all kinds pays off (not industry experience, necessarily--this tends to hinder good analysis quite often, by keeping the analyst from raising questions he needs to ask himself).

The formal analysis completed, the analyst still has two tasks in any project:

(a) development and evaluation of the alternatives for action revealed by the analysis, and

(b) development of a well-digested and summarized presentation of his analysis and recommendations to management.

The combined result is his report.

414

DEVELOPING RECOMMENDATIONS AND DESIGNING A PRESENTATION

The visible result of any project is the final report. However, a very important step comes after the analysis and before the report--a careful logical consideration of the action potentials revealed by the analysis, and choice of those options that should be most profitable for management. It is at this point that the analyst's breadth of experience, observational acuity, and breadth of knowledge of consumer behavior is most important. The figures alone really point in no direction until related to what we know of human behavior in the case of marketing (and also in matters of personnel management).

Once the analyst has arrived at his conclusions and recommendations, he still has to design a report which does the following:

1. Summarizes in a simple, and compact concise form the full results of his study.
2. Gives his conclusions and recommendations and shows why they logically follow from these findings.
3. Does so in a manner most likely to be understood and accepted by those to whom he must report.

A good report is best measured by its lack of volume. Some few studies are so extended and complex that the report may involve some considerable volume. But it is a good rule that the more voluminous and complex the presentation, the less focused the study and the more superficial the analysis, if any. By contrast, the simpler, more understandable, the more concise the presentation, the higher the quality of the analysis, generally speaking.

Given all these steps, how does the executive judge the worth of a study and make use of the results?

MAKING USE OF MARKETING RESEARCH

Marketing analysts are used for much the same reasons as accountants are: the work of assembling and summarizing the information needed to make decisions is a full-time job in itself, and often for a number of people. But in the process of collection and classification, such staff personnel create classifications and reach implicit or explicit conclusions which must be reviewed in the light of the executive's own ob-

jectives. In the case of the accountant, the conclusions which
need reviewing are primarily his statements of what should be
included in costs and value. In most other matters, his measurements do not involve any major question of judgment, and
his data has the accuracy of history. With extremely rare exceptions, even what data should be gathered is rather cut-and-
dried, and the form into which it is to be presented is likewise.

In the case of the market analyst, however, personal
judgment tends to be an important ingredient of every step he
takes. The logic of the whole operation requires review. The
basic questions the executive needs to ask himself in this case
then are:

(a) Was the study based on a research question which
dug under the action question to the basic underlying issue?

(b) Was the research plan based specifically on this
research question?

(c) Did the analyst make full use of existing information prior to developing his plan?

(d) Was the analysis of the field data thorough, and was
it based on understanding of consumer behavioral
patterns or did it simply follow standard cliches?

(e) Did the conclusions and recommendations flow logically and only from the data and from established
behavioral principles?

(f) Were all of the alternatives for action considered
and carefully weighed in the light of the data?

(g) Do the recommendations take realistic account of
the firm's own specific resources and opportunities,
its market position, and its objectives?

Making these judgments requires care and attention. Unless
they are made, the research effort may be wasted. The research analyst, like the accountant, is not responsible for the
action taken--the executive himself is, and must make the final
evaluation of the information he has requested. But the quality
of the market analyst's presentation is infinitely more dependent on his judgment and experience than is the accountant's.

SUMMARY

1. The evaluation of the results of marketing research
is more complicated than the evaluation of the accountant's

output. Every step of the process must be considered.

2. The tendency to focus on the technique side of research is so widespread as to lead to wide swings of fashion in technique popularity. It is also misplaced. Any one technique has a minor place in the results.

3. The market analyst's task is a six step one: problem formulation, data gathering planning, data collection, data analysis, data interpretation, and presentation.

4. The key step is that of formulating the research information question underlying the action-oriented management question.

5. The data collection plan should include a preliminary summary of available data, to be certain no more primary research is planned than is absolutely required.

6. Field research will normally include an exploratory phase which may involve an experience survey, depth or exploratory interviews with individuals or groups, or some kind of planned observation of selected situations.

7. Planned observation, when possible, can lead to highly valid results. But many situations and kinds of information are not open to observation, and surveys must suffice.

8. Survey techniques may involve direct question-and-answer, indirect questions, or various psychological techniques intended to get at answers the respondent would be unlikely to give directly, or could not articulate.

9. Depending in part on the technique, the analyst may use personal interview, telephoned interview, or mailed questionnaires. The type of information needed will limit this choice. Whatever the method, the results will lead only to inferential conclusions, since no possible set of questions or stimuli can hope to fully duplicate the consumer decision situation.

10. Experimental techniques are used to approximate the reality of consumer reaction. One form, the market test, is too costly to be used for much more than final testing of a well-researched promotional plan. Information needed at earlier stages must rely on some simple laboratory design.

11. Laboratory designs include consumer jury tests, psychological laboratory tests of packaging, lottery purchase simulations, accelerated purchase in-store tests.

12. All consumer research is limited to getting answers within consumer experience.

13. Whatever the method, the results do not speak for themselves, but require analysis; the search for inter-

relationships of factors.

      14. The analysis itself must be interpreted in terms of alternatives for management action, and developed into a specific presentation.

      15. The executive who uses the research must evaluate the logic of every step in the process, from problem formulation to presentation.

Exhibit 1
Instruction Outline for Exploratory Interviews
with Industrial Sales Officials

DRILL POINT DISTRIBUTION STUDY

We are making a distribution study to determine what impact the drill point specialists have made on the industry. The entire business is made up of old line manufacturers that use old fashioned methods. Traditional distribution is through mill supply houses and direct to the OEM. Specialists came into prominence shortly after World War II. These firms buy surplus merchandise, distressed merchandise, and newly manufactured goods. They are able to offer immediate delivery, competent engineering help, and a full line of drills. They sometimes offer special concessions to customers. For example, if an OEM will guarantee a certain amount of business, the specialist will warehouse the merchandise and bill as delivered. (This is called *stockless purchasing.*) Although the OEM may pay slightly more for the goods, he saves capital and warehouse space. Specialists are doing increasing amounts of the OEM business and have progressed in some cases to putting up the drills in their own packages, a practice which robs the maker of identification with the product. This is the problem in brief. We want you to interview the individuals listed, getting the following information:

1. Are drill specialists here to stay?
2. What percent of the market do they have?
3. What advantages do they have over the mill supply house and the factory?
4. In what area of the country are they strongest?
5. What disadvantages must they overcome?
6. Who owns these drill specialists? Do the manufacturers in any case?
7. Are these specialists offshoots of larger mill supply houses, or independents?
8. From whom do they buy?
9. Are they limited to large cities, or could they survive in a small area?
10. In what quantities do they buy?
11. To whom does the specialist sell?
12. What have the mill supply houses and the manufacturers done to counter the specialist?
13. Is there a trend for factories to set up additional warehouses? If so, are these warehouses being used for storage only or are they sales distribution centers?
14. What has happened to the size of the individual sale in the last five years?
15. How do these specialists finance their operations?

16. From whom do you buy your drill points?
17. Why do you buy from this particular source? (Any other reason?)
18. Do you get any special deals such as stockless purchasing, consignment purchasing, quantity discounts, etc.?
19. What types of sales aids do factories give you? Which are most valuable? What types would you like to receive that you are not now getting?

If any other idea comes to mind, or the respondent brings up a seemingly worthwhile subject, probe further. Use the questions to be answered as a guide sheet, but conduct the interview as a conference. A good part of the questions do not have to be asked directly, but just start the respondent talking. He will cover many of these points on his own.

Exhibit 2
Probing Instructions for Exploratory Interviews in a Study of Drill Point Distribution.

The word *probe* means *to investigate thoroughly.* Probing is needed (1) when a respondent's answer is not clear, (2) when the answer is not complete, or (3) when the reply does not directly answer the question or when the answer is evasive. The following suggested probes can be adapted to any of the above situations in order to explore as fully as possible the thought, feelings, reactions, and ideas of the respondent about any particular matter.

Suggested Probes

What do you suppose makes you feel that way?
Can you explain that to me?
Can you give me an example?
Anything else?
Just how do you mean?
Tell me more?
What else?
I don't see what you mean.
What would cause you to feel that way?
Any other reasons?

Some of the questions do not require probing. Other questions do require probing and the answers should be as complete as possible.

Avoid leaving short answers. Words like *new* or *quick and easy* or *fresh* are not complete answers and do not usually represent a respondent's complete answer. Answers should not be abbreviated but should be recorded fully.

The following types of generalizations are not acceptable:

good	convenient	economical
better	expensive	easy

Each of these words may have different meanings for different people, and the meaning attached to it by each respondent should be determined. Always ask for an interpretation, such as, "What do you mean by *good*?" or "What do you mean by *economical*?"

Exhibit 3
Portions of an Exploratory Interview with a Sales Representative, to Determine the Nature of the Market for Butterfly Valves

The chemical industry in this area is a potential user of butterfly valves. This is the inorganic segment of the industry—many of the applications involve the handling of high-temperature corrosive gases. Pressures are low—gases like SO_2. Valves must shut off, but not necessarily give a tight shut-off. We do not have synthetic fiber plants in our district, but the valves for Dupont's plants are brought here. Butterflies are used in the acid reclaim sections of viscose rayon production process—not ours, but they do buy from competitors. They use metal seat valves—tight shut-off is not required.

Dupont could give a lot of information on the use of butterfly valves in a number of segments of the chemical industry. You could talk to a number of people, but the instrumentation people would be best—they buy most of the butterfly valves. They are part of the plant design group at Dupont. Dupont builds most of their own plants, and this is typical of the larger producers of chemicals. They buy mostly small sizes.

。。。。。

The Healey people (a competitor) are in the petroleum field, too. They are in all of the industrial fields. Most of Healey representatives are also tied up with a diaphragm motor manufacturer—usually Zenith. It becomes a natural to put a Zenith top works on a Healey valve. The big field here, when you get into control valves, eight inches or above—a double-seated globe-type control valve price becomes prohibitive. You can usually go to the butterfly-type valve at less cost. One of the advantages is that you can use a smaller butterfly-type valve—say a 6-inch—and get the same results you get with the larger globe-type valve, in a control-type valve. In most of these applications, you are concerned with the throttling action, not the shut-off—with action in the 60 range. Can be on anything in a process control application—can be on a heat exchanger, to water, etc. Heat exchanger applications are spread throughout a lot of industries.

。。。。。

(Asked about a valve which might go as high as 400-500 psi pressure:) Can't get too excited about a high pressure valve. If you said degrees, I would be more interested. The big problems in the industrial field is designing for corrosion and for higher temperatures. Once in a while you get into higher pressures, but the only place that I have been handicapped by pressure, and that isn't high in the Eastville Water Company. I went and talked distribution valving to them. They were interested. But they get up to 250 psi in their lines, because of topography. If you had it up to 250, we would cover nearly every application. But if you could go in one direction at a time, I would rather go into temperature than into that pressure.

Exhibit 4
A TAT Cartoon Example

"The Chicago Tribune," "The Consumer Speaks about Appliances,"
Tribune Company, 1959.

ROLE PLAYING
Reveals In-Store Buying Attitudes

The drawing of a husband and wife in an appliance store was shown to women. The husband is shown as saying, "Oh, here comes the salesman." On display is a range of major appliances.

From this one situation are extracted 3 areas:

1. What the woman is actually saying *out loud* to her husband.
2. What she is thinking to herself, but probably would not say out loud.
3. What she feels he is thinking, which gives an indication of anxieties developed by the husband's attitudes as she interprets them.

27a What might SHE be thinking to herself? _____

5 What is HE thinking? _____

Through the device of a role-playing situation, respondents are actually revealing their own attitudes while feeling they are interpreting those of others.

Exhibit 5
Tabulated Interpretations of Replies to Appliance TAT Cartoon

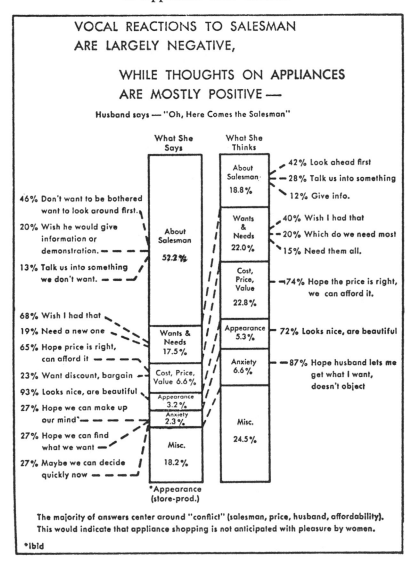

VOCAL REACTIONS TO SALESMAN ARE LARGELY NEGATIVE,

WHILE THOUGHTS ON APPLIANCES ARE MOSTLY POSITIVE —

Husband says — "Oh, Here Comes the Salesman"

What She Says | What She Thinks

About Salesman 18.8%
- 42% Look ahead first
- 28% Talk us into something
- 12% Give info.

46% Don't want to be bothered want to look around first.

20% Wish he would give information or demonstration. — —

13% Talk us into something we don't want. — — —

About Salesman 52.2%

Wants & Needs 22.0%
- 40% Wish I had that
- 20% Which do we need most
- 15% Need them all.

Cost, Price, Value 22.8%
- 74% Hope the price is right, we can afford it.

68% Wish I had that
19% Need a new one
65% Hope price is right, can afford it — — —
23% Want discount, bargain
93% Looks nice, are beautiful
27% Hope we can make up our mind — — —
27% Hope we can find what we want —
27% Maybe we can decide quickly now — — —

Wants & Needs 17.5%

Cost, Price, Value 6.6%

Appearance 3.2%

Anxiety 2.3%

Misc. 18.2%

Appearance 5.3%
- 72% Looks nice, are beautiful

Anxiety 6.6%
- 87% Hope husband lets me get what I want, doesn't object

Misc. 24.5%

*Appearance (store-prod.)

The majority of answers center around "conflict" (salesman, price, husband, affordability). This would indicate that appliance shopping is not anticipated with pleasure by women.

*Ibid

423

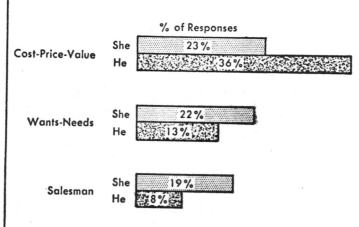

WHAT SHE THINKS
VS
WHAT (SHE FEELS) HE THINKS*

% of Responses

Cost-Price-Value
She 23%
He 36%

Wants-Needs
She 22%
He 13%

Salesman
She 19%
He 8%

*Comparisons show women tend to view their husbands as
barriers to getting an appliance.*

—He is more concerned with price
   (which may be too high and therefore she won't get it)

—He is less concerned with needs and wants
   (and therefore doesn't fully appreciate her needs)

—He has only minor concern with the salesman
   (which makes her feel it's going to be 2 against 1)

Exhibit 6
Role Playing and Word Association
(Study of travel attitudes)

I. ROLE PLAYING

1. Let's suppose I'm a friend of yours, and I'm going to St. Louis (from Tulsa). *I don't have an automobile* and I'd like your advice on how to get there. How would you advise me to go? Why? (IF RESPONDENT SAYS, "DEPENDS ON PURPOSE," SAY, "TO VISIT SOME FRIENDS.")
2. What if I were going to Seattle? How would you advise me to go? Why?
3. What if my trip were to Oklahoma City? How should I go? Why? (NOTE: OTHER THAN BY AUTOMOBILE)

II. CONVENTIONAL WORD ASSOCIATION TEST

Now I would like to read you a list of words. As I read each word, you tell me the first word that comes to mind. For example, if I said, "cat," you might immediately say, "dog." Is that clear? (BE SURE RESPONDENT UNDERSTANDS TECHNIQUE.) Here's the first word:

WORD	ASSOCIATED WORD	NUMBER OF SECONDS 1 2 3 4 5 6 7 8 9 10	Over 10	Blocked
Automobile	———	— — — — — — — — — —	———	———
House	———	— — — — — — — — — —	———	———
°Pullman	———	— — — — — — — — — —	———	———
Electric	———	— — — — — — — — — —	———	———
°°Greyhound	———	— — — — — — — — — —	———	———
Grass	———	— — — — — — — — — —	———	———
Airplane	———	— — — — — — — — — —	———	———

°IF ASSOCIATION TO PULLMAN IS "TRAIN," ASK FOR NEXT WORD THAT COMES TO MIND.
°°IF ASSOCIATION TO GREYHOUND IS "BUS," ASK FOR NEXT WORD THAT COMES TO MIND.

III. PROFILE OF CHARACTERISTICS

Here are five ways to travel (SHOW EXHIBIT OF PICTURES). Now I'll read you a list of words and phrases. Would you tell me whether or not each of these words and phrases fits each of the different ways of travel. And then I would like you to tell me which way of travel *fits best*.

	Airplane		Pullman		Bus		Rail Coach		Air Coach		Fits Best
	Fits	Does not	Fits	Does not	Fits	Does not	Fits	Does not	Fits	Does not	
Comfortable	( )	( )	( )	( )	( )	( )	( )	( )	( )	( )	———
Unpleasant passengers	( )	( )	( )	( )	( )	( )	( )	( )	( )	( )	———
Adventurous travel	( )	( )	( )	( )	( )	( )	( )	( )	( )	( )	———
Scenic	( )	( )	( )	( )	( )	( )	( )	( )	( )	( )	———
Convenient terminals	( )	( )	( )	( )	( )	( )	( )	( )	( )	( )	———
Friendly	( )	( )	( )	( )	( )	( )	( )	( )	( )	( )	———
Clean terminals	( )	( )	( )	( )	( )	( )	( )	( )	( )	( )	———
Dangerous	( )	( )	( )	( )	( )	( )	( )	( )	( )	( )	———
Reliable schedules	( )	( )	( )	( )	( )	( )	( )	( )	( )	( )	———
Modern	( )	( )	( )	( )	( )	( )	( )	( )	( )	( )	———
Poor people	( )	( )	( )	( )	( )	( )	( )	( )	( )	( )	———
Courtesy	( )	( )	( )	( )	( )	( )	( )	( )	( )	( )	———
Good service	( )	( )	( )	( )	( )	( )	( )	( )	( )	( )	———
On time	( )	( )	( )	( )	( )	( )	( )	( )	( )	( )	———

Exhibit 7
A Projective Technique Survey Form,

SURVEY ON CORNS AND CORN REMEDIES

We are making a survey on people's foot ailments. We know that almost all of us occasionally have some trouble with our feet. We are particularly interested in corns.

1. Have you been bothered with corns any time in the last year? Yes——No——DK—— (IF NO or DON'T KNOW, SKIP TO CLASSIFICATION DATA.)

2. Do you ever use a corn remedy? Yes——No—— (If NO, SKIP TO Q. 4.)

3. IF YES: Which type of remedy do you prefer? Plaster——Pad—— Liquid—— (SHOW SAMPLES.)
   IF PADS: Do you use a medicated disc with the pad? Yes——No——

4. Do you ever do anything else to relieve your corns? Yes——No—— (IF NO, SKIP TO Q. 6.)

5. IF YES: What else do you do? Cut or pare corns——File or sand—— Go to a chiropodist——Wear different shoes for a while——Other (specify)————————

6. What brands of corn remedies have you ever heard of? Which brands, if any, have you ever used? Which brand, if any, did you buy last? In what kind of store did you buy it?

	A Have heard of	B Have used	C Last bought	D Bought it in:
Brand				
Dr. Scholl's	―――	―――	―――	―――
Blue Jay	―――	―――	―――	―――
Freezone	―――	―――	―――	―――
Other――――	―――	―――	―――	―――
Don't know	―――	―――	―――	―――
None	―――	―――	―――	―――

Why did you buy (brand checked in column C)?―――――

Would you buy this brand again? Yes―No―Why?――――――

7. Now, we would like to know what a group of words and phrases makes you think of: I will read you the first part of a phrase or sentence, then you will tell me in your own words how you would finish the sentence. For example, suppose I say to you, "I buy aspirin . . . ," and then you might complete the sentence by saying, "when I get a headache." Or maybe you might say, "when my supply is down and I see a special sale." As another example, if I were to say, "Cold tablets are . . . ," you might answer, "a good way to get rid of the sniffles." Or you might say, "a very good way to cure my cold." Each sentence and phrase is about corns or corn remedies.

A. Corns are――――――――――――――――――――――

B. I buy a corn remedy――――――――――――――――――

C. I really expect from a corn remedy that it will――――――

D. Curing a corn is――――――――――――――――――――

E. I would like a corn remedy which――――――――――――

F. The worst thing about a corn is――――――――――――

8. I have here 6 statements which can be made about one or the other corn remedy. I would like you to tell me how they would appeal to you if you were buying a remedy for a sore corn. Here is how you can tell me: I would like for you to line up for me (ON A TABLE OR SIMILAR SURFACE) these six cards. Put the one farthest to the left which appeals to you most, the one second to the left which appeals to you second most, etc., so that the one furthest to the right appeals least to you. You may put two or more cards in the same spot if you see no difference in the way they appeal to you. Is that clear? (BE SURE RESPONDENT UNDERSTANDS METHOD THOROUGHLY, BUT BE EXTREMELY CAREFUL NOT TO INFLUENCE CHOICE IN ANY WAY.) INDICATE BELOW THE KEY OF THE STATEMENT IN EACH POSITION.

1_____2_____3_____4_____5_____6_____

[The statements and keys on the six cards were:
(R) Gives quick relief from the pain of corns.
(D) Contains the new effective wonder drug for corn removal, barsillium.
(WC) Gets rid of the whole corn
(S) A safe way to get rid of your corn
(X) Pushes out corns from underneath
(FS) Your drug store's fastest selling corn remedy.]

9. Is there anything else a manufacturer might say about a corn remedy which would appeal to you more?_____

10. I note that you have indicated (1)_____ appeals to you most. Why?_____

11. Are there any statements among those shown you which really have very little appeal to you? Which ones? (LIST BY KEY) _____(FOR EACH) Why?_____

CLASSIFICATION DATA

Age: Under 25_____25-35_____35-44_____45 or more_____
Occupation (head of hh.)_____
Name_____
Address_____
Date_____Interviewer_____

Socio-Economic Status
Upper_____
Upper Middle_____
Middle_____
Lower Middle_____
Lower_____

APPENDIX. SOME OF THE COMMON ABBREVIATIONS AND CONVENTIONS OF MATHEMATICAL LANGUAGE

ABSTRACT SYMBOLIC LABELS DENOTING QUANTITIES

GENERALIZED VARIABLES: x, y, z, x_1, x_2, x_3, etc. -- denote a set of quantities which can, even in the context of a specific situation, be any one of an extremely large number of values depending on the circumstances. The choice of any particular letter is quite arbitrary, and it must be defined.

GENERALIZED COEFFICIENTS AND OTHER CONSTANTS: a, b, c, d, k, a_1, a_2, a_3, etc. Are called constants when standing alone (as in $x = a$), coefficients when they modify a variable (as in $x = ay$). They indicate quantities which have a single value in the context of a particular situation and a given mathematical relationship.

GENERALIZED SUBSCRIPTS: such as 1, 2, 3, k in a_1, x_1, x_2, a_3, x_k (read as "a-sub-1", etc.)--simply differentiating labels which distinguish x_1 as denoting a quite different quantity than does x_2, for example. They have no separate quantitative significance of their own, are simply a device for economizing in the use of separate symbols.

k, when used as a subscript refers to some specific but undesignated finite value of the variable or constant. (Similarly, when used as an exponent, it denotes a specific but undesignated finite power, and when used in such expressions as "the kth term" refers to some finite end, usually, of a series of similar terms.)

i, when used as a subscript, denotes "an individual value" of whatever it modifies. When used in a formula or in a table heading (x_i, for example), it indicates that the appropriate individual numerical value is to be substituted. Σx_i would be read as "the sum of the individual values of x."

GENERALIZED EXPONENTS: 2, 3, 4, a, b, x, y, k in x^2,

y^3, a^x, etc. indicate power. That is, they indicate that the designated quantity is to be multiplied by itself as many times as designated by the exponent.

SPECIFIC STANDARD ABBREVIATIONS

UNIVERSAL:

π (pi)--a single specific irrational number (approximately 3.1416 to the 5th significant figure) which is always the ratio of the circumference of any circle to its own diameter

e--another irrational number which is the base for natural logarithms

STATISTICAL CONVENTIONS:

$\bar{x}$, $\bar{y}$, etc. (usually read as "x-bar, y-bar")--the mean of all values of the designated variable

μ (mu)--often used to indicate the midpoint of a normal distribution, or sometimes used instead of $\bar{x}$, simply indicating the arithmetic mean.

p--the probability of whatever it modifies. Thus, p(x - y), meaning "the probability of (x - y)."

q--the reverse probability. That is, the probability of not-occurring. By definition, (p + q) is always equal to 1.

n--the number of observations

σ (sigma)--the actual standard deviation of a distribution (the square root of the average of the squares of the deviations of individual items from the mean)

s--the standard error, that is, the estimate of σ calculated from a set of sample observations

SYMBOLIC OPERATING INSTRUCTIONS

+ (plus)--add the two quantities thus joined. That is, increase the first by the amount of the second

– (minus)--subtract the two quantities thus joined. That is, decrease the first of the two quantities by the amount of the second.

× or · , as in x×y or x · a, or mere juxtaposition when using letter symbols as in ab and in (a + x)(b - y)-- multiply one term by the other. That is, add the second term to itself as many times as indicated by the first term (or the other way around--it comes out the same).

÷ , /, or ——— , as in a ÷ b, a/b and $\frac{a}{b}$, --"divide by"-- that is, subtract the second term from the first as many times as possible before it reaches zero.

Σ (Sigma), as in $\Sigma(x_i - \bar{x})$--the sum of all the individual values indicated by the symbol or expression which follows.

$\sum_{X=a}^{X=b}$ ( )--the sum of all those values for the expression within the parenthesis which are between the value indicated at the bottom of the sign and the value indicated at the top.

SYMBOLS OF RELATIONSHIP

= ("equals"), as in x = a --indicates that the quantities on either side of the sign can be considered as completely substitutable for each other for the specific purpose under consideration

$\cong$ ("approximately equal to"), as in $\pi \cong 3.1416$-- indicates that the two quantities may not be quite equal, but the difference between them is not significant for the purpose under consideration

$\sqrt{}$ ("radical")--take the square root of whatever is under the sign. That is, find that number which, when multiplied by itself, will give the number under the radical. When the radical carries a number, as in $\sqrt[k]{}$, the kth root to be taken--that is, that number found which when multiplied by itself k times will give the number under the radical

> ("greater than"), as in a > b ("a is greater than b")--
indicates a significant <u>inequality</u> in the stated direction.
Can also be represented in the opposite direction, as in
b < a, meaning "b is less than a." Thus 1 > p > 0 is
shorthand for "p is some value between 0 and 1, but is
not equal to either"

≥ ("equal to or greater than," and thus also means "at
least, and may be more than")

≤ ("equal to or less than," and thus "no more than, and
it may be less")

∪, as in A ∪ B ("the intersection of set A with set
B," often read as "A cup B")--signifies all of those
items which are part of both the set of phenomena designated by A and that set designated by B

∩, as in A ∩ B ("the union of set A with set B," read
as "A cap B")--signifies all items which are part of
either set A or set B, or both.

f( ), as in f(x) ("some function of x")--signifies that
whatever is defined as equal to it has a single definable
value for each separate value of the variables enclosed
in the parenthesis

∫ f(x) ("the integral of the function of x")--an analog of
Σ f(x), but applies whenever f(x) is a continuous relationship and the number of values of f(x) thus is infinite even
for a small portion of it. ∫ f(x) is a relationship whose
solution defines the total area bounded by f(x).

$\int_{x=b}^{x=a} f(x)$ --the area bounded by f(x) between the point where
x = a and the point where x = b.

Δx -- signifies an incremental change in the value of x

dx ("differential of x")--the infinitesimal change in the
value of x as it passes through a single point in the
function.

$\frac{dx}{dy}$ ("the differential of x with respect to y")--signifies the expression which tells how to calculate the slope of the curve plotted by an equation, and thus is the equation for the rate of change in the curve from which it is derived.

Logarithmic functions: log x (the logarithm of x to the base e) and $\log_{10} x$ (the logarithm of x to the base 10). Each of these indicates a number which, when it is the exponent of the base indicated, will give the value of x. Tables of these values, and slide rules scaled from them, have long served to ease the carrying out of multiplication, division, calculation of powers, and computation of roots. These functions have another valuable property, however. A great many relationships are exponential functions (such as $y = a^x$) or approximately so over sections of their curves. Substituting the logarithmic form (log y = log a) changes the characteristically J-shaped exponential relationship to a straight line relationship which is easier to use in such computations as linear programming.

sin x, cos x ("Sine x, Cosine x")--the labels given to standard trigonometric functions which can be represented graphically by the familiar wavelike plots we call cycles.

Index